The JEWS of CHINA

The JEWS of CHINA

Volume One
Historical and Comparative Perspectives

Edited and with an Introduction by
Jonathan Goldstein

Concluding Essay by
Benjamin I. Schwartz

An East Gate Book

M.E. Sharpe
Armonk, New York
London, England

An East Gate Book

Copyright © 1999 by M. E. Sharpe, Inc.

All rights reserved. No part of this book may be reproduced in any form
without written permission from the publisher, M. E. Sharpe, Inc.,
80 Business Park Drive, Armonk, New York 10504.

Library of Congress Cataloging-in-Publication Data

The Jews of China, Volume One: Historical and comparative perspectives /
edited by Jonathan Goldstein.
p. cm.
"An East Gate book."
Includes bibliographical references and index for both volumes at the end of volume two.
Contents: vol. 1. Historical and comparative perspectives.
ISBN 0-7656-0103-6 (alk. paper).—ISBN 0-7656-0104-4 (pbk. : alk. paper)
1. Jews—China—History.   2. China—Ethnic relations.
I. Goldstein, Jonathan.
DS135.C5J49   1998
951´.004924—dc21   98-5350
CIP

Printed in the United States of America

The paper used in this publication meets the minimum requirements of
American National Standard for Information Sciences—
Permanence of Paper for Printed Library Materials,
ANSI Z 39.48-1984.

∞

MV (c)   10   9   8   7   6   5   4   3   2   1
MV (p)   10   9   8   7   6   5   4   3   2   1

This book is dedicated to the memories of

Nissim Elias Benjamin Ezra
(1883–1936)
of Shanghai

and

Dr. Avraham Iosifovitch Kaufman
(1886–1971)
of Harbin

Pioneers of Zionism in East Asia

הֵן בְּכָל דּוֹר יָקוּם הַגִּבּוֹר גּוֹאֵל הָעָם

In each generation, a hero will arise as savior of our people.

Jonathan Goldstein
Carrollton, Georgia
October 1998

Contents: Volume One

Historical Introduction
    Jonathan Goldstein   xi

I. The Kaifeng Experience

  A. Assimilation and Acculturation   3

    1. The Synagogue at Kaifeng: Sino–Judaic Architecture of the Diaspora
        Nancy Shatzman Steinhardt   3

    2. Kaifeng Jews: The Sinification of Identity
        Irene Eber   22

    3. The Confucianization of the Kaifeng Jews: Interpretations of the Kaifeng Stelae Inscriptions
        Andrew H. Plaks   36

  B. Western Response   50

    1. The Revelation of a Jewish Presence in Seventeenth-Century China: Its Impact on Western Messianic Thought
        Michael Pollak   50

    2. Memories of Kaifeng's Jewish Descendants Today: Historical Significance in Light of Observations by Westerners Since 1605
        Wendy R. Abraham   71

  C. Comparisons with Indian Jewry   87

    1. The Kaifeng Jews and India's Bene Israel: Different Paths
        Shirley Berry Isenberg   87

2. Cochin Jews and Kaifeng Jews: Reflections on Caste, Surname, "Community," and Conversion
   Barbara C. Johnson 104

3. The Judaisms of Kaifeng and Cochin: Parallels and Divergences
   Nathan Katz 120

II. Nineteenth-Century Baghdadi and Ashkenazi Experiences in India, China, and Japan

A. *Baghdadi Jews in India and China in the Nineteenth Century: A Comparison of Economic Roles*
   Joan G. Roland 141

B. *The Shanghai-Nagasaki Judaic Connection, 1859–1924*
   Lane Earns 157

III. Twentieth-Century Baghdadi and Ashkenazi Experiences

A. **Urban Profiles: Hong Kong** 171

   1. Environmental Interactions of the Jews of Hong Kong
      Dennis A. Leventhal 171

B. **Urban Profiles: Harbin** 187

   1. The Construction of the Chinese Eastern Railway and the Origins of the Harbin Jewish Community, 1898–1931
      Zvia Shickman-Bowman 187

   2. Harbin's Jewish Community, 1898–1958: Politics, Prosperity, and Adversity
      Boris Bresler 200

C. **Occupational Profiles: Shanghai** 216

   1. Silas Aaron Hardoon and Cross-Cultural Adaptation in Shanghai
      Chiara Betta 216

   2. Jews and the Musical Life of Shanghai
      Xu *Buzeng* 230

3. Jewish Musicians in Shanghai: Bridging Two Cultures
     Harriet P. Rosenson   239

D. *Zionism, the Holocaust, and the Sino-Judaic Exodus*   251

 1. The Shanghai Zionist Association and the International Politics of East Asia Until 1936
     Maruyama *Naoki*   251

 2. Zionism and Zionist-Revisionism in Shanghai, 1937–1949
     Pan *Guang*   267

 3. Who Can See a Miracle? The Language of Jewish Memory in Shanghai
     Vera Schwarcz   277

Concluding Essay
Jews and China: Past and Present Encounters
   Benjamin I. Schwartz   299

Contributors   305

An index to volumes one and two appears at the end of volume two.

Historical Introduction

Jonathan Goldstein

From August 16 through 18, 1992, the editor of this publication organized and Harvard University's John K. Fairbank Center for East Asian Research hosted an international conference to present historical and comparative perspectives on the Jewish communities of China. The conference was formally entitled "Jewish Diasporas in China: Comparative and Historical Perspectives" and hereinafter is referred to as "Conference." In number of participants and disciplinary range, the Conference surpassed previous "Jews in China" symposia held during the 1980s and the early 1990s in Antwerp, Hong Kong, Minneapolis, Munich, Hangzhou, and Beijing. The 1992 conference involved specialists in Chinese, East Indian, European, Japanese, Judaic, Persian, and Turkish studies from the disciplines of anthropology, art history, comparative literature, diplomatic history, economics, history, library science/bibliography, linguistics, musicology, political science, and religious studies. The 157 participants from Australia, Canada, China, Hong Kong, Israel, Italy, Japan, Mexico, Singapore, the United Kingdom, and the United States brought international perspectives to the Conference. There have been at least four published evaluations of the Conference.[1]

This publication is a result of the Conference. It is neither a transcript of Conference proceedings nor a collection of all the papers actually delivered. Only the best papers from the Conference, plus several submitted afterward, are published here. While not a comprehensive history of the Jews of China, this publication does contain a representative sampling of Conference presentations and papers stimulated by the Conference, all of which have been revised and edited. Drafts of all the papers that were distributed shortly before and during the Conference have been deposited and can be consulted in the Harvard-Yenching Library, 2 Divinity Avenue, Cambridge, Massachusetts 02138 (hereinafter cited as "HYL").

Both the Conference and this publication focus on two significantly different cycles of Jewish history in China, each of which brought different varieties of Jews and Judaism to China. In China, as in many parts of the far-flung Jewish Diaspora, one cannot speak of a "typical" or "standard"

Jew or Judaism. The first cycle began approximately A.D. 900, when Jewish merchants began to arrive in late Tang dynasty China. Chang'an (present-day Xian), the capital of the north, was an eastern terminus of the transasiatic "silk route" used by Jews, Muslims, Manichaeans, Zoroastrians, and Nestorian Christians.[2] Some two to three centuries later a Jewish presence was established in Kaifeng, then the capital of the Northern Song dynasty. The Kaifeng Jewish historical cycle ends in the late Qing dynasty (1644–1911). By 1860, the last Kaifeng synagogue had been destroyed by flood and was not rebuilt; there was no rabbi; and the community had lost its knowledge of Hebrew and most traditional Jewish practices. Some members of the community still continue to call themselves Jews almost exclusively on the basis of lineage. By virtue of its sheer longevity, the Kaifeng community, more than any other Jewish community in China, lends itself to analysis of Jewish interaction with Chinese culture.

A second cycle of Jewish history in China began just before the Kaifeng community's nineteenth-century disappearance. By the late 1700s, American Jewish traders had begun to arrive in the South China port of Guangzhou (Canton). Benjamin (1798–1875) and Horatio (1805–1891) Etting, Philadelphia merchants of German–Jewish origin, traded and resided in Canton and Aomen (Macao). Lionel Moses (1825–1895), from New York and apparently of Spanish– or Portuguese–Jewish origin, also traded and resided in Canton and Macao. A Joseph Moses arrived in Canton in 1842 and was still there in 1846. A Gelaustan Moses appeared in the censuses of January 1843 and 1844.[3]

These pioneers were followed by a succession of Middle Eastern migrants and immigrants, including, in the nineteenth-century, many Arabic-speaking Jews from Baghdad. The Baghdadis, who are also referred to as Levantine Jews, should not, strictly speaking, be categorized as "Sephardim," or Jews who were expelled from the Iberian Peninsula in 1492/93 who retained medieval Spanish and Portuguese as their mother tongues in varied places of exile. The Baghdadis were followed by Russian Jews seeking business opportunities in Manchuria. Russian entrepreneurs were followed by thousands of European Jews fleeing tsarist anti-Semitism, the Bolshevik revolution, and Hitler. By the mid-1950s, shortly after the establishment of the People's Republic of China, most Jewish residents had left China, and the second cycle of Jewish history in China was nearing its end. As of 1998, only a handful of Jewish descendants of the Kaifeng community and the nineteenth- and early twentieth-century migrations remained in the People's Republic. There are Jewish communities of diplomats, scholars, and businesspeople in Hong Kong, Beijing (Peking), Shanghai, and Taibei (Taipei), composed almost entirely of non-Chinese citizens.

To provide focus and a theoretical framework for the Conference and this publication, a list of questions and issues—some more applicable to the long-term Kaifeng cycle of Jewish history than to the more recent cycle of Western and Middle Eastern migrations—was circulated to contributors in advance. Authors were asked to isolate those special features of Chinese–Jewish identity, multiculturalism, and religiosity that set Jews in China apart from other Jewish Diasporas. Each participant was requested in particular to review three prominent concepts of Jewish Diaspora historians and to evaluate whether those concepts also applied in the case of China.

Acculturation

In many parts of the Diaspora, the Judaism of immigrant Jews has drawn upon and been enriched by the host country. It has also sometimes enriched the culture of the host country. By examining how Jews performed rituals and celebrated holidays, can we detect any influence from the Chinese setting? Were certain holidays or rituals added to the life cycle? Did aspects of the Jews' ritual life help them integrate into the society of China or set them apart? How did Jews in China see themselves vis-à-vis their neighbors and Jews elsewhere? Did they even know that there were Jewish communities in existence elsewhere? What was the nature of Jewish communal institutions in China, so basic to the preservation of "community" among Jews in Europe, the Middle East, and India? How did Jews represent themselves to the non-Jewish community around them? Did the Judaism of immigrant Jews enrich the culture of the host country in this case?

Economic Utility

In many parts of the Diaspora, Jews functioned as intercultural links in commerce. One of the striking aspects of Jewish economic history in India is its entanglement with colonialism, beginning with the Portuguese and Dutch even before the arrival of the British. There is a long history of direct Jewish trade from India to China and Europe, culminating in the nineteenth- and twentieth-century ventures of the Sassoons, Hardoons, Ezras, Toegs, and Kadoories.[4] In Europe itself, disabilities imposed from without combined with the desire of Jews to live within their own communities to produce a situation in which Jews perforce worked along the margins of society. European, Middle Eastern, and Indian Jews functioned as social intermediaries between city and countryside and in international trade, precisely as emigrant Chinese performed in Southeast Asia. Did Jews function as commercial intermediaries in China? Was there cooperation or conflict between Jewish and Chinese merchant enterprises in China?

Assimilation, Anti-Semitism

While Jewish communities have survived in many parts of the West and made significant contributions in such "traditionally Jewish" occupations as wholesale and retail commerce, education, medicine, law, science, journalism, and music, this achievement has often occurred while Jews were either voluntarily assimilating into the host country or experiencing the opposite of assimilation: anti-Semitic discrimination and persecution. In India, on the other hand, the caste system and a long tradition of religious/ethnic pluralism discouraged both assimilation (as distinct from acculturation) and its opposite, anti-Semitism, while Jews contributed significantly to Indian society. Was there anti-Semitism in a China under the Manchus or in a China under indigenous Chinese rule? In a China under Japanese occupation? To what extent did anti-Semitism, if it existed in China, emanate from such non-Chinese residents as White Russians, German Nazis, or Japanese? How did it affect acculturation and assimilation? How did it compare with European and Middle Eastern varieties? In the case of the Jewish community of Kaifeng, a group never larger than two thousand survived for at least seven centuries and lived without religious persecution. How is it that the Kaifeng community became so sinicized, while the twentieth-century communities in Beijing (Peking), Dalian (Dairen/Dalny), Hailar, Hankou, Harbin (Haerbin/Kharbin), Hengdaohezi, Lüshun (Port Arthur), Manzhouli, Qingdao, Qiqihar, Shanghai, Shenyang (Mukden/Fengtian), Tianjin (Tientsin), and Yantai (Chefoo) had few enduring contacts with the surrounding Chinese community?[5] Would this conclusion also apply in the case of Hong Kong, which as of 1998 hosted China's longest-lasting and largest Jewish community established during the nineteenth century? Did Jews make notable secular contributions at any point in Chinese history? If so, under what circumstances and in what specific areas? If not, does this tell us something about Sino–foreign relations? Why didn't the local Chinese society welcome them? Was it a result of Chinese resistance to foreigners?

Is Chinese anti-Semitism an issue at all? Were Kaifeng Jews, for example, seen by others as significantly different from Chinese Muslims, Zoroastrians, Christians, Hindus, and Manichaeans? Two of the underpinnings of Western anti-Semitism are the notion of Jews as Christ-killers and the perception of Jews as stateless or having dual loyalties and hence untrustworthy. If an awareness of Christian anti-Semitism and knowledge of a Diaspora were both lacking in Kaifeng up through the nineteenth century, what does this tell us about Chinese-Jewish relations? And, how did European Jewish émigrés fare during the first half of the twentieth century? Was

Chinese anti-Semitism, if it existed at all, merely a superficial imitation of European or Middle Eastern strains, as is clearly the case for early twentieth-century Japanese anti-Semitism?

Evidence to help answer these questions comes together in papers in this two-volume publication. Volume One contains historical and comparative perspectives on the Jewish communities of China. Volume Two, a sourcebook and research guide, contains articles by Chinese historians on traditional Chinese awareness about Jews; recollections of life in China by former Jewish residents, including a distinguished diplomat, an academic, an attorney, and a journalist/editor; guides to specific collections of source material about Jews in China; and a bibliography. The authors and translators of these articles are citizens of the United States (21), China (7), Israel (3), the United Kingdom (2), Japan (1), and Italy (1). Three of the historians writing in Volume One were or are long-term Jewish residents of China but do not hold Chinese citizenship (Zvia Shickman-Bowman, Boris Bresler, and Dennis A. Leventhal). Most papers in this publication, therefore, are by scholars who are not themselves participants in the Chinese–Jewish experience.

The Kaifeng experience is the first Sino–Judaic encounter analyzed in this publication. Architectural historian Nancy Shatzman Steinhardt scrutinizes the Kaifeng synagogue itself. Unfortunately, only drawings and a handful of artifacts remain, making it difficult to assess the aesthetic appeal of the structure. What Jews did in that synagogue is analyzed in articles based chiefly on the inscriptions on stone stelae, travelers' accounts, and legends. Andrew Plaks investigates acculturation: how, after arrival in Kaifeng, Jews acclimated to China by developing syncretic, that is, neo-Confucian, forms of worship and belief. Michael Pollak probes the impact on Western messianic thought of the revelation of the presence of a Jewish community in seventeenth-century China. Perhaps more than any other contributor, Pollak discusses the broad political, historical, and religious reasons for Western interest in Chinese Jews in the nineteenth and twentieth centuries. Wendy R. Abraham uses oral history interviews conducted in the 1980s to trace what Kaifeng residents of Jewish origin remember about Judaism.

Taken as a whole, these Kaifeng papers explicate a Jewish–Confucian integration of Kaifeng Judaism, a theme noted by Irene Eber. Kaifeng Jews' worship or veneration of ancestors suggests comparisons with the "Chinese rites" controversy within the Roman Catholic Church. To what extent, for example, could Chinese Jews or Catholics adopt Chinese ritual practices such as ancestor worship while maintaining the integrity of their monotheism? The evidence of material culture and written records tends to support Irene Eber's conclusion that, because of kin-centered identification, some

Kaifeng residents saw themselves as Jews even after a synagogue was no longer in existence. The distinctively Judaic quality of the practices of the community gradually disappeared as the community took on more and more of the characteristics of Chinese sectarian religion.

Indologists Shirley Berry Isenberg, Barbara C. Johnson, and Nathan Katz tackle one of this publication's primary objectives: comparing China's Judaism with the Judaism of India, the site of the one other, long-lived Jewish Diaspora of East, Southeast, or South Asia. These authors contrast acculturation, assimilation, economic activity, and anti-Semitism in both Chinese and Indian cultures and consider the extent to which the Kaifeng experience is unique within an East, Southeast, and South Asian context.

After examining Kaifeng, this work turns to the late eighteenth-, nineteenth-, and early twentieth-century Jewish experiences in China. With two major exceptions, there was nothing explicitly Judaic about the experiences of the handful of American-Jewish traders resident in Canton and Macao from approximately 1790 to 1846. Apart from the fact that they did not attend church or support Christian missionaries, they were indistinguishable from their Christian colleagues in South China. These Jews were nevertheless victims of the anti-Semitism of their Christian compatriots. In the 1840s John Heard wrote that Joseph Moses "sports now a ferocious whisker, dirty moustache, and a coat which a Christian would not be seen in."[6] At about the same time Nathaniel Kinsman wrote his wife that "I am sorry that my particular friend Mr. Moses has in my absence honoured you with a call, [sic] he is a low fellow and his visits can be dispensed with."[7] Kinsman subsequently explained Moses' "lowness" by reference to Moses' Judaism: "It is astonishing to me that Miss King permits that dissipated Jew Moses to gallant her about, [sic] there is no accounting for tastes, however, as the old woman said when she kissed the cow."[8] By the early twentieth century, Europeans in China, especially ethnic Russians, subjected their Jewish compatriots to treatment worse than the verbal abuse Joseph Moses received from his fellow Americans.

This work focuses next on mid-nineteenth to mid-twentieth century Jewish experiences in specific Chinese cities. Historian Joan G. Roland discusses the nineteenth century arrival in Hong Kong and Shanghai of Baghdadi Jews from India. She then contrasts the role of Baghdadi Jews in China with their even longer experience in India. Historian Lane Earns explains the role of the Japanese transit point of Nagasaki for Jews reaching China. By the early twentieth century Yokohama and Kobe also served this purpose. Thus, journalist Israel Epstein's father, Lazer, moved his young family from Warsaw, Russian Poland, to Kobe and thence to Harbin and Tianjin.

Perhaps the most tumultuous urban Jewish experience in twentieth century China occurred in Harbin and other towns along the Chinese Eastern Railway (CER) in Manchuria. Harbin was successively ruled by tsarist Russia, by an international coalition of allied powers, by Chinese warlords, by the Soviet Union, by Japan, by the Soviet Union again, and finally by the Chinese Communists, all in a period of sixty years. The city was originally built by tsarist Russians in 1898 as the economic hub of their 250,000–acre spread of territorial concessions associated with the CER. Bolshevik and tsarist factions battled for control of the railway zone during Russia's civil war of 1917–22, with the Bolsheviks ultimately victorious. The zone remained in Russian hands until 1935, when the Soviet Union sold it to Japan. Following the end of World War II in 1945, the Soviet Union resumed control of the zone and held it until 1955, when it was finally ceded to the People's Republic. Jews lived in the zone under various statutes and statuses throughout these turbulent periods. Their experiences are recounted by Israel Epstein and "Alexander Menquez" in the autobiographical section of this publication, in Volume Two. Zvia Shickman-Bowman and Boris Bresler analyze the same experiences in the historical section of this publication, in Volume One.[9]

While Kaifeng was the longest-lived Jewish community in China, and Harbin arguably the most tumultuous, Shanghai was numerically by far the largest. Shanghai's Jewish population was specialized enough and records abundant enough that occupational histories can be written. *Xu* Buzeng, Harriet P. Rosenson, and Chiara Betta describe individuals who happened to be Jewish but who made purely secular contributions in China. Xu and Rosenson investigate Jewish composers and performers of Western-style, and sometimes Chinese-style, music. Betta recounts the career of Shanghai businessman Silas Aaron Hardoon (1851?-1931). Hardoon energetically blended into Chinese society, eventually endowing both a Buddhist and a Confucian university. For Hardoon and Israel Epstein, both of whom moved into Chinese society, Judaism was something to move away from. Epstein at least partially attributes his progressivism and attraction to the Chinese revolution to the tenuous influence of traditional Judaic values. The journalist Vincent Sheean in his *Personal History* of 1934 recalls the secular contributions of many such Jews in China. Referring to journalist Rayna Prohme and Communist activist Mikhail Borodin (né Gruzenberg), he observes:

> The Jews I had known in China had risen so far above the prison walls of race, nation, and tradition, that their Jewishness was altogether lost in their humanity; and their special passion, the purity and intensity in which the best

of the Jewish heritage was expressed, burned itself out in a cause from which no human creature was excused. Only in such freedom could the Jewish genius give all it had to give to the developing consciousness of mankind.[10]

For Sheean, the Jews he knew in China had ceased to be Jews and evolved into something higher.

It would be impossible to discuss Jews in twentieth-century China comprehensively without mentioning the Holocaust and the unique role of Shanghai during that tragedy. The Holocaust steered thousands of Austrian, Croatian, Czech, Dutch, German, Hungarian, Lithuanian, and Polish Jews to Shanghai by varied escape routes, over land and sea, at a time when no other place in the world, including the United States, would freely accept Jewish refugees. Therefore, while certain questions that pertain to Holocaust history in general apply in the case of Shanghai, others do not. The question of "entry visas being denied," a major concern to Holocaust historians, is inapplicable in the case of Shanghai. Up to 1941, when the Japanese slammed the gates shut, having earlier kept them open, any Jew or anyone else for that matter could simply "arrive" in Shanghai. Transportation might be an obstacle, but the critical "permission to enter" could not be denied. Ernest Heppner wrote that his family, and other Austrian and German Jews arriving in Shanghai in the late 1930s, could not believe that no one asked for their papers as they passed through the customs house. Hundreds of thousands of Jews in Europe were trying to find a country permitting them entry and "here Jews could just walk ashore."[11]

Other central questions of Zionist and Holocaust history are applicable in the Shanghai case. Historians *Pan* Guang and *Maruyama* Naoki note that well in advance of the Holocaust, and in anticipation of such a disaster, Jews in China had a vibrant Zionist movement with mainstream and radical factions. While Zionists in China appreciated the unique openness of Shanghai, its sheer distance from European hotbeds of anti-Semitism made it a welcome haven but never a solution. For Zionists, a reborn Jewish homeland in Palestine was the only viable answer to European anti-Semitism. Maruyama delineates the origins of the Zionist movement in Shanghai that were simultaneous with those of the world Zionist movement. He paints a touching portrait of the indefatigable Shanghai journalist Nissim Elias Benjamin Ezra, who died in 1936 before his ambition to be part of a Jewish government in Palestine could be fulfilled. The Shanghai Zionist movement ended dramatically in 1949 when, as most Jews were leaving China, the stewards of the Shanghai Jewish Club deeded their property to their "mother land," the reborn State of Israel. The property was received by Moshe Yuval, Israel's first diplomatic representative in

China.[12] Pan and Maruyama stress the distinctive characteristics of Shanghai that enabled Zionism to thrive and permitted Zionists from China to make small but significant contributions to the founding of the State of Israel.

Ernest Heppner raises the controversial question of how much aid Diaspora Jews could and did give to their coreligionists fleeing Hitler.[13] Maruyama concludes that, at least in N.E.B. Ezra's case, the commitment to European brethren was profound.

To sum up the Shanghai experience, Vera Schwarcz discusses the meaning of memory principally for Orthodox Jewish survivors. This illustrious sub-community included Polish religious Zionist (Mizrachi) leader Zorach Warhaftig, who would become Israel's minister of religion; Pinchas Hirszprung, later chief rabbi of Montreal; David Zysman, vice-president-to-be of New York City's Yeshiva University; Rabbi Moshe Zupnick, of Brooklyn; and Shimon Kalish, a Grand Rabbi of Amshenov, Russia, and later of Brooklyn. Members of Kalish's family established an important yeshiva, or Jewish religious school, in his name in Jerusalem.[14] While in China this eminent Orthodox group maintained little contact with non-Orthodox German–Jewish refugee musicians, Bundists, Communists, or the Chinese population. In many ways it lived in a shtetl within a shtetl. Schwarcz argues that precisely for this reason the Orthodox subcommunity survived. It subsisted on memory, seeing its escape to Shanghai as but one more act of providence, comparable to Abraham's divinely inspired exodus from Ur or the fortuitous salvation of the entire Persian Jewish community from the designs of Haman. For Schwarcz, the determination of Orthodox Shanghailanders to anchor their novel Shanghai experience in the language of tradition and memory [*zachor*] accounts for their vigorous Jewish survival.

Taken as a whole, the papers on eighteenth-, nineteenth-, and early twentieth-century Sino–Judaic experiences echo a question raised in the earlier Kaifeng papers: What accounts for the survival of some Jews as Jews and the assimilation of others, in the seductively tolerant climate of China? Modern Chinese history is replete with examples of Jewish assimilation into the Chinese context (Hardoon, Epstein) or into the Europeanized cultural ethos of the Concessions and treaty ports (e.g., "Jewish" merchants in nineteenth-century Canton and Macao, or "Jewish" musicians, Communists, and journalists in twentieth-century Shanghai). But what sustained Jewish identity in China?

Schwarcz has given us one ideological paradigm to explain Jewish survival. She vividly describes the grand rabbi of Amshenov dancing with his followers in war-torn Shanghai on the occasion of the publication there of the Talmudic tractate *Gittin*. Pan, Maruyama, Bresler,

Shickman-Bowman, and "Menquez" offer another paradigm for Jewish survival. For the culturally assimilated Russian Jews of Manchuria, Tianjin, and Shanghai, and for some successful Anglophilic Baghdadis like N.E.B. Ezra, the novel, vibrant phenomenon of twentieth-century Zionism was cultural salvation. When Dr. Avraham Kaufman (1886–1971), the leader of mainstream Zionists in Harbin, ultimately reached Israel after sixteen years' imprisonment in the Soviet Union, his son asked what had kept his identity so strong. "What a question you are asking!" the father exclaimed. "We preserved our nationality because we believed in Zionism and always looked toward Erez [sic] Israel."[15] Both Jewish religious orthodoxy and a variety of Zionisms thrived in Modern China. This publication delineates the social context for fruition of both ideologies.

A Note on Transliteration

For Chinese names and terms, I have generally used the pinyin system of romanization, which is rapidly becoming universal. However, I also have been guided by Professor John Schrecker's advice to let common American usage dictate which transliteration should prevail. He asks rhetorically, "Do we use Firenze rather than Florence?" During centuries of Sino–Western relations, several formal systems plus numerous arbitrary renditions have been used to transform Chinese words into Latin characters. In both the text and index, I therefore have rendered Chinese names according to their commonest usage in American English, such as Confucius, Mencius, Harbin, Yen Fu, Liang Ch'i-ch'ao, Chang Tso-lin, Chiang Kai-shek, Sun Yat-sen, Nanking Road, Dairen, Mukden, Port Arthur, or Hong Kong. Wherever feasible I have juxtaposed pinyin transliterations of terms that appear in an original text but are less commonly used in American English, such as Shanghae or Chang-hai. Similarly, city names like Wilno or Kovno [Polish] are juxtaposed with their Lithuanian [Vilnius or Kaunas] and Yiddish [Vilna or Kovno] equivalents. As with Chinese, varieties of Arabic, Hebrew, Hindi, Japanese, Korean, Malayalam, Marathi, Russian, and Yiddish romanization may be listed initially, followed only by the spelling commonly used in American English, e.g., shtetl, tsarist, or yeshiva. Chinese and Japanese family names customarily precede personal names and are italicized in the first instance where they appear in conjunction with first names (e.g., "*Xu*" in "*Xu* Xin"; "*Sugihara*" in "*Sugihara* Chiune"). These family names are not subsequently italicized.

Acknowledgments

Lastly, I wish to thank some of the many individuals and institutions who made the Conference and its derivative publications possible.

I am grateful to State University of West Georgia History Department Chairman James S. Taylor for providing released time, which enabled me to bring this publication to fruition. I also wish to thank West Georgia's Learning Resources Committee for subsidizing part of the research cost of this publication and West Georgia librarians Nancy Farmer, Myron House, and Charles E. Beard for bibliographical help.

Above and beyond assistance from my home institution, background research for this publication was completed with subsidies from the Pacific Cultural Foundation, the Dorot Foundation, and the Association for Asian Studies. The Conference itself, of which Professor Benjamin I. Schwartz was the senior scholar, was most fortunate to receive financial backing from the National Endowment for the Humanities, the Lucius N. Littauer Foundation, the Sino–Judaic Institute, Asian Rare Books, Inc., and Lawrence E. Sheftel. Through the efforts of Charles Berlin, the Lee M. Friedman Bibliographer in Judaica in the Harvard College Library, that library's Judaica Division arranged a major exhibition of its resources for the study of Jews in China and Sino–Israeli relations. The exhibit was held concurrently with the Conference, and the Judaica Division published an exhibition catalog, which was distributed gratis to participants. The exhibition and catalog were prepared by Violet Gilboa, Judaica Technical Services Librarian in the Harvard College Library, with an introduction by Irene Eber.[16] The exhibition and catalog were funded by the Max and Irene Engel Levy Judaica Book Fund. Larsen Librarian of Harvard College Richard de Gennaro most generously arranged for the Harry Elkins Widener Room to be opened on a Sunday evening for the Conference's and exhibition's opening lecture by Professor Donald Daniel Leslie of the Australian National University, an event cosponsored by the Friends of Harvard College Library and the Levy Fund.[17]

Conference bibliographer Frank Joseph Shulman advised on the library exhibit and catalog, suggested speakers for the Conference, chaired sessions, hosted a post-Conference dinner, and helped compile and edit Conference-related bibliographies and a directory of individuals interested in the Jews and the Jewish communities of East, Southeast, and South Asia.[18] Bernard Wasserstein, dean of Brandeis University's Graduate School, gave Conference participants a tour of the University and of the American Jewish Historical Society library on the Brandeis campus. He also served as a commentator on Conference presentations. President Albert E. Dien of the Sino–Judaic Institute arranged for that group's cosponsorship of the Conference.[19] Dien, like Berlin, Shulman, and Wasserstein, was an indefatigable guide for managerial aspects of the Conference ranging from nuance of translation to subtleties of international diplomacy. Richard Matthews of the *Atlanta Journal*, and Professors Avraham Altman of the Hebrew University of Jerusalem, Peter Berton of the University of Southern California, Roger Des Forges of the State University of New York at Buffalo, Robert E. Entenmann of St. Olaf College, Steve Hochstadt of Bates College, Deborah Lipstadt of Emory University, Murray A. Rubinstein of the City University of New York, and Eber and Shulman each made substantive and much-appreciated criticisms of drafts of this publication.

I owe a final debt of gratitude to my Harvard colleagues at the Harvard-Yenching Library, Eugene W. Wu, director, and at the Fairbank Center, James W. Watson and Ezra Vogel, directors. Over a period of eight years, Harvard-Yenching staff librarian Raymond Lum routinely ferreted out the arcane background materials needed for the Conference and this publication. He also mounted a representative sampling of those materials in a Harvard-Yenching exhibit during the Conference. Fairbank Center associate Merle Goldman helped me navigate the myriad shoals of Harvard bureaucracy. Fairbank Center colleagues Paul A. Cohen, Joshua A. Fogel, William Kirby, John Schrecker, and Benjamin I. Schwartz, as well as University Counsel Frank Connors, provided expert intellectual guidance during the period of years in which the Conference and this publication were in the planning stages, at critical points during the conference itself, and subsequently. Each of the aforementioned colleagues, through discipline of mind, creativity, and personal generosity, serves as a personal and professional role model. Each typifies the combined virtues of the Chinese *junzi* and Yiddish *adele mensch:* extraordinary intellectuals of equally outstanding personal refinement.

Jonathan Goldstein
Carrollton, Georgia
October 1998

Notes

1. For published evaluations of the Conference, see Anson Laytner, "When East Meets West: A Ground-Breaking Conference Studies Jewish Diasporas in China," *Points East* 7, no. 2 (October 1992), pp. 8–11; Edith and Isidore Chevat, "Harvard Sponsors a Conference on the Jewish Diasporas," *U.S.-China Review* 16, no. 4 (fall 1992), pp. 10–12; Jonathan Goldstein, "Jews in China: A Pathbreaking Conference," *Fairbank Center News,* no. 1 (spring 1993), pp. 4–5; and "Chinese Jews intrigue experts," *Jerusalem Post,* August 25, 1992, p. 12.

2. Jerry H. Bentley, *Old World Encounters, Cross-Cultural Contacts and Exchanges in Pre-Modern Times* (New York: Oxford University Press, 1993), pp. 69, 96–98.

3. Benjamin Etting, "Journal of Voyages to Canton 1822–1837," Philadelphia Maritime Museum; Letters: Henry McKean (Philadelphia) to Benjamin Etting (Canton), July 8, 1836; Richard Coe (Philadelphia) to Benjamin Etting (aboard ship *Liberty*), June 25,

1835, Historical Society of Pennsylvania, Philadelphia; *The North American,* March 23, 1913; "Solomon Moses' Journal on a Voyage to Madras and Calcutta, January 3, 1798 to April 23, 1798"; Letter: H.? Murray (Canton) to Lionel Moses (Macao), March 15, 1855, American Jewish Historical Society Library, Waltham, Massachusetts; Letter: Mrs. Nathaniel Kinsman (Macao) to sister, November 3, 1844, reproduced in "The Daily Life of Mrs. Nathaniel Kinsman in Macao, China: Excerpts from Letters of 1844," *Essex Institute Historical Collections* 86 (October 1950), p. 316; Malcolm Stern, *First American Jewish Families* (Cincinnati: American Jewish Archives, 1978), p. 209; *Canton Press,* September 3, 1842; *China General Price Current* (Canton), September 6, 1842; *Chinese Repository* (Canton) 8 (January 1844), pp. 6–7.

    4. Joan G. Roland, *The Jews in British India: Identity in a Colonial Era* (Hanover, NH: University Press of New England, 1989).

    5. Teddy Kaufman, "Jews in Modern China," *Bulletin* of Igud Yotzei Sin in Israel (Association of Former Residents of China), no. 336 (August–September 1994), p. 13. See also p. 20 of Russian-language version of same *Bulletin.*

    6. Letter, John Heard (Canton) to "Capt. Graves," May 5, 1844, "Letters Sent 8 April 1844–10 January 1846," Heard Papers, LF-1, Heard Collection, Baker Library, Harvard University Graduate School of Business Administration, Boston.

    7. Letter, Nathaniel Kinsman to Rebecca Kinsman, December 4, 1844, Nathaniel and Rebecca Kinsman Correspondence, Nathaniel Kinsman Papers, Phillips Library, Peabody Essex Museum, Salem, Massachusetts, folder B3, F10.

    8. Letter, Nathaniel Kinsman to Rebecca Kinsman, December 17, 1844, Kinsman Correspondence. See also "Life in Macao in the 1840s: Letters of Rebecca Chase Kinsman to Her Family in Salem," *Essex Institute Historical Collections* 86 (January 1950), pp. 15–40.

    9. On the complex history of Harbin and the Chinese Eastern Railway Zone, see Søren Clausen and Stig Thøgersen, *The Making of a Chinese City: History and Historiography in Harbin* (Armonk, NY: M.E. Sharpe, 1995); Bruce A. Elleman, "The Soviet Union's Secret Diplomacy Concerning the Chinese Eastern Railway, 1924–1925," *Journal of Asian Studies* 53, no. 2 (May 1994), pp. 459–586; Elleman, "The Iurin Mission to China: The Prelude to Sino-Soviet Diplomatic Relations," *Soviet and Post-Soviet Review* 19, nos. 1–3 (1992), pp. 137–62; and David Wolff "To the Harbin Station: City Building in Russian Manchuria, 1898–1914" (Ph.D. dissertation, University of California at Berkeley, 1991).

    10. Vincent Sheean, *Personal History* (New York: Literary Guild, 1934), p. 391.

    11. Ernest Heppner, "On the Relations of the West European Refugees vs. the Shanghai Resident Jews" (paper presented at a conference on Jewish Diasporas in China: Comparative and Historical Perspectives, Harvard University, August 16–18, 1992) (hereafter, cited as "Conference"), p. 4, in HYL.

    12. Deed of Gift, Shanghai Jewish Club to the Government of Israel, February 21, 1949, Jewish Agency Records, Central Zionist Archives, Jerusalem.

    13. Heppner, "On the Relations," *passim.* See also Joseph R. Fiszman, "The Quest for Status: Polish-Jewish Refugees in Shanghai, 1941–49" (paper prepared for the Conference), in HYL.

    14. Marvin Tokayer and Mary Swartz, *The Fugu Plan: The Untold Story of the Japanese and the Jews During World War II* (New York: Paddington Press, 1976), p. 271.

    15. Kaufman, "Jews," p. 18.

    16. *China and the Jews: A Sampling of Harvard Library Resources for the Study of the Jewish Life in China and Chinese-Jewish Relations* (Cambridge, MA: Max and Irene Engel Levy Judaica Book Fund, 1992).

17. Donald Daniel Leslie, "China and the Jews: Prospects for Research" (paper prepared for the Conference), in HYL.
18. Frank Joseph Shulman, comp. and ed., *Directory of Individuals Interested in the Jews and the Jewish Communities of East, Southeast and South Asia* (1993). Available from the Sino-Judaic Institute, 232 Lexington Drive, Menlo Park, CA 94025.
19. The Sino-Judaic Institute was founded in California on June 27, 1985. It is a privately supported, all-volunteer organization composed of Jewish and non-Jewish Westerners, Chinese scholars of Jewish descent, and non-Jewish Chinese scholars. Its principal activities are the publication of the newsletter *Points East* and the journal *Sino-Judaica*. It sponsors visits to Kaifeng, Shanghai, and other Jewish settlement sites in China. It is the foremost but not the only organization promoting research and publication about the Jews of China and Sino–Israeli relations. On its history, see [Leo Gabow], "How the Sino-Judaic Institute Began," *Points East* 1, no. 1 (January 1986), p. 1; and Anson Laytner, "A Brief Review of the Sino-Judaic Institute," *Points East* 7, no. 2 (July 1992). Other organizations concerned with Sino–Judaic history include the Tel Aviv–based Igud Yotzei Sin (Association of Former Residents of China), a Jewish fraternal organization established in the 1950s that publishes its *Bulletin* in English, Russian, and Hebrew (13 Gruzenberg St., P.O. Box 1601, Tel Aviv, 61015 Israel; Tel. or Fax: 972–3–5171997); the Jewish Historical Society of Hong Kong (c/o The Jewish Club, 4th Floor, Melbourne Plaza, 33 Queen's Road, Central, Hong Kong; Tel.: 852–801–5440); the Asia Pacific Jewish Association (G.P.O. 5402 CC, Melbourne, Victoria 3001, Australia; Tel.: 61–3–828–8570; Fax: 61–3–828–8584); the Council on the Jewish Experience in Shanghai (c/o Ralph B. Hirsch, 3500 Race Street, Philadelphia, PA 19104–4925; Tel. and Fax: 215–386–1270); the Foundation for Chinese Jews (420 Lincoln Road, Suite 222, Miami Beach, FL 33139; Tel.: 305–531–7500; Fax: 305–531–0026); and the Henan University Research Center on Jewish History in China (c/o Prof. *Wei* Qianzhi, History Department, Henan University, Kaifeng, Henan, China).

A burgeoning interest in Sino–Judaica in China in the 1980s and 1990s is partly attributable to the People's Republic's shedding of its traditional pro-Arab stance in favor of military, commercial, and ultimately diplomatic ties with Israel. As a by-product of those ties, Judaic studies in China assumed sudden political respectability and expanded exponentially. China's Jews can now be studied openly, alongside China's other more numerically significant religious minorities: Muslims, Christians, Hindus, Manichaeans, and Zoroastrians. On the rapid growth of Judaic Studies in China, see *Pan* Guang, *The Development of Jewish and Israel Studies in China* (Jerusalem: Hebrew University of Jerusalem, 1992); and Jonathan Goldstein, "Israel and the Great People of China Today," *Midstream* 39, no. 6 (August/September 1993), pp. 23–25.

Part I

The Kaifeng Experience

A. Assimilation and Acculturation

Chapter I.A.1

The Synagogue at Kaifeng: Sino–Judaic Architecture of the Diaspora

Nancy Shatzman Steinhardt

The twentieth-century wooden model of a synagogue in Beth Hatefusoth (the Nahum Goldmann Museum of the Jewish Diaspora), Tel Aviv, is a frequently illustrated architectural reminder of the Jewish community in the city of Kaifeng, Henan province, China (Figure 1). The detailed Chineseness of the reconstruction stands alongside photo-archives as evidence of Kaifeng Jewry from the beginning of the Song dynasty in 960 through the nineteenth century.[1]

The earliest and only pictures of the entire synagogue complex are eighteenth-century Jesuit sketches and slightly later formalized drawings of them (Figure 2).[2] Inscriptions on stelae originally at the site of the synagogue, facing Sinew-Extracting Lane near the intersection of Earth Market Character and Fire-god Shrine Streets, provide a few more details of the buildings or their layout.[3]

The Chinese city of Kaifeng is just one of a myriad of cities where Jews have worshiped in a synagogue in the course of their wanderings since the destruction in 586 B.C. of their most famous temple, the one built by King Solomon in Jerusalem nearly four hundred years earlier. During these two-and-a-half millennia of diaspora, the Jewish house of worship has never acquired a standard form. Since it has just a few religious requirements, synagogue architecture has adopted or been adapted to the architectural spaces of its time and environment. The third-century-A.D. Roman Synagogue in Dura-Europos, Syria, the ca. fourteenth-century Abulafia Synagogue in Toledo, Spain, and the Touro Synagogue of 1760 (designed by Peter Harrison) in Newport, Rhode Island, for instance, are examples of structures distinguishable as Jewish either from formal residences or worship halls of more prevalent faiths in the same city only by Hebrew inscriptions or Jewish symbols. At the other extreme, synagogues famous for structural uniqueness such as Temple Beth Sholom in Elkins Park, Pennsylvania, designed by Frank Lloyd Wright, are equally devoid of obvious Jewish identity on the exterior.[4]

The range of possibilities in synagogue architecture is a direct result of the remarkably few structural requirements for Jewish prayer space. Outside Jerusalem, Jewish worship often occurred in houses, but wherever it took place, the forms and spaces of Jewish worship have been driven by purpose rather than by consistency to identified styles.

In standard literature on the subject, the synagogue is defined by three purposes: congregational worship, study, and community gatherings.[5] The role of community, for study, for prayer, and in and of itself, is most important. Even Solomon's Temple, although described in the Bible, did not motivate subsequent synagogue construction.[6] Simply, the form of the Jewish house of worship has been directed by functionality of space and several objects that had to be housed in it.

Because it had few spatial requirements, the construction of a synagogue should have posed no greater problem in China than in provincial Rome, Muslim Spain, or colonial North America. It perhaps should have posed a smaller problem, for one aspect of the Chinese construction system is especially suited to adaptability, even universality, of forms. All Chinese worship space, Buddhist, Daoist, and Confucian, was derived from royal residential space. The ruler's palace gave way to the earliest layouts for Chinese religious space, and thus the position of the emperor on his throne in his hall of audience was the model for the enshrinement of the Buddha in a temple or in paradise.[7]

Still, the earliest evidence of a synagogue in China, in 1163, suggests that the first designated house of worship may have been built a full thousand years after the arrival of Jews in China, possibly during the reign of Han emperor Mingdi (r. A.D. 58–75) (coincident with the destruction of the Second Temple and the expulsion from Jerusalem in the year 70). Perhaps the numbers of Jews, even during the Tang dynasty (A.D. 618–906), did not warrant more than houses for worship.[8] Yet perhaps a greater cause for the very late appearance of a synagogue in China was a fundamental conflict, in spite of the few architectural constraints of the synagogue and the adaptability of the Chinese construction system, between Jewish theology and Chinese architecture. The same building system that so readily interchanges palatial or Buddhist, Daoist, or Confucian worship space does so primarily because the gods of one religion are often found in the worship hall or an adjacent one of another Chinese religion, and because the arrangement of deities in Chinese religious space was inspired by the hierarchical positions of men, relatives or ministers, in the emperor's hall of audience. In constructing a synagogue, the premodern designer in China had to make compatible the ultimate Jewish theological issue—one God, who could not be represented in human form—with the age-old Chinese residence for a pantheon of deities.

Universalities of Synagogue Space

Not even one feature is necessary for the exterior design or form of a synagogue. The sole external indication of a Jewish house of worship is a *mezzuzah,* a parchment inscribed with the *Shem'a* (or "Hear, O Israel" prayer) and then placed in a case positioned on the doorpost on the right-hand side as one enters.[9] This feature is so small that it is visible only to someone who passes through the entryway. Inside, only three features can be called essential. The principal building component that influences a synagogue's interior plan is the *bimah,* the place where the Torah scrolls are placed for reading (Figure 3). Frequently the design and lighting focus on it, but all that is really necessary for a *bimah* is a table. The table is usually made of wood and enclosed by a railing. The use of wood dates to the time of Ezra and Nehemiah (fifth century B.C.), the former of whom is said to have read the Torah from a wooden pulpit.[10] It is also common for the *bimah* to be covered. Sometimes the floor underneath is lowered in accordance with a passage from Psalms that refers to prayers "rising out of the depths." The *bimah* is usually on the central axis of the building interior, but it can be placed at either end. For acoustical reasons, it is also occasionally placed in the center of the prayer hall.

The main competition for interior focus in a synagogue is the ark (*aron ha-kodesh*), the second necessary component of interior synagogue space. Whereas the *bimah* is the locus of instruction, the ark is the holiest space in the synagogue. It is the repository for the Torah scrolls. Initially the ark was a portable chest that could be kept outside the worship space. By the third to sixth centuries, the ark and its scrolls came to be placed in a wall niche, usually on the wall corresponding to the direction of Jerusalem (in Figure 3 they are stored in a wall cabinet).[11] Later the ark came to be placed in an apse. In certain synagogues the spaces of ark, *bimah,* and pulpit combined in an apse that was modeled after Christian church architecture. The term used by Jews of Eastern Europe to refer to the ark, *aron ha-kodesh,* took its meaning from the ark installed at the Holy of Holies in Solomon's Temple. Of course, no one knows precisely what it looked like, but because the Holy of Holies was separated by a *parokhet* from the room in front of it at

Solomon's Temple, the ark came to be covered by a curtain whose source was the veil in the Holy of Holies. The ark, too, is often on the main building axis, but at one end.

The third requirement for a synagogue today is the eternal light. It has neither specific form nor specified location. Although there was a *ner tamid* (perpetual light) in the Holy Temple, it did not become standard in synagogue architecture until the seventeenth century.[12]

Other components of a synagogue's interior are common but optional. A Jerusalem indicator is often found on the appropriate wall, the eastern wall in Europe and the western in China. A pulpit is also optional. Used as the location from which to give a sermon or read prayers less holy than those read from the *bimah,* the pulpit has been a more common feature in synagogues of Eastern Europe and thus the United States than among Jews of southern Spain or the Islamic countries, who generally conduct the entire service from the *bimah.*

Along practical lines, necessary space is always space for worshipers. Enough space and often space partitioned by a *mechitzah* (a curtain or other divider separating men from women) are required. In the Diaspora, the synagogue has served as a social, educational, and cultural center for the local Jewish community, and there is almost always classroom space. A kitchen, social hall, small chapel, and office space are often part of a synagogue complex. One can also find at least short-term apartments for visitors or the leader of worship.

The Kaifeng Synagogue

Until 1126, the city of Kaifeng was the Song dynasty capital known as Bianliang. Bianliang represented the epitome of urban life in Asia. It was a city in which a lot of money could be made and there was much to spend it on. More open than China's previous capitals, Bianliang no longer had the strict ward system that had characterized earlier cities. Instead, the city had grown almost as a boomtown, expanding beyond its walls as soon as they were completed so that before the end of the tenth century three sets of walls were constructed, of uncharacteristic irregular shape but a direct result of the tremendous rate of growth in the capital. Bianliang was joined to other cities of China by the Grand Canal.[13] The people of Bianliang spent a lot of time on the street; teahouses and shops were filled. The city offered organized public services including a fire department.

Twelfth-century court painter *Zhang* Zeduan's *Qingming shanghe tu* (Qingming festival on the river), a masterful study of the early spring festival in the city where he began his career, captures the fantastic city and the residents' fascination with it.[14] Unfortunately, no one has been able to find the synagogue or Earth Market Street in it. Nineteenth-century local records confirm the existence of the intersection of Earth Market and Fire-god Shrine Streets, but not the actual structure (Figure 4).[15]

It seems more likely that the Jews of Bianliang still worshiped in pre-synagogue quarters like a house during rule of the Song in the north, for the first date associated with the synagogue in Kaifeng is 1163, the year in which stelae inscriptions record the community was authorized to erect a house of worship.[16] By then Song rule in the north and the capital itself had fallen to the non-Chinese but quite sinicized Jin, or Jurchen, dynasty, under whom the edict was issued.[17]

That synagogue of 1163 is nowhere described. It was, according to the same stelae, repaired in 1279, by which time the area was in Mongolian hands. Other than the date, the only fact provided in the stelae inscriptions is: "It was situated southeast of the Earth Market Street, and its four sides were each 35 *zhang* in length."[18] Thirty-five *zhang* equals about 350 feet, and the inference is thus that the dimensions are of a building complex.

The third date that refers to a synagogue at Earth Market Street is 1421, when Prince Ding of Zhou, a nephew of the emperor, gave money for reconstruction of the synagogue. The prince's motivation for the contribution seems not to have been altruism. Rather, his donation is believed to have been a sort of penance for his betrayal of the emperor, a crime that had been exposed by a Jewish soldier from Kaifeng.[19] This Jew was rewarded for his fidelity to the emperor with the surname Zhao, one of the most famous Chinese Jewish surnames even down to the present.[20] Nothing of that synagogue's architecture survives either. However, one detail from the stele of 1489 is noteworthy. During the 1421 rebuilding, an imperial tablet was placed inside.[21] The tablet is important, for it acknowledges both imperial sanction of the Jewish house of worship and allegiance of the worshipers to the emperor. Figure 11 shows where the tablet might have been placed (see #4).

In 1445, two Jews with the surname Li provided funds for rebuilding the synagogue, but this version was lost to a flood in 1461.[22] The community petitioned local authorities to rebuild again and the same Lis offered money to begin reconstruction. Three members of the Gao family provided money for what became not only reconstruction but additions in the back and an enclosing corridor. These repairs took place between 1465 and 1488, and the stele recording them was dedicated the same year as the new synagogue, in 1489. The next inscription, from 1512, may have been written in conjunction with repairs.

Between 1573 and 1620 the synagogue burned down again. It was probably rebuilt in some form, but again it was destroyed. In 1642 the followers of the rebel *Li* Zicheng diverted the waters of the Yellow River, flooding the city and destroying the synagogue in the process.

A major building fund campaign occurred between 1653 and 1663 to which members of seven Jewish clans contributed. This synagogue of 1663 and its congregation are the best known. It was visited and described in letters of early missionaries including Matteo Ricci (see chapter I.B.1 by Michael Pollak in this volume) and Nicolò Longobardi.[23] It was pictured by eighteenth-century Jesuits Jean-Paul Gozani, Jean Domenge, and Antoine Gaubil.

The Kaifeng Synagogue Illustrated

The most famous drawing of the 1663 Kaifeng synagogue is the one by missionary Paul Bruker (see Figure 2) based on the sketch of Father Domenge.[24] The view is from Sinew-Extracting Lane, a reference to the customary method of preparing kosher meat and to a common Chinese epithet that referred to the Jews. At the gate marked #1, one faces west, the direction of Jerusalem from Kaifeng. At one time the words *qing zhen si* were written on the gate. Meaning "pure truth monastery," they use the same characters as those for "mosque."[25]

In the seventeenth century, stone lions stood on either side of the entry to the Kaifeng synagogue. After 1800, when the synagogue was demolished, they became the property of a Buddhist monastery.[26] Directly behind the gate (1) was a *pailou* (2), a memorial archway erected in 1678 in honor of some of the Zhao family members.[27] From here the path to the worship hall was tripartite. Two more triple-entry gateways (3, 4) led farther into the compound. Alternately, one could pass to either side of the main path through doors (5) that ultimately led to the same back courtyard. Side apartments off of the second courtyard (24) were for members of the *kehillah,* the Jewish congregation. Perhaps these were locals who helped maintain the synagogue, or perhaps the space was temporary housing for the Jewish community at large, including visitors from other cities.

The next courtyard had as its focus a free standing gateway (6) flanked by trees and stele (7). To the right as we face the west were the lecture hall (16) and kitchen (18) and to the left another lecture hall (17). North and south beyond them were clan temples, the one on our right for the Zhao clan (23) and the one on the left perhaps for the Lis (22). Beyond, right in front of the westernmost building-complex, was an incense burner (14) flanked by stone (marble) lions (13) and behind them were pots in which miniature trees and shrubs were planted (15). To the right was a well (19) and then the main building.

This multiroom, multi-eaved back structure was flanked by halls dedicated to Abraham (20) to the right, and to unspecified patriarchs (21) to the left. Inside them are said to have been incense burners for offerings to this group, to ancestors of the congregation, and to Confucius.

The spaces and arrangement of space in the synagogue complex at Kaifeng are so Chinese that they call to mind numerous religious and secular architectural compounds, including those of the Qing (1644–1911), the dynasty during which Domenge saw the synagogue. One reason for the formal similarities is the multifunctionality of Chinese architecture referred to earlier. The most common building arrangement in the Chinese structural system was used twice in the Kaifeng synagogue complex. Known as four-sided enclosure (*sihe yuan*), the space is created by four structures and adjoining walls (for example, 3, 4, and 24).[28] A second example of *sihe yuan* is formed directly behind the first. Were the front gate not present, its position would still be implied and the contained space could be labeled *sanhe yuan* (three-sided enclosure). The second extremely common Chinese spatial formation, reserved for the most eminent Chinese structural groups, consists of three buildings in a line, the middle one the smallest in plan; or two buildings joined by a connective corridor. This plan is named *gong* after the Chinese character that looks like a capital I. The building arrangement of the Kaifeng synagogue was suitable for a less eminent architectural complex than the Forbidden City, whose Three Great Halls and Three Back Halls are archetypical *gong* formations. At the synagogue, the main building line consisted of two gates and a hall, in which case the back hall should be and was the main one. The direction of space within the compound to the back hall via a triple-lane approach, here defined by the three passageways of the two gates, is found both in highest-ranking building compounds that employ the *gong* plan and in lesser ones. Thus, in terms of spatial arrangement the Kaifeng synagogue complex was decidedly Chinese. Similarly, the main hall and other individual structures are examples of the ubiquitous post-and-lintel system. The timber skeleton of Chinese construction was amendable and augmentable for religious, palatial, and humble buildings around courtyards or in the *gong* configuration referred to above. Thus revealing no Jewish sign, the three courtyards of architecture at the Kaifeng synagogue are excellent evidence of how the Chinese architectural system masks functional identity.

Brucker's illustration, however, goes a step farther. The presentation of his drawing, and of Father Domenge's on which it is based, is the standard one of a Chinese building complex in a provincial or more local record (Figure 5). The very gradual one-point perspective that shows all of the fronts and some of the sides of buildings is preserved not only in Qing-dynasty printed books but in

Buddhist paradises painted about nine hundred years before Brucker's drawing.[29] It is a clear break from the European architectural drawings that had surely been seen by missionaries in seventeenth- and eighteenth-century China.

Building by building as well, the Kaifeng synagogue complex appears to have been very much a standard residential-religious compound of Qing China, whose unassuming entry off Earth Market Street indicated little about the arrangement or scope of the courtyard architecture behind.[30] It is possible, however, to identify a more specific subset of Chinese architecture that offers models for what came to be the Kaifeng synagogue complex. This group consists of the architecture of temple complexes for paying homage to national or local heroes such as Confucius, or residential architecture of China's most powerful families. Such buildings can be found all over China. Here, examples are drawn from Shandong, Shanxi, Guangdong, and Taiwan.

One begins with the Kong family mansion in Qufu, the city known as Lüdu when Confucius was a statesman there in the sixth century B.C.[31] More than seventy generations later, Kong family descendants who lived in the same area until the founding of the People's Republic could trace their ancestry directly to *Kongzi* (Confucius). In the eleventh century, Bianliang's second century as the Chinese capital, the Song emperor enfeoffed a forty-sixth generation descendant of Confucius as duke, entitling him and all eldest-son descendants to an area that in its present form occupies fourteen hectares of land in Qufu. In the Ming dynasty, the first emperor ordered sacrifices to Confucius at Qufu and awarded funds to the Kongs to repair both their mansion and the Confucian temple. In the sixteenth century, local government offices were incorporated into the family compound so that the yamen buildings were directly in front of the family residences. Except for the Forbidden City, the Kong family mansion is unique in its structural integration of government office and private residence.[32] The historical circumstances of imperial sanction and awards to the local family are comparable to those at the synagogue in Kaifeng during the Song, Ming, and Qing dynasties.

At the Confucian complex, stone lions flank the entries to both the temple and the mansion in the manner described for the Kaifeng synagogue. Further, one finds *pailou,* the trilane approach, central incense burners, and at the temple, two enclosed courtyards (*sihe yuan*) in front of the main building complex (Figures 6 and 7).

It is in Confucian and Confucian-equivalent architectural space and the architectural space of powerful families that one finds the best comparative examples for the Kaifeng synagogue. Next to Confucius, the most important focus of native Chinese reverence is Guan Yu.[33] In the national temple to Guan Yu (Guandi), in Yuncheng, at the southern tip of Shanxi province, the Qing-period architectural arrangement is similar to that of the Confucian building complex just described. Entered via a *pailou,* the passage proceeds along a tripartite path through gateway after gateway after gateway, punctuated by incense burners but ultimately leading to the main hall of reverence (Figures 8 and 9). The layout of Confucian temples outside Qufu is similar.[34] So is the presence of structures like a kitchen, meeting room, and lecture or educational hall, all recorded at the Kaifeng synagogue. Moreover, the architectural arrangement is employed in residential space of the most powerful local families of any Chinese town, such as the Chen family mansion in Guangdong or the Lin family mansion in Banqiao, Taiwan, even though each bears signs of local style in roof construction (Figure 10).[35]

A few more structures of the Kaifeng synagogue complex can also be found in important residential or religious Chinese contexts. It is recorded, for instance, that there was a drum tower at the Kaifeng synagogue. The building, not shown in the Jesuit drawings, usually pairs with a bell tower on either side of the main monastery axis as the time-keeping devices of the religious complex. In a Buddhist context, the bell was sounded or the drum beaten to remind worshipers it was time to pray. The main worship hall, lecture hall, monks' quarters, and kitchens are always present in Chinese monastery architecture. It is a little surprising that the People of the Book did not have a separate scripture hall, another standard structure, often with fantastic interior cabinetry including revolving cabinets for sutra storage.[36]

The Kaifeng Synagogue Main Hall

The main hall of the Kaifeng synagogue measured about 40 feet wide and 60 feet deep. Like any Chinese main hall, it was raised on a platform and surrounded by a balustrade. It was a timber-frame, pillar-supported hall for which exterior pillars indicated column rows that extended across the interior. The aisle defined by the two central pillars of the front facade was wider than the side ones (Figure 11). (The description of the interior from here on follows the arbitrary lettering or numbering of published drawings.) First was a table (1) on which were placed an incense burner (A), vases, and candlesticks. Behind was a chair, termed by seventeenth- and eighteenth-century observers the Chair of Moses (2). The Torah held upright would be read from this place. In the only surviving illustration of the Chair, a sketch of Father Domenge's (Figure 12), both reader and holder are standing (such as is the case at the eighteenth-century synagogue in Amsterdam shown in Figure 3). However, in a letter of December 20, 1724, entitled "Clarification of Remarks on the Kaifeng Bible," Father Domenge included one detail about the Chair of Moses (*Chaire de Moïse*) that suggests a different function. According to the letter, when the leader of the congregation, perhaps the rabbi (*chef de la cérémonie*), was seated on the Chair of Moses, a large red satin cloth was held over him.[37] It is possible that at certain times the rabbi sat in the same position with a large red satin umbrella held over him.[38] Precisely above this chair was a sunken lattice ceiling (16). Clearly, the Chair was the focal point of the interior. Directly behind was a freestanding pavilion, labeled "dragon pavilion" (*long lou*) in Domenge's drawing, on which stood a tablet (4). If the date on the table is correct, the one seen by Domenge was from the Wanli reign period (1573–1619). A second table and tablet from the Qing dynasty is said to have stood behind it. One of these tablets made its way into a mosque in Kaifeng before 1912, when it was seen by Bishop White.[39] Above the Qing tablet were the words of the *Shem'a*,[40] here shown in the position of 15. Next was a table with a miniature *pailou* on it (7) and then the holy ark that contained the Torah scrolls (8). At one time there were thirteen of them. Cases to the right and left held (to the right) individual weekly portions *(parashot)* (9) and to the left miscellaneous scriptures owned by the congregation (10). Above the front of each of these were the first two lines of the *Shem'a* together with two words that, if properly copied, read "sun" and "moon" (14).[41] The last object of note in the sanctuary, in the lower right of the drawing, was a basin for hand washing (13).

Like the groundplan of the complex, the details of the main worship hall are found in individual Chinese structures. The timber frame elevated on a stone platform and surrounded by a stone balustrade is found in every province of China. Hypostyle construction was also standard in the Qing period and earlier. As for the interior contents, the front table, with its incense burner, bronze vessels, and candlesticks, could have been found in almost any Qing temple hall. The sunken portion of the ceiling, where one would have expected to find an eternal light in a synagogue, was in all likelihood a *zaojing* (a latticework or other decorative indentation from the ceiling toward the roof), a form known from Chinese architecture since the tenth century.[42] If so, the Chinese source of beauty may have been substituted for, or even taken on as a symbol of, an eternal light. Like most Chinese religious halls, at the Kaifeng synagogue lattice doors and windows were the sources of light.

If one were to remove the Chair of Moses and replace it with a Confucian tablet and substitute Chinese inscriptions for Hebrew, the interior space becomes that of a Chinese hall. In it, one burns incense, makes an animal sacrifice or food offering,[43] walks along the sides to the central or back focus of worship, but does not sit for a service.[44] The presence of incense burners suggests that, as was and is the case in every region of China, a Chinese Jew in Kaifeng entered at will to burn incense at least as often, if not more often, than he entered for a scheduled service.[45] Probably that is why there are no seats and why it was also possible to sacrifice to Confucius and to family ancestors in the courtyard in front of where Torah scrolls were read. Indeed, the tablets to the Zhaos and to at least one other local Jewish family point to a primary role of the Kaifeng synagogue as a temple of homage to its patrons (the Zhaos) and to Jewish patriarchs like Abraham and Moses (who had small side temples) as much as a locus of congregational worship. Again, the central role of tablets for reverence in the place of statues is confirmed in Qing and twentieth-century temple interiors (Figure 13), especially in Confucian temples, in which the statesman is more often worshiped through his tablet than as a deity (Figure 14).

Judaism in the Kaifeng Synagogue Main Hall

With such strong visual links to Confucian shrines, one legitimately asks whether this can be called a synagogue. Returning to the prerequisites for a synagogue mentioned above, no record of a *mezzuzah* on the doorpost has been found. Inside, the most serious omission is that of the *bimah*.

In the Kaifeng synagogue, scriptures were read from the Chair of Moses, located where one would expect to find the *bimah,* on the main axis near the center of the worship hall. The function of the Chair of Moses as a *bimah* was recognized by Gozani and Domenge.[46] Yet a true Seat of Moses (*k'sidrah d'Mosheh*) was different from a *bimah*. According to Wilhelm Bacher, "Seat of Moses" originally referred to the chair in which the chief justice of the Sanhedrin, the Jewish court, sat.[47] The existence of a Seat of Moses in Kaifeng and the discrepancy between it and this classical definition were realized in the scholarly literature the same year Bacher published his paper—the Seat of Moses was not intended for sitting.[48] It functioned, in fact, as a *bimah*. It is unlikely, however, that the name was arbitrary. Perhaps one could apply the definition for the Seat of Moses proposed by Israel Renov, "a symbol of Jewish legal authority conferred upon teachers of Jewish law."[49] If so, then an umbrella raised above the head of the rabbi probably was empowered with added meaning. In an Asian context, the first significance of an umbrella over a head is recognition of the East and West Asian practice of shielding the head of royalty. The Buddha Śākyamuni, for instance, when depicted during his youth as a prince, is covered by an umbrella borne by servants as was customary for an Indian prince.[50]

Besides drawing from the symbols of Asian royalty to underscore the role of the rabbi in the Jewish community, the Chair of Moses seems to suggest a second type of symbolism. The rabbi in the isolated Jewish community of Kaifeng may well have functioned as a judge, not with the power of a member of the Sanhedrin but rather as the one with authority to settle everyday matters or small disputes in the lives of his congregants. Thus even without its occupant and his red umbrella, the vacant chair suggests symbolism additional to that of a *bimah*. It was the highest authority of Jewish self-government in an isolated community.

The sun and moon, although less explicitly symbolic, were more widespread in Asian art, both native Chinese and general Buddhist. Since ancient times in China, the celestial bodies have been references to the ultimate forces in an ordered universe. The symbolism of the sun and moon in China during the last two centuries B.C. is now well documented by objects like the silk "banners" excavated at Mawangdui (Figure 15) or wall painting from the tomb of *Bu* Qianqiu in Luoyang.[51] Deities of the sun and moon were part of the Buddhist pantheon of symbols in East Asia by the eighth century, when they are found as the gods Nikko and Gakko on the Buddhist altar of the Hokkedō at the monastery Tōdai-ji in Nara, Japan.[52] On the other side of China, the sun and moon are part of the Khotanese wallpainting tradition. They appear in the hands of three-headed, multi-armed deities at Dandan-öilik and Balawaste and as wheat bread shapes in a Manichean painting found at the Uyghur capital Qoço (Gaochang).[53] The creative use of Chinese and East Asian Buddhist symbols away from their contextual origins gives way to the sort of commingling of a Western faith and Eastern motifs in evidence at the Kaifeng synagogue. Still, the words "sun" and "moon" on the wall do not mean that they are to be taken as part of a Chinese or Buddhist or Manichean or Jewish pantheon of gods; they are simply adopted members of what has become a Jewish pantheon of symbols.

As for the other components of a synagogue, the ark is present. It contains the scriptures and, as has been standard in Western Europe and in the United States, it is placed on the wall toward which prayer is directed, the wall that faces Jerusalem. Whether or not the western wall contained a Jerusalem indicator, the western orientation of the synagogue, in contrast to the standard Chinese practice of southern orientation for religious and palatial main halls, implies recognition of the direction toward which a Kaifeng Jew would pray. The pulpit, however, is missing. So, it has been noted, are seats and places where one would expect to have found them. Finally, the *ner tamid* is absent, but as has been suggested, its function may have been represented by a *zaojing*. Yet many aspects of a synagogue function are noticeably present. One is the role of the Jewish house of worship as a community center, perhaps a safe haven for Jewish socialization in an otherwise Chinese city. This purpose was the reason for the kitchen and residential apartments.

Certainly the Kaifeng building complex was a synagogue. Its primary function as a locus of Jewish worship and community is confirmed by Hebrew inscriptions, Torahs, the Seat of Moses (whatever it symbolized), and much more. Yet specific forms of the synagogue were unique in Chinese and Jewish architecture, a Sino–Judaic building group made possible both by the widespread religious compatibility of a Chinese architectural environment and by the few architectural constraints of synagogue architecture.

Finally, however, one must address the ultimate question of Judaism in a polytheistic world. What was the role of God in the sanctuary? The imperial tablets in the center clearly offered imperial Chinese sanction to this space. It was a sort of sanction similar to that offered to the Kong family at their mansions adjacent to the national Confucian temple.

The key to the identification of this worship hall as a Jewish sanctuary is the position of the *Shem'a*. It surely was not a coincidence that the *Shem'a*, in particular a passage in which the name of God occurs three times, was written in three places. Nor, furthermore, that two of the inscriptions occupied physically higher spots than the emperor's name. Since every Chinese religious hall has inscriptions, the implications of the location might not have attracted attention of a Chinese official or Jesuit as a challenge to the place of the emperor in the Jewish world. Nevertheless, the one fundamental and uninterpretable aspect of Judaism, the oneness and supremacy of God, could not be and was not questioned.

The Kaifeng synagogue was much more than simply another example of how adaptable the Chinese architectural system is that can accommodate Buddhist and Daoist and Confucian and Muslim and Nestorian and Jewish architecture within it. It is also more than another example of how few the liturgical requirements are for what constitutes a synagogue or an example of how Jews have accommodated worship to circumstances of Diaspora. The Kaifeng Synagogue was a monument of legitimacy and power expressed within the confines of Song and then Ming–Qing society by originally an ethnic and always a numerical minority. The brilliantly conceived architectural space of the Kaifeng synagogue, through its direct borrowing from Confucian or Confucian-equivalent temple architecture, legitimated the Jews as Chinese citizens, or at least the presence of Jews in China. It legitimated the Zhaos and other Chinese Jewish families as noteworthy members of their local and ethnic community. Its construction legitimated Judaism as a religion according to the Chinese understanding of the term. In other words, the message of the space was that in this place one worshiped local and national ancestors and burned incense to them with the emperor's

16   THE KAIFENG EXPERIENCE

tablet in the center. For religions like Judaism or Christianity, it was possible for the Chinese government to be tolerant probably because it was not fully understood that monotheism placed God above the authority of the emperor. The Chinese architectural context of the synagogue helped cloud the presence of God and diffuse His ultimate authority.

Yet the architecture also allowed Jewish religious observance for those to whom it mattered. The Kaifeng synagogue offered a full-service Jewish life-style including food prepared by ritual slaughter and prayer several times a day. The architecture of the Kaifeng synagogue made clear the power of God above that of the Chinese emperor or Confucius. It also made possible congregational worship, Torah reading, or bar mitzvah for any who desired them behind the facade of a simple gateway near the corner of Earth Market Street and Fire-god Shrine Street.

Notes

1. Pictures of the model of the synagogue and members of the Kaifeng Jewish community are published in, for example, Donald D. Leslie, *The Survival of the Chinese Jews: The Jewish Community of Kaifeng* (Leiden: E.J. Brill, 1972), and Michael Pollak, *Mandarins, Jews, and Missionaries: The Jewish Experience in the Chinese Empire* (Philadelphia: Jewish Publication Society, 1980). I would like to thank Professor Albert Dien of Stanford University and Professor Donald D. Leslie of the Australian National University for helpful comments about this paper and bibliographic references.

2. A fanciful Italian illustration of the synagogue is published and discussed in Rudolph Löwenthal, "An Imaginary Illustration of the Kaifeng Synagogue," *Oriens Extremus* 19, nos. 1–2 (December 1972), pp. 95–99.

3. According to Leslie, the site of the nineteenth-century synagogue was the same as that of earlier synagogues in Kaifeng, at least since 1279 (*Survival*, pp. 158–59). For inscriptions, translations, and discussion, see Jérôme Tobar, *Inscriptions juives de K'ai-foung fou* [The Jewish Inscriptions of Kaifeng-fu] (Shanghai [sic]: Imprimerie de la Mission catholique, Orphelinat de T'ou-sè-wè, 1900); William C. White, *Chinese Jews: A Compilation of Matters Relating to the Jews of K'ai-fêng Fu*, 3 vols. (Toronto: University of Toronto Press, 1942), vol. 2; and Leslie, "Some Notes on the Jewish Inscriptions of Ka'i-feng," *Journal of the American Oriental Society* 82 (1962), pp. 346–61 (based on Yitzhak Ben-Zvi, "The Stone Tablets of the Old Synagogue in Kaifengfu" [in Hebrew], *Sefunot* 5 (1961), pp. 29–66). Hereafter, Earth Market Character Street (Tushizijie) will be shortened to Earth Market Street.

4. Rachel Wischnitzer-Bernstein addresses this issue in "The Problem of the Synagogue," *Commentary* 3, no. 3 (1947), pp. 233–41. Other studies of the synagogue that I have found useful for this study are Isaac Levy, *The Synagogue: Its History and Function* (London: Valentine and Mitchell, 1963); Azriel Eisenberg, *The Synagogue Through the Ages* (New York: Bloch, 1974); Joseph Gutmann, comp., *The Synagogue: Studies in Origins, Archaeology, and Architecture* (New York: KTAV, 1975); B. de Breffny, *The Synagogue* (New York: Macmillan, 1978); and Carol H. Krinsky, *Synagogues of Europe: Architecture, History, Meaning* (New York, Cambridge, MA, and London: Architectural History Foundation and MIT Press, 1975).

5. Krinsky, *Synagogues of Europe*, p. 5. Joseph Gutmann, *The Jewish Sanctuary*

(Leiden: E.J. Brill, 1983), p. 1, defines the synagogue's functions according to the three Hebrew names for the structure, translated as "house of prayer," "house of learning (study)," and "house of assembly."

6. On the Temple of Solomon, see Joseph Gutmann, ed., *The Temple of Solomon* (Missoula: University of Montana Press, 1976), and Th. Busink, *Der Tempel von Jerusalem von Salomo bis Herodes,* 2 vols. (Leiden: E.J. Brill, 1970 and 1980).

7. Alexander Soper, *The Evolution of Buddhist Architecture in Japan* (Princeton: Princeton University Press, 1942), pp. 1–21 *passim,* notes this Chinese adaptation of palatial space into religious space.

8. On evidence of Jews in China during the Han and Tang dynasties, see Leslie, *Survival,* pp. 4–7.

9. If a Jew knows only one prayer in Hebrew, it is the first six words of the *Shem'a.* Usually the first prayer a Jewish child learns, it is recited in daily morning and evening services. The six words, "Hear, O Israel, the Lord our God, the Lord is One," reaffirm the oneness of God, the cornerstone of the Jewish faith.

10. Sources of the information about the *bimah,* the ark and its cover, eternal light, and other components of the synagogue and their locations discussed in this paragraph and the three that follow can be found in Krinsky, *Synagogues of Europe,* pp. 21–27 and 31–34, and Gutmann, *The Jewish Sanctuary,* esp. pp. 11–16. Although the presence of a *mezzuzah* on the doorpost is stipulated in the first paragraph of the *Shem'a* (after the sentence quoted in note 9), neither Gutmann nor Krinsky mention it as a prerequisite of synagogue construction.

11. Ibid., p. 12.

12. Ibid., p. 13.

13. Numerous studies of the Northern Song capital and its role as a commercial center have been written. See, for example, Edward Kracke, "Sung K'ai-feng: Pragmatic Metropolis and Formalistic Capital," in *Crisis and Prosperity in Sung China,* ed. John Haeger (Tucson: University of Arizona Press, 1975), pp. 49–77; Shiba Yoshinobu, *Commerce and Society in Sung China* (Ann Arbor: University of Michigan, Center for Chinese Studies, 1970); and on the plan of the city see Nancy Steinhardt, *Chinese Imperial Planning* (Honolulu: University of Hawaii Press, 1990), pp. 137–44.

14. For illustrations and discussion of this painting, see Roderick Whitfield, "Chang Tse-tuan's *Ch'ing-ming shang-ho t'u,*" in *Proceedings of the International Symposium on Chinese Painting* (Taibei: National Palace Museum, 1972), pp. 351–415.

15. This page is also published as Map E in White, *Chinese,* vol. 1, and Leslie, *Survival,* plate 33.

16. The date is recorded in the stelae of 1489 and 1512 and repeated in the inscription of 1663. For a translation of the passage from the stelae of 1489 see Leslie, *Survival,* pp. 23–24, and *Xiao* Xian's article in volume two of this publication.

17. The two major studies of Jin Sinicization are *Tao* Jing-shen, *The Jurchen in Twelfth-Century China: A Study of Sinicization* (Seattle and London: University of Washington Press, 1976), and Hok-lam Chan, *Legitimation in Imperial China: Discussions Under the Jurchen–Chin Dynasty* (Seattle and London: University of Washington Press, 1984).

18. White, *Chinese,* vol. 2, p. 12.

19. On this incident see *Fang* Chaoying, "Notes on the Chinese Jews of Kaifeng," *Journal of the American Oriental Society* 85, no. 2 (1965), pp. 126–29.

20. As recently as 1980, Albert Dien stood at the Kaifeng intersection where the synagogue used to stand and asked if anyone knew any Jews. He was led to the home of a family named Zhao and was told by a family member that her grandfather was in a picture from Bishop White's book that Professor Dien showed her. The story, which I

heard from Professor Dien in July of that year, also appears in Donald Leslie's review of Pollak's *Mandarins* in *Harvard Journal of Asiatic Studies* 41, no. 2 (1981), pp. 699–71. For more on the Zhao family of Kaifeng, see Leslie, "The K'ai-feng Jew Chao Ying-ch'eng and His Family," *T'oung Pao* 53, nos. 1–3 (1967), pp. 147–79.

21. White, *Chinese,* vol. 2, p. 12.

22. Ibid., p. 13. The history in this paragraph and the next two is also retold in Pollak, *Mandarins,* pp. 274–79, and Leslie, *Survival,* pp. 25–30. The stelae inscriptions recording the history are translated and analyzed in White, *Chinese,* vol. 2.

23. The best source for Jesuit accounts of the Jews of China is Joseph Dehergne, S.J., and Donald Leslie, *Juifs de Chine* (Roma: Institutum Historicum, 1984). Jesuit records are summarized in Leslie, *Survival,* pp. 174–85.

24. This drawing is illustrated and discussed in White, *Chinese,* vol. 1, pp. 2–4; Leslie, *Survival,* plate 21; and Pollak, *Mandarins,* pp. 279–82.

25. Because they have minarets, pointed arches, and, frequently, stone walls, Chinese mosques are more obvious from the outside than was the Kaifeng synagogue as a Jewish house of worship. Churches, which appeared in China centuries after mosques, are similarly obvious from the exterior, because of both stone as a building material and the presence of crosses. The mosque that seems to have led to the idea the Chinese mosques are essentially Chinese halls is the one that best fits that description, the Ming-period mosque in Xian. (On this mosque, see Jill S. Cowen, "Dongdasi of Xian: A Mosque in the Guise of a Buddhist Temple," *Oriental Art* 29, no. 2 [1983], pp. 134–47.) However, surviving mosques in Quanzhou, Yangzhou, and Guangzhou bear more signs of their Islamicness. The Kaifeng synagogue, in contrast to most mosques and churches in China, was distinctively devoid of external symbols (except, perhaps, a *mezuzah*) that might have identified it as a Jewish place of worship. For illustrations of mosques in China, see *Yang* Yongsheng, ed., *Gujianzhu youcan zhinan* (Travel guide to ancient architecture) (Beijing: Zhongguo jianzhu gongye chubanshe [China Building Industry Press], 1988), pp. 371 and 403.

26. According to White, *Chinese Jews,* vol. 1, p. 3. His caption refers to the gate where they stood. Pollak also mentions this fact in *Mandarins,* p. 280.

27. All numbers in the next four paragraphs refer to Figure 2.

28. *Sihe yuan* and other standard arrangements of Chinese residential space and their associations are explained in *Liu* Dunzhen, *Zhongguo zhuzhai gaishuo* (Notes on Chinese residences) (Beijing, 1957; repr. Taibei: Wenming Press, 1981), pp. 25–38. The *gong*-plan, mentioned later in this paragraph, is discussed and illustrated in *Liu* Dunzhen, *Zhongguo gudai jianzhu shi* (History of traditional Chinese architecture), 2d ed. (Beijing: Zhongguo jianzhu gongye chubanshe [China Building Industry Press], 1984), pp. 8 and 11–13.

29. Examples of Buddhist paradise paintings where this formation is evident are found in Mogao Caves 148, 172, and 217 at Dunhuang.

30. In a Chinese town, the size of the entrance usually reveals little about what lies behind it. The actual double-door size is the same for entrances to courtyard-style domestic architecture that survives from the nineteenth-century Taiwanese fishing village Lugang and to the most expansive gardens of Suzhou that occupy tens of courtyards of buildings plus acres of landscape architecture.

31. On the Kong family mansion, see Nancy S. Steinhardt, *Chinese Traditional Architecture* (New York: China Institute, 1984), pp. 152–57; and *Pu* Hong, "Eba dizhu shuangyuan-Qufu 'Kongfu' " (A tyrant-landlord's manor—The 'Confucian Mansion'), *Kaogu* (Archaeology), no. 4 (1974), pp. 226–33.

32. Steinhardt, *Chinese Traditional Architecture,* pp. 155 and 157.

33. For more on Guan Yu, see Prasenjit Duara, *Culture, Power, and the State* (Stanford: Stanford University Press, 1988), pp. 139–48.

34. For the layouts of Confucian temples in Taiwan see *Han* Pao-teh (Baode), *Zhanghua Kongmiao de yanjiu yu xiufu jihua* (Investigation and plans for the restoration of the Confucian Temple at Zhanghua) (Taizhong: Donghai University Press, 1975).

35. On the Lin Mansion see *Han* Pao-teh, *Banqiao Linzhai* (Lin mansion at Banqiao) (Taizhong: Donghai University Press, 1972).

36. Revolving sutra cabinets survive in the ca. tenth-century pavilion of the Revolving Sutra Cabinet at Longxing Monastery in Zhengding, Hebei, and at the Qing dynasty monastery Tayuansi on Mount Wutai, Taihuai, Shanxi. On revolving sutra cabinets, see L. Carrington Goodrich, "The Revolving Bookcase in China," *Harvard Journal of Asiatic Studies* 7 (1942), pp. 130–61.

37. Dehergne and Leslie, *Juifs de Chine*, p. 184.

38. In his study of the journals of two Chinese who visited the Kaifeng synagogue in 1850, Bishop George Smith of Victoria writes that the rabbi was said to have been seated on an elevated "position" with a large red satin umbrella held over him. Although the synagogue no longer had a rabbi when Smith's delegates visited, the umbrella was still there. See Pollak, *Mandarins*, pp. 294 and 412, whose source is George Smith, ed., *The Jews at K'ae-fung-foo: Being a Narrative of a Mission of Inquiry to the Jewish Synagogue at K'ae-fung-foo on Behalf of the London Society for Promoting Christianity Among the Jews* (Shanghai: Missionary Society Press, 1851), p. 51. White, *Chinese*, vol. 1, p. 116, also says it was a red umbrella. I suspect that the elevated position was the Chair of Moses.

39. White, *Chinese Jews*, vol. 2, pp. 24–25 and note 23.

40. See note 9 for translation of the key passage, which also appeared on the synagogue walls.

41. The Hebrew words are *kamon* and *shemesh*. As Pollak explains in his note on the subject (*Mandarins*, pp. 410–11), the interpretation of the words as sun and moon raised some skepticism in a Jewish context. Smith, *The Jews at K'ae-fung-foo*, p. 27, presented a Christian interpretation, namely, that these were the names of two angels. In 1853, Joseph Zedner accepted *shemesh* as sun but offered an explanation of *kamon* as a miscopying of a Hebraicization of *qamar*, Arabic for moon (Pollak, *Mandarins*, pp. 410–11).

42. For illustrations of the *zaojing* in Central and East Asia, see Alexander Soper, "The 'Dome of Heaven' in Asia," *Art Bulletin* 29, no. 4 (1947), pp. 225–48. White's comment (*Chinese Jews*, vol. 1, p. 7) that the ceiling formation was derived from a Persian source is perhaps based on knowledge of some Sasanian ceiling form. So far, no one has proved that the Chinese and West Asian "domes of heaven" are linked. The Chinese ceiling structure known as *zaojing* has a continuous Chinese history beginning in the tenth century.

43. There is no record of animal sacrifice in the Kaifeng synagogue. Food offerings are still fundamental for Chinese worship. In synagogue ritual, sacrifice of animals ceased with the destruction of the Second Temple, so the practice of Judaism outside Jerusalem was coincident with the termination of ritual sacrifice and with the slightly later emergence of the institution known as the synagogue. As for other practices in the Kaifeng synagogue, Jesuit accounts provide few details. Bowing and kneeling, worship toward one direction, and prayer in bare feet (see Figure 12) were repeatedly observed. (Barefoot prayer is typical of Jewish worship in the Muslim world and of Muslims in China.) So was the wearing of skull caps (but not prayer shawls), the use of exclusively vocal music, and bathing before holidays or on festivals. According to White (*Chinese Jews*, vol. 1, p. 4), the Kaifeng synagogue complex had a building for ablutions that was not pictured in Domenge's sketch. Pollak, *Mandarins*, p. 292, interpreted the purported ablutions structure as the location of a *mikveh* (ritual bath house). On Chinese Jewish

ritual, see Leslie, *Survival*, esp. pp. 86–96 and notes to those pages for sources of this information from Jesuit diaries.

44. In my observation in Confucian, Buddhist, and Daoist temples in North and South China, Inner Mongolia, Hong Kong, and Taiwan during eight different years between 1976 and 1993 I have seen worshipers seated only once (in Tainan, Taiwan, in 1977). At that time folding chairs were brought into the temple hall for a ten-minute service. It is conceivable that Jews prayed from the floor, as is the practice in Jewish worship in the Muslim world. Yet, based on Chinese religious precedent, I believe that it is just as likely that on the majority of occasions when a Jew entered the Kaifeng synagogue his stay was short enough to stand throughout. (Perhaps the reason no *mechitzah* has been observed is the lack of permanent seating.)

45. According to the Jesuit accounts, there were some scheduled holiday observances. Jews in Kaifeng celebrated what was referred to as the Feast of Unleavened Bread and Paschal Lamb and an autumn festival that has been called Simchat Torah. However, as Leslie (*Survival*, p. 87) points out, the times of the year when major Jewish festivals are celebrated correspond to the seasons, when native Chinese observance would also bring its devotees into a religious building.

46. Leslie, *Survival*, pp. 83 and 93. I thank Professor David Stern of University of Pennsylvania for helpful information about the history of the Chair of Moses in ancient synagogues and its possible counterpart in church interiors. See also Marilyn Chiat, "The Synagogue at Kaifeng, Henan Province," in *East Gate of Kaifeng: A Jewish World Inside China*, ed. M. Patricia Needle (Minneapolis: China Center, University of Minnesota, 1992), pp. 59–63.

47. Wilhelm Bacher, "Le siège de Moïse," *Revue des études juifs* 34 (1897), pp. 299–301.

48. Mayer Sulzberger, "Encore le siège de Moïse," *Revue des études juifs* 35 (1897), pp. 110–11.

49. Israel Renov, "The Seat of Moses," in *The Synagogue*, ed. Joseph Gutmann (New York: KTAV, 1953), p. 233.

50. Famous examples in relief sculpture of this image are found in the late-fifth-century Cave 6 from Yun'gang, Shanxi province. The custom of protecting the head of Asian royalty originated much farther west and much earlier. One of the earliest depictions is a fragment of Akkadian relief sculpture from about 2400 B.C. in the Musée du Louvre. (See Anton Moortgat, *The Art of Ancient Mesopotamia* [London and New York: Phaidon, 1969], plate 125.)

51. At least twenty studies of the interpretation of the silk "banners" from Mawangdui have been written. See, for example, Annelise Bulling, "The Guide of the Souls Picture in the Western Han Tomb in Ma-wang-tui near Ch'ang-sha," *Oriental Art* 20, no. 2 (1974), pp. 158–73; Chow Fong, "Ma-wang-tui: a Treasure-Trove from the Western Han Dynasty," *Artibus Asiae* 35, no. 1–2 (1973), pp. 5–24; Michael Loewe, *Ways to Paradise* (London: George Allen & Unwin, 1979); and Anna Seidel, "Tokens of Immortality in Han Graves," *Numen* 29, no. 1 (1982), pp. 79–122. On the tomb of *Bu* Qianqiu and interpretation of its wall paintings see *Sun* Zuoyun, "Luoyang Xi Han *Bu* Qianqiu bihua kaoshi" (Analysis of the wall paintings in the Western Han tomb of Bu Qianqiu in Luoyang), *Wenwu* (Cultural Relics), no. 6 (1977), pp. 17–22.

52. The deities on the altar of the Hokke-dō (or Sangatsu-dō) (Lotus Law Hall or Hall of the Third Moon) are found in almost any history of Japanese art. See, for example, Penelope Mason, *History of Japanese Art* (Englewood Cliffs, NJ: Prentice-Hall, 1993), p. 69.

53. It may not be a coincidence that the sun and moon were found at the Kaifeng synagogue and in Khotanese painting. Khotan was one of the Central Asian oases with a

Jewish population at the time of the Tang dynasty (618–906) in China. The Judeo–Persian manuscript found there by Aurel Stein was published by D.S. Margoliouth in *Journal of the Royal Asiatic Society* in 1903. (For a reference see Leslie, *Survival,* p. 165.) For an illustration of the painting from Dandan-öilik, see Benjamin Rowland, *The Art of Central Asia* (New York: Crown, 1975), p. 131. For the painting from Balawaste, see Mario Bussagli, *Painting of Central Asia* (Geneva: Albert Skira, 1963), p. 60. The Qoço painting is published in Herbert Härtel et al., *Along the Ancient Silk Route: Central Asian Art from the Western Berlin State Museums* (New York: Metropolitan Museum of Art, 1982), pp. 176–77. All these paintings are dated between the sixth and tenth centuries.

Figure 1. Model of the Kaifeng Synagogue, Beth Hatefusoth, Tel Aviv. Published with permission of Beth Hatefusoth, the Nahum Goldmann Museum of the Jewish Diaspora.

Figure 2. The Kaifeng Synagogue. Redrawn by Joseph Brucker, S.J., based on the sketch of Father Domenge, eighteenth century. After White, *Chinese Jews*, vol. 1, p. 2.

Figure 3. *The Portugese Synagogue in Amsterdam*, 1583. Engraving of Bernard Picart, Amsterdam, 1725. Collection of Alfred Rubens, London. After Alfred Rubens, *A Jewish Iconography* (London: Nonpareil, 1982), p. 79. Published with permission of Alfred Rubens.

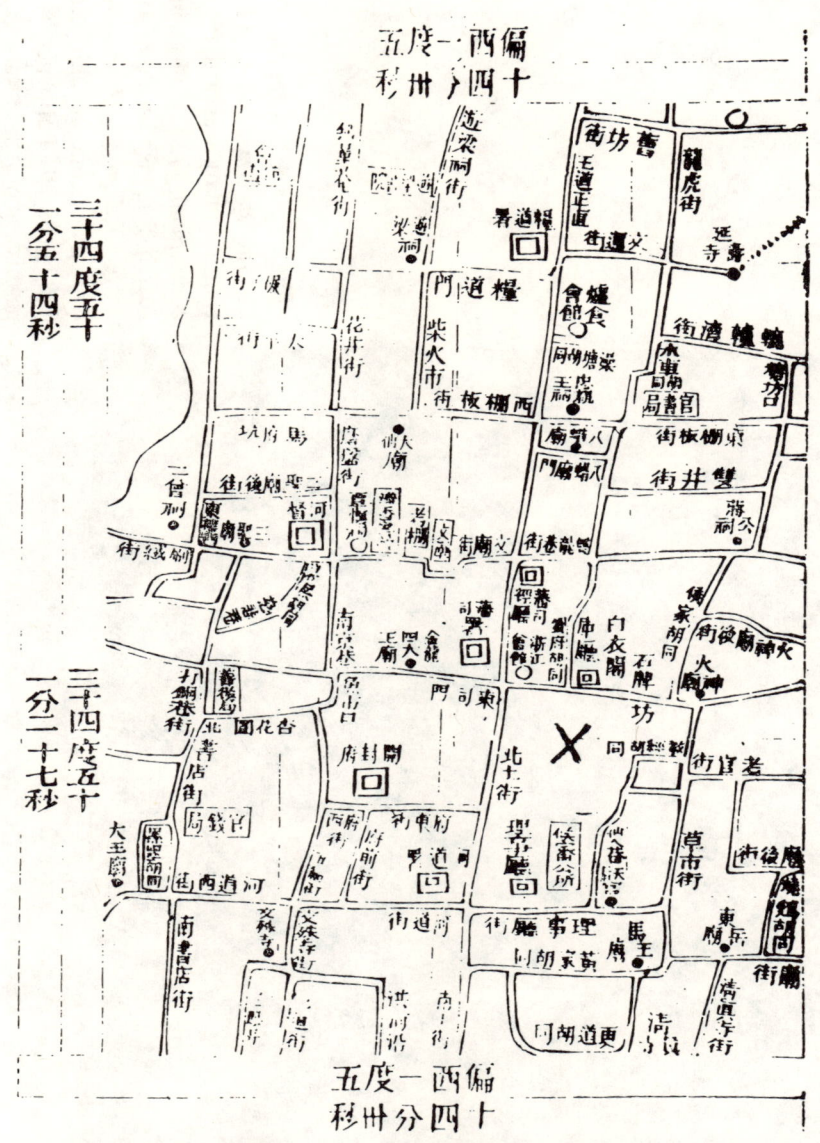

Figure 4. Map of portion of Kaifeng showing street intersection where synagogue was located. *Xiangfuxian zhi* (Record of Xiangfu county), 1898.

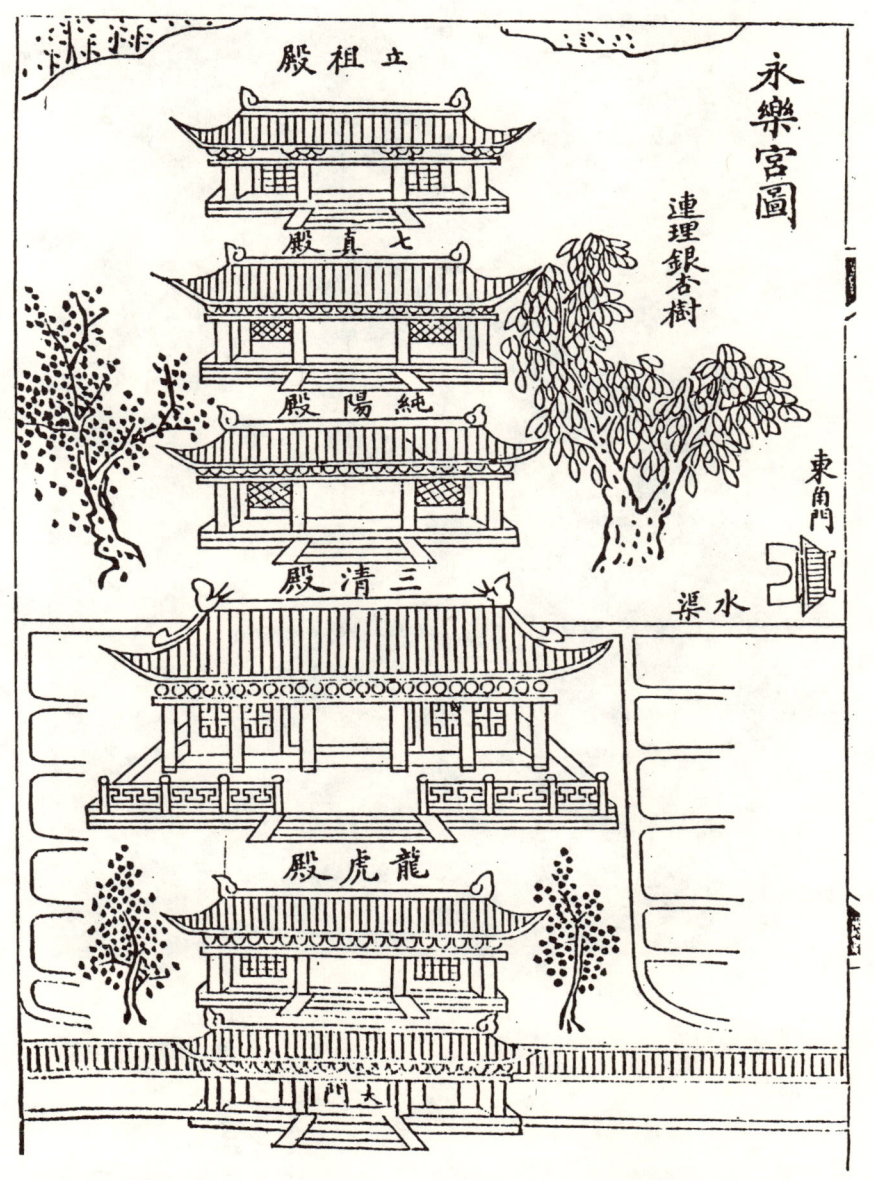

Figure 5. Main building compound of Yongle Daoist Monastery, Shanxi. *Yongjixian zhi* (Record of Yongji county), 1886.

Figure 6. Triple-entry Archway of Virtue Equal to Heaven and Earth, Confucian Temple, Qufu, Shandong, Ming period (1368–1644). After Kong and Jiang, *Qufu* (Shandong: People's Publishing House of Shandong, 1982), plate. 5.

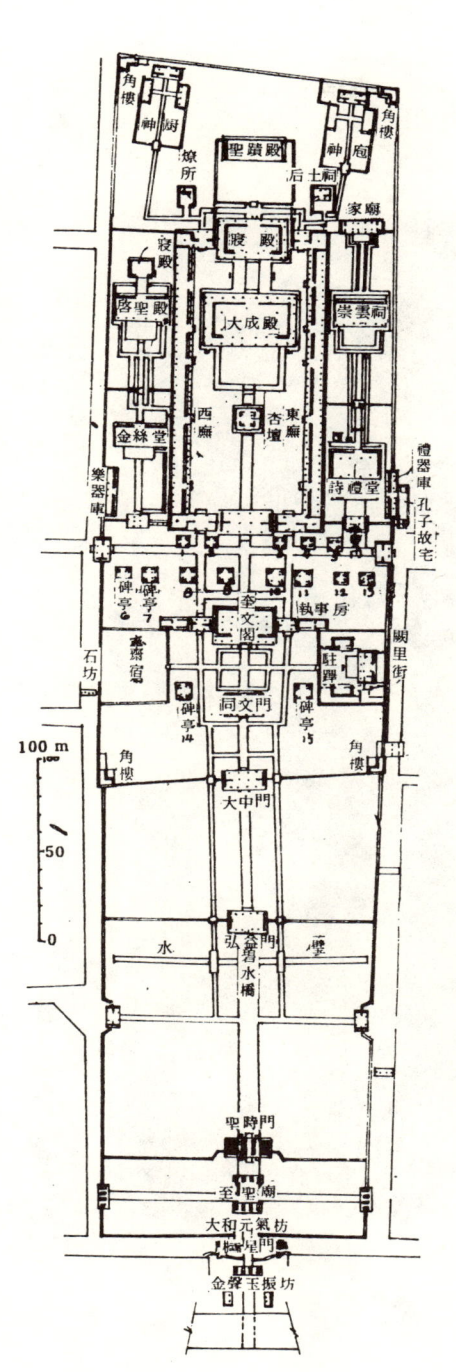

Figure 7. Plan of Confucian Temple, Qufu, in Qing period (1644–1911). After Ye Dasong, *Zhongguo jianzhu shi* (History of Chinese architecture), vol. 2 (Taibei: Zhongguo dianji jishu chubanshe [China Electrical Technology Publishing Company], 1977), p. 958.

Figure 8. Wumen Pavilion. Guan Yu Temple, Yuncheng, Shanxi, Qing period (1644–1911). Steinhardt photograph.

Figure 9. Approach to Spring and Autumn Hall. Guan Yu Temple, Yuncheng, Qing period (1644–1911). Steinhardt photograph.

Figure 10. Entry to Chen Family Residence. Guangzhou, Guangdong, Qing period (1644–1911). Steinhardt photograph.

Figure 11. Interior of Kaifeng synagogue. Joseph Brucker, S.J., after sketch by Jean-Paul Domenge, S.J. After White, *Chinese Jews*, pt. 1, p. 6.

בְּוָה, שֵׁמוּ, בּ-יְוָוֵי אֱלֹהֵנוּ אֲהָדּ

בְּרוּךְ שֵׁם כָּל הוּד רְעָלָם וָעֶד

Figure 12. Chair of Moses. Jean-Paul Domenge, S.J., 1720s. After Dehergne and Leslie, *Juifs de Chine*, plate 11. Published with permission of D.D. Leslie. Caption by Domenge reads, in translation: "A Kaifeng Jew reading the Bible [Torah] on the Chair of Moses, with two prompters."

Figure 13. Tablets on altar of one-room shrine, Lugang, 1977. Steinhardt photograph.

Figure 14. Tablet to Confucius, Dacheng Hall, Confucian Shrine, Tainan, Taiwan, 1977. Steinhardt photograph.

Figure 15. Detail of sun and moon, silk "banner," excavated at Mawangdui, Changsha, Hunan, ca. 193–177 B.C. After *Xi Han bohua* (A Western Han silk painting) (Beijing, 1972), detail 1.

Chapter I.A.2

Kaifeng Jews: The Sinification of Identity

Irene Eber

The origin, history, and condition of the Jews of Kaifeng has been discussed in scholarly and popular writings by Jews and non-Jews alike ever since news of a Jewish community in Kaifeng first reached Europe in the seventeenth century.[1] This chapter addresses one aspect in the life of the Kaifeng Jews that has so far not received much attention, namely, the process of sinification. By sinification I mean the gradual adaptation of customs from the Chinese environment that led not to assimilation and disappearance but to the strengthening among at least some Jews of their Jewish identity. A transformation of Jewish identity took place that, rather than keeping them as strangers, allowed Jews to integrate into Chinese society. Sinification permitted their survival within the Chinese environment.

The history of the community has been preserved in fragments, and because of the limited source material the process of sinification cannot be recaptured in detail. The general pattern over a period of roughly seven hundred years can, however, be outlined as follows:

(1) From the time of their arrival early in the twelfth century until the mid-fifteenth century, Kaifeng Jewry was apparently strengthened and reinforced by contacts with other Jewish communities within and without China. Its numbers may also have been augmented by new arrivals. In the course of this three-hundred-year period, kinship organization in accordance with the Chinese lineage system was adopted.

(2) Contacts with communities outside China probably ceased by the mid-fifteenth century. Moreover, sometime around the beginning of the seventeenth century, the Jewish presence in Chinese cities other than Kaifeng disappeared, and the community continued in complete isolation. In spite of an ongoing sinification, a life-style that included the taking of Chinese secondary wives and concubines, and the successful integration of

members into Chinese society, the Jewish identity of this community persisted. Neither in these nor in later centuries is there evidence of discrimination against the Jews.

(3) In the eighteenth century and thereafter, the Kaifeng Jews were identified and, in turn, identified themselves as a religious sect, not dissimilar from other popular syncretic sects present in Chinese society. This sectarian identity persisted into the twentieth century and, instead of obliterating Jewish identity, reinforced it. To this day many Kaifeng families still refer to themselves as Jews, even if they are in no sense practicing Jews. The following, first, briefly outlines the history of the Kaifeng Jews and, then, offers some clarification of the process of sinification together with the persistence of Jewish identity resulting from kinship and sectarian identity.

History

Although Jewish traders probably first came to China in the late eighth or early ninth century, there is no evidence that they established a permanent Jewish community anywhere. Some two centuries later, but probably before 1120, when war began to engulf North China, Jews began to arrive in Kaifeng, the capital of the northern Song dynasty (960–1126). In the 1120s northern China was threatened by invasion from China's Inner Asian neighbors, the Jurched, and it is highly unlikely that groups of strangers would have tried to travel to the inland capital overland from the coast or from elsewhere during the disturbances. Hence it should be assumed that the Jews came no later than 1120 and that some years of settling in passed before they built a synagogue.[2] According to the 1489 account, the synagogue was built in 1163. By that date northern China was ruled by the foreign Jurched (Jin) dynasty, while Chinese rule was confined to the area south of the Yangzi River.

Jewish merchants came to Kaifeng for several obvious reasons. During the Northern Song dynasty, Kaifeng was a multifunctional metropolitan center of more than a million people. It was a commercial and industrial city, at the hub of an overland and river communications network. A vigorous import–export trade connected Kaifeng to the eastern seaboard and to the Yangzi delta with its flourishing port cities.[3] Therefore, Jewish traders arriving in, say, Hangzhou or Ningbo on the southeastern coast might have found it desirable to have permanent business representatives in the capital, especially since it is likely that Jewish communities were also established in the twelfth century in Yangzhou and Ningbo.[4]

Between the Jews' arrival early in the twelfth century and the first notice about a Jewish presence in Kaifeng by Matteo Ricci in 1605, the community underwent a process of integration into Chinese society. Jews received Chinese surnames and were apparently organized into lineage families. Members of these lineages had careers in Chinese official life as military men or in the civil service. The synagogue, built in 1163, was in use until around 1849, when it was severely damaged by floods. Until 1810 there was a community leader or head of the religious sect (*zhangjiao*).[5] After he died, there apparently was no one remaining with a knowledge of Hebrew. The Jews celebrated seasonal festivals, even if there seems to have been a gradual sinification of festival practices by including ancestor worship and seasonal foods common to Chinese festivals, as is indicated by the 1663a inscription.[6] Polygamy and concubinage were practiced. The first wife, at least until the end of the seventeenth century, was Jewish; secondary wives and concubines were Chinese.

Sometime between 1851 and 1866, the synagogue was dismantled. Whatever Jewish practices remained gradually fell into disuse, although some form of *kashrut* continued as late as the beginning of the twentieth century. Abstinence from pork (possibly as a result of Muslim influence) is a persistent memory into the 1980s.[7] In the 1990s, as well as in previous decades, visitors to Kaifeng, when meeting members of the Shi, Zhao, or Ai families, are invariably told that these families are Jewish. [On recollections by Kaifeng's Jewish descendants in the 1980s, see Wendy R. Abraham's article in this volume —*Ed.*]

Jewish Identity and Kinship Organization

By what means was this identity retained? Is not, we are inclined to say, Jewish identity in part connected to Jewish practices? Is identity linked only to practice? Have not Jews, dispersed in Western culture, ceased to be Jews within a generation or two when they were no longer practicing Jews? Is it the strength of a particular group's Judaism, something within Judaism, that allows Kaifeng families to cling to their Jewish memory? Or should the answer be sought more specifically in Chinese culture and society as well as in the Kaifeng setting on the North China Plain?

It is of no small significance that early in the fifteenth century the surname Zhao was bestowed by imperial decree on one An San (Hassan?)[8] and that other Jewish families probably acquired their Chinese surnames at about the same time. The use of Chinese family names by the Jews of Kaifeng suggests that, more or less contemporaneously, they adopted the Chinese lineage family organization. Chinese lineages generally trace their origin to one ancestor, go by one surname, are domiciled in one locality, and hold some properties, including burial grounds, in common. The following evidence can be cited to support the assumption of a lineage family organization in Kaifeng. First, there are the various terms used for family on the five stone inscriptions. In the 1489 inscription the term *shi* is used for families, indicating surnames, rather than individual families.[9] (The 1512 inscription discusses individuals rather than families and, therefore, furnishes no further evidence.) The 1663a inscription mentions for the first time the "seven surnames" (*qi xing*), clearly referring to lineages.[10] The most obvious example is found in the 1679 inscription, in which seventy-three names (*xing*) are said to consist of five hundred families (*jia*).[11] The 1663b inscription further distinguishes blood relations (*zu*), or immediate family from more remote family.[12]

Further evidence may be adduced from burial customs. According to *Wang* Yisha, the Jews date the use of family cemeteries variously to the late seventeenth century (1875–1908) or after the 1642 flood. The latter is a more likely date and, furthermore, reaffirms the increasing adoption of lineage and agnatic forms of family organization according to which burial, particularly in North China, customarily took place in family cemeteries. He lists a number of sites in Kaifeng's suburbs or in adjoining hamlets and notes that *Jin* Ziru's family cemetery and *Li* Enshou's family cemetery have each a "foremost" grave marked "Old Ancestor's Grave."[13] "Graveyards in the north China pattern," writes Myron L. Cohen, "constituted the major symbols of agnatic affiliation that were on permanent public display."[14] He also points out that the triangular arrangement of graves, reflecting genealogical relationships, had the (Old) ancestor's grave at the apex. But the ancestral remains were not buried in this grave; rather, the ancestor's second grave provided a symbolic linking to the lineage's earlier origins.

The importance of the ancestor in the lives of lineage families can be also seen in the keeping of ancestor portraits. Sixty-year-old *Shi* Zhongyu remembered in 1982 that his mother owned several ancestor portraits.[15] Phyllis Horal visited Kaifeng and saw one such portrait, painted in the manner of conventional Chinese ancestor portraits and showing a distinguished man in official robes.[16] However, none of the nineteenth- and twentieth-century visitor accounts mention family ancestral halls, although an ancestral hall (*citang*) was apparently part of the synagogue. According to Anglican missionaries, the Jews did use ancestral tablets.[17] Finally, Bishop White, writing in 1919, makes reference to an ancestral scroll (*jia pu*), which was kept by the Shi family.[18] The Zhaos, whose lineage (literati) status dates to the seventeenth century, apparently also had an ancestral scroll, which presumably was taken away by an Englishman.[19] Such scrolls were owned by families with lineage status and previous or present wealth;

they recorded horizontally the genealogical arrangement of names together with dates of birth and death.[20] They were, therefore, completely different from the genealogy register of the dead (now in the Hebrew Union College Library, Cincinnati, Ohio) in which all seven lineages appear.

The transformation of a community of families, or even clans, into a group of lineages has significant implications for the question of identity. When Jews acquired Chinese surnames and began to adjust family and community organization to lineage and family organization, identification with the larger and amorphous community became less important than identification with the lineage and agnatic group. Thus individuals identified first with the family and second with the lineage. As long as lineages remained Jewish, individual Jews were unlikely to abandon their Jewish identity. Although Jewishness could be forgotten and abandoned by an entire family, especially if that family left Kaifeng, Jewishness would continue within the lineage as long as the lineage remained intact and was domiciled in the same locality. What then bound Kaifeng Jews together was not community, but family identity.

This is not to negate the importance of the synagogue in Kaifeng Jewish life. As long as the synagogue was in existence, it was a center for housing the all-important scriptures and for meeting in worship. Jews met in the synagogue, however, as members of Jewish families and not as members of a Jewish community. But it was not the building that determined or even sustained the identity of the congregations. Indeed, because of the kin-centered identity that evolved, Jews could identify as Jewish even after there was no longer a synagogue.

The gradual weakening of Jewish practices in the late eighteenth and nineteenth centuries, especially the loss of Jewish learning that accompanied the general intellectual decline among Kaifeng Jewish families, did not also lead to a weakening of Jewish identity among all the families. The intellectual decline among what were, no doubt, elite families was, however, a serious problem. Men like *Zhao* Yingchen (1619–1657?), or his younger brother, *Zhao* Yingdou, were actively engaged in maintaining Judaism in Kaifeng, but they were also degree holders and served in provinces other than their native Henan.[21] Although they periodically returned to Kaifeng, either at the conclusion of their tour of duty or to observe mourning periods, their working lives and their Jewish lives did not coincide. While this is not exactly a brain drain, it nonetheless indicates that those most versed and most vitally interested in the maintenance of Jewish practices in Kaifeng were men whose status and position required them to be elsewhere. They could not be counted on to maintain Jewish learning in Kaifeng in a sustained fashion.

Jewish Identity and Sectarian Identity

Whereas Jewish identity was eroded at one level, at another it was reinforced because Jewish religious practices came to be regarded as similar to those of a popular religious sect. Like other sects, the Jews were called a *jiao* (translated variously as religion, religious sect, or teaching), they had a shrine and a religious leader, and they engaged in certain practices that differentiated them from other sectarians. Their Judaism, as can be partially gleaned from the stelae inscriptions, was evolving into a Judeo–Confucian syncretism. As a popular sect, Jews did not have to be regarded by others as espousing a religion of strangers, but could be seen to fit into a mosaic of syncretic sectarian groups that characterized Chinese religious life in the north as well as in other parts of China. Identifying with a sect together with family identity, rather than undermining or obliterating Jewish identity, served to maintain it even after the synagogue fell into complete ruin and was dismantled in the mid-nineteenth century.

To understand this sectarian identity it will be useful first to examine how the Jews were referred to and how they referred to themselves. As noted above, between the seventeenth and the twentieth centuries, Kaifeng Jews were referred to and identified themselves as a *jiao*. Two different names were in use; one was *Tiaojin jiao* (the sect that extracts the sinews); the other was *Jiaojing jiao* (the sect that teaches the scripture). According to the Jesuit Jean Domenge, the Jews were also called *Lanmao huihui* (blue-cap Muslims).[22] These designations do not appear on the stone inscriptions. Nor does the term Israel (*Yicileye*) appear as the name of the people. When used in the 1489, 1512, and 1663a inscriptions, Israel refers to the founding or the establishment of the teaching (*jiao*).[23] Thus the 1489 inscription opens with the statement, "The founder (*zishi*) who established the teaching [religion] of Israel was Abraham." The term *zishi* is generally used for founders of religious sects. When the adherents of this religion, that is, the Jews, are referred to, the term Israel is not used and they are simply called the followers of the teaching (*jiao rong* or *jiao ren*).[24] Quite probably "sinew-plucking sect" and "scripture-teaching sect" were popularly used by their Chinese neighbors and, though accepted by the Jews, were avoided in official statements, which these stones represent. The Jesuit Jean-Paul Gozani seems to imply just this when he wrote in 1704 that the "idolaters first gave them this name [*Tiaojin jiao*]."[25]

Whether called "sinew-plucking" or "scripture-teaching," the Jews considered themselves and were considered by others a *jiao*. In this particular context, *jiao* is probably best translated as religious sect, for their Chinese neighbors may very well have thought of Jews as belonging to one of the many popular sects that Judaism in part resembled. By the nineteenth century, place and religion were linked and the alley in the vicinity of the synagogue where they lived was called the "sinew-plucking sect" alley. The term *Youtai ren* or Jew is of more recent usage; only in the twentieth century do Kaifeng families refer to themselves as *Youtai ren*.

To understand the significance of this designation as a sect, the prevalence of popular sectarianism in Chinese society requires some explanation. Sectarian religions, consisting of mixtures of Buddhist, Daoist, Confucian, and folk elements, had appeared for the first time in the fourteenth century. Often considered "unorthodox" by the official establishment, syncretic sectarianism came to be both localized and highly fragmented and the sects were known by many different names. Depending on local conditions, sectarian religious groups frequently developed millenarian and political aims. At such times, local officials took notice of their activities, and when they reached a militant stage, the rebellious sectarians were suppressed. Several of the great popular rebellions of the past seven hundred years—beginning with the rebellion that led to the overthrow of the Mongol (Yuan) dynasty in 1368—had their origin in religious sectarianism turned politically militant. However, as long as these sects pursued the purely religious goals of gathering adherents, meeting in prayer, and observing ceremonials in their meeting houses and shrines, they generally escaped the notice of local officials. This accounts for the paucity of information about their more quiescent phases.[26]

In spite of the widely varying syncretic combinations among the sectarian groups, there were nonetheless several shared characteristics. A sect had a leader or sect master (*jiao zhu*), a set of sacred writings or scriptures generally referred to as "precious books" (*bao juan*) or "holy books" (*jing*), and a meeting place for worship and prayer. A set of distinct doctrines differentiated one sect from another, and membership was conferred in acts of initiation.[27] Many sects also had dietary practices, including vegetarianism. Members of sects were usually recruited from among the lower strata of the population, peasants, small-town artisans and merchants, although lower-grade officials, clerks, and military men were also known to be members of religious sects.

Susan Naquin describes White Lotus sects in which hereditary transmission of sectarianism within families assured the sect's longevity as well as cohesiveness: "There, sect patriarchs were simultaneously lineage ancestors (both termed *zi*), parent-children relationships reinforced those between teachers and pupils, and the intimate and double-stranded connection between generations slowed the dilution of religious doctrine and the loss of organizational control."[28] However, even when sect adherence was not hereditary, sects generally were not merely associations of individuals. Those who joined tended to bring in other members of their households. Sect membership frequently was family membership.[29]

In the eighteenth century and at the beginning of the nineteenth, sects were widely dispersed throughout China, in the Yangzi Valley, along the southeastern coast, as well as on the North China Plain. Before the great Eight Trigrams Uprising of 1813, popular religious sects flourished in the vicinity of Kaifeng within a circumference of one hundred to two hundred kilometers.[30] Popular religious sects on the North China Plain, in parts of Henan and Hebei, existed well before 1813. They were a part of the rural as well as the urban scene.

City and countryside were not rigidly isolated from each other: People traveled to and fro in pursuit of livelihood and met in day-to-day activities. However, establishing a clear connection between sectarianism and Kaifeng Jews is not easy. As long as a religious sect did not develop political aims, thereby becoming a real or imagined threat to the established order, it was considered harmless and escaped official attention. Throughout its history, the "sinew-plucking sect" apparently had no political ambitions.

By the eighteenth and nineteenth centuries, the Jews had blended into their environment so completely that they were indistinguishable from their Chinese neighbors. Their religious practices also were not too dissimilar from those of their neighbors. If their Chinese neighbors assumed that the Jews belonged to a harmless religious sect, they would consider the sinew-pluckers not much different from members of other sects with which they were familiar. Like other syncretic sects, the "sinew-plucking sect" had a meeting place; it had a set of sacred writings shared only by those who participated in sectarian worship; it had a leader who was the keeper of the scriptures; and it had dietary and other practices. In all likelihood, this sectarian identity suited the Jews and they perpetuated it as a remembered identity, even after the synagogue disappeared, the scriptures were sold, and Jewish practices were discontinued.[31] When the Jews were identified as and accepted the identification of a *jiao* of scripture teaching or sinew-plucking, on the one hand they severed the connection to a foreign and universal religion and on the other, forged a link to the native and local religions. Identifying as Jewish in eighteenth-, nineteenth-, and even twentieth-century Kaifeng meant not underscoring difference or outsider status; rather, it meant emphasizing particularity within universality, being a particular group among any number of other groups that were also particular. *Shi Zhongyu* described himself in 1982 as a Jew and a "descendant of the Yellow Emperor," thus expressing quite accurately his forebears' and his own identity.[32]

Sectarian identity, both conferred and accepted, seems more important than the fact that sometimes Jews were considered Muslims because of obvious but superficial similarities. In any event, the acceptance of Muslim identity appears to be a relatively recent phenomenon, related to the weakening of kin and sectarian identity and the severing of links to their native place, Kaifeng. In the periodic rebellions, wars, and conquests of the twentieth century, families dispersed and moved to various parts of China, thus losing their connection to place that figures importantly in maintaining family identity.

The Jin family is a case in point. At some time, early in the twentieth century, Jin family members came to identify themselves as Muslims, without apparently being practicing Muslims. *Jin* Xiaojing, now of Beijing, accidentally rediscovered her Jewish origins when she traced her family background to Kaifeng, where Muslim Jins were not known, but Jewish Jins certainly were.[33] Not mistaken ascription, but the weakening of both native-place ties and family identity contributed to some Kaifeng Jewish families eventually becoming or being considered Muslim.

Sectarian identity was, furthermore, affirmed in those portions of the stelae inscriptions that discuss the Jews' religious and historic beginnings. These statements, though unfortunately sparse, show that Kaifeng Jews saw themselves as part of the broad stream of Chinese tradition and culture, with merely some divergent developments in the past.[34]

Inscriptions from 1489, 1512, and 1663a reveal interesting variations. According to the first, "The Patriarch (*zishi*) Abraham, who established the religion (*jiao*) of Israel, was the nineteenth-generation descendant of Pan Gu Adam." The 1663a inscription has it somewhat differently: "The establishment of the Israel religion is in the distant past. It began with Adam, the nineteenth descendant of Pan Gu, and continued through Noah and Abraham." The 1512 inscription does not mention Pan Gu, but distinguishes between the first ancestor (*shizi*) of the Israel religion, Adam, "who originally came from the West country of India in the Zhou period" (1122–221 B.C.), and Abraham, who founded the religion and is, therefore, the religion's ancestor (*jiaozi*).[35]

The joining of Adam and Pan Gu, and in the 1489 inscription even with Abraham, is quite amazing, for the Pan Gu myth bears absolutely no similarity to the Adam or Abraham stories. Pan Gu was a giant whose body after he died became the created world and everything within it. The Pan Gu myth is thus a creation story and presents creation as transformation, made possible by the act of dying, whereas in the biblical Genesis story, Adam was created after the creation of the world. In the 1489 inscription Pan Gu and Adam are, so to speak, contemporaries, although having the two names side by side could also mean that Pan Gu and Adam are one and the same person. Whatever the case may be, Abraham is a descendant of both, and here and elsewhere in the inscriptions the succession is patrilineal, in accordance with Chinese usage, in which women do not figure.

The several terms used for Adam and Abraham indicate how their functions are perceived. Both the 1489 and 1663a inscriptions place Abraham's name in close relationship with the development of the religion, and he is, therefore, referred to variously as the patriarch (of the religion) and its ancestor. Among the characteristics ascribed to Abraham that allow him to occupy this exalted position are understanding the correct teaching (*zheng jiao*) and understanding the true heaven (*zhen tian*).[36] Adam as the first ancestor has no contact with religious developments and is, therefore, not given the title of patriarch (*zishi*), which is reserved for those who have contributed to the transmission of the teaching. The inscription assigns a pivotal role to transmitters like Moses, who is called the "master of the law" (*shifa*), and to Ezra, under whom the law shone with renewed brightness (*fuming*).[37]

Finally, in addition to Pan Gu, the 1489 inscription also refers to the "creation (*kaipi*) of heaven and earth," following which the patriarchs transmitted the teaching.[38] The term *kaipi*, however, has none of the Genesis implications. It means literally "separation [of heaven and earth]" and thus conforms to the Chinese view that the world began as an "opening up," when heaven ascended and earth descended. Nonetheless, it is also stated that the "great origin comes from Heaven" (*dayuan chu yu tian*).[39]

None of the five inscriptions introduce a new and strange god, for when referring to the Jewish God they use Heaven (*Tian*).[40] Reference to Heaven is made in various contexts and is frequently coupled with the important Confucian term for respect or reverence (*jing*), admonishing believers to revere Heaven or show reverence for Heaven.[41] Both the 1489 and 1663a inscriptions sometimes join reverence for Heaven with honoring (*zun*) ancestors. According to the 1489 inscription, sacrifices cannot be offered to the ancients if only Heaven is revered without also honoring ancestors. The 1663a inscription stresses revering Heaven and observing the regulations (*fa*) of the ancestors. Belief in God was, therefore, clearly seen as an integral part of filial piety and ancestor worship.

Heaven is also sometimes referred to in conjunction with the Way (*Dao*), that is, Heaven's Way. Although it might seem occasionally that Dao and Heaven are used synonymously, this is not in fact the case. Revere Dao, admonishes the 1489 inscription, but do not forget Heaven; or, in another place, Dao has no form similar to the Way of Heaven above. In the 1663a inscription, Abraham is said to have known that the Way of Heaven has neither sound nor smell. Heaven–God is thus not awesome, inspiring fear and dread. Only the 1512 inscription mentions fear of Heaven's decree (*wei Tian ming*), which is not the same as fearing Heaven.

The scriptures (*jing*), that is, the Torah, are frequently mentioned, but their divine origin is referred to only once. According to the 1489 inscription, Moses's devotion touched the heart of Heaven (*Tianxin*) and the true scriptures came forth (*zilai*).[42]

In these inscriptions, Jewish and Chinese beliefs about beginnings, creation, and what happened thereafter are obviously intertwined in a useful syncretism. It is useful because the inscriptions reveal a compatible accommodation that allowed Jews to be Chinese without ceasing to be Jews. Center stage is occupied by the men (not women)—Adam, Abraham, Moses—who make the history that eventually brings the Jews to Kaifeng. According to the inscriptions, this might have been during the Zhou or during the Han dynasty (206 B.C.–220 A.D.). There is no divine guidance and no God who punishes or makes promises, but there is also no backsliding and there are no complications. The inscriptions imply that the God of the Jews and the Heaven of the Chinese are one and the same. What matters in those portions dealing with the history before to the building of the synagogue in Kaifeng is the account of handing down the tradition. As seems to be the case in some other sectarian traditions, these inscriptions attempt to show legitimate succession and transmission.[43]

This chapter contends that the Kaifeng Jews' process of integration into Chinese society—their sinification—has not led to assimilation and extinction of all Kaifeng Jews. In fact, because of its rather unusual features, this process led to the maintenance of Jewish identity and to the persistence of Jewish memory. After a patrilineal kinship organization of lineages evolved among Kaifeng Jews, Jewish identity was shifted from a people and community to lineage and family. Jewish identity was linked to Kaifeng since Chinese lineages are always associated with specific localities. When individual Jewish families dispersed, as has been the case especially in the twentieth century, the tie to both lineage and place was severed, leading to the cessation of Jewish identity. On the other hand, families who remained in Kaifeng and who may also have had stronger and longer-lasting kinship associations, like the Shi and Zhao families, continue to identify themselves as Jewish. To account for the persistence of Jewish memory, religious identity was also considered. Jewish practices in Kaifeng, no matter how much was lost or forgotten in the course of time, had most of the earmarks of Chinese sectarian religion. Like the members of other sects, the "sinew-pluckers" had a shrine, scriptures, and practices that distinguished them from adherents to other sects. A transformation of religious identity from a foreign universal religion to a syncretic sectarian religion that was no longer foreign had taken place.

The syncretism consisted in combining, or in fusing, Confucian and Jewish concepts, as pointed out by Andrew Plaks in the next chapter. It also consisted in establishing a history that was commensurate with Chinese history, and a transmission of the tradition that verified the religion's legitimacy. Without having to bother themselves (and others) about such matters like sin, punishment, or divine intervention, Jews affirmed that their history began with a first ancestor, and continued through worthy men thereafter. These men knew the correct religion, or teaching (*zheng jiao*), were benevolent (*ren*) and righteous (*yi*), and, as in Abraham's case, were not misled by ghosts and spirits (*gui shen*).[44]

The combination of family and sectarian identity was so durable that even if successive generations forgot increasingly more after the synagogue disappeared, the memory of a Jewish past did not cease. Because of a unique process of acculturation and transformation, which began probably some two hundred years after their arrival in Kaifeng, the identity of the Kaifeng Jews was strengthened rather than destroyed, allowing for its persistence into the twentieth century.

Notes

This paper is based on a lecture delivered at the Ben-Zvi Institute, Jerusalem, in December 1988. The present paper is an abridged version of a paper that appeared in *Monumenta Serica*, 41 (autumn 1993), pp. 231–47, as "K'aifeng Jews Revisited: Sinification as Affirmation of Identity."

The author thanks Dr. Steven Kaplan for his helpful comments on an earlier version of this paper and the Ben-Zvi Institute, the Louis Frieberg Research Fund, and, the Truman Research Institute for their partial support of this research.

1. For an exhaustive summary and analysis of accounts about Kaifeng Jews that were available to both Jews and non-Jews, see Michael Pollak, *Mandarins, Jews, and Missionaries: The Jewish Experience in the Chinese Empire* (Philadelphia: Jewish Publication Society, 1980).

2. On the other hand, the Jews may not have wished to settle permanently, but may have remained in Kaifeng since they were unable to return home because of the unsettled conditions in the north. I am grateful to Dr. Steven Kaplan for this suggestion.

3. The high degree of commercial and industrial development in the Northern Song dynasty is discussed by Robert Hartwell, "Markets, Technology, and the Structure of Enterprise in the Development of the Eleventh-Century Chinese Iron and Steel Industry," *Journal of Economic History* 26, no. 1 (March 1966), pp. 29–58.

4. The existence of a Jewish community in Ningbo in the fifteenth century is well established. Sometime between 1457 and 1465 (following the 1461 flood?), several Kaifeng Jews obtained a Torah scroll there that they brought back to Kaifeng. Another scroll, also from Ningbo, was brought to Kaifeng by *Zhao* Ying. Early in the sixteenth century, a certain *Jin* Pu from Yangzhou obtained an additional scroll for the Kaifeng Jews. The Yangzhou and Ningbo Jews disappear from view sometime in the seventeenth century. Donald D. Leslie, *The Survival of the Chinese Jews: The Jewish Community of Kaifeng* (Leiden: E.J. Brill, 1972), pp. 29, 146. Toward the end of the fifteenth century,

Jewish Jin surnames were, however, also found in the far northwestern Gansu province. A *Jin* Ying from Ningxia together with a *Jin* Li from Kaifeng set up the 1489 stele. Twenty-three years later, in 1512, another Ningxia man, *Jin* Jun, again participated in similar events. See William C. White, *Chinese Jews: A Compilation of Matters Relating to the Jews of K'ai-fêng Fu* (Toronto: University of Toronto Press, 1966), 2d ed., pt. 2, pp. 39, 54.

5. It might be misleading to translate *zhangjiao* as rabbi since wider and different responsibilities are implied by the Chinese term.

6. White, *Chinese Jews*, pt. 2, pp. 81–82. The 1663a inscription speaks of filial piety (*xiao*) as the subject of the scriptures; sacrifices to ancestors that take place in summer and winter with seasonal foods; and foods at the mid-autumn sacrifice that are without seasoning.

7. *Qu* Yinan, for example, remembers her grandfather's refusal to eat pork. Quoted by Mathis Chazanov, "Chinese Jew Traces Her Heritage," *Los Angeles Times*, December 8, 1985.

8. Leslie, *The Survival*, p. 26.

9. White, *Chinese Jews*, pt. 2, p. 38.

10. Ibid., p. 94.

11. Ibid.

12. Ibid., p. 95.

13. *Wang* Yisha, "The Descendants of the Kaifeng Jews," in *Jews in Old China*, ed. Sidney Shapiro (New York: Hippocrene, 1988), pp. 183–84.

14. Myron L. Cohen, "Lineage Organization in North China," *Journal of Asian Studies* 49, no. 3 (August 1990), p. 513. See also White, *Chinese Jews*, pt. 1, p. 16, who writes that burial in family cemeteries was practiced after the 1642 flood.

15. Michael Weisskopf, "Judaism Only a Dim Memory to Chinese Descendants," *Washington Post*, April 9, 1982.

16. Mrs. Horal kindly made a photograph of the portrait available to the Department of East Asian Studies at the Hebrew University, Jerusalem. The photograph is in the Phyllis Horal Collection, London.

17. "Missionary News," *Chinese Recorder* 50 (November 1919), pp. 780–82.

18. According to the Anglican missionaries in Kaifeng, only the Shi family kept a scroll, which was discovered in 1919 (ibid.) See also Wang, "Descendants of Kaifeng Jews," p. 186, according to whom the scroll cannot be located.

19. *Zhao* Yunzhong's account to *Mikami* Teicho, who visited Kaifeng in October 1940. Mikami Teicho, "Kaifeng yudakyoto no Genjo hokoku" (Report on the present-day status of Kaifeng Jews), *Shina kukkyo shingaku* 5, no. 1 (June 1941), pp. 76–77.

20. Cohen, "Lineage Organization," pp. 515–16. Cohen adds that in the Hebei village that he studied, ancestral scrolls had been prevalent whereas ancestral tablets were usually found only in better-off households.

21. After the disastrous 1642 flood, when most of Kaifeng was inundated and the synagogue was completely destroyed, the Zhaos were, according to the 1663b inscription, prime movers in the rebuilding of the synagogue and in the restoration of the water-damaged Torah scrolls. It is regrettable that the two books—one by *Zhao* Yingcheng, *Shang jing ji bian* (A record of the disaster of the holy scriptures), the other by *Zhao* Yingdou, *Mingdao xu* (Preface to the illustrious way)—are no longer extant. White, *Chinese Jews*, pt. 2, p. 84. Personal statements, in addition to the official inscriptions, might have thrown light on the problem of literati status and Jewish identity. Leslie, *Chinese-Hebrew Memorial Book*, pp. 227–30.

22. Leslie, *Survival of the Chinese Jews*, p. 108.

23. White, *Chinese Jews*, pt. 2, pp. 35, 52, 80.

24. Ibid., for example, pp. 83, 94, 104, in the 1663a and b and 1679 inscriptions.

25. Leslie, *Survival of the Chinese Jews*, p. 49.

26. The two major accounts on popular sectarian religions are by Daniel L. Overmyer, *Folk Buddhist Religion, Dissenting Sects in Late Traditional China* (Cambridge: Harvard University Press, 1976); and Susan Naquin, *Millenarian Rebellion in China: The Eight Trigrams Uprising in 1813* (New Haven: Yale University Press, 1976).

27. Stevan Harrell and Elisabeth J. Perry, "Syncretic Sects in Chinese Society: An Introduction," *Modern China* 8, no. 3 (July 1982), pp. 286. The authors point out that all sectarians met the latter two criteria.

28. Susan Naquin, "Connections Between Rebellions: Sect Family Networks in Qing China," *Modern China* 8, no. 3 (July 1982), p. 339.

29. Susan Naquin, "Millenarian Rebellion in China: The Eight Trigrams Uprising in 1813" (Ph.D. dissertation, Yale University, 1974), p. 128 n. 101, p. 427.

30. Sects were reported in Shangqiu county, approximately 200 km. southeast of Kaifeng; in Hua county, approximately 100 km. northeast; and in Jun (Yu) county, approximately 200 km. southwest. Naquin, *Millenarian Rebellion,* maps, pp. 132, 149, 257.

31. In 1940 *Zhao* Yunzhong, having adopted twentieth-century nomenclature, referred to Judaism as *Youtai jiao* and to himself as a *huichang*. See *Mikami*, "Kaifeng yudakyoto" (Report on the present-day status of Kaifeng Jews), p. 76.

32. Shih quoted by Weisskopf, "Judaism."

33. *Jin* Xiaojing, "Wo shi Zhongguo Youtai ren" (I am a Chinese Jew), *Shehui kexue zhanxian,* no. 4 (1981), pp. 35, 37.

34. The 1489 inscription was composed by a Kaifeng Jew, *Jin* Zhong. White, *Chinese Jews,* pt. 3, p. 124. Zuo Tang, who composed the 1512 inscription, may have been a Yangzhou Jew, according to White, pt. 2, p. 47, note. Leslie, however, writes that he was "almost certainly not a Jew" (*Survival of the Chinese Jews,* p. 29). Leslie, furthermore, suggests that the inscription was not written in Kaifeng, and that the inscribed stone was brought to the city by a group of non-Kaifeng Jews. The 1663a inscription was composed by *Liu* Chang, a non-Jewish scholar and court minister.

35. White, *Chinese Jews,* pt. 2, pp. 35, 80, 52.

36. Ibid., p. 35.

37. Ibid., pp. 52–53. However, the 1512 inscription in another place takes up the topic of transmission with Adam as the first patriarch, who transmitted the teaching to Noah.

38. Ibid., p. 35.

39. Ibid., p. 38.

40. I am grateful to Professor Lauren Pfister for repeatedly raising the question of the term used for God in the inscriptions. Apparently the Jews were not troubled by which Chinese term to use.

41. See, for example, the comments on *jing* by Julia Ching, "What Is Confucian Spirituality?" and Wm. Theodore de Bary, "Human Rites: An Essay on Confucianism and Human Rights," in *Confucianism: The Dynamics of Tradition,* ed. Irene Eber (New York: Macmillan, 1986), pp. 63–80 and 109–32.

42. White, *Chinese Jews,* pt. 2, pp. 35–39, 51–54, 80–85.

43. Daniel L. Overmyer, "Attitudes Toward the Ruler and State in Chinese Popular Religious Literature: Sixteenth and Seventeenth Century *Pao-chuan*," *Harvard Journal of Asiatic Studies* 44, no. 2 (1984), p. 369.

44. The reference may be to witchcraft, perhaps to such activities as spirit calling or spirit writing, which were not condoned by elite Confucians. But the reference may be also to Confucius's statement about keeping one's distance from the spirits. *Analects,* XI:11, trans. in *The Four Books,* James Leege (Shanghai: Chinese Book Co., n.d.).

Chapter I.A.3

The Confucianization of the Kaifeng Jews: Interpretations of the Kaifeng Stelae Inscriptions

Andrew H. Plaks

There are many approaches to the study of the Jews of China. A majority of scholars interested in this subject come to it from the perspective of Jewish history, taking this far-flung Diaspora community as a remarkable test case of a process of linguistic, cultural, and religious adaptation leading to gradual assimilation and ultimate submergence as a functioning cultural entity. A few sinologists, on the other hand, have attempted to put this topic into the broader context of Chinese history, considering the minimal record of the survival of this minuscule minority within the ocean of Han culture as an example of such factors as social mobility, relations between competing minorities, government policy in the post-Song imperial system, or perhaps as a chapter in the local history of Henan province.[1] This chapter explores the area of intersection of these two perspectives, that is, the written evidence of cultural and intellectual interaction brought about by the disproportionate encounter of these two communities. I am limited in this inquiry to a fairly narrow band of time out of the thousand-year history of the Jewish settlement in Kaifeng—that which falls after the community had become sufficiently sinicized to participate fully in Chinese social, political, and cultural life, but before the process of assimilation had reached the point at which they lost virtually all substantive knowledge of Jewish learning and practice. This covers roughly the period from the mid-fifteenth to the early eighteenth centuries.

It is certainly not accidental that the unique extant documents providing insight into the cultural consciousness of the Chinese Jews—the surviving stone stelae inscriptions dated 1489, 1512, 1663, and 1679—happen to fall precisely within this period. This was, after all, the only time when the explanation in Confucian literary terms of Jewish origins and beliefs was both technically possible and intellectually meaningful. These documents have already been scoured by a number of scholars, notably Jérôme Tobar, William Charles White, *Chen* Yuan, Donald Leslie, Yitzhak Ben-Zvi, and Michael Pollak, with an eye toward uncovering scraps of information about the history of the community.[2] Along the way, they have also occasionally taken the time to point out certain fragmentary pieces of evidence for reconstructing some of the religious practices of the Chinese Jews during this period: their knowledge of Hebrew texts and sources, deviations from normative rabbinic prescriptions, possible affinities with Karaites, and so on.[3] For example, the stelae inscriptions make explicit mention of a number of Torah narratives and precepts, while they give a picture of ritual cycles and worship services that are somewhat at variance with standard practice elsewhere but still easily recognizable.[4] Here, however, I am more interested in the world of ideas and belief, in particular, the ways in which these were modified through contact with the prevailing neo-Confucian intellectual currents of the Ming and Qing periods.

As soon as we begin to take seriously the idea-content of the Kaifeng inscriptions, the question arises as to whose ideas these really were: How representative were they of Jewish beliefs of the time? There is some uncertainty about precisely who wrote the texts of the inscriptions. Most scholars accept *Jin* Zhong, named as author of the 1489 inscription, as a member of the Jewish community, but there is a difference of opinion regarding *Zuo* Tang credited with the 1512 document, and all agree that *Liu* Chang, author of the 1663 text, was a prominent non-Jew in Kaifeng. The fragmentary 1679 stele seems to have been executed by members of the Jewish Zhao clan, but it is of less importance as a substantive document.[5] Even if some or all of these texts were actually composed on commission by non-Jewish literati, according to the established Chinese custom of the time, I still maintain that they reflect primarily Jewish input, whether in the form of preliminary drafts or of discussions with the writers, so that they can be taken as evidence of Jewish thinking on various subjects.

In attempting to gauge the degree to which these pieces are representative of the Jewish consciousness of the Kaifeng community, we must add a few further qualifications. First of all, a good many of the statements contained in the inscriptions are clearly not much more than self-serving propaganda, designed to find favor in the eyes of Chinese neighbors and Confucian authorities with some fine-sounding rhetoric about gratitude to the nation, loyalty to the throne, and the like.[6] In some passages, we get unabashed apologetics, such as the following claiming the compatibility of the Jewish faith with Confucian teachings:

> Although there are some minor discrepancies between Confucian doctrine and our own, in their main focus of ideas and established practices both are exclusively concerned with honoring the Way of Heaven, venerating ancestors, valuing the relations of ruler and subject, obedience to parents, harmony within families, correct ordering of social hierarchies, and good fellowship among friends: nothing more than the "five cardinal relations" of mankind.
>
> Although it differs from Confucian texts in its writing system, if one scrutinizes the basic principles [of Judaism] he will find that it is the same, as it contains the Way of constant practice.[7]

The 1663 inscription goes on to proclaim that the Jewish scriptures are identical to the "Six Classics" in their basic meaning, even if they are written in a strange script; and the 1679 text asserts that the teachings of their scriptures are in full accord with the ideas of Confucius and Mencius.[8] This sort of Confucian apologetics, punctuated by frequent citations from the appropriate Confucian sources, is more prominent in the two seventeenth-century stelae, products of a period in which pious pronouncements of Confucian verities were even more desirable than they had been in the more free-thinking age of the late Ming.[9]

In a similar sense, we must be careful not to overinterpret every point at which loaded philosophical terms are inserted into these texts, since such usages may often be taken as examples of the obligatory decorative touches of formal prose style. This is clearly the case in many references to "Heaven," the *Dao,* "the correct teachings," and various specific Confucian virtues, as well as the automatic condemnation of heretical thinking. It applies just as well to the use of certain heterodox terms, such as the notion of "sudden enlightenment" [*wu*] mentioned in the 1489 text.[10] This does not necessarily indicate any measure of Buddhist influence, since by this period such expressions belong to a large common pool of philosophical vocabulary shared by all of the schools of thought under the syncretic umbrella of neo-Confucianism. The 1489 inscription, in fact, makes an explicit appeal to the idea of "unity of the three teachings" [*sanjiao heyi*] in order to claim a piece of the syncretic pie for this one additional school of thought.[11]

In general, the idea of accommodation to prevailing modes of discourse and conceptual models has primarily negative connotations, a kind of watering down of cultural purity. Thus, the examples of "contamination" by Confucianism reflected in Chinese Jewish life—whether in matters of external style such as the curved roofs and tilework of the Kaifeng synagogue sketched by Domenge in 1722, or internal substance such as the puzzling ritual calendar debated by scholars[12]—are usually taken as symptoms of the irreversible process of terminal assimilation. The most notorious example, of course, is the issue of ancestor worship in the synagogue, the same issue that caused so much grief for the Jesuit missionaries who were trying to convince the Chinese of the compatibility of their own faith with Confucianism in this same period. I argue below, however, that these instances may be better understood as examples of creative cultural interaction than as simple submission to the norms of the majority culture.

In the remainder of this study, I consider some of the specific conceptual bridges built by the Kaifeng Jews, as expressed in the three main stelae inscriptions. To begin at a more superficial level, we can already observe an interesting process of linguistic and conceptual mediation (on the part of the authors/or their patrons) at work in the particular Chinese terms chosen to render the proper names of the Jewish tradition. I would like to suggest that at least a few of the renderings of the biblical names (as opposed to the phonetic transcriptions of Hebrew and Judeo–Persian personal names and titles) may reveal a certain sensitivity to the cross-cultural implications involved. Take, for example, the conflating of Adam (transcribed *Adan*) with the mythical figure Pan Gu at the head of the chain of transmission "nineteen generations" before Abraham given in the 1489 inscription (this is, by the way, a rare early reference to the Pan Gu figure, known widely in the popular Chinese tradition, in a formal prose text).[13] At first sight, these two "fathers of mankind" are a bit ill matched, since Pan Gu is usually thought of as an agent rather than a product of the process of creation. But this process of creation is conceived of as a spontaneous dissolution of a pre-existing body, along the lines of cosmic-egg myths in a wide variety of cultures.[14] The chicken-or-egg question of where this first man came from is not altogether irrelevant to the creation of Adam, the sixth day of creation notwithstanding, in light of certain metaphors of autochthonous generation that creep into Adam's story ("dust of the earth," etc.).[15] If, as a number of recent sinologists have insisted, the Confucian tradition may be unique for its lack of a sanctioned creation myth, then this linking of the progenitor of the Jews to another progenitor in the folklore of the host culture shows a certain degree of ingenuity.

An even more ingenious linking of mythical figures occurs in the transcription of the biblical Noah by using the two characters *Nü wa* (alternate reading *Nügua*). In this case as well, despite the nice coincidence in sound, we see an initial discrepancy between the two figures, since Nüwa is only indirectly linked to the Chinese flood myth, being better known in the popular tradition in connection with the "repair of Heaven" [*bu tian*] after the flood has already subsided.[16] A greater resonance between the two figures does emerge, however, when we take a closer look at the aftermath of the Great Deluge in the Chinese and biblical versions. Here, we immediately notice the striking resemblance between the rainbow of the renewed covenant and the five-colored stones fused by Nüwa to restore the vault of Heaven, two metaphors both conveying a common sense of the harmonious ordering of spectral divisions.[17] In both sets of myths, moreover, the post-deluge order is associated with the re-creation of mankind, one of the major tasks assigned to the Nüwa figure in early Chinese texts.[18] In the Kaifeng inscriptions, however, the mythological associations of Noah/Nüwa are left unstated. Instead, the figure is simply named as the key link in the chain of transmission from Adam to Abraham, precisely matching the well-known formulation of Jewish origins in the classic, five-chapter portion of the *Mishna* called *Pirkei-avot* (Sayings of the Fathers), 5:2.[19]

Most of the other biblical names given in the inscriptions are rendered with more or less predictable syllabic transcriptions. Perhaps the rendering of the name of Abraham as *A-wu-luo-han* (in which the *wu* may well have had a dialect pronunciation as *mu* or *bu*) with the Buddhist term *luohan* was not entirely accidental. At least, the fact that Abraham is described as having experienced a "sudden enlightenment" [*wu*] of the true way makes this possible association with an *arhat* of Buddhist attainment quite appropriate.[20] One example in which the transcription of a Hebrew name is clearly intended to represent more than the sound is seen in the characters *yicileye* used to render the name Israel. To say the least, this is an unusual choice of words for syllabic transcription. That these may not be meant as empty syllables is supported by the fact that nearly the same sequence occurs later in the 1489 inscription, where they describe the grant [*ci*] of joyful domains [*le ye*] by the Ming founder to pacify his new empire. Thus, it may not be too farfetched to translate these four characters literally as something like "the one [God] has bestowed a joyful enterprise."[21]

Let us now review some of the basic ideas expressed in the Kaifeng stelae inscriptions in order to reconsider the degree of cultural accommodation they reflect in the light of their neo-Confucian intellectual background. Beginning as early as Tobar's study, scholars have pointed out that the authors of these texts scrupulously avoid any transcriptions of the name of God (the ancient term *shangdi* later adopted by the Christians is conspicuous for its absence, occurring only in one quotation from the *Shijing*).[22] They instead choose various combinations of the indeterminate Chinese terms *Tian* [Heaven] and *Dao* [the Way].[23] One of the most frequently stated points in the inscriptions is the denial to the divinity of any corporeal form. One could dismiss some of these examples as simple lip-service to Confucian prejudices against popular religious cults, with their flagrant idolatry, as in the following line from the 1512 inscription: "For if one fashions it into physical shapes, or traces its image in tangible forms ... this is tantamount to heresy."[24] But, of course, revulsion toward idolatry is also the central thread of the entire Hebrew scripture, which needs hardly be justified in Confucian terms. The 1489 inscription begins to sound more Confucian when it goes on to deny concourse between Heaven and man and insists on the nonvolitional spontaneity of the workings of Heaven, alluding directly to *Analects* XVII:19 ("Heaven does not speak . . . ").[25] In the following line, it then expands upon the idea of spontaneous being by the emphatic repetition of the adverb *zi* ("in and of itself," "without external causation"): "processes of generation go on by themselves; processes of transformation proceed by themselves; things take on shape and form in and of themselves."[26]

The conception of the spontaneous generation and functioning of the universe (the same idea expressed as the "opening up of the cosmos" [*tiandi kaipi*] in both philosophical and mythical formulations, including the opening lines of this inscription)[27] would appear to clash irreconcilably with the doctrine of volitional creation *ex nihilo* upon which the entire structure of Jewish theology is held to rest. In fact, Confucian cosmological thinking seems to provide a perfect example of the doctrine of pre-existing (i.e., uncreated) matter (*kadmut*)—even better than that of the neo-Aristotelians, against whom Maimonides is at such pains to direct his arguments in his great philosophical treatises.[28] But, at the same time, to the extent that the bulk of Jewish exegesis, from Philo and Onkelos through the major medieval thinkers, is preoccupied with depersonalizing lingering anthropomorphisms of divine will and power in the Old Testament, the gap between these two systems of thought may not be as unbridgeable as it seems. After all, literal expressions of the "will of Heaven" are not entirely absent in the Confucian Classics either (e.g., *tian ming*). In any case, the rejection of any notion of corporeal divinity, or even the reification of the divine will, as idolatrous is as much in line with Jewish thinking as with Confucian. One need only think of Maimonides' statement of this principle in his Thirteen Principles of Faith, widely known in the verse formulation in the prayer *Yigdal:* "He has no bodily form, for He is incorporeal." A similar narrowing of the gap between Judaic and Confucian thought can be seen in the various formulas for the oneness of God invoked in the Kaifeng inscriptions (e.g., "He is One, pure and inimitable").[29] In early Confucianism the concept of primal oneness is not very prominent—it is more a catchphrase of the Daoists, and later the Buddhists. But by the time of the Neo-Confucian centuries we are dealing with here, doctrines of primal unity (e.g., *tai ji*) were very much a part of Confucian philosophical discourse.

A second point of interest in the discussions of Heaven in the Jewish inscriptions has to do with the relationship between *Tian* and *Dao*. In a few passages, *dao* seems to be presented as a logically secondary dimension of being with respect to the priority and primacy of Heaven, somewhat along the lines of the logical movement from *Tian* to *Dao* in the opening passage of the *Zhongyong*.[30] At least at such points, what I believe the Chinese Jewish thinkers have in mind is an equation of *Dao* and Torah, in accordance with the various sources (e.g., Proverbs 8:22, Midrash Rabbah on Genesis 1:1, etc.) that speak of the Torah as a pre-existing design of universal creation. A slightly modified statement of this idea is expressed in the following passage at the beginning of the 1512 inscription: "If the Way were not incorporated into scripture it would have no basis for continuing existence; if the scripture were without the Way, it could not be put into practice." In formulations such as this in Confucian texts, we must normally understand the term *tian* as a kind of abbreviation for *tian di* ["heaven and earth," i.e., the entire given universe], also referred to as "the myriad things" [*wan wu*], of which *dao* is the sum total of all underlying principles of intelligibility. This gives rise to the notion of the omnipresence of *dao* (as in the well-known passage in the *Zhongyong* 1: "One can never be separated from the *Dao*, even for an instant," which is, by the way, cited in a different context in the 1663 inscription). I suspect that this notion of omnipresence is behind the ambiguous description of praying to every direction in the 1489 and 1663 inscriptions.

There are two other ideas cited in connection with Heaven in these texts that I believe reflect specifically neo-Confucian conceptions. One of these is the notion of the infinite generative force of the universe (*shengsheng zhi de*, in various Confucian texts)[31] that finds expression in a few passages in the 1489 and 1663 stelae, as well as in some of the synagogue inscriptions.[32] Although the Chinese Jews were most likely unaware of medieval Jewish philosophical texts (often under neo-Platonic influence) that reinterpret such concepts as providence (*hashgacha*) or the "divine presence" (*shechina*) in comparable terms, similar ideas can be readily derived from scriptural sources.

A final neo-Confucian implication that we can perceive in these documents is the notion of the refraction or replication of the "mind of the universe" (the *Dao* of the *tian di* cosmos) within the mind [*xin*, literally, "heart"] of the conscious individual. This major point of neo-Confucian metaphysics derived from passages in the Four Books is most frequently cited in the so-called intuitionist writings of the "School of Mind" [*Xinxue*] from Song through Ming, but it is equally crucial to the "rationalists" of the "School of Principle" [*Lixue*].[33] In the Kaifeng Jewish documents we see a number of discussions that grow out of this basic idea. For example, the original "enlightenment" of Abraham is described in a few places as a "communion" with, or a "conjunction" with the truth of Heaven.[34] Elsewhere, the same understanding surfaces in discussions of the act of prayer, which, we are told, must be preceded by a purification of the Heavenly mind, and seeks to attain a "vision of Heaven from the human perspective."[35]

This brings us back to the problem of ancestor worship in the Kaifeng synagogue. At a number of points in the stelae inscriptions, the worship of (literally, "sacrifice to," *ji*) the ancestors is cited as the principal form of religious expression in the community.[36] As mentioned above, the specter of idolatry associated with this practice was a serious sticking point for the establishment of Christianity in China, but this simple statement may be a bit misleading, since Chinese "ancestor worship" is a religious phenomenon with basically no sacred text, no formal doctrine, and no set liturgy; even the occasional use of portraits or other effigies is a far cry from heathen idol-worship.[37] Thus the worship of "ancestors" by the Kaifeng Jews was not necessarily an alien graft onto their tradition, since homage to the forefathers of the Jewish people (i.e., the patriarchs Abraham, Isaac, and Jacob) is such a central element in Jewish liturgy. In fact, it is worth mentioning that the opening section of the "Eighteen Benedictions" of every liturgical service (the section referred to as the "fathers," *avot*) is often held to be the most important part of Jewish prayer.[38] In any event, the authors of the stelae inscriptions manage to bypass this issue by linking these practices, in certain passages, to more broadly defined objects of worship. For example, the 1663 text tells us that the purpose of worship is "to requite with reverence the munificence of the powers that 'shelter and support' mankind" (the expressions "shelter" and "support" being standard epithets for Heaven and earth).[39] In both Chinese and Jewish thought, the basic idea of homage to the ancestors lies in the continuous chain of descent linking the past, present, and future of the community. This constitutive function finds expression in the following line in the 1489 inscription: "To revere Heaven without paying homage to the ancestors is not the proper way to worship the ancients."

Once again, lines like these may be taken as simple lip-service to Confucian values, but I prefer to see in them serious attempts to reconcile Chinese and Jewish sensitivities.

The other side of the coin of ancestor worship is the Confucian emphasis on the honoring of parents and elders [*xiao*, conventionally translated as "filial piety"]. In many contexts, *xiao* refers to little more than the ethical value of filial obedience, but in some texts it is elevated to the central term in the network of cardinal human relations [*wu lun*] defining human existence, sometimes abstracted as a kind of metaphysical cement holding Heaven, earth, and man in a harmonious balance.[40] In one place, the 1663 inscription shows an awareness of some of these implications by citing the argument of Mencius that filial devotion, along with the other cardinal virtues, is an inherent element of human nature rather than an externally imposed mode of behavior.[41] It is questionable whether the Kaifeng Jews had any awareness of the texts of medieval Jewish philosophy and exegesis that also raise the commandment to "honor thy father and mother" to a kind of metaphysical status (emphasizing the participatory role of human generation in the work of continuous creation). But they would certainly have understood the significance of the placement of this commandment in the Decalogue, alongside the principle of the sabbath as a celebration of the creation of the universe.

It is interesting that the concept of the sabbath is not emphasized in these inscriptions as much as one might expect. Could it be that the notion of a seven-day week was a bit too alien or perhaps suffered from negative associations with the Buddhist seven-day funeral cycles? In any event, the descriptions of observance of the Sabbath, while certainly recognizable, present considerable ambiguity. First of all, the line in the 1489 text that mentions "four days of observance each month" is grammatically imprecise, and could even be interpreted as a four-day period at the end of each month if the context did not require otherwise.[42] Moreover, the term *zhai* [literally, "fast-day"] applied to the sabbath observance is a bit surprising in view of the great importance attached to joyful eating and drinking on the day (*oneg shabbat*).[43] But, of course, the contradiction disappears as soon as we go on to explain that this Chinese term, as used in various contexts, refers more to a period of quiet meditation than to abstinence. In both the 1489 and the 1663 inscriptions, this day of meditation is directed toward contemplation of deeper patterns of meaning in the universe.[44] In pursuing this idea, the 1663 text makes its most clever linkage between Chinese and Jewish sources by citing the twenty-fourth hexagram *Fu* in the *Yi jing* [Book of Changes] as a conceptual model of the idea of the restorative temporal cycle underlying the institution of the sabbath. Not only does the name of this hexagram (literally, "return") capture the notion of periodic return and renewal, but the structure of the hexagram itself, traditionally interpreted as the reappearance of a strong *yang* line in the first position after having moved through a sequence of six prior stages of temporal process, provides an almost uncanny parallel to theoretical discussions of the meaning of the sabbath in Jewish sources.[45] The inscription, in fact, goes even further, emphasizing that this sabbath meditation is directed toward a restoration of vision: a renewed communion with the mind of the universe.[46]

From here, it is not very much of a leap to transfer the idea of restoration and renewal to the annual renewal of the New Year season, the highest point of which is the fast-day of Yom Kippur. In both the 1489 and the 1663 inscriptions, the discussions of the sabbath lead directly into the description of Yom Kippur observances. The details of this description all conform fairly well to expectations. The time, specified as "the end of autumn," may sound a little late, but the fixed date in the Hebrew calendar (tenth day of seventh Jewish lunar month, by Torah reckoning) falls just a few days before the Chinese Mid-autumn Festival (fifteenth day of eighth Chinese lunar month). The explanation of the observance as a day of "great abstention" and "confession to Heaven" is backed up by another appropriate quotation from the *Yi jing* in the 1489 text: "He acknowledges his faults and corrects them."[47] The linkage between the Sabbath and the Day of Atonement is deepened in the 1663 text by associating the meditative aspects of these days with the neo-Confucian notion of self-cultivation: "preserving the mind to nourish the inner nature,"[48] presented as the culmination of a description of the cessation of all worldly activity that seems to echo a passage in the "Image Commentary" on the *Fu* hexagram in the *Yi jing*.[49]

The view of spiritual cultivation through ritual observances presented in the Kaifeng inscriptions has both its external and its internal aspects. On the external side, the text insist in several places that the process of cultivation must take place within concrete acts of daily existence [*riyong*], as in this passage: "What is the Dao? It means the principles commonly followed by all men, past and present, in the abiding practices of daily life."[50] One might well take these claims of down-to-earth ethical roots as simply denials of heretical superstition, but I prefer to understand them as reflections of the central Jewish concept of the performance of prescribed observances (the "commandments," *mitzvot*) within the circumstances of day-to-day reality.[51] When formulated in this way, the entire range of prescribed *mitzvot* (i.e., what adds up to the system of *halacha*) sounds quite a bit like the range of prescribed behavior covered by the Confucian term *li*, often translated as "ritual propriety"), and the 1663 text, in fact, cites the *Li ji* at several points to bring out this conception.[52]

On the internal side of the dual cultivation of the inner and outer self, the key terms of neo-Confucian discourse cited in the stelae inscriptions are *jing* and *cheng*. Both of these terms are subject to misinterpretation, since their common translations as "reverence" and "sincerity" respectively, based on usages in the modern language, do not really capture their significance as philosophical concepts. In neo-Confucian contexts, both of these expressions come to mean a state of inner equilibrium, free of the disruptive influence of selfish desire, in which one can experience the deepest commonality of the self [*xin*] and the universe.[53] When the inscription-texts touch upon such matters, they tend to settle for throw-away quotations from the *Four Books,* but in a few passages they do seem to reveal a sensitivity to the implications of these concepts in Ming–Qing neo-Confucian thought.[54] For example, the 1512 text sums up a long review of the major concepts of the Jewish faith by stating: "all of the above are uniformly rooted in the qualities of *jing* and *cheng.*"[55]

I have attempted to mine the Kaifeng stelae inscriptions for examples of the substantive accommodation of the Chinese Jews to their Confucian intellectual environment. Over the past ten years, in the wake of the reopening of China to extensive foreign travel and the explosion of Western reports on the Kaifeng Jews, many Jewish and Chinese readers have been fascinated by the chance intersection of the histories of what are arguably the two oldest continuous civilizations in the world today.[56] Under these circumstances, many simplistic comparisons between these two traditions have been aired, ranging from overstatements of the conceptual incompatibility of theistic and nontheistic philosophical systems (which to my mind misunderstand both the noneschatological character of Judaism and the religious dimension of Confucianism) to various facile analogies between Chinese and Jewish sociological factors: role of education, elevation of the scholar, philanthropic institutions, family structure, merchant organizations and business practices, and the like (which often lose sight of the crucial differences in the historical experience of the two peoples). Such comparative speculations remain for us an endless source of fascination. But for the Jews of Kaifeng in the Ming and Qing periods, these were vital questions that determined the very identity and survival of their community.

Notes

Earlier versions of this article appeared in *Sino-Judaica: Occasional Papers of the Sino-Judaic Institute* 1 (1991), pp. 47–62, and in M. Patricia Needle, ed. *East Gate of Kaifeng: A Jewish World Inside China* (Minneapolis: China Center, University of Minnesota, 1992), pp. 29–38. The article is republished with permission of both publishers.

1. The most important studies of the Kaifeng Jews from the perspective of Jewish history include Donald D. Leslie, *The Survival of the Chinese Jews: The Jewish Community of Kaifeng* (Leiden: E.J. Brill, 1972); Yitzhak Ben-Zvi, "The Stelae of the Ancient Synagogue in K'ai-feng-fu" (in Hebrew), *Sefunot* 5 (1961): 29–66; and Michael Pollak, *Mandarins, Jews, and Missionaries: The Jewish Experience in the Chinese Empire* (Philadelphia: Jewish Publication Society, 1980). The most substantive Chinese study of the Chinese Jews is that by the prominent twentieth-century historian *Chen* Yuan, *Kaifeng yicileye jiao kao* (Investigation of the Israelite Religion in Kaifeng) (Shanghai, 1923). Leslie's *Survival* also deals with Chinese documents to a considerable extent.

2. In addition to the studies mentioned in note 1, see also Bishop William C. White, *Chinese Jews: A Compilation of Matters Relating to the Jews of K'ai-fêng Fu* (1942; repr. of 2d ed., New York: Paragon, 1966); P. Jérôme Tobar, S.J., *Les inscriptions juives de K'ai-fong-fou* (Shanghai: Mission Catholique, 1912); and Leslie, "Some Notes on the

Jewish Inscriptions of K'ai-feng," *Journal of the American Oriental Society* 82 (1962): 346–61.

3. See Leslie, *Survival,* p. 20. On the other extant written documents of the community, see Tobar, *Inscriptions,* pp. 92–110; White, *Chinese Jews,* vol. 2, pp. 155–77; and Leslie, *Survival,* p. 141–59.

4. These include mention of Moses's forty-day fast, and his "just and compassionate" nature; descriptions of the practices of ritual purification, funeral societies, *sha'atnez* [the use only of permissible fibers in the manufacture of garments], honesty in weights and measures, and charity; and prayer three times a day. The forward and backward steps, facing four directions, and so on, show the greatest discrepancy. See Leslie, *Survival,* pp. 92f. for discussion.

5. See Leslie, *Survival,* pp. 28–30, 39–40, 47; Tobar, *Inscriptions,* p. 54; White, *Chinese Jews,* vol. 2, pp. 32, 47, 77, 103; and Pollak, *Mandarins,* pp. 61f. and 70.

6. The most blatant propaganda appears at the end of the 1489 inscription. See transcription in White, *Chinese Jews,* pp. 38, lines 12–13, and 39; lines 1–2.

7. See 1489 inscription (White, *Chinese Jews,* p. 38, ll. 9–10), and 1512 inscription (ibid., p. 52, l. 7).

8. See, for example, 1663 inscription (ibid., p. 82, l.10), and 1679 inscription (ibid., p. 105, l. 1).

9. Of course, it is difficult to trace the evolution of ideas from stele to stele, since the later ones are all to one extent or another based on the earlier ones.

10. See 1489 inscription (ibid., p. 35, ll. 4–5). The same applies to the appropriation of characteristically Muslim usages, such as the "pure and true faith" [*qingzhen jiao*].

11. See 1489 inscription (ibid., p. 38, ll. 8).

12. For the issue of the ritual calendar, see Leslie, *Survival,* pp. 86–90, and "Some Notes," pp. 356–60, where he refutes earlier speculation by James Finn in *The Jews of China* (London, 1843). See also Tobar, cited in White, *Chinese Jews,* pp. 198f. For descriptions of the synagogue, see Tobar, pp. 1–7, and Leslie, *Survival,* pp. 79–83.

13. For sources and discussion of the Pan Gu myth, see Derk Bodde, "Myths of Ancient China," in *Mythologies of the Ancient World,* ed. Samuel Noah Kramer (New York: Anchor-Doubleday, 1966), pp. 382–84; Yuan Ke, *Zhongguo gudai shenhua* [Ancient Chinese Myths] (Shanghai, 1950); Norman Girardot, *Myth and Meaning in Early Taoism* (Berkeley: University of California Press, 1983), pp. 192–94, etc. The 1663 inscription separates the names of Adan and Pan Gu, making Adam a nineteenth-generation descendant of Pan Gu himself. Chen Yuan regards this as a textual error and emends the text accordingly.

14. The inscriptions conspicuously avoid use of the term *zaowu zhe* for the creator. Cf. the occurrence of the term in Zhuangzi, "Da zongshi" chapter (where it also refers to a secondary molder of physical forms). For discussion, see my *Archetype and Allegory in the Dream of the Red Chamber* (Princeton: Princeton University Press, 1976), p. 18. For general discussion of Chinese creation myths, see Frederick W. Mote, *Intellectual Foundations of China* (New York: Knopf, 1971), pp. 17–20; and Bodde, "Myths," p. 405.

15. See Genesis 2:7 and 3:19.

16. On the Nüwa mythical materials, see Bodde, "Myths," pp. 386–89; and Plaks, *Archetype and Allegory,* pp. 27–42. The Chinese flood myths are more directly related to the figures Gun and Yu, and to Gong Gong (See Bodde, "Myths," pp. 398–403).

17. Genesis 9:12–16. See Plaks, *Archetype and Allegory,* pp. 28, 81f.

18. Genesis 10. See Plaks, *Archetype and Allegory,* pp. 37–40.

19. The citation reads: "ten generations from Noah to Abraham." Nüwa is first

mentioned in the 1512 inscription (White, *Chinese Jews*, p. 53, l. 10), repeated in the 1663 and 1679 texts. See also Vertical Inscription 27 (ibid., p. 138).

20. The character *wu* (literally, "without"), of course, may also be more than a phonetic rendering.

21. Or perhaps: "the One Man (i.e., the Emperor) . . . "

22. The *Shi jing* quote is found in the 1663 inscription (ibid., p. 81, l. 8). See, for example, *Zhongyong* 18 for another "Confucian" usage.

23. For a discussion of the usages of the term *tian*, see Tobar, *Inscriptions*, pp. 104f. Legge occasionally translates *Dao* as God in his *Chinese Classics*.

24. See 1489 inscription (White, *Chinese Jews*, p. 35, l. 2), and 1512 inscription (ibid., p. 53, l. 8). See also Vertical Inscriptions 28 (ibid., p. 139) and 35 (ibid., p. 146).

25. See also 1663 inscription (ibid., p. 80, l. 2).

26. 1489 inscription (ibid., p. 35, l. 4).

27. See 1489 inscription (ibid., p. 35, l. 1), and Vertical Inscription 26 (ibid., p. 137).

28. I have in mind discussion of the philosophical theory of *kadmut* in such texts as *Moreh-n'vochim, Sefer haKuzari*, etc.

29. See 1489 inscription (ibid., p. 35, l. 10).

30. "That which is endowed by Heaven is called Nature; what conforms to Nature is called the Way."

31. See, for example, the *Yi jing, Xici zhuan* 5, translated in Richard Willhelm, *The I Ching* (Princeton: Princeton University Press, 1950; repr. 1980), p. 299.

32. See also 1663 inscription (White, *Chinese Jews*, p. 80, l. 3), and Vertical Inscriptions 16 (ibid., p. 137), 33 (ibid., p. 144), and 39 (ibid., p. 150).

33. For an introductory discussion of the concept of *xin* within Zhu Xi orthodoxy, see *Fung* Yu-lan, *History of Chinese Philosophy*, trans. Derk Bodde (Princeton: Princeton University Press, 1953), vol. 2, pp. 586–607.

34. See 1489 inscription (White, *Chinese Jews*, p. 35, l. 5), cf. *Zhongyong* 22 for possible sources of allusion. See also 1663 inscription (ibid., p. 80 11.2–4).

35. See 1489 inscription (ibid., p. 36, l. 2), and 1663 inscription (ibid., p. 81, l. 5).

36. For example, 1489 inscription (ibid., p. 36, ll. 7, 11) and 1512 inscription (ibid., p. 52, l. 10). See also Vertical Inscription 38 (ibid., p. 149).

37. We are all familiar with the amusing story of *Ai* Tian's toleration of Matteo Ricci's "idolatry," reported in Leslie, *Survival*, pp. 31f., and Pollak, *Mandarins*, pp. 7f.

38. See *Babylonian Talmud*, Tractate Rosh Hashana, 4.

39. See 1489 inscription (White, *Chinese Jews*, p. 36, l. 7). For preceding citation, see 1663 inscription (ibid., p. 81, l. 11).

40. For example, *Lunyu* 1:2, *Xiaojing*, etc.

41. See 1663 inscription (White, *Chinese Jews*, p. 81, l. 1).

42. See 1489 inscription (ibid., p. 36, l. 9). Tobar has some trouble with the imprecise grammar and translates: "la purification de quatre jours gardée chaque mois," but he immediately goes on to qualify this: "c'est-à-dire en quatre semaines" (p. 42).

43. See also Vertical Inscription 37 (White, *Chinese Jews*, p. 148). Cf. the notion of "purification of the mind" (*xinzhai*) in *Zhuangzi*, "Renjian shi" chapter.

44. See 1489 inscription (ibid., p. 36, l. 9), and 1663 inscription (ibid., p. 82, l. 3).

45. For translation, see Willhelm, *The I Ching*, pp. 97–100, 504–9.

46. See 1663 inscription (White, *Chinese Jews*, p. 82, l. 4).

47. See *Yi jing*, hexagram *Yi*, Image Commentary (Willhelm, *The I Ching*, p. 163). See also 1663 inscription (White, *Chinese Jews*, p. 82, l. 6).

48. See 1663 inscription (ibid.).

49. See Willhelm, *The I Ching,* p. 98.
50. See 1512 inscription (White, *Chinese Jews,* p. 51, l. 1), and 1489 inscription (ibid., p. 36, l. 1).
51. Cf. 1489 inscription (ibid.).
52. See quotations from *Li ji* in 1663 inscription (ibid., p. 81, ll. 10–13).
53. See, for example, *Shu jing:* "Yao dian," *Li ji:* "*Li qi*" 35, "*Li yi*" 17, 18, 31–33, and *Zhongyong,* 20–22, 25.
54. See, for example, 1663 inscription (White, *Chinese Jews,* p. 81, l. 8), and 1512 inscription (ibid., p. 52, l. 9).
55. 1512 inscription (ibid., p. 52, l. 11). See also 1489 inscription (ibid., p. 36, ll. 2, 9), and 1663 inscription (ibid., p. 81, ll. 6, 11).
56. Of course, no Greek or Indian scholar will accept this characterization, but on the point of *both* age and continuity I will stand by it.

B. Western Response

Chapter I.B.1

The Revelation of a Jewish Presence in Seventeenth-Century China: Its Impact on Western Messianic Thought

Michael Pollak

The startling announcement from China of the discovery in 1605 by the Jesuit missionary Matteo Ricci of a small Jewish community in the city of Kaifeng produced a chain of bizarre reactions in European intellectual circles that tell us substantially more about the Western settings in which they arose than about the people by whose existence they were prompted.[1] The myths, moreover, that were concocted around the Jewish experience in old China, mostly by individuals who sincerely believed that what they were saying was absolutely true, provide a prime illustration of how fact transformed into fantasy can generate illusions that soak into the fabric of the historiographic process and become difficult or impossible to wash away. "How many pens are worn out," a venerable Jewish text asks resignedly, "how many bottles of ink are used up, to write about things that never happened?"[2]

It must be made clear that the revelation that Jews had been found in faraway China came to a Europe in which considerable numbers of Christian and Jewish thinkers had already convinced themselves that the messianic age could not be far off. Believing also that the conversion of the Jews throughout the world was a *sine qua non* to the arrival of the redeemer who would inaugurate that glorious epoch, many of the Christians among these savants concluded that the discovery of a branch of Israel in the land beyond the Great Wall provided a unique opportunity for effecting the mass conversion that would herald his coming. It need scarcely be pointed out, in any event, that the Jewish and Christian perceptions of the nature and content of messianism were, and remain, profoundly different from one another: To the Jews, the messiah was a human being of uniquely charismatic and ethical stature who, upon his first and only appearance on earth, would return them to their ancient homeland and inspire them to renew and reinvigorate their commitment to the Judaic teachings their ancestors had received at Sinai; to the Christians, the messiah was a divine figure whose *second* appearance on earth, and the multitudinous blessings that this would confer upon those who trusted in him, would take place only after the Jews, having been brought together from the ends of the earth, recognized the error of their ways and acknowledged him as their savior.[3]

Suffice it to say that when the news of Matteo Ricci's discovery of the presence of Jews in China reached Europe, theologians of both faiths were searching avidly through scripture, as well as through cabalistic and other seemingly pertinent sources, for texts that would enable them to holster their particular eschatological views, while indulging in endless speculations as to the year that would mark the beginning of the messianic era.[4] Our interest here lies, however, in: (1) explaining why the celebrated Rabbi Manasseh ben Israel of Amsterdam saw fit to inject Ricci's Chinese Jews into an apocalyptic scenario that, although solidly grounded in the messianic lore of Judaism, was designed to appeal to an English readership steeped in the traditions of Christian millenarianism; and (2) explaining the rationale behind a succession of Catholic and Protestant efforts to acquire a Torah scroll from the Kaifeng synagogue and make its text serve as the linchpin in a novel plan for accelerating the conversion of world Jewry to Christianity and, with that, the second advent of Jesus of Nazareth.

Throughout the centuries, the extent to which Christians and Jews have sought comfort in the messianic promise may well be said to have varied directly with the degree of insecurity in which they lived. Messianic zeal, in other words, reached its heights when people faced severe persecution, wars, famine, pestilence, and the like, and diminished when times grew better, so that the sixteenth and seventeenth centuries, eras of exceptional turmoil throughout Europe for both Christians and Jews, proved especially conducive to the propagation of redemptionary predictions.[5] The Jews, who were still absorbing the wrenching consequences of their expulsions from Spain and Portugal, had also to cope with the crossfire, in which they were caught throughout the endless clashes that went on between the Church Militant and a burgeoning Protestantism. Deprived of even the right of residence in many European countries, and denied civil and religious liberties in virtually all the others, their lives were further embittered by the slaughter of perhaps as many as 300,000 of their brethren during the widespread fighting and frenzied pogroms that erupted in 1648, when Bogdan Chmielnicki's Cossacks, supported by Tatar forces from the Crimea, rebelled against their Polish overlords. "It is said," Manasseh ben Israel ruefully observed in 1650, "that although the Messiah were lame, he might have come by this time."[6] Still, his very next sentence demonstrates that his impatience had not led to hopelessness. "Though we cannot exactly shew [sic] the time of our redemption," he wrote, "yet we judge it to be near." Here Manasseh was echoing a sentiment that had been, and would continue to be, sufficiently commonplace to produce a climate in which such pseudo-messiahs as David Reubeni (ca. 1490–1541?), Solomon Molko (ca. 1500–1532), and Sabbatai Zevi (1626–1676) could attract myriads of followers from the ranks of their coreligionists.[7]

Christianity, too, was enduring trying times: peasant revolts on a grand scale, Henry VIII's disputes with Pope Clement VII and the subsequent establishment by Edward VI of an independent English church, the Reformation and the Counter-Reformation, the horrors inflicted by the Thirty Years' War and numerous other conflicts, perennial outbreaks of fanaticism, which resulted in the legalized slaughter of thousands upon thousands of men and women on charges of heresy or witchcraft, and so forth. And with all this came a powerful upsurge in the yearning for the better world that, it was felt, only the second coming of the messiah who had died on the cross and was three days later resurrected could bring to a suffering humanity. Before long, this upsurge enveloped both England and large portions of the continent, thereby exerting considerable influence on the shaping of Western religious thought and, inevitably, on the consequences thereof. Although the nature and impact of this messianic activity seem now to be increasingly addressed in specialized scholarly publications, they tend to be overlooked or given short shrift in the general run of historical works whose readership extends beyond the confines of the academic community.

One reason—and, in my opinion, the most compelling reason—for the interest that Christian messianists exhibited in the Jewish community of Kaifeng can be traced to patristic writings going as far back as the second century. Such early Church fathers as Justin Martyr, unwilling to believe that the Jewish scriptural texts (Hebrew, *Tanakh*) would not have included verses foretelling the birth, ministry, crucifixion, and resurrection of Jesus of Nazareth in terms so unequivocally spelled out that not even the most obstreperous of Jews could fail to understand them, raised the charge that while many passages of this nature had in fact been part of the Hebrew biblical literature of pre-Christian times, they had been altered or excised by a venal rabbinate bent on eliminating all biblical prophecies related to his coming.[8] On the other hand, Jerome (ca. 337–420), translating the *Tanakh* into Latin, rejected the "corrections" that certain Christian exegetes were proposing to make in the old Jewish writings. However, this did not keep him from challenging the accuracy of at least one biblical verse when he discovered that it did not conform to a theological interpretation that he was then advocating. As the centuries passed, in any case, and Christian attacks on the integrity of the *Tanakh* continued unabatedly, Jewish scholars, including even Maimonides, responded forcefully, though without notable success.[9] So it was that hundreds of years after the death of Judaism's most illustrious medieval scholar, Catholic and Protestant theologians found it possible to inject the Torah scrolls of the synagogue of Kaifeng into the old dispute, proclaim these scrolls to be key factors in demonstrating that the *Tanakh* had been "corrupted" by the rabbinate, and endow the Kaifeng Torahs with apocalyptic overtones that, had the Chinese Jews who owned these texts been made aware of what was going on, would have left them in a state of utter bewilderment.

A Lost Tribe's Migration from China to Peru

To his dying day, as we know, Christopher Columbus remained firmly convinced that the transatlantic regions to which he made his four epic voyages were part of the Asian continent. But they were not, of course; and once the monumental scope of what Columbus had actually accomplished was finally recognized, the theologians of Europe suddenly found themselves confronted with the daunting problem of explaining his discoveries in terms that could be reconciled with scripture.

When he sailed west from Palos in 1492, Columbus, anticipating that he might encounter components of the Lost Tribes in the Indies that were his destination, took along as interpreter the converted Jew Luís de Torres, whose linguistic repertory included Hebrew and Aramaic, as well as a smattering of Arabic, a language then thought to be akin to Chinese. When Columbus landed in Cuba, he even dispatched Torres on a fruitless mission to seek out the Great Khan, in whose court he might be expected to find someone with whom he could converse in Arabic, and perhaps someone who could speak Hebrew, or at least point him in the direction of others who could—with people, that is, of the Lost Tribes of Israel.[10]

Who then, Europe's theologians now began to ask themselves, are the American Indians? Scripture does not mention them or the lands in which they live. Like the rest of us, they must obviously be descended from Adam and Eve. We have absolutely no reason to believe, moreover, that the flood that covered the entire earth and killed off all its inhabitants except Noah and his immediate family would have spared any members of the human race who might have ventured as far as the Americas. Accordingly, the Indians—again, like the rest of us—are necessarily descended from Noah.

Does this mean then, as certain learned people are now suggesting, that the ancestors of the Indians made their way to the Western Hemisphere from a starting point that, depending on whose arguments you find most palatable, may have been Phoenicia, Troy, Carthage, China, the Lost Continent of Atlantis, Norway, or even the pre-Israelite Land of Canaan? Or—most intriguing of all—could these American Indians be descended from one or more of the Ten Lost Tribes of Israel?[11]

With the passage of time and the accumulation of experience in dealing with them, the question of the origin of the Indians became central to many Christian scholars, even obsessive. If it turned out that the Indians were indeed of Jewish extraction, and if they could then be ingathered and converted to the faith, this would contribute immeasurably to hastening the onset of the most wondrous event Christianity looked forward to—the second coming of Christ.

The first published attribution of a Lost Tribes origin for the Indians appeared in Joannes Fredericus Lumnius's *De extremo Dei iudicio et indorum vocatione* (Antwerp: Antonium Tilenium Brechtanum, 1567). The conviction that the Amerindians were Jews of the Lost Tribes then spread quickly throughout the Western world, in time including among its proponents such men as John Dury, Thomas Thorowgood, John Eliot, Roger Williams, William Penn, and, later, an array of commentators on the Book of Mormon. There were also Pedro Simón and Antonio Vazques de Espinosa, who narrowed down the line of descent of the Amerindians to only one of the Lost Tribes—Issachar. The American Israelitism thesis was not, however, shared by all scholars. Hamon L'Estrange, for example, objected to it strongly, constructing as one argument against its legitimacy an Aristotelian syllogism of bemusing dimensions. Everyone knows, L'Estrange observed (in his *Americans No Iewes* [London: Henry Seile, 1652]), first, that Jews are forbidden to marry harlots and, second, that all Indian women are harlots. Whence it follows, he triumphantly declared, the Indians can under no circumstances be Jews.

This study is not the place in which to delve into all the theological questions that were raised by the discovery of the Americas. We will, however, examine here the means through which the question of whether the Indians were of Lost Tribes origin was linked to the Jews of China, and what came of this.

The man responsible for making this linkage was the enterprising Manasseh ben Israel, who proposed an explanation that enlisted the unwitting assistance of the Jews of Kaifeng in the campaign that brought him to London in 1655 for the purpose of persuading Oliver Cromwell's Puritan government to permit Jews to settle again in England, from which they had been expelled in 1290.[12] In the course of his negotiations with the English, Manasseh took the position that the earliest inhabitants of America were not the Indians but, rather, Jews—members of the Ten Lost Tribes of Israel who, fearful of being overrun by advancing Tatar forces, left their homes (and a core of seemingly less apprehensive coreligionists) in Kaifeng and fled to the then totally uninhabited Western Hemisphere, either by way of a land bridge or by ferrying themselves across the "Streight of Anian." The Tatars, who crossed into America after them, Manasseh's argument went, became the people who were now known as Indians. As for the Jews whom they pursued—the people who would have been the first to set foot on the American landmass—they still lived there, and still thought of themselves as members of the House of Israel. In fact, Manasseh had an affidavit in hand that was composed in Amsterdam on 18 Elul 5404 (= 19 September 1644), and in which the Portugese Marrano [secret Jew] Antonio Montezinos told the amazing story of how he had recently discovered a community of three hundred members of the Lost Tribes of Reuben in the Cordillera mountains of Peru.[13]

What Manasseh was driving at, and was to express again in 1656 in his *Vindiciae Judaeorum,* though without doing violence to his own passionately held Judaic understanding of the content and promise of messianism, was that the Puritan government of Oliver Cromwell would have to permit the resettlement of Jews in England as a prelude to the coming of the messiah. And the time was now ripe, Manasseh realized, for an approach on behalf of the resettlement cause to be made to the English, whose apocalyptic leanings had by then produced, as Lucien Wolf would observe in 1901, not only "a very widespread philo-Semitism," but also "a strong conviction that, inasmuch as the conversion of the Jews was an indispensable preliminary to the Millennium, their admission to England, where they might meet the godliest people in the world, was urgently necessary."[14]

Manasseh's theological argument for the readmission of the Jews to England was essentially based on three separate and seemingly unrelated sources: a verse from the Book of Isaiah, Matteo Ricci's discovery of an old Jewish community in the heart of China, and Antonio Montezinos's reported encounter with members of the Lost Tribes in the wilds of South America. These he put together ingeniously, though not, one suspects, without a touch of guile.

Manasseh starts with Isaiah, 49:12. Here Isaiah (Deutero-Isaiah, to be more precise), picturing the return of the dispersed of Israel to their homeland, tells his listeners: "Look! These are coming from afar, These from the north and the west, And these from the Land of Sinim." But what, asks Manasseh, does the prophet mean by the Land of Sinim? After acknowledging that the authoritative biblical commentator Abraham ibn Ezra had placed the Land of Sinim on the southern border of Egypt, Manasseh merely notes that in this ibn Ezra was "mistaken," accepting instead Ptolemy's identification of Sinim as the land inhabited by the Chinese people. Manasseh's interpretation of this verse from Isaiah thus "proves" that there must already have been Jews in China as far back as the era in which Isaiah prophesied—in the sixth century B.C., that is.[15] In Manasseh's opinion, Matteo Ricci's announcement of the continuing presence of Jews in China simply corroborates both the Isaiah placement of their ancestors in that country and the more recent disclosure by Antonio Montezinos of the presence of Reubenites in the Americas—Reubenites, Manasseh contends, who came to the New World by way of Kaifeng as refugees from their Tatar foes.

Drawing upon Deuteronomy and the Book of Daniel for prophecies concerning the events that would precede the coming of the messiah, Manasseh writes,

> I conceived, that our (the Jews') universal dispersion was a necessary circumstance, to be fulfilled, before all that shall be accomplished which the Lord hath promised to the people of the *Iewes,* concerning their restauration, and their returning again into their own land, according to those words (in) *Dan.* 12.7. *When he shall have accomplished to scatter the power of the holy people, all these things shall be finished.* As also, that this our scattering, by little, and little, should be amongst all people, from the *one end of the earth* (ketsei ha-arets), *even unto the other;* as is written (in) *Deut.* 28.64. I conceived that by the *end of the earth* might be understood this *Island* (England).[16]

In short, Manasseh's use of the old argument that coupled the Deuteronomy and Daniel verses to the chain of events that would precede the coming of the messiah stressed to his English readers that if they were serious about speeding that coming, they must realize that the Jews would have to be ingathered not alone from that end of the earth which is America—where, thanks to Montezinos, it was now known that they could be found—but also from that other end of the earth—the *ketsei ha-arets* called England, that is—from which they had so long been barred. Precisely how the coming of the Jewish messiah would fit in with Christian expectations regarding the "end of days," Manasseh did not say. Given, however, the prevailing messianic fervor of the time, I think that what Manasseh had in mind was that his Christian readers would somehow deduce—as many actually did—that the Christian messianic era that they envisaged would never come into being unless the Jews were first readmitted to England.

How else, after all, can one explain why Manasseh chose to construct a thesis advocating a course of action for expediting the advent of a Jewish messiah in a book directed to an audience that was non-Jewish? Moreover, why he would suddenly start identifying the biblical *ketsei ha-aretz* as England, when he had previously identified it as Portugal?[17]

In the end, neither Manasseh's messianic stratagems nor his more worldly political and economic arguments brought a formal revocation of the ban on Jewish immigration to England, but they did play an important part in persuading the English to turn an unseeing eye toward the quiet and persistent influx of Jews into the country that ensued. When full de jure recognition of the Jewish right to residence and civil equality was finally attained during the nineteenth century, few Jews realized how much they owed to Manasseh and to the strained messianic lore that he so zealously dispensed throughout the England of his day.

Essentially, Manasseh introduced the Chinese Jews into the arguments with which he hoped to gain the readmittance of their Western coreligionists to England merely to add credence to his thesis that Montezinos was telling the truth about having found traces of the Lost Tribes of Israel in South America. Manasseh's linking of the Chinese Jews to the messianic expectations of his Christian readers was consequently intended to be no more than a supportive tactical maneuver. The Christian interest in the Torah scrolls of the Kaifeng synagogue, to which we now turn our attention, was, however, another matter. Here the motivation was plain, bluntly stated, and, in the minds of those who were swept up by it, quite likely to lead to the most exhilarating prospect that they and the rest of humanity could look forward to—the return to earth of the savior for whom they had so long been waiting.

The Chinese Torah Scrolls and the Second Coming

Matteo Ricci learned of the existence of an old Jewish community in Kaifeng from the mandarin *Ai* Tian, a member of that community who visited him at his church in Beijing during the last week of June 1605. He also learned that the Kaifeng congregation, whose first synagogue was built in 1163, owned several Torah scrolls, one of which was alleged to have been written around the year 1000.[18] It was to be the destiny of these scrolls—and of the copies made following the loss of most of them in a flood that destroyed the synagogue in 1642—to be injected into the ongoing disputes over the textual purity of the Hebrew scriptures available in the West and, consequently, into the mainstream of Christian millenarian thought.

The story starts with the acceptance by a succession of European savants of two presumptions concerning Chinese Jewish history from which they constructed a hypothesis that would lead, they hoped, to the substantiation of the old Christian contention that the Jews had nefariously altered the texts of their Torahs. These two presumptions—both of which, it must be stressed, proved in the end to be utterly without merit—were, in short: (1) that the Jews came to China before the beginning of the Christian era;[19] and (2) that they had ever since their arrival in the country been *totally* cut off from contact with coreligionists in other lands. The first premise was apparently derived from a vague statement by Ricci that Jews had arrived in China "at an early period," and from an assortment of fantasies that had been built up regarding early Jewish diasporic history.[20] The second was born out of the fact that China was so far away that it seemed unlikely that its Jews would have been able to communicate with coreligionists outside the nation, and perhaps also as the result of a faulty attribution of an early Ming ban against travel beyond the country's borders to a much more remote period in Chinese history. Whatever the case, the conclusion drawn from these two premises was that the texts of the Torah scrolls that would have been brought to China by the Jews who came there in pre-Christian times must have been "pristine." From this it followed that these texts would necessarily have contained the lost messianic prophesies for which Christian theologians had so long been searching. The Chinese Jewish copyists of all succeeding generations would accordingly have enjoyed the advantage of working from wholly uncorrupted source texts. Hence, each of the Torahs used by the Jewish congregation of Kaifeng could be expected to contain the messianic passages that the rabbinate had changed or erased in the opening years of the Christian era.

The next step, of course, would be to secure at least one of the Kaifeng Torahs, bring it to Europe, and let the Jews of the West read with their own eyes the prophetic verses that had been withheld from them and from all humanity outside China for more than a millennium and a half. Once they realized how grossly they had been betrayed by their rabbis, this line of reasoning went, they would be left with no choice but to renounce their old religious ties, become believing Christians, and, in so doing, pave the way for a speedy coming of the redeemer to whom they had at last turned.

Actually, it was Ricci himself who first tried to determine whether the texts of the Kaifeng Torahs were identical to those in Western lands. In 1608, two Chinese he had sent to Kaifeng—one of whom had become a Jesuit lay brother—returned to Beijing with copies of the opening and closing portions of the individual books of the city's synagogal Pentateuchs, but no textual inconsistencies could be found between these small samplings and the corresponding verses contained in the Hebrew bibles in use outside China.[21] What was needed, it was decided, was a complete Torah scroll that could be compared word for word with the scrolls known to the West.

An early summing up of the reasons behind the Christian interest in the Kaifeng Torahs comes to us from Alvarado Sem(m)edo's *Imperio de la China,* which was published in Madrid in 1642. "Father *Julius Alenes,*" an English version of this work states,[22] "one of our company [the Jesuit order], was among them [the Kaifeng Jews] for some time [in 1613]; they shewed him their *Synagogues* [more correctly, their *Synagogue*], but would not draw their curtaines [sic] and let him see the Bible. Father *Mattheus Riccius* affirmeth, that according to the relation which the *Jews* themselves made to him thereof in *Pekim,* it was not at all differing from ours. They have no knowledge at all of *Christ,* so that it seemeth, they were entred [sic] into *China* before he came into the World; or at least, if they have heard of him, the memorie [sic] of it is quite lost: and therefore it would be of great consequence to see their *Bible;* for perhaps they have not corrupted it, as our Jews have done, to obscure the glorie [sic] of our *Redeemer.*"[23]

Perhaps the most illustrious figure who shared Semmedo's line of thought regarding the Kaifeng Pentateuchs, and also made a concerted effort to have them studied, was none other than Wilhelm Gottfried von Leibnitz, who in a letter dated January 1, 1700, informed Father Antoine Verjus that he had recently asked Father Charles le Gobien to urge his Jesuit colleagues in China to arrange for a thorough examination of "the Old Testament of the Chinese Jews in order to collate its text with that of the Hebrew Scriptures employed in Europe." His reason for wanting this done, Leibnitz explained, was that he considered it "possible to come upon certain hitherto unknown details in the Chinese texts, since it would seem that for a long time the Chinese Jews have had absolutely no contact with the Jews of Europe." He suspected, he also told Verjus, that the Chinese Jews "might still hold some of those books or passages which the European Jews have perhaps altered or suppressed out of hatred for Christianity." That Leibnitz's interest in securing the Chinese texts was not a passing fancy is demonstrated by the fact that he is known to have written at least two other letters of a similar nature, one in 1705 or thereabouts, and the other in 1707.[24]

In 1707, le Gobien, concurring with Leibnitz, put his feelings about the Chinese–Jewish texts—and about Jews in general—into a scurrilous preface to one volume of a large collection of reports received from Jesuits stationed or traveling in far-off lands, the *Lettres édifiantes et curieuses écrites des missions étrangères.*[25] The Jews of Europe, he declared, stood accused, and with good reason, of having "altered the Scriptures—perhaps by omitting or transposing entire chapters; perhaps by merely changing several verses or words; perhaps by revising those passages that did not suit them; or perhaps by altering the punctuation in various passages in order to make them support their own views." This would have been done, he went on, "to confirm the interpretations already arrived at by their sect."[26] Then, in a scathing attack on the Talmud, he suggested that if it were possible to "make the Jews see that the tenets of Judaism as they comprehend them are not necessarily the same as those held by Jews living in certain other regions—regions, that is, to which the teachings of the Talmud have never penetrated—we will have convinced them to stop venerating their Talmud. We might also be able to do likewise with regard to those Jews who now live in China by demonstrating to them that the faith to which they subscribe differs greatly from the faith of their brethren in the West."

Included in the correspondence published in the Lettres édifiantes was a letter dated November 5, 1704, that was sent from Kaifeng to Father Joseph Suarez by the Jesuit priest Jean-Paul Gozani.[27] In this letter, Gozani reported that he and the rabbi of Kaifeng had actually compared a series of Hebrew scriptural passages, beginning with Genesis 1:1, as they occurred in a text belonging to the city's synagogue and in a European biblical text that Gozani owned. Although Gozani knew no Hebrew, the two men, speaking Chinese, succeeded in checking out "the descendants of Adam down to Noah, with the age [at death] of each," a procedure suggested by Leibnitz in his 1700 letter to Verjus. They then compared "in a summary manner the names and main points of chronology" of each of the books of the Pentateuch. In the end, Gozani wrote, they discovered that "all was in agreement." Notwithstanding this, Gozani remained "suspicious that they have among them Talmudic Jews and have corrupted the Bible." His reasoning? Rodrigo de Figueiredo and Christiano Enriquez, two Jesuit priests who were stationed in Kaifeng before Gozani's first assignment there and were known to have visited the synagogue on a number of occasions, had made no effort to secure a copy of a congregational Pentateuch. To Gozani, this indicated that the two men had seen no point in wasting their time on a text that had already been "corrupted by the Talmudists" and was no longer "pure, as it had been before the coming of the Savior."

Nevertheless, Gozani urged caution. "As to whether their Bible is true or corrupted, complete or partial," he wrote apologetically, "I, who am ignorant in these matters, would not be able to say: I will do and am doing my best, but I am doubtful of success." Nonetheless, continuing his efforts to procure one of the synagogal Torahs, he suggested in a letter written in

Beijing on August 25, 1712, that "some part of the Bible, especially a Hebrew version of the Pentateuch, might be obtained from them discreetly [discrètement], and with not a little amount of money."[28]

"It is unlikely," Donald Daniel Leslie writes, "that any books of the Talmud were held in Kaifeng, though we have almost no evidence.... However, there is a remarkable page in the *Fonds Brotier* 123, fol. 55, autographed by Gozani, dated 12 Sept. 1713 (see plate 20 [of the Leslie work from which this quotation is excerpted]). It is not certain, but I believe that this list of chapter titles was not copied in Kaifeng, but that Gozani was sent it (from Rome?) to check if the Jews would recognize it. That the Jews actually had some knowledge is evidenced by Gaubil (1725): 'Ils ont des fragmentes de la *Mischne,* qu'ils n'entendent pas, et ils ne firent que me dire le titre de quelques chapitres'. Domenge's suggestion that four books of the *Mishna* were held is based on his erroneous identification of *Minha* (afternoon service). Neubauer (p. 129) writes: 'There is no quotation in their books from the Gemara [the more recently compiled, and more voluminous, section of the Talmud], but parts of the Mishnah [the older portion of the Talmud] are to be found in their Prayer-book.' "[29]

The inference that may be drawn from Neubauer's statement is that because Christianity was already approaching its second century when the old ban was lifted against transmitting mishnaic texts in any manner other than orally, the possession by the Kaifeng Jews of written passages from the Mishnah would represent still another blow against the claim for a total Chinese Jewish isolation going back to pre-Christian times.

Curiously, neither Gozani's reports nor those of his colleagues who visited the Kaifeng synagogue tell us whether the city's Jews celebrated, or even knew of, the Hanukkah festival, which, as the writers of these reports were surely aware, commemorates the great Maccabean victory of 165 B.C. This is surprising, for a display of ignorance by the Jews of the existence of the holiday would have meant that if their ancestors came to China in the pre-Christian era and were absolutely cut off thereafter from Jews in other lands, their arrival would have taken place before the establishment of the holiday. On the other hand, if the congregation was aware of the existence of the festival, this would indicate an arrival after 165. In any event, whatever the reason may have been for the apparent failure of the Jesuits to make the necessary inquiries, the fact remains that the collection of Kaifeng synagogal texts held by the Hebrew Union College (Cincinnati) includes three Hanukkah liturgical fragments (mss. 3, 4, and 14).[30]

Still, the old illusion would not fade away entirely, and it was now the turn of the French Jesuit Jean Domenge, acting on instructions from his superiors in Europe, to try his hand at approaching the Jews of Kaifeng in quest of a copy of one of their Torahs. When the congregation refused to sell, Domenge struck a bargain with the Jew *Gao* Ting, who agreed to provide the priest with a Bible that he had inherited from his uncle and then deposited in the synagogue. In a letter written to Paris in 1722, Domenge tells Father Etienne Souciet that when Gao tried to fulfill his end of the agreement, the sexton "to whom he went straightforwardly to ask for it flatly refused to give it to him." To sell a Bible to "a European who eats the black beast [pig]," was bad enough, the sexton told Gao, but what it really came down to, he went on angrily, was that to sell the scriptures was "the same thing as to sell the Lord."[31]

Domenge was persistent. In the same letter, he advises Souciet that he had later arranged for a Jew named *Ai* Wen to sell him four synagogal books, but "being caught in the act one festival [on a festival] as he was carrying them off, he was compelled to leave them behind and sent away with a rebuke." Moreover, "he has not been permitted to come and see me since, and give me hope of obtaining them sooner or later."[32]

Eventually, Domenge, who is reported to have known Hebrew—though apparently not well enough to keep from making the glaring error of confusing "Minha" with "Mishnah"—and had for an interval been granted access to the synagogal books, came to the conclusion that the contents of both the Kaifeng Torahs and those available elsewhere were identical. He discovered numerous spelling errors in the former and certain variations in scribal style, but in no case was the sense of the text different in even the slightest manner.

In March 1723, an offer to buy a synagogal Torah was made by the Jesuit Antoine Gaubil who, traveling to Beijing, stopped over for two days at his order's mission house in Kaifeng and, while there, made a point of visiting the synagogue of the city's Jews. This offer too was rejected. Instead, Gaubil was permitted to commission a Kaifeng scribe to copy either an entire Pentateuch or the Book of Genesis—it is not clear which—and have him give the product of his work to Gozani for transmission to Beijing.[33] Shortly after Gaubil's departure from Kaifeng, however, the Jesuit order was expelled from nearly all of China. The expulsion decree included those members of the order who were stationed in Kaifeng, among them Gozani. Whether the synagogal scribe had enough time to carry out his assignment is not known; what is known is that Gaubil, who was granted authorization to stay on in Beijing, never received the copy he had hoped to get.

That Gaubil did not lose all hope that the Torah scrolls of the Kaifeng synagogue were "pristine" seems quite probable, for he remained convinced that the Jewish entry to China predated the birth of Jesus by at least three hundred years.[34] It was this conviction, it appears, that induced him to ask two Chinese princes to instruct the Kaifeng Jews to send one of their Torahs (or perhaps a copy) to Beijing. In this he did not succeed: The prince who agreed to transmit such an order died before he could do so; the other was not interested. Gaubil wondered whether he might not have fared better with the surviving prince. "Had we approached him 'in the Chinese way,' however," Gaubil later wrote "this also would have failed. But now that I think about it, perhaps we should have worked the problem out along that line."[35]

One would expect that the reports of Gozani and Domenge, weakening as they did the case for finding "pristine" Torah texts in the ark of the synagogue of Kaifeng, should have put a damper on the European eagerness to obtain these Torahs; and so they did—but not entirely. The Abbé Brotier, for example, would write in the 1750s that "the agreement of their [the Kaifeng Jews'] Pentateuch with ours adds new validity to the proofs that have hitherto been adduced with so much profit from the Mosaic literature in favor of our religion."[36] Nevertheless, he hoped that the Chinese texts would become available in Europe, though for study purposes rather than for reasons having to do with apocalyptic thought. Here, it becomes obvious, he was tacitly disowning the old discredited "corrupt text" argument that still fascinated so many of his contemporaries and trying to repair the damage by introducing a directly contradictorily thesis, which, he must surely have recognized, could be anticipated to yield a far more modest recompense than the earth-shaking redemptionary thesis it was intended to replace.

From 1724, when the Jesuits were driven out of Kaifeng, until 1850, when two Chinese representatives of the London Society for the Promotion of Christianity Among the Jews arrived in the city, there was, as far as we know, absolutely no contact, direct or indirect, between the Kaifeng Jews and even a single Westerner. There were even, for that matter, numerous expressions of doubt by Westerners as to whether the old community still existed. These did not, however, totally rein in the imaginations of those who still aspired to acquire the Kaifeng scrolls and use them for conversionary and messianic ends. A prime example of this kind of thinking is provided by Claudius Buchanan, who as late as 1812 still found it possible to write that "a copy of the Scriptures belonging to the Jews of the East, who might be supposed to have had no communication with Jews in the West, has been long considered a desideratum in Europe; for the Western Jews have been accused by some learned men of altering or omitting certain words in the Hebrew text to invalidate the arguments of Christians. But Jews in the East, remote from the controversy, would have no motive for such corruption."[37]

In 1851, a quarter of a millennium after the Western desire for the acquisition of a Chinese Torah was first expressed, the two agents of the London Society—the Chinese delegates as they came to be called—made a second trip to Kaifeng and succeeded in taking possession of the "desideratum" for which Buchanan longed. In fact, desiderata would be the better term, for the two men acquired no less than six synagogal Torah scrolls, several dozen scriptural and liturgical texts, and a memorial book listing the names of more than a thousand members of the congregation who died between ca. 1400 and ca. 1670. Whether, as the delegates and their principals reported, these texts were legally purchased from the Jews for the sum of 400 taels of silver or were procured fraudulently, as several Kaifeng Jews later claimed, is a question that remains unanswered.[38]

When all is said and done, the careful examinations to which the manuscripts obtained from the Kaifeng Jews were subjected by Western scholars made it abundantly clear that there were no significant differences between the Chinese texts and those in general use. There were, however, as Domenge had discovered from his inspections of scattered sections of the Kaifeng Pentateuchs, many misspellings and an assortment of unconventional stylistic usages, all attributable to the understandable erosion of Hebraic knowledge experienced by the minuscule Jewish community of Kaifeng with the passing of generations. The centuries-long expectation that the Chinese scrolls might play a pivotal role in bringing on the second coming had in any event finally been brought to an end. And, leaving aside those few diehards who still accept Manasseh ben Israel's placement of Jews in China during the prophetic era as historically correct,[39] the consensus has at last been reached that Jewish settlements did not exist in China before the beginning of the Christian era, and that the isolation of those Jews who later crossed into China and organized communities there was, at least in the first centuries of their presence in the country, not as unbroken as so many Western theologians have chosen to believe.

Notes

The present study sums up, makes corrections to, and elaborates upon my previously published descriptions and analyses of the impact of the discovery of an old Jewish community in Kaifeng on Western millenarian thought. Pertinent bibliographical references are provided as called for in the text and notes that follow.

1. For the story of Ricci's contacts with the Jews of Kaifeng, beginning with his 1605 meeting in Beijing with the Chinese Jew *Ai* Tian, see pp. 3–12 of my *Mandarins, Jews, and Missionaries: The Jewish Experience in the Chinese Empire*, 2d ed. (Philadelphia: Jewish Publication Society, 1983).

2. *Tanhuma Shoftim*, 18.

3. Because the overview presented here of the Jewish and Christian approaches to messianism is necessarily brief and very broadly drawn, it does not address the differing interpretations that evolved within each of the two religious communities with regard to

the innate character of the concept and the process through which it was to be transformed into reality. In Judaism, for example, the early messianic ideal, as Abba Hillel Silver writes, tended to be "temporal and political, colored by that intense mystico-religious imperialism of the nation which was the legacy of prophetism. The ideal evolved into supernaturalism as the task of national redemption and universal conversion appeared progressively more difficult of accomplishment through human effort alone. While the human character of the Messiah and his religio-political mission were never entirely lost sight of, certain miraculous potencies were added to his personality, in proportion to the nation's realization of its own impotence" (*A History of Messianic Speculation in Israel* [New York: Macmillan, 1927]), p. ix. The messianic viewpoints of Judaism and Christianity are compared and contrasted in Joseph Klausner's *The Messianic Ideal in Israel,* ed. W.F. Stinespring (New York: Macmillan, 1955); see especially pp. 519–31. For discussions of the messianic climate prevailing in Europe during the period covered by the present study, see Silver, *History of Messianic Speculation,* pp. 110–92, and Richard H. Popkin, "Jewish Messianism and Christian Millenarianism," in *Culture and Politics from Puritanism to the Enlightenment,* ed. Perez Zagorin (Berkeley: University of California Press, 1980), pp. 67–90. As an indication of how intense the messianically inspired Christian interest in proselytizing the Jews was, Popkin notes (p. 69) that one of the two stated purposes underlying the founding of the Jesuit order was to convert the Jews. The other, Popkin adds wryly, was "to save fallen women." An in-depth discussion of Christian messianic beliefs is provided, *inter alia,* by Sigmund Olaf Alytt Mowinckel, in his *He That Cometh,* trans. G[eorge] W[ishart] Anderson (Nashville: Abingdon Press, 1954).

4. Although Jewish scholarship has since talmudic times discouraged the practice of calculating the date of the arrival of the messiah, such speculations occur frequently in rabbinic literature. Abba Hillel Silver was accordingly able to tell of more than five dozen Jewish scholars, many of them quite prominent, who engaged in that practice (*passim*).

5. Maimonides (1135–1204), who repeatedly cautions his readers against attempting to set a time for the coming of the messiah, nevertheless excuses Saadiah Gaon (882–942) for doing precisely that, explaining that Saadiah was attempting to provide hope to demoralized fellow Jews in a time of distress (*A Maimonides Reader,* ed. Isadore Twersky [New York: Behrman House, 1972], p. 452). Maimonides also cites several talmudic injunctions against the making of messianic computations and discusses what the world will be like once the long-awaited messianic era arrives (ibid., *passim*).

6. *Menasseh ben Israel's Mission to Oliver Cromwell,* ed. Lucien Wolf (London: Macmillan, for the Jewish Historical Society, 1901), p. 46. This volume contains facsimile reprints of Manasseh's *Hope of Israel, Vindiciae Judaeorum,* and other publications and correspondence pertinent to both Manasseh's understanding of messianism and his efforts to have the Jews readmitted to England. A lithographic reproduction of the *Hope of Israel,* as it appears in the Wolf work, is included in Lynn Glaser's *Indians or Jews* (Gilroy, CA: Roy V. Boswell, 1973).

7. During this period, Christian counterparts to the pseudo-messiahs who rose to prominence in the Jewish world were exceedingly rare. One reason was, of course, that because the Jewish messiah was by definition a human being rather than a divine figure, it was simply easier for a Jew than for a Christian to declare that he was the messiah and to seek out followers. Diasporic Judaism, moreover, does not possess a hierarchical structure akin to those of Catholicism and certain Protestant denominations, nor could a rabbinical court hand over condemned heretics to "the secular arm" for execution, as the Inquisition did. Any Christian who dared assert that he was a divine figure would

accordingly lay himself open to charges that would almost certainly lead to his death. The burning at the stake of a gentile pseudo-messiah is thus reported—though perhaps not altogether truthfully—in a collection of hundreds of letters dealing with life in Western Europe that appear to have been composed for the most part by a perceptive and erudite Italian novelist named Giovanni Paolo Marana but were attributed to a fictitious character identified merely as "the Turkish Spy." In one such letter, written in 1663, the Spy tells an equally fictitious correspondent, designated as "Codarasrad Cheik, a Man of the Law," that "thou wilt approve the Sentence that was yesterday executed on a *Frenchman* in this City [Paris], who said he was the Son of God, and had persuaded a great many poor ignorant People to believe him. He was burnt alive for his Blasphemy, and his Ashes kick'd into a Ditch" (*Letters Writ by the Turkish Spy*, vol. 6, 23d ed. [Dublin: 1736], p. 121).

8. For a review of the other theological matters that aroused the interest of Christian thinkers in the Jews of China, primarily the dispute over whether Chinese converts should be permitted to carry over any of their old Confucian practices to the Catholicism they had adopted (the rites controversy) and the problem of determining which Chinese designations for the deity conformed to the Catholic concept of the nature of God (the terms question), see my *Mandarins, passim*.

9. See *Jewish Encyclopedia* (New York: Funk & Wagnall, 1901), vol. 4, pp. 80–86, and vol. 7, pp. 115–18, for the accusations made by the Church fathers that the *Tanakh* had been corrupted by the rabbinate, and for an examination of Jerome's life and work. B. Graffin's "Kitab al-Ulvan ('Histoire Universelle'), écrite par Agapius (Mahboub) de Menbidj," *Patrologia Orientalis* 5, fasc. 4, pt. 1 (Paris: 1947), pp. 645–57, contains a variant of the story of how the Jewish scriptures were supposedly altered, with the culprits being the high priests Caiaphas and Annas rather than the rabbis. Interestingly, the advent of Islam brought condemnations of the authenticity of *both* the Hebrew and the Christian scriptures on the ground that prophecies of the coming of Muhammad had been impiously removed from each. A list of allegedly corrupted biblical passages compiled by Islamic polemicists is contained in Moritz Steinschneider's *Jewish Literature from the Eighth to the Eighteenth Century* (London: Longman, Brown, 1857); repr. New York: Hermon Press, 1970) pp. 129, 318–19 n. 39. See also my *Mandarins*, pp. 368–69 n. 31. *Jewish Encyclopedia*, vol. 10, p. 637, notes a Jewish convert to Islam, one Sa'id ben Hasan of Alexandria, who in the thirteenth or fourteenth century accused "the Jews of corrupting the Biblical text, and of substituting other names for those of Mohammed and Ishmael." Maimonides refers to Islamic charges of this nature in his "Epistle to Yemen" (Twersky, *Maimonides Reader*, pp. 429–30).

10. Glaser, *Indians or Jews*, p. 21. "The language of Ishmael"—that is to say, Arabic— is identified as the medium through which contact was initially made with the Indians by the explorers from Spain in *Divrei ha-Yomim l'Malkhei Zarfat u'Malkhei Beit Ottoman ha-Togar* (A Chronicle of the Kings of France and the Sultans of the Ottoman Turks), a work printed in 1554 at Sabbionetta for its author, Joseph ha-Kohen, the leader of the tiny Jewish community of Genoa. In this work (which was republished at Amsterdam in 1733, and at Lemberg in 1859), not only does ha-Kohen present a garbled account of Columbus's first voyage, but the year in which that voyage took place is misstated, Columbus's name is left conspicuously absent from the text, and the commander of the expedition is identified as Amerigo Vespucci. C.H.F. Bialloblotzky's English translation of the *Divrei ha-Yomim*, issued under the title *The Chronicles of Rabbi Joseph ben Joshua ben Meir, the Sphardi* (London: Oriental Translation Fund of Great Britain and Ireland, 1835–36), contains ha-Kohen's account of the "Vespucci" voyage to America (vol. 2, pp. 4–12). (Bialloblotzky's rendition of this account can also be found in my study, "The Ethnic Background of Columbus: Inferences from a Genoese–Jewish

Source: 1553–1557" [*Revista de Historia de América* 80 (July–December 1975): 155–57].) Shortly after they first sighted the coast of America, ha-Kohen relates, "The men rejoiced much, and rowed towards the dry land, and went on shore. And they came into a small city, whose inhabitants were few and naked; yet they were not ashamed. And the Spaniards spake unto them, but they understood nothing except a little of the language of Ishmael." However, in his later writings, ha-Kohen sets the date right and correctly identifies the discoverer as his townsman Christopher Columbus (*Revista,* pp. 147–50 nn. 2, 3, and 5)..

11. The eschatological implications of these questions are considered in detail in Lee Eldridge Huddleston, *Origin of the American Indians: European Concepts: 1492–1729* (Austin: Institute of Latin American Studies, University of Texas Press, 1967). Glaser (*Indians or Jews, passim*) also takes note of other problems that troubled certain scholars in the aftermath of the discovery of the New World: Were the Americas to be considered a Mundus Alterius—a second and totally distinct world, that is, in which God's laws did not apply?; were these lands ruled by God or by the Devil?; and so forth.

12. The expulsion of the Jews from England and the tacit institution in the Cromwellian era of a policy of readmitting them to the country are discussed in numerous specialized and general English and Jewish historical works. Lucien Wolf's edition of Manasseh's readmission writings, referred to above in note 6, contains an excellent overview of these events.

13. The story of Antonio Montezinos's alleged discovery of a settlement of members of the tribe of Reuben in South America has been reprinted many times and in many languages. I have summarized the details, as best as I could reconcile them from the slightly differing accounts presented in the early editions of Manasseh's *Hope of Israel* and elsewhere, in my *Mandarins* (pp. 44–46). Elisabeth Levi de Montezinos, a collateral descendant of Antonio Montezinos, has been able to prove from Inquisition records that she consulted in the Archivo Historico Nacional, Madrid, that from September 3, 1639 until shortly after February 19, 1641, Antonio was, as he claimed, imprisoned by the Inquisition in Cartagena, Colombia. Her article, "The Narrative of Aharon Levi, alias Antonio de Montezinos," which appeared in *The American Sephardi* 7–8 (autumn 1975), pp. 62–83, also presents a previously unpublished English translation made by Elias Hayyim Lindo in 1853 of Manasseh's recounting, in a 1650 Spanish edition of his *Hope of Israel,* of Montezinos's adventures in South America.

14. Wolf, *Menasseh ben Israel's Mission,* p. xxii. However, that not all Englishmen anticipated an early conversion of the Jews is manifested, *inter alia,* in Andrew Marvell's well-known poem, "To His Coy Mistress." Here Marvell pleads with the lady of his affections to refrain from making him wait "till the Conversion of the Jews" before confessing that she reciprocates his love for her.

15. Manasseh also overlooks or ignores the identifications of the Land of Sinim as "the Land of the South" that are made in such standard biblical commentaries as those of Rashi and David Kimchi, and in the Targum Jonathan. For that matter, terms phonetically close to *Sin,* such as *Zin* and *Azin,* meaning China, first appeared in Hebrew literature in the ninth century A.D., when they were used by Saadiah Gaon and Eldad ha-Dani. (The term *Sinim,* which was probably adopted at approximately the same time, indicates the people of Sin—the Chinese.) Moreover, a Dead Sea exemplar of the Book of Isaiah displays the word *Sevaniyim* (samekh-vav-nun-yod-yod-mem) rather than *Sinim* (samekh-yod-nun-yod-mem) in chapter 49, verse 12, suggesting that scribal errors are responsible for the introduction of the spelling *Sinim* in later copies, including those now in use. The Sevaniyim were the Syenians, a people who lived in the region of southern Egypt that later came to be called Aswan, and we know that large numbers of Jews also lived in that region during the years in which the Isaiah prophecies were

enunciated. See *The Interpreters' Bible* (New York: Abingdon Press, 1956), vol. 5, p. 575, and my *Mandarins,* pp. 50–51.

16. *Vindiciae Judaeorum* (Wolf, *Menasseh ben Israel's Mission,* p. 143). For a critical analysis of the stages through which Manasseh ben Israel's approach to the problem of persuading the English to readmit the Jews to their country proceeded, see Ismar Schorsch's authoritative study, "From Messianism to Realpolitik: Menasseh ben Israel and the Readmission of the Jews to England," *Proceedings of the American Academy for Jewish Research* 45 (1978), pp. 187–208.

17. Schorsch points out (ibid., p. 204 n. 43) that although Manasseh chose to translate the biblical *ketsei ha-arets* as England in his dealings with the English, he had originally employed the term—as he had himself seen it used in one of his major sources, Samuel Usque's classic *Consolations for the Tribulations of Israel*—to indicate Portugal. Usque's threnody was written in classical Portuguese and published in Ferrara in 1553 as *Consolaçam as Tribulaçoens de Israel.*

18. The Kaifeng Torah scrolls are described in my book, *The Torah Scrolls of the Chinese Jews: The History, Significance and Present Whereabouts of the Sifrei Torah of the Defunct Jewish Community of Kaifeng* (Dallas: Bridwell Library, Southern Methodist University, 1975).

19. The most ancient placement of Jews in China, though as transients rather than as settlers, appears to have been made by the Russian churchman Aleksei Vinogradov, who in his *Istoria biblii na wostoke* (History of the Bible in the East) (St. Petersburg: Panteleevykh, 1889–95) says that "it is very likely that Jews as travelers frequented China at the time of the Kings of Israel," and even that some Jews may have gotten there before the birth of Moses(!). (Cited in S[aveli] M[aximovich] Perlmann's *History of the Jews in China* [London: R. Mazin, 1913]. The Perlmann work is reprinted in Hyman Kublin's *Jews in Old China: Some Western Views* [New York: Paragon, 1971], pp. 118–211; see, specifically, pp. 124, 139.)

Nearly a century and a half after Ricci's discovery of the Kaifeng community, the Jesuit missionary Antoine Gaubil, writing from Beijing, would tell the Academy of Sciences of St. Petersburg that "in the city of Kaifeng, a metropolis in the province of Honan, I saw a Jewish synagogue [in 1723]; they [the Jews] came to China 300 and more years before Christ" (letter dated 11 June 1746, *Correspondance de Pékin 1722–1759,* ed. René Simon [Geneva: Librairie Droz, 1970], p. 563. Additional details regarding Gaubil's visit to the synagogue of Kaifeng are provided below, in the text of the present study and in notes 33–35.) The consensus among modern historians, derived from a statement occurring in the text of a stele erected in 1489 in the courtyard of the synagogue and now held in the Kaifeng Municipal Museum, is that the Jews arrived in that city between 960 and 1126, the years during which it served as the Song capital of China.

20. *China in the Sixteenth Century: The Journals of Matthew Ricci: 1583–1610,* ed. and trans. Louis J. Gallagher (New York: Random House, 1953), p. 107.

21. Ibid., p. 109.

22. Alvarado Sem[m]edo. *The History of That Great and Renowned Monarchy of China....* (London: J. Crook, 1655), p. 153.

23. In his 1605 talks with Matteo Ricci, *Ai* Tian made it clear that his background in Judaic studies was minimal. The only other Chinese Jews whom Ricci ever met personally were three young men who visited Beijing in 1610. Like Ai, the three were merely superficially acquainted with the basic literature of their people, and surely would not have remembered enough of the Tanakhic texts stored hundreds of miles away in Kaifeng to be able to determine how closely these corresponded with whatever Jewish scriptural works Ricci may have showed them. Semmedo appears to have made more than he should have of Ricci's

remark, no doubt based on an examination of the few verses of Pentateuchal text acquired (in transcript form) by the latter's two Chinese agents during their 1608 visit to Kaifeng.

24. Pertinent selections from each of the three letters may be found in *The Sino-Judaic Bibliographies of Rudolf Loewenthal*, ed. Michael Pollak (Cincinnati/Palo Alto: Hebrew Union College Press/Sino–Judaic Institute, 1988), p. 184. In the same month that Leibnitz was urging Verjus to do his utmost to have the Jesuits procure a Kaifeng text, doubt was being expressed as to whether the Chinese Jews retained any religious works at all. "I do not know," wrote François Froger in January 1700, "if these Jews are indigenous to China, and since they are so few in number, it would seem improbably that they could have succeeded in preserving their books" (*Relation du premier voyage des François à la Chine, fait en 1698, 1699, et 1700, sur le vaisseau "L'Amphrite"* [Leipzig: Verlag der Asia major, 1926], p. 140).

25. The *Lettres édifiantes et curieuses* were published several times, and in several languages. The le Gobien excerpt presented herein is taken from vol. 7 of the 1707 edition, published in Paris by Nicholas Le Clerc.

26. Le Gobien was obviously unaware of the absolute ban against the use of punctuation or vowel symbols in Torah scrolls read in synagogal services. As a matter of fact, the *Lettres* specifically state that "tous les Takings du Bethel sont sans point" [all the Torah scrolls, that is, of the Kaifeng synagogue are without punctuation]. (Paris: J.G. Merigot, 1781 ed.), vol. 24, p. 66. Markings of this kind, for that matter, were not introduced into Hebrew texts until several centuries after the appearance of the first accusations by patristic writers that the rabbinate had corrupted the Jewish scriptural texts.

27. *Lettres édifiantes* (1781 ed.), vol. 18, pp. 31–55.

28. Joseph Dehergne and Donald Daniel Leslie, *Juifs de Chine* (Rome: Institutum Historicum S.I., 1980), pp. 56, 59.

29. Donald D. Leslie. *The Survival of the Chinese Jews: The Jewish Community of Kaifeng* (Leiden: E.J. Brill, 1972), pp. 153–54. Another reproduction of the talmudic list in the *Fonds Brotier* (Archives des Jésuites de Paris) may be found in Dehergne and Leslie, *Juifs de Chine*, plate 4. Fathers Domenge and Gaubil, both mentioned in the citation from Leslie, appear later in the present study. The Adolf Neubauer essay alluded to by Leslie is entitled "The Jews in China," *Jewish Quarterly Review* 8 (October 1895), pp. 123–139; it is reprinted in Hyman Kublin, ed., *Studies of the Chinese Jews: Selections from Journals East and West* (New York: Paragon Book Reprint Corp., 1971), pp. 139–57.

30. *The Hanukkah Texts from the Synagogue of Kaifeng*, a keepsake published by the Sino-Judaic Institute in 1991, provides facsimiles selected from mss. 4 and 14, with comments by David J. Gilner.

31. See Dehergne and Leslie, *Juifs de Chine*, pp. 139–51, for the French text of Domenge's letter and an English translation; for the French and English portions of the letter describing Domenge's negotiations with *Gao* Ting, see pp. 140 and 147.

32. For the portion of the letter listed in n. 31 that tells about Domenge's dealings with the Kaifeng Jew *Ai* Wen, see Dehergne and Leslie, *Juifs de Chine*, pp. 141 (French) and 149 (English).

33. Gaubil's visit to the Kaifeng synagogue, as well as his subsequent efforts, in Beijing, to obtain one of its Torah scrolls, are described in my *Mandarins*, pp. 106–12.

34. Gaubil to de Mairan, November 8, 1749, *Correspondance de Pékin*, pp. 598–600.

35. Ibid.

36. *Lettres édifiantes* (1781 ed.), vol. 24, pp. 56–100. See p. 99.

37. Claudius Buchanan, *Christian Researches in Asia* (New York: Richard Scott, 1812), p. 122.

38. The two journeys of the Chinese delegates to Kaifeng, the tactics they employed to obtain the synagogal manuscripts, and the reactions of Jews and Christians both within and outside China to the acquisition of these works are discussed in my *Torah Scrolls,* pp. 26–32, and my *Mandarins,* pp. 146–63.

Of the Torah scrolls that were procured from the Kaifeng Jews in 1851 and in succeeding decades, seven are known to have survived, there being one in each of the following institutions: British Library, Bodleian Library, Cambridge University Library, Österreichische Nationalbibliothek [Austrian National Library], Bridwell Library (Southern Methodist University), Library of the Jewish Theological Seminary of America, and American Bible Society. One of the three Kaifeng Torah scrolls brought to Beijing in 1867 was reported by the Austrian diplomat Karl von Scherzer to have been acquired by a mosque (unnamed) located in the city (according to Leslie, *Survival,* p. 143). In addition, the first twelve skins of another Kaifeng Torah scroll are presently owned by an anonymous collector and are thought to be held in Michigan. Virtually all the other surviving texts of the Kaifeng synagogue are preserved in the library of the Hebrew Union College Jewish Institute of Religion, Cincinnati. There is good reason to suspect, moreover, that the Dongda Mosque, in Kaifeng, holds a number of the city's old synagogal manuscripts, concerning which it prefers, for one reason or another, to remain silent. (See my *Mandarins* [1983 ed.], p. xviii.)

39. P. (Père?) Azoulay, in his "La présence juive en Chine," a study submitted on September 4, 1957, in Munich to the XXIVe Congrès Internationale d'Orientalisme, upholds Manasseh's claim for the presence of Jews in China in Isaiah's time. Azoulay's paper was reprinted in "Rapports culturels de la Bible et de la Chine" (Paris, 1957, mimeographed). Rabbi Josef Zeitin takes the same position vis-à-vis the Manasseh claim in the *Miami Herald,* August 1, 1975.

Chapter I.B.2

Memories of Kaifeng's Jewish Descendants Today: Historical Significance in Light of Observations by Westerners Since 1605

Wendy R. Abraham

Reports that, as late as 1985, there were still Chinese Jewish descendants claiming to remember the celebration of a holiday when rooster's blood was painted over the family's doorpost, followed by a week when cakes of unleavened bread were consumed, all during the springtime in Kaifeng, are often greeted with both fascination and intense skepticism. But there remain many with memories of these and other identifiably Jewish religious practices or aspects of growing up with an awareness that they were different from the surrounding Han Chinese. Reminiscences like these were reported by men then between the ages of 50 and 75 of events that would have taken place in the 1920s and 1930s, just when Anglican Bishop William Charles White of Canada was living in Kaifeng, working and compiling his notes for his three-volume magnum opus, *Chinese Jews*. Other Western visitors between 1850 and 1933 recorded their observations of the Chinese Jews, which coincided with memories of events or practices supposedly handed down by these descendants' fathers and grandfathers.

This chapter presents a brief historical overview of Westerners' observations of the Chinese Jews made over the centuries, thereby putting the memories of Kaifeng's Jewish descendants today in their historical context and leaving open the question of whether or not there are still memories worth preserving and recording in Kaifeng today.

Western Contacts with the Chinese Jews, Tenth Century to 1850

Information about the Chinese Jews of Kaifeng before the first recorded meeting in 1605 by the Jesuit Matteo Ricci (1552–1610) comes from four main sources: accounts by early Arab travelers and historians, those by early European missionaries, and information gleaned from native Chinese and Jewish sources, in particular the three stelae dating to 1489/1512 (a single stele), 1663, and 1679, only two of which are still extant. All have been amply documented and discussed by Donald Leslie and Michael Pollak.[1] [See Michael Pollak's article in this volume –*Ed.*]

The reports of the early Jesuits after Ricci–Jean-Paul Gozani (1659–1732), Jean Domenge (1666–1735), and Antoine Gaubil (1689–1759)—remain the only sources of firsthand information on the daily life of the Chinese Jews that captured their existence in both the heyday and the twilight of their lives as a religious community. They reported a full religious life, observance of the laws of kashrut, circumcision of infant sons, and a synagogue facing westward, toward Jerusalem. The synagogue had by now stood for six hundred years. Although obvious signs of assimilation into their Confucian surroundings abounded, ties to their Jewish ancestry proved strong enough for attempts to purchase copies of the Kaifeng Torah to be rebuffed. After proselytizing was banned by the Yongzheng emperor in 1724 and all missionary work retreated from the interior, it was more than a century before Westerners would meet face to face with the Chinese Jews again.

In the meantime, attempts were made to reach the Kaifeng Jews by letter. With the exception of that sent by Isaac Nieto in 1760, an answer to which was actually said to have been received, presumably none reached their destination until the time of James Finn.[2] Letters from foreigners residing in China relayed word of the existence of a synagogue, the observance of the Sabbath and of dietary laws, but also of the Jews living in a dispersed manner and displaying an ignorance of their own religion.[3]

Finn's letter of 1847 posed twenty questions concerning their history and origins, the types of religious and prayerbooks they possessed, their degree of observance of Jewish law, and whether or not they were free to practice Judaism in China. Before their reply was received, however, Finn heard that all together eight families of Jewish descent still lived in Kaifeng, totaling about one thousand people. Although the head of the Shi family was said to no longer observe Judaism, he nevertheless repaired the synagogue. Much intermarriage had taken place, and knowledge of their history and religion had faded considerably. It was related, too, that "strangers and carriers of pork cannot pass" in front of the synagogue, to the right of which still stood the stelae. Not one Jew was said to be able to read or write Hebrew, even though they still refused to sell their sacred texts.

In April 1870, after a twenty-year hiatus most likely due to the dislocations caused by the Taiping Rebellion [the Taiping was the largest of a series of rebellions that convulsed China between 1850 and 1873 –*Ed.*], Finn finally received a reply to his letter. The response, written by *Zhao* Nianzu in 1850, revealed that the community had been without rabbis for quite a while, and the synagogue was in need of great repair.[4] Zhao further asked for ministers to be sent and for their temple to be "put in order."

Zhao related the many achievements of the members of his own clan and answered Finn's questions about the festivals and days of worship celebrated in the synagogue, as well as his own recounting of the history of Judaism. The letter ended with Zhao naming those willing to mortgage or sell the temple buildings and materials, evidence of the contentions in the Kaifeng community. This was the only letter a Westerner ever received from the Chinese Jews of Kaifeng.

Western Observations of the Chinese Jews, 1850-1949

By the time *Qiu* Tiansheng and *Jiang* Rongji, two Chinese Protestant converts from Shanghai sent by the London Society for Promoting Christianity Among the Jews,[5] arrived in Kaifeng in 1850, the religious life among the Chinese Jews had come to a virtual halt. Although the synagogue still stood, it was in ruins, and the last rabbi had died several decades before, taking with him the last bits of knowledge of Hebrew. Some of the synagogue material had already been sold,[6] and circumcision was said to no longer be practiced.

The delegates succeeded in buying eight Hebrew manuscripts on their first short visit to Kaifeng in December 1850. On their second and last trip the following year, they returned with six Torah scrolls and between fifty and sixty more Hebrew manuscripts in addition to the Chinese–Hebrew Memorial Book of the Dead. During the second trip the delegates learned that the population was not estimated at 200, as they had heard on their first trip, but, rather, was more in the vicinity of 300 to 400. They discovered that circumcision was indeed still being performed.

Zhao Wenkui and *Zhao* Jincheng, both circumcised Jews, were persuaded by the two delegates to go to Shanghai to relearn Judaism and bring this knowledge back to Kaifeng. *Zhao* Jincheng stayed only briefly, while *Zhao* Wenkui remained until he died, and was buried in the Jewish communal cemetery in Shanghai. Joseph Edkins later wrote of his contacts at Shanghai with members of the Kaifeng community, saying:

The last among them that could read Hebrew died nearly a century ago. They evince no wish to recover the knowledge of that language, nor do they seem to have any idea of a future revival of their condition, which could occur only in the case that the Emperor may be induced to command their synagogue . . . to be rebuilt at the public expense.[7]

Edkins added that they still observed the Sabbath and some traditional festivals.

Yellow River floods of 1841, 1849, and 1860 contributed greatly to the destruction of the synagogue and the religious life of the community as well—whatever was left of it by the time the two Chinese Protestant delegates visited Kaifeng. The Taiping Rebellion also contributed to the scattering of the Jews. [Estimates of those killed during the twenty years of the Taiping Rebellion alone range from twenty to thirty million. If one adds in losses due to other rebellions, droughts, and floods, China's population dropped by sixty million and did not recover to prerebellion levels until almost the end of the dynasty in 1911. *–Ed.*]

The mistrust of foreigners and dangers inherent in communicating with the remnant community of Jews in Kaifeng exacerbated by the Taiping Rebellion, inhibited contact with the Chinese Jews throughout much of the nineteenth century. Their already desperate situation now seemed almost hopeless to the few who did manage to make contact.

After the Reverend W.A.P. Martin visited Kaifeng on February 17, 1866, he related learning that the Jews seriously debated leaving one of their Torah scrolls in the marketplace after the last rabbi had died in the hopes that a Jew from afar who might pass through Kaifeng would notice it and teach them again.[8] He was told that the Jews themselves were impoverished and had scattered to other cities. When Martin was finally taken to the site of the old synagogue, all that he reported standing was a solitary stone. He was asked questions about their Torah, which they could not read. He learned that their population was estimated to be between 300 and 400, and by now they neither met as a community nor kept any registers. Some had recently converted to Buddhism or Islam. Martin met the son of the last rabbi, who had died in Gansu province some thirty or forty years before, and learned that none of them knew Hebrew any more.[9]

The first Western Jew to visit Kaifeng, in 1879, was the Austrian merchant Jacob Liebermann, who lamented their degree of assimilation. He noted that at one point "by order of the Government, Scrolls of the Law were exhibited in the open market place, and an advertisement in Chinese was inscribed by the side, offering a reward and leading position to anyone who would be able to explain the wording of the Scroll."[10]

China's Millions, a missionary journal, published an article in 1891 by the Reverend Dennis J. Mills, who had visited the Kaifeng Jews a year before. In "Ho-nan Province: An Eventful Itineration," Mills relates that about 200 families were scattered about the city and that the synagogue was demolished around 1855. A member of the Gao clan who had been to Beijing told Mills that he alone possessed one of the remaining Scriptures, which he intended to take to Shanghai to give to the Jews there. Although one of the Chinese Jews he met was later baptized in Nanjing, no converts could be made in Kaifeng.

Even during Mills's brief stay of two days in Kaifeng he observed the feuding and dissension among the Jews. One Jew was even said to be in prison awaiting trial for the murder of another. Pollak notes that the murder "may have been related to the blood feud that . . . [broke] out between the Chang [Zhang] and the other clans, the Chang having been accused of selling the old synagogal ark to a mosque."[11]

The ostracism felt by the Zhang clan is attested to only a few years after Mills' visit, in 1893, by A.S. Annaud of the National Bible Society of Scotland, who first stated that only six clans remained in Kaifeng. Annaud had met a young Jew named *Gao* Huigui, who estimated that about 500 Jews remained in Kaifeng. Pollak adds that the Zhang may have moved away or become completely assimilated by then.[12]

In 1899 the Apostolic vicar of the Henan Mission, Monsignor Volonteri, bought a Torah and other smaller documents from an elderly Chinese Jewish widow in Kaifeng, prompting the Shanghai Jewish community to respond. The Shanghai Jews, led by S.J. Solomon and David Ezekiel Abraham, offered help to the Jews of Kaifeng to return to Judaism, in particular by reconstructing the synagogue. On October 24, 1900, the Jew *Li* Jingsheng replied, stating that the ongoing Boxer Rebellion, begun in Shandong province in 1898, made the present an inappropriate time to reconstruct the synagogue. The site of the synagogue was said to remain, but the Jews were "very much scattered."[13]

In reply to the Society's next letter, however, Li mentioned in January 1901 that he would come to Shanghai the following spring. On April 6 of that year, fifty-two-year-old Li arrived in Shanghai with his twelve-year-old son, *Li* Zongmai. They stayed this first time only three weeks, before returning to Kaifeng with a letter from the Society. While in Shanghai, Li told the Western Jews that only about 140 families of Jewish descent remained in Kaifeng. He said that they no longer observed the Jewish dietary laws, except for abstention from pork, no longer observed the Sabbath or the festivals, and did not circumcise their infant sons.[14] On March 10, 1902, the Lis returned to Shanghai with six other Jews from Kaifeng. They visited the home of Edward I. Ezra soon after their arrival, on March 26, and noted that for a long period before the Taiping Rebellion they were gradually declining in number and their faith was rapidly being forgotten. "At present they do not observe any of the ordinances of the Jewish religion, nor do they observe the idolatrous practices of the heathen."[15]

Li's observations about his community were reported also by B.L. Putnam Weale, a traveler who visited Kaifeng in the early 1900s and, with the help of a local Muslim, visited Kaifeng. He was told that the Jews had for years intermarried, no longer circumcised their infant sons, and no longer had a synagogue in which to worship.[16]

However, the oldest among them was said to possess a family record dating back two hundred years. They stressed that the flood and the Taiping Rebellion had hastened their demise as a community, and the new generation was ignorant of everything connected with the religion and history. Edward I. Ezra noted the shame they appeared to feel without a rabbi, synagogue, or school for their children. Yet further on in his account he related that they indeed still observed some of the laws of *kashrut* and that one even allowed his eldest son of fifteen to be circumcised in the home of D.E.J. Abraham. Ezra's account ends by noting that the money collected by the Jews of Shanghai and London to rebuild the Kaifeng synagogue was soon diverted to aid the Jews in Russia facing pogroms.

Severely disappointed that nothing could be done to help their community, six of the Kaifeng Jews returned home only three months after their arrival. *Li* Jingsheng remained in Shanghai until his death in 1903, when he was buried in the Jewish cemetery. As his body was being prepared for burial, it was noted that Li Jingsheng "bore the covenant of Abraham," even though he told the Shanghai Jews that he was ignorant of this rite. Since he was born in Kaifeng on July 18, 1851, this "confirms the Chinese delegates' announcement of their discovery, only two weeks before Li's birth, that 'circumcision also appears to be practiced, though the traditions respecting its origin and object appear to be lost among them.' "[17] The younger Li was raised by the family of D.E.J. Abraham and when he was circumcised was given the name Shmuel.[18] Shmuel was educated at the Shanghai Jewish School and was employed as a clerk in D.E.J. Abraham's firm.[19] Not until fifty years later, after World War II, did he return to Kaifeng where he died. It was said that after 1949 his son was sent from Shanghai to the interior.

The Reverend Robert Powell further relayed information to the Shanghai Society that he had been visited by the brother of a Jew who had become a Buddhist priest, and that the Jews were said to know little about their religion. While they did not intermarry, and their numbers had diminished, there were still representatives of the eight clans. "All have dwindled, but none are extinct."[20]

Writing in 1930, Allen Godbey mentioned a James A. Thomas, who helped gather various historical materials for him. Thomas reported that "he frequently heard the local community spoken of as 'Black Jews,' a regular term in India for Judaized natives."[21] Dr. W.B. Pettus of Beijing was also said by Lloyd to have visited Kaifeng and found the Chinese Jewish descendants waiting for an opportunity to sell a rubbing of their stelae. He related that the Jews would charge him nothing, however, since he was "a friend of our people."

In 1906 the English writer Oliver Bainbridge visited Kaifeng, reporting the existence of eight Jewish families with approximately fifty people, who were quickly assimilating into Islam, even though there seemed to be much animosity between the Jewish descendants and the Muslims. His report failed to speculate on the reason such assimilation might be occurring. Bainbridge photographed some of the Jews he met and was given a petition by one of them asking for the help of Western Jews in rebuilding Kaifeng's synagogue and looking for a way out of their poverty. One man recounted the history of the Kaifeng Jews to Bainbridge and described in detail the structure of the former synagogue as well as various religious practices. After proclaiming that their ancestors suffered many hardships because of the objections of the Chinese officials to their religious practices, he added "even to-day they object to our circumcision, which they denounce as a barbarous and cruel practice."[22] Clearly, then, circumcision was still practiced at the turn of the century, this statement having been made in 1906. It would appear, too, that ignorance of the meaning behind certain Jewish customs by Chinese officials of the time led to increased suspicion of the Jewish descendants, but it would be difficult to conclude that this exemplified a form of anti-Semitism among Chinese officials.

In sum, a tale of poverty, intermarriage, and conversions among the Chinese Jews is told by the handful of Western visitors to Kaifeng during the first decade of the twentieth century. Assimilation was now taking place at an accelerating rate, although the "eight families with seven Jewish surnames," as the Jews were known, were still identifiable in Kaifeng. Poverty had reduced them to attempting to sell their religious scrolls, even while they petitioned the Western Jewish community to help them rebuild their synagogue and regain some semblance of Jewish life.

Bishop William Charles White, the Canadian Church of England's first Anglican bishop of Henan province, who lived in Kaifeng from 1910 to 1933, succeeded in getting the heads of the seven clans to agree to have his church take over protection of the two extant stone inscriptions in 1912, soon moving them to the cathedral compound. Two years before this, the Jews refused to give up legal title to the synagogue site. A year later, however, in 1911, after a conflict over the possession of the stelae with the local authorities, White was able to purchase the stones on the condition that they never leave Henan province. In 1914 the site of the synagogue itself was sold by the Jews to the mission. This was the first time in more than seven centuries that someone other than the Chinese Jews owned the site.

By this time no more scrolls of the law were left and parts of the synagogue were already being used by others in Kaifeng. A Confucian temple had one of the marble balustrades of the former synagogue for more than fifty years; two stone lions were said to be outside one of the Buddhist temples; and even the green roof tiles were now part of the local mosque.

In May 1919, Bishop White held a series of meetings with the Reverend J.H. Blackstone, attended by all seven clans to try to educate them and revive some kind of communal spirit among them. The Jews were for the most part uninterested, however, since they had no social relationships, and were said to follow no Jewish practices of any kind. Only the Shi clan was said to have kept family records.[23]

Living among the Chinese Jews for almost a quarter of a century, Bishop White was in the prime position to give a detailed firsthand account of the life of the remnant community of Chinese Jews in Kaifeng. Writing in 1913, he noted that there were about fifty individuals. "They do not trust each other and have no brotherly feelings for one another, while they have no religious observance of any kind, and evince not the slightest desire to resuscitate the religion of their forefathers."[24]

In 1920 Charles D. Tenney, an American diplomat, noted the small number of Jews remaining, all of whom were in great poverty, as well as some "Jewish physiognomies" he spotted on the street occasionally. On the process of assimilation, he noted, "the Jews have established themselves, but little by little the tenets and ceremonies of their religion have been modified and adapted to the hereditary beliefs and superstitions of the surrounding Chinese population."[25]

In 1923 the traveler Harry A. Franck wrote that the Chinese Jews seemed to have lost every vestige of Jewish identity. "No one in Kaifeng, as far as is known, can read Hebrew, and the clan seems long ago to have lost any interest in Judaism. Several portions of Hebrew scriptures have been found on the streets for sale, evidently as mere curios."[26]

During the summer and autumn of 1924, the Shanghai Society briefly resuscitated itself and finally managed to send someone to Kaifeng. David Levy Wong, a Chinese from Xinjiang province claiming to be a Jew, was chosen to go and assess the situation. Wong related that on August 13 he was photographed in the garden of the Anglican bishop's compound with more than ten heads of Jewish families present. He later asked one member of the Zhao clan and *Shi* Zhongyong to make a plan of the synagogue property and write a report. This report, which Wong enclosed and sent back to the Society, said that only ninety-nine Jews, most of whom were poor, were left in Kaifeng.

After Wong returned to Shanghai, he reported that he had been to the homes of many of the Jews, and they all seemed eager to reorganize the community. They even suggested that a school be built first, so that the younger generation could learn Judaism. He noted that, although they had not met as a community for many years, they recognized *Zhao* Yunzhong as their communal leader and still considered themselves Jewish.[27]

Also in 1924, Arthur Sopher of the Shanghai Society went to Kaifeng and reported meeting a man he only knew was surnamed Zhao, who was delighted that Sopher was a member of the same tribe as he was. On July 4 of the same year, A. Horne, in an article in *Israel's Messenger,* expressed his utter dismay and disappointment upon reaching Kaifeng, only to find a totally assimilated group of people who lived in different quarters of the town, never met for religious or communal purposes, and observed no Jewish customs. He claimed that they no longer even circumcised their sons.[28]

Of all the reports received by firsthand Western observers during this period of the twentieth century, that of David A. Brown, written in 1933, sheds the greatest light on the subject. Brown visited Kaifeng in November 1932 with Bishop White and met representatives of five of the seven clans. In a five-part series of articles for *The American Hebrew and Jewish Tribune* in 1933, Brown wrote of the history of the Chinese Jews and of the Western visitors they had had in the previous several hundred years.

Brown was told by a member of the Ai clan that the Jews' most pressing need was a school for their children. In response to a further question, they all indicated their eagerness to return to Judaism itself if they could relearn it. Of their own identity as Jews, Brown wrote that "they know they are Jews, but know nothing of Judaism. They realize they are Chinese, completely assimilated, yet there is pride in the ancient people who are different from the other Chinese in Kaifeng."[29] His report implied that the Chinese Jews were still very much aware of and eager to renew their ancient heritage.

Brown met the oldest member of the Chinese Jews from the Zhao clan, born in 1858. This man had "only a hazy recollection of the past history of his people. But his son, ... a young man of twenty-seven years, quite Jewish in appearance, with a good education, had acquired considerable knowledge of the history of the Jews of Kaifeng."[30]

Of their racial features, "all but those of the Chao's and the Widow Shih were definitely and distinctly Chinese."[31] The Widow Shi turned out to be a goldmine of information for Brown. "Greatly pleased" when she learned that he had been to Palestine twice, she lamented the fact that the Chinese Jews had lost their Bible. Her husband and her husband's family were said to have lived near the synagogue for a very long time.[32]

Four years after Brown's visit, the American journalist Harrison Forman went to Kaifeng.

Although he took many photographs of them, Forman's only comments on the Jews were that, when he visited them in 1938, he could find only a handful, perhaps a dozen, families of Jewish descent who had "preserved nothing in written Hebrew, nor could any of them have read it if they had. . . . When questioned, all they knew of their Hebrew heritage was that it was 'different' from the Chinese."[33]

In 1940 two Japanese who had been involved in the occupation of Kaifeng, which began in 1938, made semiofficial reports about the Jews. *Sogabe* Shizuo and *Mikami* Teicho reported that between 80 and 100 people of Jewish descent remained in Kaifeng, of six families. Another 100 were said to live in Shanghai and elsewhere. The Jews were said to be impoverished and rarely intermarried with other Chinese. Mikami stated that the Zhang clan had left the city after much quarreling with the other Jews.[34] Lowenthal reported that Sogabe also spoke of learning that in 1918 a foreigner had bought a family register from the Jews. Lowenthal also mentioned receiving a letter from a missionary living in Kaifeng, Father Antonio Cattaneo, in 1943, stating that "there were a few Jews left within and outside of that city and the Shih family had become Catholic in 1924."[35]

Other direct observations made about the Chinese Jews in the 1940s add little to the above accounts. Little contact was made with Kaifeng's Jewish descendants immediately after the founding of the People's Republic. The sparse accounts of encounters between 1949 and 1979 reflect only various discrepancies in the number of descendants, reported variously between 200 and 2,000. In 1980 the UPI journalist Aline Mosby traveled to Kaifeng, then closed to tourists, and was told of the existence of dozens of Jewish descendants in the city, none of whom were said to observe any of the Jewish customs or rituals. The former curator of the Kaifeng Municipal Museum, *Wang* Yisha, concluded from a survey that he had conducted among the Jewish descendants in Kaifeng that there were still 140 former Jewish families from Kaifeng in China with six surnames. Of these, 79 families were said to live in Kaifeng and 61 other families moved to different parts of China. The 79 Jewish families in Kaifeng number all together 166 people.[36]

Amid all the reports that appeared over the preceding three centuries, however, none had ever been able to share accounts of the lives of the

Kaifeng Jews or what they were taught about their heritage, in their own words.

The Chinese Jewish Descendants in 1985

In the summer of 1985 I met with six heads of households and spoke with about twenty members of their families. In addition to displaying knowledge of certain Jewish holidays and practices of kashrut in varying degrees, several of these descendants provided me with interesting new information, a few times unknowingly corroborating one another's stories.[37]

Two of the descendants maintained that their families used to celebrate Passover, but they did so during the Chinese New Year. One said that the only way they distinguished Passover from Chinese New Year was to eat flat cakes instead of fish and pork. This same man, a member of the Zhao clan, claimed that the Shi family he knew in his youth used to put lamb's blood over their doorposts as well. The member of the Shi clan to whom he was referring later told me independently that his father did put lamb's blood, chicken blood, or cinnabar mixed with water over the doorpost during Chinese New Year as late as 1928. However, this ritual was separated by two weeks from the holiday he called the "Wheat Festival," during which his mother would make only flat cakes that did not rise.

One man mentioned that during certain Chinese festivals his family put offerings of mutton rather than pork in front of the ancestral memorial tablets out of respect for the fact that his ancestors never ate pork—a tradition his family still retains.

A member of the Shi clan related seeing several yarmulkas kept in the family's chest, which he described in great detail. They were dark blue in color with a black trim around the edge and had Hebrew writing embroidered on them with yellow thread. They were made up of six parts, his mother told him, to commemorate the fact that the earth was created in six days. It is unknown when these yarmulkas were made, but they must have been made by someone who could at least imitate Hebrew writing quite well or dated back to the early 1800s, when knowledge of Hebrew was all but extinguished.

Later on, a daughter from the Zhao family gave me one of the yarmulkas that she had begun making in the hope of selling to Western tourists. The yarmulka she gave me was dark blue and, interestingly, had a black trim all around it. Although literature on the subject has often noted the fact that the Jews were called "blue-capped Muslims," as a way of distinguishing them from the Muslims, who wore white skull caps, nowhere has there ever been mention of a black trim. Whether or not this is merely an unusual coincidence is open to speculation.

The descendants knew about circumcision, but had no idea why it would still be considered necessary by foreign Jews. Only one of them knew for sure that his grandfather had been circumcised. This would have occurred in the late 1800s.

Concerning the meeting for the descendants held by Bishop White with David Brown in the 1930s, suspicions were expressed by the descendants as to White's true motives for getting them together. This lent credence to the speculation by the Chinese historian *Shi* Jingxun that White's activities in Kaifeng were in some instances more suspect than noble, as other literature on the subject leads us to believe.[38]

A descendant from the Shi clan, *Shi* Zhongyu, related a story about his aunt, who attended that meeting. He said, "This old Westerner invited her to eat once. While they were eating, she heard it was a conference of Jews. . . . The synagogue was no longer standing . . . but there were still Jewish relics. . . . *Zhao* Pingyu's second uncle sold these things. . . . Even though he sold them he didn't dare use the money he got for himself so he invited Shi, Li, Gao, Ai, Jin, and Zhang, all the older ones, to sign their names. After he asked them to sign their names to this agreement, this Westerner took these relics and said that the Jews sold them to him."

Most curious of all, one of the descendants noted that his grandparents spoke of not being able to go to synagogue daily because they had to work hard just to have enough to eat from day to day. If in 1985 this descendant was seventy-one years old, then his grandparents were probably born between 1844 and 1870. In either case, by the time his grandparents would have been old enough to remember attending synagogue themselves, the synagogue was either in such a state of disrepair as to be effectively useless, noted by the 1850 delegates, or it no longer even stood, as observed by W.A.P. Martin in 1866. If, however, they were born even earlier than 1844, then it becomes clear that a religious life was maintained in Kaifeng several decades after the last rabbi had died. This would be supported by the 1848 letter from *Zhao* Nianzu, which listed the festivals and worship days still celebrated, as well as the 1859 Taiping document noting that the Jews performed ceremonies without understanding the Hebrew letters and their meaning.

Based on these and many other stories I heard, the following general observations can be made about the Jewish descendants today: Their ethnic identity appears to remain quite strong vis-à-vis their Jewish heritage. Most of those with whom I spoke noted that they were all registered as *youtai houdai,* or

"Jewish descendants," on their Certificates of Registry. One member of the Zhao clan, who had only daughters, insisted that any children his daughters might have must all be registered as Jewish as well, going against the Chinese custom of patrilineal religious descent.

While the extent of their knowledge of Jewish history, both in and out of Kaifeng, and Jewish religious practices varied greatly, they all strongly insisted that, if nothing else, their children must know that they are Jewish descendants. None had any interest whatsoever in reviving Jewish religious practices. They felt that this was not necessary, yet still strongly identified themselves as Jewish descendants. Their attitudes in this regard support Irene Eber's thesis that the process of sinification actually strengthened their Jewish identity along the way and that their identification as Jews was based on their identification with a particular lineage, rather than observance of the religion itself.

A second observation is that they were at great pains to relate how good relations with the Muslim minority have always been. They made a point of relating how none among them had ever converted to Islam, however. One member of the Zhao clan said that any such conversions were "just a rumor." The ones who really became Muslim, he said, were from Hangzhou, Suzhou, Shanghai, calling them "the Jews who had dispersed." This directly contradicts statements made by various Western visitors to Kaifeng over the years such as Oliver Bainbridge, as noted earlier, and leads me to suspect a possible undercurrent of, at best, ambivalent feelings remaining between the two groups.

Third, attitudes about their status as national minorities, or rather their nonstatus, were most interesting to hear. Across the board I was told with equal certainty that, on the one hand, they do not officially count as national minorities and, on the other, that they are nevertheless accorded that status by the Chinese government. One said that the Jewish descendants have official representation at the National People's Congress and that they receive special food subsidies for meat like the Muslims. However, since they no longer have life-styles setting them apart, as do other minorities, the government cannot officially call them one.

The possibility that they were once close to being officially declared a national minority soon after Liberation was clear from the statements of two descendants in particular. A member of the Shi clan noted that the United Front Department recommended him for admission to the National Minorities Institute, and a senior member of the Ai clan, who has since passed away, took part in the 1952 National Day celebrations in Beijing, to which he was sent as an official representative of the Jewish descendants by the local authorities. There he met and shook hands with *Mao* Zedong, *Zhou* Enlai, *Zhu* De, and *Deng* Xiaoping.

Conclusion

The conversations I gathered on tape are significant in several respects. First, and perhaps most poignantly, they consist of words spoken by the last generation of Jewish descendants who can even purport to have memories dating back to the early part of this century. Their children and all future descendants can never claim the same place in Chinese Jewish history.

It has been shown that in the 1920s and 1930s many descendants had a clear understanding of their heritage and their place in Kaifeng's Jewish history. This knowledge could have been handed down to their children, who in 1985 were still able to remember these stories and pass this knowledge to their children. The taped conversations open up the question of just how reliable previous reports claiming to be the "final word" on the subject—including those of Bishop White—really are, both in terms of when remnants of Jewish practices actually ceased and the number of descendants still left.

While it is ultimately impossible to prove the veracity of each of the stories told by the descendants, the fact that several key bits of information, noted earlier, were unknowingly corroborated by several other descendants leads me to conclude that there are still bona fide memories worth searching out and preserving among Kaifeng's Jewish descendants today. They appear to put to rest the reports that have intermittently emerged chronicling the process of acculturation and assimilation of the Chinese Jews over the past three centuries.

Notes

1. See especially Donald D. Leslie, *The Survival of the Chinese Jews: The Jewish Community of Kaifeng* (Leiden: E.J. Brill, 1972), and Michael Pollak, *Mandarins, Jews and Missionaries: The Jewish Experience in the Chinese Empire* (Philadelphia: Jewish Publication Society of America, 1980).

2. See James Finn, *The Orphan Colony of Jews in China* (London: James Nisbet, 1872), p. 15. See Pollak, *Mandarins, Jews and Missionaries,* for interesting details on letters by Benjamin Kennicott (1769), Olav Gerhard Tychsen (1777 and 1779), Solomon Joseph Simpson and Alexander Hirsch (1795), and an 1815 letter in Hebrew from the Jews of London.

3. See *Chinese Repository* 1 (1832), p. 44; 15 (1846), pp. 43-44; and 13 (1844), pp. 79 and 468 (letters by Robert Morrison, Joseph Rizzolati, William C. Milne, and an anonymous author whom Leslie, in *The Survival of the Chinese Jews,* surmises to have been Walter Macon Lowrie).

4. Although the original Chinese text of this letter is now missing, Finn is believed to have had it from 1870 to 1872. A copy was also sent to the bishop of Victoria, George Smith.

5. For background information on the London Society, see Pollak, *Mandarins, Jews, and Missionaries,* pp. 146-49.

6. See Bishop George Smith, ed., *The Jews at K'ae-fung-foo: Being a Narrative of a Mission of Inquiry to the Jewish Synagogue at K'ae-fung-foo on Behalf of the London Society for Promoting Christianity Among the Jews* (Shanghai: Missionary Society Press, 1851), p. vii.

7. Joseph Edkins, *Religion in China* (Boston: Houghton Mifflin, 1878; and London, 1893), pp. 181-83.

8. See "Account of an Overland Journey from Peking to Shanghai, Made in February and March 1866," *Journal of the North China Branch of the Royal Asiatic Society III* (December 1866), pp. 26-39.

9. Martin's account was reprinted in *The Chinese: Their Education, Philosophy, and Letters* (New York: Harper & Brothers, 1881), and later in *A Cycle of Cathay* (New York: F.H. Revell, 1896). A summary of this account can also be found in Martin's *The Awakening of China* (New York: Doubleday, Page, 1910), pp. 41-44, and in White's *Chinese Jews: A Compilation of Matters Relating to the Jews of K'ai-fêng Fu,* 2d ed. (New York: Paragon, 1966 [1942], vol. 1, chapter 9, pp. 184-87.

10. *Jewish Chronicle* (London), July 11, 1879, p. 12.

11. Pollak, *Mandarins, Jews, and Missionaries,* p. 395 n. 5.

12. See Ibid., p. 200.

13. See *Jewish Chronicle,* January 4, 1901, p. 15.

14. See Pollak, *Mandarins, Jews, and Missionaries,* p. 212.

15. Edward Isaac Ezra, "Chinese Jews," *East of Asia Magazine,* 1 (1902), p. 294. Another account of this visit was given by S.M. Perlmann, in *The History of the Jews in China* (London: R. Mazin, 1913), pp. 23-27.

16. See B.L. Putnam Weale, *The Re-Shaping of the Far East,* vol. 1 (New York: Macmillan, 1905), pp. 152-53.

17. Pollak, *Mandarins, Jews, and Missionaries,* pp. xxxi–xxxii.

18. See Pollak, *Mandarins, Jews, and Missionaries,* p. 213.

19. See *Jewish Chronicle,* October 12, 1962, p. 20, for Mrs. R.D. Abraham's (D.E.J. Abraham's daughter-in-law) letter to the editor.

20. Robert Powell, "The Jews in K'ai-feng Fu, Ho-nan," *China's Millions* 11 (January–March 1903), p. 9.

21. Allen H. Godbey, *The Lost Tribes: A Myth* (Durham: Duke University Press, 1930), p. 417.

22. Oliver Bainbridge, "The Chinese Jews," *Israel's Messenger* (1906), pp. 8-10.

23. See William Charles White, "An Attempt to Reorganize the Chinese Jews of Kaifeng," *Chinese Recorder* 50, no. 11 (November 1919), p. 780.

24. William Charles White, "The Jews of Kaifengfu, in Honan," in *Chinese Mission Year Book* (Shanghai: Christian Literature Society for China, 1913), p. 165.

25. Charles Tenney, *Millard's Review of the Far East* 12, no. 1 (March 6 1920), p. 6. ["Taken from an address delivered at a Peking Medical Conference"].

26. Harry A. Franck, *Wandering in Northern China* (New York and London: Century, 1923), pp. 335-36.

27. See George E. Sokolsky, "The Jews in China," *Menorah Journal* 15, no. 5 (November 1928), p. 454.

28. A. Home, "Kaifengfu," *Israel's Messenger,* July 4, 1924, p. 18.

29. David A. Brown, "Brown Rediscovers China's Ancient Jews," *American Hebrew and Jewish Tribune* (January–March 1933), p. 229.

30. Ibid., p. 237.

31. Ibid., p. 242.

32. See David A. Brown, "The Chinese Jews: Lost to the World for 1700 Years, Discovered Over 300 Years Ago, What Is to Be Their Fate?" *American Hebrew and Jewish Tribune* (January–March 1933), p. 242.

33. Harrison Forman, *Changing China* (New York: Crown, 1948), p. 147. See Pollak, *Mandarins, Jews, and Missionaries,* p. 247, for information on the French diplomat Pierre Gilbert's 1938 visit to Kaifeng, which was later related to Israel's president Yitzhak Ben-Zvi.

34. Related in Leslie, *Survival of the Chinese Jews, passim.*

35. Lowenthal, *Supplementary Bibliography,* p. 56. Lowenthal also reported that three years after this the American journalists Jimmy Burke and Archibald Steele wrote articles about their visit to Kaifeng on July 10, 1946, published in *Liberty Magazine* and *The New York Herald Tribune.* However, these articles have not been located.

36. See *Wang* Yisha, "The Descendants of the Kaifeng Jews," in *Jews in Old China: Studies by Chinese Scholars,* ed. Sidney Shapiro (New York: Hippocrene Books, 1984), pp. 171-72.

37. Excerpts from the transcriptions of these tapes, made with the full knowledge and consent of the Chinese Jewish descendants in August 1985 were published in the newsletter of the Sino-Judaic Institute, *Points East* 8, no. 2 (June 1993).

38. *Shi* Jingxun wrote a series of articles in 1913 describing possible secret deals by Bishop White to buy the 1489/1512 stele and smuggle it and other items out of China. See *Kong* Xianyi, "Delving into the Israelite Religion of Kaifeng: The Patriotic Scholar Shi Jingxun and His Study of the Origins of the Plucking the Sinews Sect of Henan," trans. Albert Dien, *Sino-Judaica,* 1 (1991), pp. 63-77.

C. Comparisons with Indian Jewry

Chapter I.C.1

The Kaifeng Jews and India's Bene Israel: Different Paths

Shirley Berry Isenberg

Mainstream Judaism has focused too long on Jewish communities of the West. Ignoring the various social–cultural–historical backgrounds of non-Western Jews has had some serious negative consequences. Among reasons for not overlooking the dynamics of culture change as revealed in comparative studies especially of Jews in China and in India—the world's most populous and, at the same time, extremely ancient civilizations—is the fact that we find in these two distinctly different Asian cultures medieval and modern examples of fairly large native Jewish communities that were never subjected to anti-Jewish (per se) discrimination or persecution.

A comparison of India's Bene Israel[1] with that of China's Kaifeng Jews shows that, while there are some similarities (most of which are not contemporaneous), the two histories of record exhibit opposite progressions spanning the time between a vestige of Jewish life, at one end, and vital community and Jewish life, at the other end. I shall refrain from elaborating on facts gleaned from the literature regarding the Kaifeng Jews while discussing at some length the Bene Israel parallels with which the present audience is likely to be less familiar.

There is no proof of the origins of either the Kaifeng Jews or Bene Israel even though, respectively, several different theories and approximate dates of origin have been suggested by Jews and non-Jews. As for the Kaifeng Jews, their own 1512 inscription states that the Jewish religion came to China during the Han dynasty (206 B.C.–A.D. 221), while the 1489 inscription dates the advent of Jews even earlier. In any case, they came from places west of China (even those Jews who may have arrived in China by sea) and settled in Kaifeng, which is located on the Yellow River about 300 miles from the river's mouth. It is likely that the Jewish community developed there between 960 and 1126 while Kaifeng was the capital of the Song dynasty. In the seventeenth century, Jesuit missionaries "discovered" the Kaifeng Jews and informed Europeans about them. The Jesuits described and made drawings of the Kaifeng synagogue and of the items therein. Certain details about Kaifeng Jewish history were recorded on Chinese inscriptions (dated 1489, 1512, and 1679) on two extant stone stelae, in a rubbing from a different stone dated 1663, and on several wooden tablets originally located in the Kaifeng synagogue complex. These inscriptions tell about the congregation's religious observances, doctrines, and important personalities. In 1163 the Kaifeng Jews were authorized by the then-rulers to build a structure for worship. Over the centuries the synagogue was repaired and rebuilt several times after damage by Yellow River floods and fire. There are many gaps in our knowledge about the history and life of the Kaifeng Jews; but the overall picture shows that Kaifeng Jewry for about five centuries constituted a distinct, respected, observantly Jewish middle-class group. In mid-seventeenth century their prosperity and their Jewishness began to decline. The 1848 flood fatally damaged the synagogue and its contents. By 1866 the synagogue had been totally demolished; the Kaifeng Jews were living in poverty; and no one among them knew Hebrew or Jewish liturgy, or how to perform Jewish rites. Their pleas to outsiders for Jewish teachers, Holy Scriptures, prayerbooks, and Hebrew–Chinese grammars were all thwarted by fate or indifference. Intermarriage with other Chinese was widespread. What was left to the Kaifeng Jews was only their knowledge that their ancestors had been Jewish.

Bene Israel persistently retell a tradition that their ancestors came by ship "from a country to the north"; that they were shipwrecked off the coast of Navgaon (about thirty miles south of Bombay); that only seven men and seven women survived; that all belongings were lost; and that at Navgaon they buried their dead. The survivors were succored by and settled among the local population. This tradition has been published as such in the two fullest early accounts about the Bene Israel: one by the Scottish missionary Reverend John Wilson in 1838 in the form of a paper read before the Bombay Branch of the Royal Asiatic Society;[2] the other by Haeem Samuel Kehimkar (himself a Bene Israel) in a manuscript completed in 1897 but published only posthumously in 1937 as a book entitled *The History of the Bene Israel of India* (Tel Aviv: Dayag Press).

The earliest document as yet known concerning the Bene Israel takes us back only to the seventeenth century. The heartland of Bene Israel settlement was Kolaba district of India's Maharashtra state.[3] There they lived a rural life, scattered among more than 100 villages, often with less than a handful of Bene Israel families per village. Bene Israel were endogamous, thoroughly Indianized, and practicing their own very limited version of Judaism. Their hereditary occupation was oil-pressing, but many were farmers and some were carpenters. Locally they were known not as Bene Israel, but as *Shanwar Telis* (*Shanwar* = Saturday, *Teli* = oil-presser) because they did no manner of work on Saturdays. There are a few eighteenth-century references to these people as *Israel Teli* or as *Israel Lok* (*Lok* = people). Neither they themselves nor other Indians referred to the Bene Israel as Jews or *Yehudim*. It is interesting to note that the Kaifeng Jews' designation of themselves in Chinese was *Yicileye* meaning "Israelites"; and that *youtai,* the Chinese word for "Jew," is said to have been introduced by Jesuits.[4]

Bene Israel say that, after having lived for many centuries in India, their ancestors were "discovered" by one David Rahabi,[5] a Jew new to the Konkan who noticed women selecting from a fisherman's catch only fish with fins and scales, that is, according to Jewish dietary law. This aroused his curiosity. He further learned that these people strictly observed the Sabbath by not even kindling fire; that they possessed no book or scroll and knew nothing about Jewish history or about the Torah;[6] but that on every occasion for prayer and at every rite of passage they pronounced in Hebrew the first sentence of the *Shem'a* (from Deuteronomy 6:4: "Hear, O Israel, the Lord our God, the Lord is One"); and that they circumcised all their male infants on the eighth day after birth. David Rahabi saw in these customs the vestiges of a former Jewish heritage. He undertook to re-Judaize these people, first by teaching three of their young men, from three different families, how to read and write Hebrew, how to conduct Jewish ceremonies for rites of passage, and how to serve as judges among their people according to basic tenets of Jewish law. He called these three men *Kazis*. He helped them copy whatever prayers and Hebrew writings he himself had then in his possession. He urged the *Kazis* to travel from village to village to minister to their people. The role of *Kazi* became an hereditary position from father to son, entailing privileges and honor. Ezekiel Rahabi's *Letter of 1768* to Moses Tobias states that "there are Jews called Bene Israel in Maratha and Mogul areas where Bene Israel make oil, some are soldiers; they know nothing but the *Shem'a* and keep the Shabbat."[7]

Physically, the Bene Israel and the Kaifeng Jews had become virtually indistinguishable from the respective local populations. It was their religion and claims of foreign origin that marked them as different. Kaifeng Jewry had thoroughly adopted typical Chinese clan structure. Each clan consisted of many family lineages, was exogamous, and observed patrilineal residence. Bene Israel divided themselves into two separate endogamous groups: The *Kala* (black) were always much fewer in number than the *Gora* (white). These terms did not reflect actual skin color. The *Kala* were the offspring, and their descendants, of Bene Israel men with non–Bene Israel women, never as wives, but sometimes as concubines. There was a ban on marriage between *Gora* and *Kala;* they did not eat together; and *Kala* were buried in a separate section of the *Gora* cemetery. During the past few decades, the restrictions have gradually been dying out. The *Gora–Kala* subdivision is a good example of how Hindu caste mentality suffused the social structure of non-Hindu groups in India, including India's Jews, Muslims, and Christians. India's all-pervasive system of *jati* (subcaste or subgroup) endogamy, coupled with strict social stratification, had helped the Bene Israel, a group so insignificant in numbers, not only to persist but to keep the Bene Israel *Gora* stock "pure." On the other hand, among the Kaifeng Jews marriage with women of non-Jewish origin had steadily increased. By the end of the sixteenth century in Kaifeng Jewish households more than one-quarter of the married women were non-Jewish by birth.[8]

More often than not, both the Kaifeng Jews and the Bene Israel were assumed by others to be part or a sect of the local Muslim minority; and, both in China and in India, the Muslim minority was/is large. Relations between the Bene Israel and Muslims were very cordial and neighborly. Bene Israel homes in villages and in towns often, though not always, were located within Muslim residential areas. In villages with very few Bene Israel residents and with no Bene Israel cemetery within accessible distance, when a Bene Israel died, he/she was buried in the local Muslim cemetery. Coexistence among Bene Israel, Muslims, and Hindus in Kolaba district was without friction. Bene Israel never suffered discrimination because of their Jewishness. They did suffer, with the rest of the population, whenever there were droughts, severe monsoon rains, epidemics, or warring armies or pirates ravaging villages. Thousands of villagers, including the Bene Israel, are known to have fled eastward from the man-made dangers, some taking refuge in safer villages, and some establishing new villages. This is how Bene Israel became dispersed throughout Kolaba district and many new Bene Israel village-linked surnames came into existence.

In typical Indian fashion, Bene Israel always showed respect and obedience to their elders, but they observed nothing comparable to the Kaifeng Jewish remembrance of and place of honor accorded to ancestors. They did, however, believe that on the eve of Yom Kippur (the Jewish Day of Atonement) the souls of their departed relatives visited their homes and did not depart until a full day after Yom Kippur. Bene Israel lived in patrilineal joint-family households. Security lay in one's joint family, in one's extended family, and in one's hereditary occupation and its concomitant status. Bene Israel status was low but respectable, that is, that of a farmer owning a little land or working as a tenant farmer. As a group they were unorganized, widely dispersed, uneducated, and typically rural people. They were largely self-sufficient, requiring very little cash, and bartering or peddling their produce.

After 1674, when Bombay became the headquarters of the British East India Company, Bombay mushroomed into a huge city, quickly became a very large and important port, and attracted thousands of villagers from the countryside. By the mid-eighteenth century, many Bene Israel had also moved to Bombay, where they found work as carpenters, construction laborers, and contractors. Other Bene Israel joined the Bombay Navy or enlisted in the so-called Native Forces, as Sepoys, of the British East India Company, in numbers out of proportion to the then total Bene Israel population of about 5,500 souls.[9] Many Bene Israel rose to the highest ranks possible for Native Soldiers.[10]

Although we know that, even in the seventeenth century, clusters of Bene Israel were living in coastal towns such as Alibag, Janjira, and Cheul, there is no indication that Bene Israel on the coast were involved in foreign trade or in commerce (except for petty trading).[11] On the other hand, Kaifeng's river traffic made it an important commercial center in which Kaifeng Jews were deeply engaged. However, even when large numbers of Bene Israel were living in Bombay (comparable to Kaifeng as a commercial and cultural center), with remarkably few exceptions, its Bene Israel were not involved in commerce. Most Bene Israel in Bombay lived lower middle-class lives.

From time immemorial, foreign merchants, foreign and Indian navies, armies, colonizers, and rulers have frequented the Konkan coastline; but it seems that until the late 1760s the Bene Israel had had no contact with other Jews, with the exception of a David Rahabi's discovery of them (whenever that occurred). In Kaifeng Jewry's long history, there were periods when excessive Chinese xenophobia forbade entry of foreigners. But the particular Kaifeng Jewish way of life, with and without contact with other Jews, did not merely survive. It was able to revive after several disasters and to thrive for centuries. Like the Bene Israel, they too circumcised their male children on the eighth day after birth, and on the Sabbath they lit no fire and did no cooking. But, unlike the Bene Israel, the Kaifeng Jews had a long history of celebrating *all* the biblical Jewish holidays and of maintaining certain Jewish rituals. What were the stages that led to the development of a community with a synagogue such as theirs? For many centuries the synagogue-oriented aspects of Kaifeng Jewishness must have been sophisticated and well organized. Most Kaifeng Jews lived in the immediate neighborhood of the synagogue compound. The synagogue was their shrine.

Their successive rabbis and learned religious leaders with specialized knowledge of the Hebrew scriptures and Jewish observances and rituals proved the vital force capable of maintaining Kaifeng Judaism intact for more than five centuries.

The layout and construction of the entire synagogue complex were typical of Chinese temple architecture, with the exception that the four successive courts of the synagogue complex were all oriented toward the West in the direction of Jerusalem. The synagogue's Holy Ark contained thirteen Torah scrolls, the one standing in the middle representing Moses,[12] the others representing the Twelve Tribes. In the seventeenth century, visiting Jesuits were told that one of these scrolls was then six hundred years old. The Sabbath and Jewish holiday liturgies of the Kaifeng Jews were most akin to Persian Jewish tradition.[13] According to Chinese and Indian Jewish and non-Jewish custom, all worshipers removed their shoes before entering a holy place. Inside the Kaifeng synagogue the men wore blue caps. One hall in the synagogue complex was devoted to Confucius and to Jewish ancestors, inclusive of some biblical characters, honored a few times a year in a typically Confucian ritual with food offerings and with burning of incense, but minus the presence of any images and not blatantly in contradiction to Jewish concepts.[14]

In 1642 rebel forces destroyed the Yellow river dikes at Kaifeng, flooding most of the city, ruining the synagogue and washing away its sacred scrolls and books, only some of which were later found complete or in part, wet and damaged. In preparing replacements of the scrolls, the scribes made many errors. The Kaifeng synagogue was rebuilt for the last time in 1653.

As for the Bene Israel, until the nineteenth century they had no Torah scrolls, Bibles, or prayerbooks; nor did they observe the four Jewish fast days of national mourning, and they did not know about Sukkot (the holiday of Tabernacles), or Purim (the story of Esther), or Chanukkah (the story of the Maccabis). But they did in their own ways observe the Bene Israel equivalents for Rosh Ha-shanah (Jewish New Year) and for *Pesach* (Passover).[15] It is impossible to know which old Bene Israel holiday customs date back to pre–David Rahabi times and which were introduced or reconstituted by him. One Kaifeng Jewish observance on Yom Kippur, as mentioned in the 1663 stele, namely, that the Kaifeng Jews "close their doors for a whole day and give themselves up to the cultivation of purity"[16] is strikingly reminiscent of the old Bene Israel custom that on Yom Kippur they would fast and sit at home *with locked doors,* dressed in white, and would not touch or talk to any non-Jew.[17] The Bene Israel called this holiday "Darfalnicha San," which literally means "holiday of the closing of doors."[18] The Bene Israel and their *Kazis* had only a few loose pieces of paper on which some prayers and a few brief excerpts from the Torah had been copied in Hebrew. The average Bene Israel, like their *Kazis,* knew many prayers by heart; Jewish rituals and group prayer, if any, took place in the home. When *Kazis* officiated, they received fees in cash or kind for their services. Their hereditary rights were recognized by local governments.[19]

The Bene Israel had, and still have, a special affinity to the Prophet Elijah, invoking his presence and help during a peculiarly Bene Israel ritual called *Malida.*[20] Bene Israel perform this *Malida* ceremony during certain rites of passage; in connection with the making and fulfillment of vows; and in times of crisis or danger, as well as on all happy occasions. A few features of the Bene Israel *Malida* ceremony resemble a specific Jewish, Muslim, or Hindu custom, as the case may be, but the ceremony as a whole is unique to the Bene Israel.[21] The importance that the Bene Israel attributed to the making of vows, combined with the *Malida* offering of a platter containing a special combination of rice, different kinds of fruit, bits of meat (fowl), and flowers are features cited by some in support of the theory that Bene Israel left the Holy Land *before* the destruction of the Second Temple, when offerings, as prescribed in the Book of Leviticus were still customary.[22] With some modification of the items being offered, the Bene Israel were observing all but three of the prescribed biblical offerings, omitting only those requiring animal sacrifice at the temple altar. The Bene Israel had no temple, no altar, and no *Cohanim* (priests) or Levites to perform the sacrifices. In the ancestral hall within the Kaifeng synagogue compound, the offerings made to Confucius and to Jewish ancestors also involved no animal sacrifice, and they too contained meat and foods in season. The burning of incense was part of the ritual at most Bene Israel observances, and always during a *Malida* ceremony, until their use of incense was forbidden by Cochini (South India) Jewish instructors in the early nineteenth century, as being contrary to *halacha,* the code of civil and ritual Jewish customs for which there is no explicit authority in the Old Testament, but which have been accepted as traditional Jewish law. Incense-burning is prevalent all over India and China. The Kaifeng Jews regularly used incense as part of their own rituals.

The first-ever Bene Israel synagogue, Shaarei Ha-Rachamim, owes its founding to a Bene Israel, namely, Commander Samaji Hassaji Divekar (Samuel Ezekiel Divekar), who, during the last two decades of the eighteenth century, led his contingent of Native Sepoys, fighting beside the British troops in the Mysore Wars against Hyder Ali and his son Tipu Sultan. In a disastrous battle, Samaji, together with the surviving British and Indian officers and men, was captured. Most of these captives were slain in captivity. Samaji had vowed that if ever he survived and were set free, he would build a synagogue in Bombay for his people. He was a second-generation Bombay resident and had learned from military and Cochini contacts that other Jews conducted group worship in synagogues. Eventually he was released from captivity.[23] With his accumulated officer's pay and retirement money, the first Bene Israel synagogue was built in 1796.

By mid-nineteenth century almost every Bene Israel family in Kolaba district had at least one family member living in Bombay for reasons of employment or education, or both. And since the 1820s many Baghdadi Jews and some Cochin Jews had also settled in Bombay. But Bene Israel in Bombay, as well as in India as a whole, have always greatly outnumbered all non–Bene Israel Jews in India. By 1837 the Bene Israel population in Bombay had grown close to 2,000; in the entire Konkan, including Bombay, it was estimated that there were about 8,000 Bene Israel. Estimates for peak totals for Kaifeng Jewry vary from 2,500 to 4,000. In 1849 informants reported only 1,000 Jews in Kaifeng, six of their eight clans having thoroughly intermarried with Muslim women. Also in 1849 Kaifeng had suffered a very destructive flood—the ultimate cause for the religious, communal, and economic collapse of the Kaifeng Jewish entity—while the Bene Israel population was continuously increasing and their Jewish community life as such was developing. The catalyst was education. The impetus for secular education among the Bene Israel occurred concurrently with their Jewish religious revival. It was not a case of competition between the two. Rather, they reinforced each other.

Two groups of dedicated and learned Jewish teachers came from Cochin to Bombay and Kolaba district in 1826 and 1833, in order to instruct the Bene Israel how to follow the numerous rules of *Halacha,* how to observe all the Jewish holidays, and how to read Hebrew; and they introduced the Bene Israel to the complete Sephardic synagogue liturgy and a plan for synagogue administration. During the nineteenth century, the Bene Israel established one more synagogue and two prayer-halls in Bombay and twelve synagogues in Kolaba district. Each Bene Israel synagogue had its own general assembly of the entire membership (membership fees were very low); a leader assisted by four or five Bene Israel elders as councilors; a treasurer; a cantor (*hazan*) who usually was a Cochini, Yemenite, or Baghdadi Jew and who not only chanted the liturgy but often also performed the duties of ritual circumcizer (*mohel*), scribe (*sofer*), teacher and slaughterer of animals (*shokhet*) for kosher meat; and a sexton (*shamash*) to sweep and light the synagogue, prepare the *kiddush* grape juice, distribute invitations to all religious and social functions, and to announce community meetings. There was no rabbi. The position of *Kazi* gradually lost prestige, but sometimes a *Kazi* was engaged to assist the cantor. Only the cantor,

Kazi, and sexton were paid a salary for their synagogue duties. No fees were charged for funeral services. Each synagogue was independent and was owned by its congregation as a whole. Income was derived from synagogue properties, rentals, investments, fines, marriage fees, and so on. The record books of the Bene Israel synagogues provide us with much information about the congregation, not only regarding financial, but also social and religious aspects. Each synagogue owned its own pots, eating utensils, and so on, for kosher catering (according to strict Jewish dietary laws) for large numbers of wedding guests and for other big social and religious affairs. Each Bene Israel synagogue became a vibrant center of community life.

None of the Bene Israel synagogues ever became a place for Talmudic studies.[24] Synagogue leadership typically remained in the hands of its nonprofessional laity, even after many Bene Israel had become doctors, advocates, teachers, engineers, and so on, and even though the professionals continued to be observant Jews and synagogue members. After the days of the Cochini teachers, every Bene Israel congregation had, and continues to have, some members, including professionals, who can and do read from the Torah scroll. They lead the prayers when and if necessary. Growing numbers of Bene Israel, employed in civil or military services in or near the cities of Thana, Ahmedabad, Pune, and Karachi settled, together with their nuclear families, in these distant cities, where, starting with a prayer hall, each of these new Bene Israel communities eventually built its own synagogue. No Bene Israel synagogue can compare with the Kaifeng synagogue complex. The Bene Israel synagogue structures varied in appearance. Only a few were rather imposing edifices. In Kolaba district the synagogues were of modest, sometimes thatched-roof, village-style construction. In the cities each synagogue had its *mikveh* (ritual bath house); in villages for ritual purification the Bene Israel immersed in a nearby stream. It is not clear whether or not the Kaifeng synagogue complex actually had a *mikveh* built according to orthodox Jewish specifications.

The Bene Israel were faced with a wholly new kind of experience when, beginning in 1813, Christian missions of various Protestant denominations became extremely active in Bombay and Kolaba district.[25] The primary purpose was to convert India's "heathens" to Christianity. At the same time many missionary efforts and successes were in the fields of medicine and education. In 1829 the American Mission alone had already set up five Native Free Schools in Bombay and thirteen other schools throughout Kolaba district, only one of which, at Alibag, was a high school. The latter already had thirty pupils, all of whom were Bene Israel, and six of whom were Bene Israel girls at a time when high-school education for girls was rare even in the West. Pupils in mission schools were taught to be literate in both Marathi (their mother-tongue) and in English. Secular subjects were emphasized as much as was the Christian religion. Among the pupils in most of the mission schools were Hindus, Jains, Parsis, Muslims, and Bene Israel.

From 1829 until his death in 1875 the Reverend John Wilson headed the Scottish Mission based in Bombay. He was not only a doctor of divinity but a prolific writer and scholar of linguistics, philosophy, the lands of the Bible, Indian archaeology, caste in India, and comparative religions. He saw in the Bene Israel a remnant of the Lost Tribes of Israel. As such, they "have never as a body proved averse to Christian education and . . . have always been ready to receive and peruse the Bible."[26] It was through Reverend Wilson, rather than from a Jewish preceptor, that most Bene Israel of that generation first became really familiar with the Bible. By 1831 Reverend Wilson had compiled and published his *Rudiments of Hebrew Grammar in Marathi*, "intended for the benefit of the Native Israelites in the Bombay Presidency" (which was the book's subtitle).[27]

Jesuit Father Antoine Gaubil recorded in 1723 that he had been asked by Kaifeng Jews to write out for them in Chinese the rules of Hebrew grammar; much later the same request was made again. Both times it was ignored. In Bombay, however, by using Reverend Wilson's *Grammar*, the Hebrew language was taught to Bene Israel pupils. Because of their experience of missionary emphasis on Bible texts, thereafter the Bene Israel tended to depend upon the Old Testament text as a self-sufficient guide for the Jewish religion,[28] and they neglected the study of rabbinical teachings and commentary. When confronted with Christian arguments concerning Jesus as the messiah, or when challenged on other religious topics, the usual Bene Israel reply was: "I myself am not learned enough, but there *are* Jews who know how to refute these Christian claims." In the seventeenth century the Jesuits found the Kaifeng Jews polite and amicable, ignorant about the Jewish faith, yet adamantly refusing to consider Jesus the messiah.

Many Bene Israel pupils who had studied at Reverend Wilson's schools went on to Bombay University (founded in 1857, where the study of Hebrew was accepted as a subject for matriculation and for higher examinations). During the second half of the nineteenth century fifty-eight Hebrew–Marathi books of synagogue liturgies and books on various Jewish religious subjects were published in Bombay, the works of a dozen Bene Israel prolific Hebrew scholars. Several Bene Israel periodicals flourished, mostly in Marathi but with occasional articles on Jewish subjects reprinted in their original English from U.S. and British publications. The Bene Israel periodicals also served as a forum for airing their community problems, controversies, announcements, and so on.[29]

Ultimate conversion to Christianity of mission schools pupils, or of their parents, was so rare that the missions gradually stopped offering free schooling to non-Christians. After twenty-five years of effort, even Reverend Wilson had not yet converted a single Bene Israel.[30] For the Bene Israel and other Indians, the teaching of English at mission schools had opened up the world of English writings and of contacts with the West. There was an additional bonus for Reverend Wilson's Bene Israel students: Their knowledge of Hebrew had led them to full participation in, and to the ability to conduct and to understand, Jewish prayer services; had introduced them to the wealth of Jewish writing; and had fostered lasting contacts with mainstream Judaism. No such opportunities materialized for the Kaifeng Jews.

In Bombay during the second half of the nineteenth century, just trying to earn a bare living took precedence over education. Yet, with great difficulty, Haeem S. Kehimkar managed to collect just about enough funds in 1875 to establish for the Bene Israel a primary, later also a secondary, coeducational school, called the Israelite School,[31] where no classes were held on the Sabbath or on Jewish holidays; and Hebrew, Marathi, and English were part of its regular curriculum. Thanks to their secular education, many Bene Israel obtained government jobs in towns and cities, working as clerks, draftsmen, accountants, telegraph signalers, policemen, railway and postal employees, nurses, hospital assistants, and printing compositors—jobs that offered real security. The British were wont to give preference for such types of work to the Anglo–Indian and to the Bene Israel minority communities. Some Bene Israel not in government service worked as skilled mechanics, carpenters, masons, construction laborers, cart drivers, and timber or grain merchants. Only a minority of Bene Israel, women included, went on to university and the professions.

Since the last quarter of the eighteenth century, during British rule and later on in independent India, several Bene Israel rose to responsible civilian positions; and many Bene Israel rose to officer ranks in the army, navy, air force, merchant marine, and police services.[32] These jobs usually entailed being stationed far from the Konkan, similar in this respect to the Kaifeng Jews who served in imperial Chinese military and civil positions, stationed far from Kaifeng. Most of those Bene Israel stationed all over India lived there with their nuclear families, often being the only Jews in the area. They made their home-away-from-home the focus of at least some Jewish observances. The family would usually return to their native place and to their joint-family's gathering in the Konkan, in order to celebrate together with them the High Holidays, Passover, and the rites of passage. If going back to the Konkan was not feasible for them, the Bene Israel would travel to the nearest Jewish prayer-hall (often at least a day's journey away) and would be put up in that city or town in order to properly observe the Jewish holiday or ritual together with other Jews because it remained important to them to do so. Did those Kaifeng Jews in the imperial Chinese services do likewise when stationed far from Kaifeng, or did they completely lose touch with their Judaism?

In some respects, and without themselves realizing it, the Bene Israel were behaving like "Conservative" American Jews, who, since early twentieth century, were veering away from rigid orthodoxy and were adapting to the times. In all but one Bene Israel synagogue,[33] however, the Bene Israel maintained traditional Orthodox customs, except for shortening the Sabbath service, mainly by omitting repetition of certain prayers, and by beginning the services early enough to enable them to get to their respective places of work by the usual opening hour of 10 A.M. Also, because so many Jewish homes in Bombay were not within walking distance of a synagogue or prayer-hall, the Bene Israel took advantage of the system (introduced, implemented, sanctioned, and used by the Orthodox Baghdadi Jews of Bombay)[34] of buying on weekdays the special public transport tickets for Jews, to be used only on the Sabbath and Jewish holidays, so that Jews would not have to handle money on those days for buying tickets in order to get to the place of prayer.

As in the villages, so also in the cities, Bene Israel got along well with Hindus, Muslims, and Christians. In India only the Baghdadi Jews discriminated against the Bene Israel, alleging that the Bene Israel were halachically pure Jews by descent nor sufficiently kosher in their observances. Another Bene Israel problem that manifested itself after their urbanization was fissiparousness among themselves. Splitting up into two separate (and sometimes mutually unfriendly) groups became characteristic of Bene Israel organizations, evident in their urban synagogue congregations, charitable institutions, periodicals, and so on. With few exceptions, Bene Israel individuals did not get involved in any but intra–Bene Israel politics.

From 1910 until 1933 Kaifeng was the see of Anglican Bishop William Charles White. In his prolific writing, his interest in archaeology, and his failure to make converts of the local Jews, Bishop White resembles Reverend Wilson. Bishop White deserves credit for his three-volume study entitled *Chinese Jews: A Compilation of Matters Relating to the Jews of K'ai-feng Fu,* and for the preservation of certain Kaifeng Jewish objects.[35] But he did not resuscitate the Kaifeng Jewish community in any way. Lacking any religious guides of their own or inspiration to continue at least some Jewish observances even without being able to read Hebrew, Kaifeng Jewry desperately needed Jewish contacts from outside. In the mid-nineteenth and again in early twentieth century a few Jewish leaders in the

United States and Europe, and some Baghdadi Jews in Shanghai, separately were moved to set up a society aimed at rebuilding the Kaifeng synagogue, re-Judaizing the Kaifeng Jews, and reversing their sad plight. But none of these societies got any further than collecting pitifully inadequate donations.[36]

In 1940 Bene Israel began to join the Bombay Zionist Organization (founded by Baghdadi Jews in 1919). Jewish agency representatives in Bombay provided classes in modern Hebrew and information about Jewish resettlement in Palestine. India became independent in 1947, Israel in 1948. Since then most Bene Israel, for a combination of idealistic and complex economic reasons, have left India to settle in Israel. Fewer Bene Israel left India to settle in English-speaking countries. Today about 5,000 Bene Israel remain in India, mostly in Bombay. Both in Israel and in Diaspora countries, in spite of not infrequent intermarriage with other Jews, Bene Israel identity is being maintained through their active local Bene Israel social organizations and, in varying ways, within each family. Several Bene Israel, not only in India, still perform the traditional *Malida* ceremony.

Among Bene Israel remaining in India, there is a preponderance of elderly persons, and for the younger generation the pool of likely marriage partners is small. Unlike the Bene Israel of the nineteenth century, with their almost total resistance to proselytization and intermarriage, in today's India Bene Israel intermarriage with non-Jews is no longer a rarity. However, a few international Jewish organizations, such as the Organization for Rehabilitation Through Training (ORT) and the American Jewish Joint Distribution Committee, are beginning to revitalize Jewish community life there. It remains to be seen which path the Bene Israel who continue to live in India will follow.

The self-imposed task of Cochin Jewish teachers to thoroughly Judaize the Bene Israel eventually created among the latter the milieu and a continuing do-it-yourself capability for the conduct of group prayer services and for synagogue organization. One wonders whether there ever was a period when the Kaifeng Jewish laity also had been thus prepared. Particularly auspicious for the Jewish as well as for the secular development of the Bene Israel was the advent of Reverend John Wilson. The British preference for employing Bene Israel, often in charge of records, accounts, correspondence, and so on, in effect prepared the laity to assume the administration of their respective synagogues, which they turned into active centers of Bene Israel Jewish and social life. On the whole the Bene Israel had demonstrated remarkable ability at every turn.

There is no doubt that the fate of the Kaifeng Jews was related to the vicissitudes of China's political and military conditions when these impinged on Kaifeng, especially in isolating its Jews from contact with other

Jews. Song Nai Rhee stresses that because of their wealth and power, from the fourteenth to the eighteenth century those Kaifeng Jews in imperial China's services had greatly influenced the rest of the congregation toward amalgamation of Judaism and Confucianism in the synagogue and also toward acceptance of intermarriage with non-Jewish Chinese women.[37] He sees these two aspects as having been the important factors that led to the total disintegration of Kaifeng Judaism. However, in the light of the Bene Israel experience, I suspect that Kaifeng Jewry's rabbis and spiritual leaders had gradually become too formal and too remote a *religious* élite, in addition to their civil service élite, and that from generation to generation there had been insufficient instruction for, and lack of participation by, the Kaifeng Jewish laity in the conduct and understanding of synagogue services and of Jewish customs and rituals. I suspect too that, inadvertently or otherwise, over the centuries the two élites had prevented the synagogue from becoming also the center of the congregation's social and cultural life. In doing so, they deprived the Kaifeng Jewish laity of the prerequisites for self-perpetuation of a functioning Jewish community—as indeed became clear once the need for such self-perpetuation actually arose.

Both the Kaifeng Jews and the Bene Israel had become thoroughly acculturated and assimilated to the patterns of life and to the social norms of their respective host cultures. Furthermore, in Kaifeng as well as in the Konkan, two factors made anti-Semitism an irrelevancy: namely, the numerical and economic insignificance of their respective Jewish populations; and, most important, the essential characteristic socioreligious emphases that permeated the ways of life at all levels of the host population. The Kaifeng Jews had been easily absorbed into China's multisectarian *clan* social structure. And it was India's all-pervasive endogamous caste and sub-*caste mentality* that accommodated its Jews and made them feel perfectly at home amid a heterogeneous population. In the West the presence of Christians has too often gone hand in hand with violent and non-violent forms of anti-Jewish behavior. But this did not happen in Kolaba district or in Bombay with their large Indian Christian minority, even though until 1947 these areas had been so long under Christian (British) rule. A combination of influences entirely new to the Bene Israel—namely, the Cochin Jewish teachers, the Christian mission schools, and British rule—had completely changed Bene Israel lives, having opened for the Bene Israel new secular as well as new Jewish horizons. If the ruling colonial power had been the Portuguese instead of the British, the Bene Israel saga would have been very different.

Regarding the Kaifeng Jews, intermarrying with non-Jews and the process of forsaking Judaism gradually accelerated during a long history of isolation from other Jews, natural disasters, and other factors. Internally the community suffered from a progressive inability to maintain Jewish spiritual leadership of high caliber and continuing expertise in Jewish tradition and in the Hebrew language. When the situation became critical, somehow the Kaifeng Jews as a group lacked anything akin to the original Bene Israel tenacity and determination to cling to their meager few (then) vestigial Jewish elements—until the remarkable and fortuitous combination of external circumstances (as described above) led the Bene Israel into assimilation with mainstream Judaism.

However, nobody can predict what contexts of situation will arise and affect the future course of Bene Israel Jewry, whether in India, Israel, or elsewhere.

Notes

1. There are three different and separate Jewish ethnic groups in India: (1) the *Bene Israel;* (2) the *Cochin Jews* with a documented history on India's southwest coast (i.e., today's Indian state of Kerala) going back at least to A.D. 1000 and during which they were in occasional contact with mainstream Jewry; and (3) the so-called *Baghdadi Jews* (referring to all Jews from Arabic-speaking countries, or from Persia and Afghanistan) almost none of whom settled in India together with their families (mainly in Calcutta and Bombay) until early in the nineteenth century. The Bene Israel have been, and continue to be, far more numerous than the other two groups combined.

2. A lengthy abstract of it was published in *The Oriental Christian Spectator* (Bombay) (January 1840), 11, no. 1, pp. 27–36. See also Shirley B. Isenberg, *India's Bene Israel: A Comprehensive Inquiry and Sourcebook* (Berkeley: Judah L. Magnes Museum; and Bombay: Popular Prakashan, 1988), pp. 74 and 327–38.

3. Kolaba (today called Raigad) district, with Greater Bombay and Thana district as its northern border, stretches about 160 miles south along the Arabian sea as far as the mouth of the Savitri River, and 40 to 60 miles eastward to the foothills of the Western Ghats and the border of Pune district. The central part of India's western coastline and coastal plain, extending from about 50 miles north of Bombay southward as far as Goa (formerly a Portuguese colony) is called the Konkan. Kolaba district is part of the Konkan.

4. Rudolph Loewenthal, *The Nomenclature of Jews in China* (Peiping, 1944), reprinted in Hyman Kublin, ed. *Studies of the Chinese Jews: Selections from Journals East and West* (New York: Paragon, 1971), pp. 72–73.

5. See note 7.

6. Torah (Hebrew): The first five books of the Old Testament collectively (Genesis, Exodus, Leviticus, Numbers, and Deuteronomy), which, especially for use in synagogue worship, have been hand-inscribed onto a parchment scroll, portions of which, in sequence, are chanted aloud to the whole congregation and completed in its entirety during the course of a full year.

7. Ezekiel Rahabi I was a Jewish merchant from Syria who settled in Cochin in 1647. His son was David Rahabi I (1646–1726), whose son was Ezekiel Rahabi II (1694–1771). David Rahabi I was very influential with the maharajah of Cochin, but Ezekiel Rahabi II was an even more important person, being the chief agent in Cochin for

the Dutch East India Company. His son was another David (Ezekiel) Rahabi II (1721–1791). These Rahabis are well-known historical figures and there are a few incidental references of a contact with Bene Israel, but the references are inconsistent. See Isenberg, *India's Bene Israel*, pp. 3, 24, 44–45, and 318. Worth pondering is Benjamin J. Israel's statement: "If the David Rahabi of Bene Israel tradition is the David Ezekiel Rahabi who visited them in the middle of the eighteenth century, it is inconceivable that in the early years of the nineteenth century when several persons who had met him must have been still alive, his coming had been put back in the communal memory more than eight hundred years. The possibility is that the name was transferred to the legendary teacher who, if he ever existed, was an entirely different person." Benjamin J. Israel, *The Bene Israel of India: Some Studies* (Bombay: Orient Longman, 1984), p. 56. Incidentally, there is a letter written by Ezekiel Rahabi II that mentions that "There are Jews in the Chinese Empire."

8. According to Donald D. Leslie, *The Survival of the Jewish Community of Kaifeng: The Jewish Community of Kaifeng* (Leiden: E.J. Brill, 1972), pt. 2, p. 7.

9. By 1838 it was estimated that there was a total of 8,000 Bene Israel. The peak of Bene Israel population growth in India occurred during the late 1940s, when their number was estimated at 20,000. For information about Jewish demography in India, see Isenberg, *India's Bene Israel*, pp. 279–306.

10. See Sir Patrick Cadell, *History of the Bombay Army* (Bombay, 1938); and Haeem S. Kehimkar, *History of the Bene Israel of India* (Tel Aviv: Dayag Press, 1937), pp. 187–225.

11. Cheul: The same site was once called Simylla or Saimur. It was an important trade center even in Roman times. Early in the sixteenth century local rulers had given permission to the Portuguese to establish a trading post and a fort of their own in Lower Cheul, but Cheul was never part of Portuguese territory as such. I am not aware of any Bene Israel having lived under the Portuguese in India. The Portuguese converted many Indians to Catholicism.

12. See Michael Pollak, *Mandarins, Jews, and Missionaries: The Jewish Experience in the Chinese Empire* (Philadelphia: Jewish Publication Society, 1980), p. 86.

13. See Berthold Laufer, "A Chinese-Hebrew Manuscript: A New Source for the History of the Chinese Jews," in Kublin, *Studies*, pp. 164–65.

14. "The argument that Judaism is wholly compatible with Confucianism is restated in various (Kaifeng) synagogue inscriptions, not only because those Jews believed this, but also to allay the suspicion that they, as foreigners, might be hostile to the virtues inherent in Confucianism" (Pollak, *Mandarins, Jews, and Missionaries*, p. 294).

15. For details about the ways in which Bene Israel had traditionally observed Bene Israel holidays, see Kehimkar, *History of the Bene Israel*, pp. 16–23.

16. See Pollak, *Mandarins, Jews, and Missionaries*, p. 293.

17. Author interviews with former Bene Israel villagers.

18. Kehimkar, *History of the Bene Israel*, p. 18.

19. See translations into English of two complete official documents that relate to Bene Israel *Kazis*, in ibid., pp. 45 and 46.

20. For a full discussion about the *Malida* Ceremony, see Isenberg, *India's Bene Israel*, pp. 111–17.

21. See ibid., pp. 114–15.

22. After the year A.D. 70 when the Romans destroyed the Second Temple in Jerusalem, including its sacrificial altar, these sacrifices were permanently discontinued.

23. For further details, see ibid., pp. 314–24.

24. *Talmud*: The compilation of, and commentaries on, all Jewish civil and religious laws, being the collective work of several generations of Rabbis, from about 450 B.C.

until about A.D. 500. Whatever, if any, Talmudic writings had ever been in the possession of Kaifeng Jews, had been lost in the 1642 flood. See Pollak, *Mandarins, Jews, and Missionaries,* pp. 284 and 296.

25. Catholic missions were not active among Bene Israel.

26. *Oriental Christian Spectator,* 11, no. 1 (Bombay) (January 1840), p. 35.

27. Ibid., 2, no. 7 (July 1831), p. 9, presents a prepublication announcement *cum* summary of the book's contents and the biblical topics used "so as to form a set of useful and constructive exercises."

28. As pointed out by Benjamin J. Israel in his chapter "Religious Evolution Among the Bene Israel of India Since 1750." Benjamin J. Israel, *Bene Israel,* p. 68.

29. See the lengthy list of Bene Israel publications (books and periodicals) according to year of publication, in *The Bene Israel Annual and Year Book, 1919–1920,* vol. 3, ed. Rebecca Reuben (Junagadh, India), pp. 56–80.

30. In extensive searches through missionary and other records, I have learned of only three Bene Israel individuals who had converted to Christianity during the nineteenth century, and two of these later renounced their conversion and were ritually reinstated into Judaism.

31. In 1931 the Israelite School was renamed the Sir Elly Kadoorie School, after one of its then-recent benefactors.

32. See E.M. Jacob Gadkar, *The Religious and Cultural Heritage of the Bene-Israels of India, Book II,* published for the Gate of Mercy (Shaar Ha-Rachamim) Synagogue (Bombay, 1984). This book devotes most of its 182 pages to biographical sketches, with dates (and usually with a photograph) of 111 Bene Israel individuals who have distinguished themselves, documenting a great variety of fields of endeavor.

33. A Bene Israel woman, Dr. Jerusha Jhirad, who held important positions in the field of medicine in India, in 1925 founded a Reform Jewish congregation in Bombay called Rodef Shalom. As a synagogue congregation it was one of the founder members of the World Union of Progressive Judaism. Rodef Shalom was the only Bene Israel congregation that ever had had an ordained rabbi when, for a total of about six years in the 1950s, a few successive visiting rabbis from England and the United States ministered to the congregation. The services of these rabbis were very much appreciated not only by the members of Rodef Shalom but also by many other Indian Jewish residents of Bombay.

34. See *American Jewish Yearbook,* 54 (Philadelphia: Jewish Publication Society, 1953), p. 420.

35. See Pollak, *Mandarins, Jews, and Missionaries,* pp. 217–18.

36. See ibid., pp. 173, 181, 210–12, and 215.

37. Song Nai Rhee, "Jewish Assimilation: The Case of the Chinese Jews," in *Comparative Studies in Society and History* (London and New York: Cambridge University Press, 1973), vol. 15, pp. 115–26.

Chapter I.C.2

Cochin Jews and Kaifeng Jews: Reflections on Caste, Surname, "Community," and Conversion

Barbara C. Johnson

A first-time visitor to the Paradesi Synagogue in the section of Cochin known as Jew Town cannot help thinking of China. The entire floor of the sanctuary is paved with exquisite blue and white Chinese tiles, painted in a Weeping Willow pattern, probably imported to this southwestern coast of India during the seventeenth century. Several cultural elements unique to this part of India give signs of early contact with China. The pagoda-style tiled roofs on some older houses and the "Chinese" butterfly-style fishing nets in Fort Cochin and along the backwaters to the north are popularly believed to demonstrate the connection. There is even some evidence that Cochin Jews of the eighteenth and nineteenth centuries had knowledge of Jews in China.[1]

Although it is fascinating to speculate about contact between Cochin Jews and Chinese Jews, the comparisons to be developed here do not depend on proof of direct connections between Cochin and Kaifeng. Rather, they are based on important parallels in the history and cultural adaptations of these two ancient communities of Asian Jews. In the days of their glory, both Cochin and Kaifeng were major commercial centers in which Jews played a significant (though admittedly minor) role as merchants. Both were royal cities—ancient Kaifeng an imperial capital and Cochin the home of a once-powerful maharajah—and the Jews of both places enjoyed good relations with the rulers. Both Jewish communities existed for many centuries in an atmosphere free of anti-Semitism, free to follow their own beliefs and practices without interference from rulers or non-Jewish neighbors. As has been pointed out to me by more than one of the Cochin Jews now living in Israel, "In India we were not just tolerated, we were respected!"

The difference between acculturation and assimilation is vitally important for understanding each community. Both communities acculturated by adopting forms of local sociocultural organization—caste in India and surnamed patrilineal descent groups in China—which they apparently did not perceive as threatening the integrity of their Jewishness. In both places Jewish men married and converted women from the local population, following marriage patterns that were acceptable to the surrounding culture.

In Kaifeng, acculturation gradually turned into assimilation, as the Jews finally lost their synagogue, their knowledge and ritual practice of Judaism, and the communal institutions that made them a distinct community. Cochin Jews as a group never assimilated in these ways, perhaps because they had a number of different congregations, or perhaps because they never lost regular contact with Jews from other places. But the Kaifeng Jews have not completely "disappeared"; just a decade ago, 166 of them still identified themselves as Jews.[2] Irene Eber analyzes this persistence of Jewish ethnic identity in terms of their adherence to the Chinese patrilineal descent system and to their recognition by outsiders as an acceptable religious sect, or *jiao*.[3]

As for the Cochin Jews today, the threat to their survival as an identifiable social group is not a loss of Jewishness through assimilation into Indian culture, but a loss of Indianness through assimilation into Israeli culture. After probably 2,000 years of community life in India, almost all of them have moved to Israel during the past forty years. The following ethnohistorical comparisons are concentrated on the Cochin Jews before they left India and on what is known of Kaifeng while it was still the home of a thriving Jewish community, or at least a community of distinctly Jewish families.

After a background summary of Cochin Jewish history, this chapter focuses on several aspects of their social organization. First, their overarching identity as one South Indian caste within an entire caste system was vital in preserving their Jewish identity in Kerala society—perhaps comparable in some ways to the identification of Kaifeng Jews as a religious sect among many sects in China. Second, internal divisions within the Cochin Jewish caste are re-examined. Rather than labeling these internal distinctions castes or subcastes (as other scholars have done), I describe their eight separate "communities" or congregations, suggesting comparison with the surnamed patrilineal descent groups of the Kaifeng Jews. The chapter concludes with a brief discussion of another internal social distinction in Cochin—that between Jews of higher status in each community, who claimed "pure" Jewish descent, and a subgroup sometimes called *mshuchrarim* or "manumitted slaves," whom they did not marry, and who were denied certain ritual privileges in the synagogues. This discussion also raises questions about the status of converts in the Kaifeng Jewish community.

Jews in Kerala History

Although the Cochin Jews are not all from the city of Cochin, they derive their name from centuries of residence in that part of the Malabar coast once ruled by the maharajah of Cochin. Now known as the modern Indian state of Kerala, the Malabar coast is a narrow stretch of fertile land cut off from the rest of India by the Western Ghat mountain range, with its economy oriented toward the sea. The Jews were just one group of traders from the West who settled down in Kerala and whose descendants and converts account for a large proportion of Kerala's 29 million people today; approximately 20 percent are Muslim, 20 percent Christian, and 60 percent Hindu. Although tradition has it that there once were many thousands of Jews in Kerala, no more than 2,500 were recorded in recent centuries, and only about fifty remain there today.

There has been a Jewish community on the Malabar coast for at least a thousand and probably two thousand years.[4] Tradition has it that the first Jewish merchants came to the coast with the ships of King Solomon's fleet around 1000 B.C., and Dravidian loanwords in the Hebrew Bible attest to that possibility. The first Jewish settlers may have been merchants on Roman ships that traveled to ports up and down the coast, carrying spices, cloth, and other luxuries back to the Middle East and Europe. Legends of the "St. Thomas" (Syrian) Christians of Malabar claim that their founder came as a missionary to an established Jewish colony in the ancient port of Cranganore almost two thousand years ago, and some of these Christians count themselves as descended from Kerala Jews.

In A.D. 1000 Joseph Rabban, leader of the Jews in Cranganore, received from the Hindu ruler a set of copper plates detailing special economic and ritual privileges, including exemption from paying taxes, the right to collect tolls, and the honor of using particular lamps, umbrellas, drums, and trumpets associated with high ritual status. These are the famous copper plates kept in the Paradesi Synagogue at Cochin. Cochin Jews maintain a certain attachment to their ancient home in Cranganore, which they refer to as "Shingli" (also spelled Shingly), though by the sixteenth century all of them had left for other places in Kerala.[5]

Literary evidence shows a rather egalitarian social order in Kerala during the early centuries of the Common Era—a situation in which it would not have been difficult for Jews and other newcomers to achieve social prominence and perhaps marry women from wealthy families in the area. Between the eighth and the eleventh centuries, Brahmins from the north came southward and began to dominate Kerala society. They lent their ritual authority to the political dominance of the small ruling caste of Kshatriyas. A much larger caste called the Nayars actually ran things, as administrators and soldiers for the two highest castes. The Nayars and several other high castes in Kerala are noted for their traditional custom of matrilineal inheritance.

By the eleventh century, when the Jews were granted their copper plate privileges, the Kerala caste system had become rigidly structured. Farming and artisan labor was carried out by low-caste Hindus and by outcaste groups, many of whom were bound to the land as agricultural serfs (called "slaves" by the British). Social procedures to avoid intercaste pollution were developed to a high degree. In addition to agricultural "slavery" there was a system of individual servitude, in which children from poor families (and sometimes women who had been outcasted from higher-status groups) were sold into personal bondage.

It seems clear that a Jewish community was firmly established by this time, fitting into a social niche between the land-owning Brahmins and Nayars, on the one hand, and the low-caste and "untouchable" laborers, on the other. No indigenous merchant castes had developed in Kerala to parallel the Vaisya (merchant) castes of North India. Trade remained largely in the hands of immigrant groups from western lands and from other parts of India. Thus the Jews were easily incorporated into this respected commercial stratum of Kerala social structure, not singled out from other groups or stigmatized because of their middleman role as they were in Europe. Descendants of the early Jewish settlers made up seven of the eight Jewish congregations or "communities" that were still thriving in Kerala up to the time of their mass migration to Israel in the mid-twentieth century.

Beginning in the early sixteenth century there was a new migration of Jews to Kerala. A report by Dutch visitors a century later reveals that some of the newcomers were Sephardic Jews, direct and indirect refugees from the Spanish and Portuguese expulsions, who came to India by way of Aleppo, Constantinople, and the Land of Israel. Others were from Iraq, Persia, Yemen, and Germany. Some apparently came in family groups, and some men married high-status Jewish women from the "first families" of Cranganore. In 1568 these newcomers, who were called Paradesis (foreigners), built a synagogue of their own on land granted to them by the maharajah of Cochin. They adopted the Malayalam language and Kerala customs, but at some point they stopped marrying the much more numerous Malabari Jews who had been there many centuries before them. In written accounts, especially by Western visitors, the Paradesis often were referred to as "white Jews" and the Malabaris as "black Jews," though there is not always a clear distinction between them in terms of skin color. A 1520 rabbinic Responsum from Cairo addressed a question about the status of converts and so-called manumitted slaves in Cochin—a topic addressed below.

A few Paradesi Jews rose to high positions as agents or brokers in foreign trade and as economic and political advisers to Hindu and colonial rulers. After a period of Portuguese persecution, the Jews in general were favored under Dutch and English rule. Some Paradesis and some Malabaris became relatively wealthy landowners; some achieved positions as clerks, teachers, doctors, and lawyers under the British colonial system; and others were bookbinders or small merchants, dealing especially in fish and poultry.

Most of the Cochin Jews migrated to Israel, beginning in the 1950s. Some were seeking improved economic conditions; some emphasized their desire to live a more religious life or to be involved in building the new Jewish state; but none were forced to leave.

Jews as a South Indian Caste, or *Jati*

Along with many other scholars,[6] I find the category of caste to be appropriate for understanding Cochin Jewish social organization, but (unlike them) only insofar as it elucidates the status and identity of the Jews as a whole within Kerala culture. The caste system throughout India embodies the assumption that one's personal identity is bound up with a group known as a *jati*—first translated by the Portuguese as *casta* or "caste." A *jati* is an endogamous group that maintains external boundaries and orderly marriage patterns; the Jewish practice of marrying only other Jews qualifies them thoroughly for being regarded as a *jati*. Traditionally, each *jati* had a specialized occupation, part of a network of interrelated jobs that assured the economic order; as noted, the Jews filled a merchant role in the Kerala economy. Traditionally, the various *jatis* were hierarchically ranked; in Kerala society the Jews were probably ranked quite high, after the Brahmins and Nayars, in a position comparable to that of the St. Thomas Christians.

Another aspect of caste is the practice of ritual purity and pollution, involving elaborate rules about food preparation and exchange along with frequent ritual bathing for purification—another set of customs that were familiar to the religiously observant Jews of Kerala. Finally, there were many *jatis* (like the Jews) that had their own deity or deities and their own religious rituals, sometimes including scriptures and songs in a special language. Each *jati* respected the customs of other *jatis,* and the ruler was responsible for overseeing their relations.

It is easy to see how this social system preserved Jewish identity rather than threatening it. No Indian would criticize the Cochin Jews for marrying endogamously. Other than foreign Christian missionaries and their converts (never the ancient St. Thomas Christians), no one in Kerala would try to persuade the Jews to change their beliefs or customs or to worship any deity but their own. Never would they be branded as peculiar for following their own ways, as long as they did not interfere with the customs of other *jatis*.

Like the *jiao,* or "sect," status of the Kaifeng Jews discussed by Eber, *jati* gave the Cochin Jews a way to become acculturated into Kerala society.[7] Of course there are important differences between a *jati* and a *jiao*. (For example, the *jiao* category in Chinese society does not imply occupational status or hierarchic ranking.) But in both Asian settings the Jews were accepted as a group because they acted like other social groups of the same primary social classification—*jati* in India and *jiao* in China.

Internal Divisions Within the Cochin Jewish *Jati*

Anthropologists and many other visitors to the Cochin Jewish communities have been intrigued by another set of social boundaries—those between the more ancient Malabari Jews and the Paradesi newcomers, the two groups of Jews labeled by outsiders as "black" and "white." Scholars have also commented extensively on the status of yet another group or groups of Cochin Jews, sometimes called *mshuchrarim* ("freed slaves" in Hebrew). At issue is how to interpret the fact that these three divisions did not intermarry, nor did they share certain ritual honors. When I first began studying the Cochin Jews, I did not question the anthropological interpretation that these were three different Jewish castes.[8]

But many years of research and personal acquaintance with Cochin Jews in India and Israel have led me to reject the label of caste or *jati* as a definition or explanation of these internal distinctions. It is true that Paradesi and Malabari Jews have not married each other, even down to the present time, and that on some occasions in the past some of them quarreled with each other, to the extent of sometimes not counting each other in the minyan of ten males required for prayer. But similar quarrels and exclusions were at times observed between different congregations or "communities" of Malabari Jews, which scholars have not labeled as separate castes. It is also true that in the past each of the two groups, Malabari and Paradesi, developed a subgroup of persons who were denied ritual and sexual equality because they were thought to descend from converts. But I do not believe that these distinctions (which are no longer practiced) were extreme enough to warrant the label of separate Jewish castes or subcastes.[9]

For me the most obvious constraint on the use of a "caste" label is that I have not heard Cochin Jews use the concept of *jati* difference to refer to any of their fellow Jews. At least among Paradesis, when they speak of "other *jati* people" they are clearly referring to non-Jews; all Jews from India and even foreign Jews are seen as members of the Jewish *jati*. Once my attention was turned away from differences and boundaries among the groups, I found ample evidence of similarities and lack of boundaries. Most conspicuously, Cochin Jews of all groups do *not* maintain barriers of ritual purity and inter-caste in relation to one another—barriers that are essential to traditional definitions of caste. Even though certain groups have not intermarried at certain times in history, they have continued to eat at the same table, sharing sanctified ritual wine and even Passover *matzoh*, which they do not share with gentiles. The clearest boundaries of purity and pollution that I experienced in the Cochin Jewish community involved preparations for Passover, particularly restrictions on non-Jewish participation in the making of *matzoh*—a process in which Jews of all groups work together.

Although the Hindu caste system must have influenced Jewish attitudes toward social difference, focusing on this influence is just one approach to understanding internal divisions within the Cochin Jewish *jati*. Two additional perspectives presented here may lead to more fruitful comparisons with the situation of the Kaifeng Jews.

Cochin "Communities"

If separate Cochin groups do not describe themselves as castes, what categories do they use? My fieldwork among the Cochin Paradesi Jews in India and Israel revealed that the most meaningful category in their expression of identity is "our community"—in colloquial Jewish Malayalam, *nammodu kambolam*. The literal meaning of *kambolam* is "street," referring to the section of Cochin known as Jew Town, where they lived for four centuries. On another level the community could be seen as a congregation, associated with the Paradesi Synagogue at the end of their street. But the social reality and vitality of "our community" persists in Israel, where the Paradesi have neither a street nor a synagogue of their own.[10]

For the past few centuries there were eight separate Jewish "communities," each with its own synagogue building and congregational organization, among the approximately two thousand Jews in Kerala. These eight synagogues were located in five different towns and villages in Kerala, and each community was identified by the name of its synagogue.[11]

In Kerala each separate community was a corporate entity, owning property and administering grants and loans as well as ritual honors for its members.[12] Governed by a council (*yogam*) of the five or seven oldest (and eligible)[13] men, it oversaw marriage, circumcision, and burial. The community was the source of political and economic power as well as religious activity for its members—and thus the arena for demonstrating and negotiating personal and family status within the Jewish caste. In addition it was also the primary small unit of warmth and support and group pride.

"Community" membership was inherited patrilineally, each bride joining the congregation of her husband, in contrast to the matrilineal inheritance of Jewishness itself. Perhaps this balance between matrilineal and patrilineal inheritance (characteristic of rabbinic Judaism) was easier for Jews to maintain in Cochin than in Kaifeng because of the mix of matrilineal and patrilineal descent patterns in the surrounding Hindu culture of Kerala, unlike the strong patrilineal tradition in China.

After the late sixteenth century members of the Paradesi community married only among themselves or with Jews from outside Cochin, not with Malabaris; hence anthropologists labeled them a separate caste. Until the late nineteenth century all of the other seven congregations seem to have intermarried with one another. Then a quarrel over the propriety of intermarriage resulted in the "excommunication" of the Kadavumbagam–Cochin community by the other six Malabari communities, so that a man marrying a woman from Kadavumbagam lost membership in his own community. Yet I have not heard anyone suggest that Kadavumbagam–Cochin was a separate caste. Surely the phenomenon of divisions and quarrels between Jewish congregations and factions is not unique to Cochin and can be discussed without the "exotic" label of caste.

Despite the marriage restrictions that set apart two of the eight congregations, and despite sometimes bitter quarrels between some of them, there is ample evidence of social contacts among the various communities—including close friendships, business relationships, invitations to each other's life-cycle rituals, women lending and borrowing jewelry and songs, and the sharing of ordinary and ritual meals without regard to barriers of purity and pollution. Cochin Jews (both Paradesi and Malabari) who moved to Bombay or Calcutta could still keep membership in their congregations back in Kerala, and these ties seemed to be an element in their maintaining a strong sense of Cochin identity, even though they worshiped in Bene Israel or Baghdadi synagogues.

In the case of the Cochin Paradesis today, it is clear that their *kambolam* (community) continues to provide a primary identity for its members now scattered in various locations in Israel. There seems to have been a pattern of Malabari congregations settling together geographically when they migrated to Israel, in some cases building their own separate synagogues; but research is needed on the extent to which they have continued their sense of "community" identities.

Comparison with Kaifeng Descent Groups

In Kaifeng there was just one synagogue—thus one *kehillah* (congregation)—for all the Jews in the city, who probably totaled about eight hundred people in the seventeenth century.[14] The existence of just one synagogue would seem to indicate a strong contrast to Cochin, but, on further thought, the surnamed descent groups of the Kaifeng Jews might be seen as carrying out some of the same social functions as the congregational "communities" in India.

In Kaifeng, Jewish marriage was regulated according to Chinese custom, by a division into exogamous patrilineal descent groups identified by surname. By the seventeenth century there were seven of these Jewish descent groups in Kaifeng: Zhao, Li, Ai, Zhang, Jin, Gao, and Shi.[15] The importance in Chinese culture of marrying out of one's descent group cannot be overstressed. Appropriately, one of the earliest mentions of a Jewish presence in Chinese records is a 1340 warning that both Jews and Muslims are prohibited from marrying their paternal cousins.[16]

Like the eight patrilineally organized congregations in Kerala, the surnamed lineages were corporate groups with property in the form of burial grounds. They traditionally kept genealogical records of their members (comparable in some ways to synagogue record books in Cochin and other Jewish communities), and they organized ritual activities associated with veneration of the ancestors. The lineages depended on one another for exchange of marriage partners, with a bride joining the descent group of her husband but probably retaining social ties with her lineage of origin.

As explained by Eber, these surnamed descent groups have been the major vehicle for preserving Kaifeng Jewish identity down to the present time.[17] Organization by lineage kept Jewish families tied to Kaifeng, and thus to their Jewish identity, for generation after generation. Even when various members and families moved far away from the city, they returned to the ancestral burial grounds for important religious rituals. And veneration of their ancestors was always a reminder of their ethnic identity as Jews. Here again I see a parallel between the function of the "community" for Cochin Jews (even those living in Bombay) and the descent group in Kaifeng.

Being aware of various factions among the Cochin Jews, we might ask how these seven Kaifeng Jewish descent groups functioned within the one congregation. The prominence of two particular lineages, at least in the seventeenth century, is illustrated by the presence of two large memorial arches in the courtyard of the synagogue, under which worshipers would pass before going through the main entrance. One bore an inscription honoring the Zhao lineage and the other honored the Ai group. The walled compound of the synagogue also included two ancestral halls, one for the Zhao lineage and one probably dedicated to those of the Li surname.[18] But further evidence suggests that different descent groups were "important" in different ways. Examination of the seventeenth-century Kaifeng Memorial Book shows that ritual leaders in the synagogue came primarily but not exclusively from the Ai and Li lineages. In contrast, members of the Zhao lineage were prominent in the larger Chinese society, including several men who achieved high positions in the government.[19] However, evidence of the economic, political, or ritual prominence of two or three lineages at particular times in history does not tell us whether there were ritual or other distinctions made among them within the Jewish *kehillah*. Nor can we determine whether late nineteenth-century reports of dissensions among various Kaifeng Jewish "clans" reflect earlier conflicts or divisions.[20]

Incorporation of Non-Jews

The remaining issue to be explored is the status of converts and their descendants in both Asian Jewish communities. This seems to be a particularly important question in view of the small size of each community overall, the proportionally large number of converts within each group, and their concern for maintaining clear boundaries around their Jewish identity.

Much more is known about the status of converts among the Kerala Jews than among the Jews of Kaifeng. However, both the historical record and ethnographic studies of the Cochin Jews are muddied by the recent practice of lumping together all Cochin Jewish converts and their descendants under the category *mshuchrarim* including (1) agricultural serfs bound to the land in traditional Kerala fashion; (2) personal servants, who may not have been slaves; (3) *yelide bayit* ("children of the house"), who were the sons and daughters of white Jewish men and "slaves," servants, or non-Jewish women; (4) all other persons who were converted to Judaism in Cochin; and (5) the descendants of persons in any of these categories.

Documentary evidence going back to the sixteenth century mentions Jewish converts in Cochin who were regarded as being of lower status than *myukhasim* (Jews of "pure" lineage). In a 1520 rabbinic Responsum from Cairo, the non-*myukhasim* included converts, *mshuchrarim*, and *yelide bayit*.[21] An early nineteenth-century record from the Paradesi community recorded a census of more than six hundred Jews attending their synagogue. About a third were identified as "white," a third were "slaves" and *mshuchrarim,* and the remaining third were *yelide bayit*.[22] A school census of that period showed that *yelide bayit* boys and girls studied in the same class with the "whites," whereas the "slaves" had a separate school.[23] Yet all three categories of converts were humiliated by the same restrictions—no marriage with "pure" Jews and exclusion from community leadership and from many ritual privileges in the synagogue. Other nineteenth-century records show that non-*myukhasim* were denied ritual equality in certain Malabari synagogues too and that the allegedly "pure" Jews in their communities would not marry them.[24]

It is startling to note that converts from outside Cochin were accepted as ritual equals, at least in the Paradesi synagogue. In contrast the Cochin Jews developed the peculiar custom of accepting local converts into Judaism only through the ritual for manumission and conversion of slaves—whether or not the convert or his or her ancestors had ever been slaves. Thus the local convert would have no choice but to be identified with the lower-status "freed slaves" and their imposed disabilities. I was told of one wealthy Paradesi man in recent years who decided not to have his Hindu wife and children converted to Judaism because they would be counted as *mshuchrarim*; instead the whole family became Christian. Another anecdote concerns a high-caste Christian who wanted to become a Jew, so the elders of the Paradesi community sent him to Calcutta to be converted; when he returned he was counted as their social equal. Such distinctions are no longer practiced today in relation to marriage or synagogue honors, but the memory of these injustices still rankles among the older generation in the Paradesi community. Some contemporary descendants of the so-called *mshuchrarim* seem to believe that their ancestors were slaves, but others insist that they were not.[25]

It is obvious that the lower status of converts in the Cochin Jewish communities must be understood in light of the nature of caste ideology and practice, as well as the history of slavery in Kerala. For example, the local model of a union between social unequals was that of women from the matrilineal Nayar caste who had children by higher-caste Brahmin men. Their children were socially recognized as belonging to the Nayar caste (incidentally, a quite respected status). In a similar fashion, the children of "white" Paradesi men and "slave"/convert women were labeled according to their mothers', not their fathers', status—though in this case they remained within the Jewish *jati* and also within the Paradesi community.[26] Thus Cochin Jewish practice was less restrictive than Hindu caste practice, but more restrictive than the laws of rabbinic Judaism. Outside rabbinic authorities were called to Cochin, and they denounced the Paradesi elders for refusing to grant full equality to the so-called *mshuchrarim*.[27]

Turning to China, much less information is available on incorporation of converts into the Jewish community of Kaifeng. Apparently there was an early practice of converting slaves to Judaism, as a Mongol decree of 1280 forbade both Jews and Muslims to "take dependents or slaves and circumcise them by force."[28] It is not known whether these converts were accepted as full and equal members of the community, or whether the practice of converting male slaves continued after the Mongols prohibited carrying it out by force. Nor is it known what category of "slaves" these were.

The seventeenth-century Memorial Book of the Dead for the Kaifeng Jewish community records only two male converts, one listed in the Zhao lineage (#259, p. 54) and one in the Gao (#240, p. 50).[29] These men may have been adopted into families that had no sons to inherit and carry on the patrilineal line.[30] But, if so, they were still identified as "sons of Adam" rather than as the sons of their adopted Jewish parents. We might ask whether this designation indicates that they (or their descendants) were not accepted as full and equal members of the Jewish community. Clearly a male convert in one's ancestry was not a barrier to social prominence, judging by *Zhao* Yingzheng (born 1619), a grandson of one of the two identified male converts. This prominent scholar and government official, whom Leslie identifies as "the most successful of the Kaifeng Jews in Chinese society," was also an important and respected Jewish communal leader.[31] His situation must be contrasted to that of the prominent Cochin Jewish attorney and politician A.B. Salem, who was excluded from leadership or even ritual equality within the Jewish community because he was labeled as *mshuchrar*.[32] Yet the designation "son of Adam" remains in the Kaifeng Memorial Book, leaving us to wonder about its significance.

What about descent from a female convert? Can we assume that there was absolutely no form of matrilineally inherited ritual status among the Kaifeng Jews? Almost a third of the 380 women in the Memorial Book are labeled "daughters of Adam." Although they are grouped by husbands' (or sons') surnames in the register, in most cases their own lineage of origin is also indicated. Why was it important to record also that these women were not Jewish by birth, given that Jewishness was inherited only through males? Surely a record book does not record unimportant data, but the significance of this designation also remains a mystery—along with the puzzle of how to interpret the Hebrew letter *kaf* accompanying the names of 101 of the women (about a third converts and the rest nonconverts).[33] Likewise, no information is available on conversion practices for women. Did they formally convert at all? Perhaps they were converted through the ritual of immersion in the "ablutions chamber" adjoining the synagogue. Or perhaps a woman was presumed to take on a Jewish identity through marriage itself, as she took on her husband's surname.

Why would a Jewish man marry the daughter of a non-Jew? Some of the female converts may have been from high-status non-Jewish families, bringing prestige and wealth into the Jewish descent groups of their husbands—as demonstrated in a recent oral history interview with a descendent of the Kaifeng Jewish community: "The [Shi] clan had lots of property. Its men selected their brides from clans of important scholars or contributors to the Imperial Court."[34] In her comparative study of early twentieth-century Chinese wives, concubines, and maids, Rubie Watson notes the importance of property brought into a lineage by the dowries of wealthy wives, as well as the benefit of important and prosperous matrilateral kin for the sons of the lineage.[35]

But it also seems possible that some of the women converts were concubines rather than primary wives. For example, there are five "daughter of Adam" wives of *Zhang* Mei, whose first wife was the daughter of a Jew.[36] Perhaps his primary wife died young or failed to produce a son, or perhaps he was simply wealthy and prominent enough to support and enjoy five extra sexual partners. Monogamy was the official marriage practice in China after the Han dynasty, but many wealthy men also took concubines and legitimized their children. A concubine mother would be mourned by her sons (hence recorded in the Memorial Book), though in other respects she usually had a far inferior status in the household, according to Watson.[37]

Finally, there is no firm evidence about the conversion of slaves into the Jewish community after Mongol times. As with the study of India, we must note that there were various categories of slavery and servitude in China. But one surprising entry in the Memorial Book is #551 (p. 85)—*Guo* Shi, "daughter of Adam," nursing-mother (*nai mu*) of (*Zhang?*) Hsiang-yu, whose natural mother is not listed. Presumably she was a servant or slave of some sort, perhaps a convert, who earned a position in the Memorial Book through the devotion of her foster son.[38] I cannot resist mentioning one of the four scriptural passages with which the Memorial Book closes, noting its reference to servitude: "The small and great are there, and the servant (slave) is free from his master (Job 3:19)."[39]

These unanswered questions about social organization among the Kaifeng Jews indicate an urgent need for more historical data. *Wang* Yisha mentions the discovery of additional genealogical material, along with the completion of more oral history interviews.[40] The seventeenth-century Memorial Book itself may reveal further information about historical patterns of marriage and conversion, if it is re-examined in light of such new data.

This ethnohistorical comparison of the Cochin and Kaifeng Jewish communities focuses on issues of social organization, at the levels of individuals (including converts), family, descent group, Jewish "community," and caste. Ongoing comparisons of these two ancient communities of Asian Jews should contribute to broader insights on acculturation and assimilation by Jewish communities, especially in cultures where they have had a secure economic and political place, and where they have not had to contend with anti-Semitism.

Notes

An earlier version of this paper appeared in Hebrew translation in *Pe'amim* 60 (1994), pp. 32–48.

I thank Irene Eber, Maram Epstein, Michael Glatzer, and Itzhak Bezalel for their careful reading of early drafts and for their helpful suggestions.

1. A.B. Salem, *Jew Town Synagogue* (Ernakulam, India, 1929; repr. Haifa: Eliya ben Eliahu, 1972), pp. 21f; Shabdai S. Koder, "A Hebrew Letter of 1768," *Bulletin of the Rama Varma Research Institute* 15 (April 1949), pp. 1–6; Claudius Buchanan, *Christian Researches in Asia* (Boston: Samuel T. Armstrong, 1812), p. 120; Walter Fischel, *Unknown Jews in Unknown Lands* (New York: Ktav, 1973), pp. 115f.

2. Wang Yisha, "The Descendants of the Kaifeng Jews," in *Jews in Old China*, ed. Sidney Shapiro (New York: Hippocrene Books, 1980), pp. 167–86. These contemporary ethnic Jews of Kaifeng are perhaps more comparable to the Bene Israel of India, before they were discovered and re-educated in Judaism by Cochin Jews and English missionaries, than to the Jews of Cochin. See Shirley B. Isenberg, *India's Bene Israel: A Comprehensive Inquiry and Sourcebook* (Berkeley: Judah L. Magnes Museum, 1988), and chapter I.C.1 in this volume, "The Kaifeng Jews and India's Bene Israel: Different Paths."

3. Irene Eber, "K'aifeng Jews Revisited: Sinification as Affirmation of Identity," *Monumenta Serica*, 41 (1993), pp. 231–47, and chapter I.A.2 in this volume, "Kaifeng Jews: The Sinification of Identity.

4. Sources for the following summary of Kerala and Cochin Jewish history are detailed in Barbara Cottle Johnson, "'Our Community' in Two Worlds: The Cochin Paradesi Jews in India and Israel" (Ph.D. diss., anthropology, University of Massachusetts, 1985), chap. 2.

5. For the earliest and most comprehensive survey of scholarship on the copper plates, see Walter J. Fischel, "The Exploration of Jewish Antiquities of Cochin on the Malabar Coast," *Journal of the American Oriental Society* 87 (1967), pp. 230–48. See also Elamkulam P.N. Kunjan Pillai, *Studies in Kerala History* (Kottayam, India: National Book Stall, 1970), pp. 377–88; and M.G.S. Narayanan, *Cultural Symbiosis in Kerala* (Trivandrum: Kerala Historical Society, 1972). For a detailed discussion of the Cochin Jews' relationship with Cranganore (Shingli), see Barbara C. Johnson (Barbara J. Hudson), "Shingli or Jewish Cranganore in the Traditions of the Cochin Jews of India, with an Appendix on the Cochin Jewish Chronicles" (M.A. thesis, Smith College, 1975), and "The Emperor's Welcome: Reconsideration of an Origin Theme in Cochin Jewish Folklore," in *Jews in India*, ed. Thomas Timberg (New York: Advent, 1986), pp. 161–76. In this volume see chapter I.C.3 by Nathan Katz, "The Judaisms of Kaifeng and Cochin: Parallels and Divergences."

6. See note 8.

7. See note 3.

8. The first influential anthropological study of the Cochin Jews was David G. Mandelbaum, "The Jewish Way of Life in Cochin," *Jewish Social Studies* 1 (1939), pp. 423–60, which he revised and expanded as "Social Stratification Among the Jews of

Cochin in India and in Israel," *Jewish Journal of Sociology* 17 (1975), pp. 165–210. Schifra Strizower (*Exotic Jewish Communities* [London: Thomas Yoseloff, 1962] and historian J.B. Segal (*A History of the Jews of Cochin* [London: Vallentine Mitchell, 1993]) follow Mandelbaum's lead in discussing the internal Cochin Jewish divisions as three separate castes. Louis Dumont, *Homo Hierarchicus,* trans. Mark Sainsbury (Chicago: University of Chicago Press, 1970), p. 328, cites both Mandelbaum and Strizower in discussing endogamous groups among the Cochin Jews, which he terms "quasi-castes." Nathan Katz and Ellen S. Goldberg, *The Last Jews of Cochin: Jewish Identity in Hindu India* (Columbia: University of South Carolina Press, 1993), refer to the three divisions as subcastes.

9. I am influenced by a new generation of postcolonial scholars who are questioning the primacy of caste as a basic category for thinking about social and religious organization in India. See, e.g., Arjun Appadurai, "Putting Hierarchy in Its Place," *Cultural Anthropology* 3 (1988), pp. 36–49; Gyan Prakash, "Writing Post-Orientalist Histories of the Third World: Perspectives from Indian Historiography," *Comparative Studies in Society and History* 32 (1990), pp. 383–408. In addition to challenging the assumption advanced by Dumont and his followers that ritually based "hierarchy" is the overwhelming principle in Hindu society as opposed to individualism and equality in the West, these scholars stress the importance of listening to indigenous self-descriptions rather than relying on theoretical models.

10. See Johnson, "Our Community." Also " 'For Any Good Occasion We Call Them': Community Parties and Cultural Continuity Among the Cochin Paradesi Jews of Israel," in *Studies of Indian Jewish Identity,* ed. Nathan Katz (New Delhi: Manohar, 1995), pp. 42–72.

11. One synagogue was located in each of the villages of Parur, Chennamangalam and Mala; three (Kadavumbagam, Tekkumbagam, and Paradesi) were in Cochin; and two (Kadavumbagam and Tekkumbagam) in Ernakulam. Three additional synagogues (Muttath or Muttam, Tirtur, and Palur) have closed since the seventeenth century.

12. See Naphtali Bar-Giora, "Sources-Material for the History of the Relations Between the White Jews and the Black Jews of Cochin," *Sefunoth* 1 (1957), pp. 243–78; "A Note on the History of the Synagogues in Cochin," *Sefunoth* 2 (1958), pp. 214–45.

13. Members of the lower-status factions within each congregation were not eligible to serve on the *yogam.*

14. Michael Pollak, *Mandarins, Jews, and Missionaries: The Jewish Experience in the Chinese Empire* (Philadelphia: Jewish Publication Society, 1980), pp. 317f.

15. Stone inscriptions of 1489 and 1679 note the existence of 70, 73, or perhaps 17 surnames in early times, but only seven are recorded in the much more detailed seventeenth-century Memorial Book. Ibid.

16. Donald D. Leslie, *Islam in Traditional China: A Short History to 1800* (Belconnen: Canberra College, 1986), p. 90. These marriage restrictions are not found among the Cochin Jews; both cross-cousin and parallel cousin marriages are allowable in Jewish law and in many Kerala castes (in contrast to other parts of India, where parallel cousin marriage is also prohibited).

17. See note 3. Some ancestor rituals may still be carried out by Kaifeng Jewish descent groups today; it is hoped that ongoing research will reveal more details and the extent to which members of separate Jewish lineages now intermarry.

18. William C. White, *Chinese Jews: A Compilation of Matters Relating to the Jews of K'ai-feng Fu* (Toronto: University of Toronto, 1942), vol. 1, pp. 2–4.

19. Donald D. Leslie, *The Survival of the Chinese Jews: The Jewish Community of Kaifeng* (Leiden: E.J. Brill, 1972), pp. 42–47.

20. Pollak, *Mandarins, Jews, and Missionaries,* pp.199–200, p. 395 n. 5.

21. Alexander Marx, "Contribution à l'histoire des Juifs de Cochin," *Revue des études juives* 89 (1930), pp. 293–304.
22. Bar Giora, "Sources," p. 251.
23. Michael Sargon, "Letters to Thomas Jarrett," *Jewish Expositor,* vol. 7 (1822), pp. 27–35.
24. Bar-Giora, "Sources," pp. 255–58.
25. Ruby Daniel discusses her family's rejection of the label *mshuchrar.* Ruby Daniel and Barbara C. Johnson, *Ruby of Cochin: An Indian Jewish Woman Remembers* (Philadelphia: Jewish Publication Society, 1995), pp. 11–22. See Johnson, "Our Community," pp. 60–64, 83–87, for the history of A.B. Salem and his family and another perspective on the issue.
26. A 1757 regulation in the Paradesi record book stated: "If an Israelite or a *ger* [apparently, a convert from outside Cochin] marries a woman from the daughters ... of the *mshuchrarim,* the sons who are born to them go after the mother; but the man, the Israelite or *ger,* he stands in the congregation of our community and he has no blemish." Bar Giora, "Sources," p. 252.
27. Ibid., pp. 260–65.
28. Leslie, *Islam in Traditional China,* p. 89, quoting the *Yuan dian jian* of c. 1320. The decree went on to warn: "If the slave lodges a complaint, he can be freed from the place where he serves and the goods and chattels (of the wrongdoer), no matter what, must be handed over to him (the slave)."
29. Donald Leslie has arranged the approximately 1,046 names in this book into family trees reaching back from 1670 into the fifteenth century. See *The Chinese-Hebrew Memorial Book of the Jewish Community of Kaifeng* (Belconnen: Canberra College of Advanced Education, 1984). The Memorial Book is also translated in White, *Chinese Jews,* vol. 3, pp. 28–72.
30. For a discussion of male adoption, see Arthur P. Wolf and Chieh-shau Huang, *Marriage and Adoption in China, 1845–1945* (Stanford: Stanford University Press, 1980), chap. 15. When possible, adopted sons were taken from the same descent line, so these two converts may have been taken from non-Jewish families of the appropriate surnames. Or perhaps they would have been adopted sons-in-law from other lineages, though uxorilocal marriage was not highly regarded (see ibid., chap. 16).
31. See Leslie, *Survival,* pp. 44–46; Pollak, *Mandarins, Jews, and Missionaries,* pp. 328–29.
32. Johnson, "Our Community," pp. 83–87.
33. White, *Chinese Jews,* vol. 3, pp. 24–25, speculates that the "*kaf*" referred to adoption (*ch'i*). Leslie, *Memorial Book,* disagrees but offers no solution to the puzzle.
34. Wang Yisha, "Descendants," p. 174.
35. Rubie S. Watson, "Wives, Concubines, and Maids: Servitude and Kinship in the Hong Kong Region, 1900–1940," in *Marriage and Inequality in Chinese Society,* ed. Rubie S. Watson and Patricia B. Ebrey (Berkeley: University of California, 1991), pp. 231–55.
36. See #541, 542–545 and 556 on pp. 84–86 in the Memorial Book.
37. Watson, "Wives, Concubines, and Maids," p. 243.
38. A discussion of wet-nurses appears in an eighteenth-century novel by Cao Xueqin, *The Story of the Stones,* trans. D. Hawkes (New York: Penguin, 1973). I am grateful to Maram Epstein for this reference.
39. White, *Chinese Jews,* vol. 2, p. 72.
40. Wang Yisha, "The New Trends and Achievements of the Study of Ancient Chinese Jews," trans. Yu Zhiqi (paper presented at a conference on Jewish Diasporas in China: Comparative and Historical Perspectives," Harvard University, August 16–18, 1992).

Chapter I.C.3

The Judaisms of Kaifeng and Cochin: Parallels and Divergences

Nathan Katz

From the perspective of the discipline of religious studies, a comparative study of the religious life of the Jewish communities of Kaifeng, China, and Cochin, India, is particularly instructive. By examining these "exotic" Judaisms, we learn about the cultures in which they flourished, China and India, at the same time as we learn about the mechanisms by which a religion, in this case Judaism, becomes acculturated into its environment.[1]

Jewish religious life is governed by the ethical and ritual code known as *halacha*. This code of law defined the requirements of traditional Jewish life: its dietary code (*kashrut*); system of family purity (*taharat mishpacha*); the observance of Shabbat and Judaism's festivals, fasts, and commemorations; the performance of rites of passage; and ethical and spiritual norms.

Halacha, however, is too generalized to provide explicit guidance in all matters of religious observance. Therefore, local customs (*minhag;* pl. *minhagim*) evolved that enabled Jews to practice *halacha* in the societies in which they lived. In other words, *minhag* is the way *halacha* is observed according to local customs, and *minhagim* vary from place to place. *Halacha* is incomplete without *minhag,* which guides many Jewish observances—especially the life-cycle rituals. *Halacha* provides the framework, but one would be unable to celebrate a *brit milah* (circumcision ritual), a bar mitzvah (the celebration of a male child's religious coming of age), a wedding, or a funeral, unless one relied upon local *minhagim*.[2] To put this point in a more traditional metaphor, *halacha* as oral Torah is God's imperative, and *minhagim* are creative, human responses to that imperative.

In addition to providing the details of Jewish observance and tradition, *minhagim* were especially important in the acculturation of Judaism into the cultures in which it has been found. So long as halachic principles were not breached, Jewish communities adapted local customs, whether Hindu, Confucian, Muslim, or Christian in origin, into their *minhagim*.

As Jewish religious acculturation was manifested in ritual practice through *minhagim,* so Jewish religious thought was influenced as well. How the Jews understood their religion and, perhaps more important for our discussion of the Judaisms of Kaifeng and Cochin, how they understood Judaism's relation to other religions—the dominant, host religion in particular—was another essential aspect of Judaic acculturation.

This chapter examines how Judaism became acculturated into Hindu and Confucian societies; that is, how the Judaisms of Kaifeng and Cochin differed and how they were similar. It explores some of the practices and the religious ideas of the Kaifeng and the Cochin Jews. The contribution to theoretical issues in the study of religions this chapter offers is in the domain of religious acculturation. Any religious tradition, in particular, Judaism, is a complex organism—so much so that some contemporary scholars prefer to analyze traditions in the plural rather than the singular: This chapter defines its subject as "the Judaisms of Kaifeng and Cochin," for example, and not "Judaism in Kaifeng and Cochin." Within the richly diverse symbolic, ritual, and ideational complexes that comprise Judaism are found such clusters of images as the priestly, prophetic, communal, ethical, ascetic, philosophical, and regal. Depending on the values of the culture in which Judaism finds itself, and whether or not that host culture was hostile to Judaism, certain of the clusters rise to the foreground, to borrow the metaphor from Gestalt psychology, and others recede to the background. By examining the foreground/background configurations of the Judaisms of Kaifeng and Cochin, we see reflected Confucian and Hindu sensibilities.

Just as the prophetic threads from Judaism's religious tapestry became foregrounded in Protestant America, so the priestly and regal threads were emphasized in Cochin, and those threads most resonant with Confucian values—familial including ancestral piety, the idealization of the life of the scholar, and civic loyalty—were evident in Kaifeng. It is proposed that this foreground/background reconfiguring of a religious tradition (or, how these configurations establish Judaisms in different host cultures) is a most useful tool for understanding the complex process of religious acculturation.

The Data

Unfortunately, the data from Kaifeng and Cochin are asymmetrical. There remains a Jewish community in Cochin, albeit an attenuated one. As recently as 1986/87, one could observe the full cycle of annual Jewish observances there, and life-cycle rituals were fresh in memory. The rich folklore of the community is still alive, Cochini elders can still be consulted, and many of their *minhagim* have made the transition into an Israeli context.[3]

Not so in Kaifeng, where the Jewish community was said to have been in precipitous decline as long as four centuries ago.[4] Despite the (often ill-informed) observations of Christian missionaries and the scholarship of Donald D. Leslie, many Kaifeng *minhagim* are obscure and many more forgotten—and there is no one to whom to turn for edification.

For this reason, comparisons are difficult and must be tentative. In sum, we are comparing the living tradition of Cochin with the extinct Judaism of Kaifeng. In the former case, we can observe rituals firsthand, but, in the latter case, we have to rely upon speculative reconstructions of what communal life might have been like. Cochin's ritual and liturgical texts are still regularly enacted, but little of Kaifeng's literature remains—although some of its stelae (stone tablets) are suggestive of what the religious life of the community must have been.

Despite these huge variations in the quality of our data, there remains a compelling rationale for comparing the Judaisms of these two most distant outposts of the Diaspora. In both Confucian and Hindu culture, Jews were welcome guests who practiced their religion in freedom. Yet the Jews of Kaifeng ceased to exist as a community more than a century and a half ago, and the Jews of Cochin abandoned their beloved homeland three decades ago. However, even their demises differed. Kaifeng's community assimilated itself out of existence, while the Jews of Cochin made mass *aliyah* (emigration to Israel) and to some extent maintain their identity as an *edah* (ethnic group) in Israel today.[5]

Origins, Welcomes, and Displayed Gifts

The Jews of Cochin and Kaifeng were similar in three ways. They claimed an ancient origin in their homeland, each during the first century of the Common Era. They tell of being welcomed by local kings who gave them land to construct their synagogue and encouraged them to practice their religion. And in their synagogues they prominently displayed gifts from local royalty.

Elite groups in both India and China claim an external origin and longstanding residence in their adopted homes; this is the case in both the Brahmin castes' claim to extrinsic, "Aryan" origin, and the foreign dynasties that ruled from Beijing. Over the centuries, it became a matter of course for nonindigenous communities to claim an ancient entry into their new countries.

This pattern was especially pronounced in India, modeled after both the royal and priestly elites. Modeling themselves after the Brahmins and the maharajahs, Jews, Christians, and Muslims spatially and temporally located their migration into India from their holy lands during their sacred times.

The oldest Christian community in India, the Nazaranee Mapillas of Kerala, trace their origin to the Apostle Thomas, whose arrival at Cranganore, then capital of Kerala, they place in the year 52. Moreover, the textual authority for this claim, *The Acts of Thomas,* has Thomas in Jerusalem receiving Jesus's commission for his mission. The events described in *The Acts of Thomas* were relocated explicitly into Kerala by Maliekel Thoma Rambam in the 1601 Malayalam epic poem, *Thoma Parvam*.[6] Linked together in this legend are sacred time (the era of the Christ), sacred space (Jerusalem), extrinsic origin, and long-standing residency in India (nearly two thousand years).

These four key elements are also found in the origin legend of Kerala's Muslim community, as recorded in the sixteenth-century Arabic historical work *Tohfut-ul-Mujahideen,* by the Kerala Muslim, Shaikh al-Malbari Zain al-Din.[7] Al-Din's narrative locates the origin of Kerala Islam in eighth-century Mecca, Arabia, when a trio of pious pilgrims set out for Adam's Peak in Sri Lanka, stopping in Cranganore en route. Contemporary local Muslims go one better: The Cheraman Juma Masjid, named for Cranganore's dynastic rulers, bears a sign proudly proclaiming it the oldest mosque in India, having been established in 621. This would date the mosque from the lifetime of the Prophet himself, thus connecting Kerala's community directly with Muslim sacred time, in accord with local legend.

Similarly, the Cochin Jews narrate an origin legend connecting them not only with sacred space—Jerusalem—but also with sacred time—the era of the Second Temple.[8] Their claim is that they came to Cranganore in the year 70, fleeing the Roman occupation of Jerusalem and the destruction of the Temple.[9] Their claim is graphically asserted: In the Cochin Synagogue hang paintings depicting the Temple in flames and Jews setting sail for India.[10]

All three legends go a step further in narrating a most hospitable welcome from the Cheraman dynastic maharajah of Cranganore.[11] Several popular Malayalam-language wedding songs have the Indo–Bactrian king Gundaphorus sending for Thomas, a carpenter, to build him a temple as grand as Solomon's. Local traditions claim Gundaphorus to have been a Cheraman maharajah. Like the Muslims and the Jews, the Christians' narrative continues with a royal welcome from "Cheraman Perumal" and the bestowal of a copper-plate–inscribed land grant, bestowing upon them sovereignty at Mahadevapattanam, "the city of the great god," in Cranganore, and rights to the seventy-two traditional privileges of royalty.[12]

The welcome claimed by the Muslims is even more grand. According to their traditions, the king secretly accompanied the three pilgrims back to Mecca, where he converted to Islam.[13] Interestingly, this apostasy is corroborated in local Hindu legends: the quasi-historical Malayalam text the *Keralolpatti*,[14] records the conversion to Islam of the last Cheraman Perumal king, who left for Mecca and thereafter became known as "makkattupoya perumal," the emperor who went to Mecca.[15] As ritual recompense for this familial apostasy, the maharajahs of Travancore used to recite, on receiving their sword of office at their coronation: "I will keep this sword until the uncle who has gone to Mecca returns."[16] In this tradition of royal welcome and patronage, there is a stone inscription at the Muccanti Masjid of Calicut according to which a thirteenth-century Zamorin granted an income for the maintenance of the mosque.[17]

Among the most prized possessions of the Cochin Jews are two inscribed copper plates, kept in the synagogue's *aron ha-kodesh* (holy ark).[18] According to the Cochin Jews' narrative, the plates were given to the leader of the Jews, Joseph Rabban, by "King Cheramanperumal" (a dynastic name; the individual monarch was Bhaskara Ravi Varman) in A.D. 379 (most modern scholars date the plates from the beginning of the eleventh century). Local traditions hold that the plates chartered an independent Jewish principality at Anjuvannam, believed to have been a section of Cranganore, known to the Jews as Shingly (also spelled Shingli). Sovereignty was symbolized by privileges granted to Rabban, including such aristocratic symbols as the use of a parasol and an elephant, the sounding of a trumpet salute, and the commercial prerogative to levy duties and tolls.

Folk songs and wedding rites underscore the importance for future generations of this archetypal relationship between King Bhaskara Ravi Varman and Joseph Rabban. When various circumstances forced the Jews to flee Cranganore and re-establish themselves at Cochin, the local maharajah similarly welcomed the Jews, granting them a plot of land to build their synagogue and residences, adjacent to his palace and temple. This patron/adviser relationship between Hindu maharajahs and Jewish leaders remained essentially unaltered until 1947, when the Princely State of Cochin was amalgamated into an independent Republic of India.

As is the case with the Jews of Cochin, the origin of the Jews of Kaifeng is obscure. The presence of Judeo–Persian words in Kaifeng chronicles led some early writers to conclude a Persian origin for the community, but it demonstrates not Persian origin so much as Persian influence.[19]

The 1663 stele from the Kaifeng Synagogue offers the community's own tradition regarding its origin: "The religion started in T'ien-chu (India), and was first transmitted to China during the Chou. A *tz'u* (ancestral hall) was built in Ta-liang (i.e., Kaifeng). Through the Han, T'ang, Sung, Ming, and up till now, it has undergone many vicissitudes."[20] The Zhou dynasty corresponds roughly to the first millennium B.C., an antique origin indeed. The inscription is also not clear as to the meaning of "T'ien-chu," which usually means India but could be any country to the west of China,[21] possibly Persia or even ancient Israel. Most indigenous traditions date their origin to the Han dynasty (206 B.C.–A.D. 221), as noted by Perlmann: "The Jews themselves, as far as their traditions go, asseverate that their ancestors immigrated to China at the time of the Han Dynasty, i.e., towards the end of the reign of Ming-ti of the East-Han Dynasty, which lasted from 25 to 75 C.E.. The Emperor reigned from 58 to 75 C.E. and is renowned for having introduced Buddhism into China."[22]

The best assessment of modern scholarship is Leslie's:

> It seems legitimate to assume that some Jews, coming via, if not from India, settled in the Chinese ports, and that some of these spread inland. There can also be little doubt that others came in via, if not from Afghanistan, and spread to Ningsia [Ningxia] and Peking [Beijing]. . . . The inscriptions, incidentally, give no hint that they might have come to Kaifeng from anywhere else in China. On the contrary, they imply that the community arrived directly in Kaifeng from a foreign country.[23]

Whenever and from wherever they came to Kaifeng, the Jews took pride in being welcomed by the emperor, much as did the Cochin Jews. The 1489 stele from the Kaifeng Synagogue reads:

> Indeed, the transmission and handing on of the Way of the Religion has an origin. It came from T'ien-chu "India"; in obedience to the (divine?) command it came. There were Li, An, Ai, Kao [Gao], Mu, Chao [Zhao], Chin [Jin], Chou [Zhou], Chang [Zhang], Shih [Shi], Huang, Li, Nieh, Chin [Jin], Chang [Zhang], Tso [Zuo], Pai [Bai], 17 surnames (*hsing* [xing]) in all. They brought western cloth as tribute to the Sung [Song]. The Emperor said: Come to our China, honour and preserve the customs of your ancestors, remain and hand them down in Pien-liang.[24]

Besides admonishing the Jews to practice their religion faithfully, the emperor gave the community through Yen-Tcheng, a Jewish physician, "a present of incense and permission to repair the synagogue. Then was received the grand tablet of the Ming dynasty to be placed in the synagogue. The emperor bestowed honors and titles upon Yen-Tcheng."[25]

The tablet was, of course, displayed in the synagogue as a mark of the emperor's favor. As in the Cochin Synagogue, in the Kaifeng Synagogue were displayed a variety of gifts from their non-Jewish neighbors. But there the similarity ends. In Cochin, with the exception of the copper plates all donated objects were Jewish ritual implements; in Kaifeng, to the contrary, the gifts were essentially Chinese, not Jewish, and in a generous, humanistic spirit symbolized the similarities between Confucian and Judaic beliefs and practices. Overall, they had the unintended consequence of undermining Judaic distinctiveness.

The most prized gentile gifts in the Cochin Synagogue are the copper plates, neither Hindu nor Jewish but establishing the relationship that was to ensue between Hindu maharajahs and Jewish subjects formally until 1947 and informally into the 1990s.[26] Memorialized in folk songs are gifts of land, usually the land upon which Kerala's synagogues were built. Most intriguing is one of the *keterim* (Torah crowns) in the Cochin Synagogue. Made of twenty-two-carat gold and studded with sapphires, rubies, and emeralds, it was donated to the synagogue by the Hindu maharajah of Travancore in 1803. And so it goes: In nearly all of Kerala's synagogues is a list of donations for its construction or refurbishing. And prominent among the donors are Hindu nobility, as well as an occasional Christian, Muslim, or Jain.

The point to note is that in Kerala, gentile gifts to the synagogues were synagogal items. Not so in Kaifeng. In the synagogue courtyards were a number of steles erected by Confucian officials. Reverend Finn was entirely correct when he wrote:[27] "[T]he tablets erected by Gentile neighbors in their very synagogue, open to the world, and challenging contradiction, bear witness to the esteem which this community in general had maintained, and the honors to which members of it have arrived in various pursuits of life."[27] Senior Confucian officials also donated horizontal inscriptions that were displayed in the synagogue itself.[28]

In displaying these steles and inscriptions, the Kaifeng Jews displayed the honor and esteem in which their neighbors held them, just as did the Cochin Jews. But what was written upon these steles casts them in a different light, from a Judaic point of view. For example, the 1663 stele, erected by a Mandarin minister of state, read in part: "They scarcely differ from us in the worship of heaven, in the duties of civil life, or in honouring the dead."[29] This generous spirit of the Confucian minister, which elevated Judaism to a level of his own Confucianism, betrayed a syncretism, an unconscious blending of Jewish and Chinese values and precepts, which came to be adopted by the Jews themselves and which played a role in their ultimate assimilation.

It was not the presence of stelae and inscriptions that was most striking about the Kaifeng Synagogue, however; it was the presence of censers and incense before "ancestor shrines," which, more than any single factor, defined the *minhag* of the Kaifeng community. Not coincidentally, the incense and censers were donated to the synagogue by an emperor of the Ming dynasty (1368–1644).[30] We shall return to the issue of "ancestor worship"; for the present the point to note is the similarity and the difference in the display of items donated by gentiles in the Cochin and Kaifeng synagogues.

Whether from the Han or Song (960–A.D. 1279) eras, the Kaifeng Jews, like the Cochin Jews, claimed ancient origins. When indigenous histories of this sort are confronted, "Not only are the data scattered, equivocal, and all too often poorly presented; but the mode of interpreting them, a matter largely in the hands of philologist, has been . . . sociologically unrealistic in the extreme. . . . [These accounts] have led to a picture . . . which, though not without its element of plausibility, perhaps even truth, has about it the unmistakable air of fantasy systematized which derives from attempting to know what one has no way of knowing."[31] But therein lies the power of these legends; as with all aspects of religion, that power "derives from attempting to know what one has no way of knowing." These narratives from Cochin and Kaifeng, in order to be understood, need to be interpreted not as knowledge itself but as a cognitive framework that organizes, which is to say that (without denying or affirming their factuality) they are truly myths. And this is why origin and welcome legends form essential component in the religious life of the Jews of Cochin and of Kaifeng; why such legends are part and parcel of any Judaism.

Ancestor Worship Versus Enacting Purity and Nobility

Perhaps there is no more dynamic mechanism for Jewish acculturation than embellishments to a community's traditions of religious observance, or *minhagim*. The central ritual strategies for adaptation to life in China and India were ancestor worship in the first case, and the ritual enactments of purity and nobility in second.

As in the case of Cochin Judaism's acculturation to its Hindu context:

> Among the most distinctive features of Indian civilization are two separate sources of power, of social prestige and position . . . the priestly-ascetic and the noble. . . . In their *minhagim* the Cochin Jews have foregrounded the symbols of purity and nobility inherent in Judaism at the same time as they have adapted some of the priestly and royal symbols of Hinduism, making for one of the most exotic systems of Jewish observance found anywhere in the Diaspora. On the one hand, they have appropriated certain Brahmanical symbols of purity in their unique Passover observances. On the other hand, they have adapted aspects of the Nayar's [Kerala's nobility] symbols of

royalty and prosperity in their unique Simchat Torah observances as well as in their marriage customs. Moreover, they managed this syncretism judiciously so as not to contravene *halacha*.[32]

Passover is known among secularized Jews for its ritual meal, the seder, and for family get-togethers. But, among the observant, it has a distinctly ascetical flavor. Preparations for the festival—the systematic, ritualized removing of all foods containing leavening agents from the household, the arduous "spring cleaning," and the expensive substitution or difficult preparation of special foods—are difficult at best. The restrictions that Passover imposes—avoiding grain products and eating dry, flavorless *matzoh*; avoiding almost all social contact with non-Jews—adds an unmistakable asceticism that is reinforced by complaints, jokes, and annually repeated discussions of pertinent laws and statutes. In Cochin all these ascetical elements of Passover are retained, some are exaggerated, and yet other restrictions are added. This practice of Jews to layer restriction upon restriction, religious duty upon religious duty, is known as the "additional observances"—*hiddur mitzvot* that "express the Jew's love of the *mitzvot* by embellishing them."[33] We have detailed these Passover observances elsewhere;[34] the point to note is that by foregrounding Passover's inherent ascetical threads, the Cochin Jews approximated the status-generating ascetical life-style of the Brahmin hereditary priests. This was one of the key strategies by which Cochin Judaism became acculturated into its contexts without jeopardizing its halachic integrity.

As for the second pole of Indian civilization, that of the maharajahs and the nobility, Cochin Judaism foregrounded its "other resources comparable to the noble-kingly symbols of the Nayars, including: (1) the royalty symbolism (*malchut*) of the High Holy Days; (2) the resemblances between the Torah processions (*haqafot* or rodeamentos) of Simchat Torah and Hinduism's deity processions; and (3) the royalty symbolism traditionally ascribed to brides and bridegrooms."[35]

Most significant is the distinctive manner of observing Simchat Torah in the Cochin *minhag*. "Three aspects of the Cochin *minhagim* for Simchat Torah are creative responses to their Hindu environment in Kerala: the displaying of Torah scrolls on a temporary ark, the addition of afternoon *haqafot* outside of the synagogue building, and the ritual dismantling of the ark. Specifically Hinduized symbols of royalty and nobility have been appropriated."[36]

For this festival, not only is the Cochin Synagogue magnificently decorated with silks and satins and bedecked with strands of jasmine, but a temporary ark, covered with rich Benarsi brocades, is constructed in front of the *aron ha-kodesh,* and the synagogue's seven Torah scrolls are displayed on it. This practice reflects the annual (or periodic) removal of a Hindu temple's deity from the *sanctum sanctorum* and its public display on a cart. The addition of, and emphasis placed upon, three *haqafot* during afternoon prayers—striking because this is done nowhere else in the Jewish world— reflects the riotous deity processions of Hindu temples. Finally, the ritualized dismantling of the temporary ark reflects the Hindu practice of disposing of the deity in a body of water, often quite unceremoniously.

It is important to appreciate that, in Cochin Judaism, these "compromises" with Hinduism were not compromises at all. All that was required for their religious acculturation was "an exaggeration of ritual themes inherent in Judaism, not the adoption of alien symbols."[37]

One wishes it were possible to analyze the ritual behavior of the Kaifeng community in as much detail as has been done in the case of Cochin, but it is not. The Kaifeng community has been in decline for four centuries, if we can take *Ai* Tien at his word, and a full cycle of Jewish observances has not been enacted in more than two centuries. Instead of the direct participant-observation possible in Cochin, in Kaifeng we have the often distorted perceptions of missionaries, indirect evidence, and attenuated memories.

Nevertheless, if the accounts available to us are accurate at all, the most striking aspect of Kaifeng's *minhag* is ancestor worship. Our question is whether this practice compromised Kaifeng Judaism's halachic integrity, or whether it was as judicious an acculturation as was the enactment of the symbols of purity and nobility in Cochin Judaism, which was unproblematic from an halachic standpoint. To put the question more pointedly: did ancestor worship (if that is the right term for the Confucian practice) reflect and model assimilation rather than acculturation? Was ancestor worship a metaphor for the ultimate demise of Kaifeng Judaism?

The Jesuit missionary Jean-Paul Gozani, who lived in Kaifeng between 1698 and 1718, noted the role of the ancestors in Kaifeng Judaism, when he wrote in 1704:

> At our going out of the synagogue is a great hall,[38] which I had the curiosity to look into. I saw nothing in it except a great number of incense bowls. They told me this was the place where they honoured their holy men (*sheng-jen*) or great men of their Law. The largest of these incense bowls, which is for the Patriarch Abraham, stands in the middle of the hall. After this stand those of Isaac, of Jacob, of his twelve children, called by them the Twelve Descents or Tribes of Israel. Next are those of Moses, Aaron, Joshua, Ezra, and of several illustrious persons both men and women.[39]

Based upon his studies of Jesuit records, the nineteenth-century British missionary and diplomat, the Reverend James Finn was also intrigued by the role of ancestors in Kaifeng Judaism:

In the matter of venerating the dead, it is still uncertain whether or not the Chinese carry it to the extent of adoration; but, like them, the Israelites in that country burn lamps before the names of their ancestors; and the sacrifices of incense, accompanied by the former at the parental graves at certain recurring periods, are nearly paralleled even among Jews in Europe and Palestine, when they visit the burial-places upon the Day of Atonement, reciting the names of departed friends or relatives, and praying to them according to a ritual called "The answer of the tongue."[40]

Two knowledgeable Jews who wrote about the Kaifeng community around the turn of the century, the German-born, English-raised Marcus Nathan Adler and an Austrian trader, J.L. Liebermann, discussed this ancestor worship from quite a different point of view from Gozani's or Finn's. Perlmann, who probably visited Kaifeng, cited the relevant passage from the synagogue's 1489 stele:

> But to venerate Heaven and to neglect ancestors is to fail in the services which are their due. In the spring and autumn, therefore, men sacrifice to their ancestors, to show that they serve the dead as they do the living, and pay the same respect to the departed that they do to those who survive, they offer sheep and oxen, and present the fruits of the season, to show that they do not neglect the honour due to ancestors, when they are gone from us.[41]

And Adler, based on his readings, described the ancestor hall in the synagogue:

> In the second division of the court was the hall of ancestors (*Tsoo-tang* [Zutang]). Here were venerated—probably at the high festivals in the spring and autumn—the Patriarchs of Old Testament history after the Chinese manner. The name of each was recorded on a tablet; there were no pictures; to each of them was assigned a censer for incense, the largest being for Abraham, others for the other patriarchs, Moses, Aaron, Joshua and Ezra.[42]

In attempting to account for this custom, which appears unique from a Jewish point of view, Perlmann commented upon the practice of displaying gifts from local notables in the synagogue:

> Although this custom is hardly compatible with Jewish law, it may be excused when taking into consideration that the censers were presented to them by the Emperor (of the Ming Dynasty, 1368–1644 A.D.) And it was the Emperor himself who gave them the necessary instructions for burning the incense; and after all it was not used for idolatrous purposes.[43]

Gozani wrote that the custom was entirely Chinese, except for avoiding the use of images: "They honour their dead in the Tz'u-t'ang, or Hall of the Ancestors, with the same ceremonies as are employed in China; but without tablets, they being forbidden the use of images and of everything of that kind."[44] Being more familiar with Jewish practices, Leslie noted the very strong parallel between Confucian ancestor worship (if, indeed, that is an accurate name for the practice) and Jewish memorial services: "The Jewish Yiskor and Jahrzeit services for the dead are similar to Chinese ancestor worship, even though the Jewish theologians insist that it is only God who is prayed to."[45]

Kaifeng Jews adopted some other Confucian practices as well, including the use of Jewish "sacred books in casting lots, and their literary men pay the same homage to the memory of Kung-foo-sze (Confucius) as their neighbors do."[46] Such a practice, like the foregrounding of the thrice-annual *yizkor* rite for the dead and annual marking of relatives' death anniversaries, do not seem to compromise Kaifeng Judaism. As with the foregrounding of ascetical and noble symbol complexes in Cochin Judaism, the Kaifeng Jews were emphasizing certain Judaic rituals that approximated Confucian practices. But what of the reverence for Confucius, mentioned by Finn? Did that practice, about which we know so very little, indicate a compromise beyond acceptable Judaic boundaries?

Ethics of Religious "Civilness"

The Kaifeng Jews' reverence for Confucius must be viewed in the context of the Chinese ethical teachings with which he is most closely associated. As recorded in the stele of 1488, the Jews found in Chinese traditions a system of ethics deeply resonant with their own:

> Although our religion agrees in many respects with the religion of the literati [Confucianism, Buddhism, and Taoism], from which it differs in a slight degree, yet the main design of it is nothing more than reverence for Heaven, and veneration for ancestors, fidelity to the prince, and obedience to parents, just that which is included in the five human relations, the five constant virtues, with the three principal connections of life.[47]

It is not difficult to see the relationship between Judaic and Confucian values. For examples: Reverence for "Heaven," the Confucian value, corresponds to reverence for God, as *Tian* (Heaven) is the Chinese character used by Jews, Muslims, Christians, and Confucians alike to translate "God."[48] Veneration for ancestors, as noted, is a value underlying both Confucian ancestor worship and Judaic *yizkor* and death anniversary rite. Obedience to parents is cardinal in both traditions and is one element in the Mosaic decalogue. The five human relationships were Confucius's model for harmonious human interactions, both in the home (*shalom ha-bayit*) and in society at large.

From a Confucian point of view, fidelity to the prince is an extension of the principle of obedience to parents. From a Judaic perspective, the halachic principle is that the law of the land in which Jews live is binding upon Jews, so long as the law of the land does not contravene *halacha*.[49] Jews emphasize this sort of patriotism, quite naturally, in nations that treat the Jews well, such as India and America. This sentiment is clearly expressed in the stele of 1488: "[S]eeing that we have received the favors of the prince, and enjoyed the emoluments conferred by him, we carry to the utmost our sincerity in worship with the view of manifesting fidelity to our prince, and gratitude to our country."[50] In Confucian society, fidelity to the prince was understood as a prerequisite for civilized life, a view endorsed in Chinese Judaism. But more generally, as Leslie aptly summarized, it was in the domain of ethics that Confucianism and Judaism have the greatest similarity, as perhaps do all of the great religions of the world, and it was in the domain of ethics that acculturation was least problematic:

> To turn to ethics, there is sufficient similarity between the customs and beliefs about good and evil in almost all civilized communities for harmony [between Jewish and Confucian ideas] to be easily achieved. One has no difficulty in finding parallels between the Confucian and Jewish classics. Manchus, the Li-chi, the I-Ching, are quoted to demonstrate the similarities. We may note, in particular, filial piety and ritual, reliance on tradition and the written word, all strongly emphasized in both cultures.[51]

Indigenous "Theologies"

Apparently, however, the Jews' religious acculturation into Confucian society did not end with ethics. There was, rather, an increasing identification with Confucian and Daoist concepts and practices, and gradually they maintained less and less religious distinctiveness. For example, a painted board in the Kaifeng Synagogue proclaimed: "From the time of Alo (Abraham), when our religion was first established, and ever afterwards, China has diffused instruction and obtained the knowledge of the whole system propagated by Confucius, Buddha, and Lautze [Laozi]."[52] Leslie gives several examples of this religious identification:

> Here are some examples of the conscious attempt to demonstrate the close similarity of Judaism to Confucianism. "The Confucian religion and this religion agree on essential points, differing only on secondary ones (1489) ... these

principles do not go beyond the Five Relationships (of Confucianism) (1489).... Although the written characters of the Scriptures of this religion are different from the script of the Confucian books, yet on examining their principles, it is found that their ways of common practice are similar (1512)."[53]

This identification of Judaic with Confucian religious ideas, according to some scholars, was the model of and model for their assimilation.[54]

Perlmann was the first to suggest that this religious identification with Confucian tradition, spurred by the very high cultural and ethical standards prevalent in Chinese society, was a factor that contributed to the demise through assimilation of the Kaifeng community:

> Two forces combined worked simultaneously towards the doom of the Jews in China, one of them being of a physical character, and the other of a purely spiritual one. By the physical force I mean the overwhelming majority of the native people, which, in a case of being not of a lower cultural standing than the alien minority, and if in intercourse with the foreigner treats him kindly, not making him feel to be a stranger, must in course of time, by quite a natural process grind the minority, crumble off parts of them and gradually absorb them. This normal process, which acted upon the Jews of China had been considerably accelerated by inundations and revolutions which time after time decimated them and lessened their power of resistance. By the spiritual force I understand the high ethical and philosophical standing of the religions of China at that time, which ... caused the Jews to abdicate their superiority, to take up Chinese learning, and to assimilate to and mingle with the dominant majority.[55]

A similar point was later emphasized by Wendy Abraham. Having considered the many scholarly explanations for the assimilation of Kaifeng Jews, she more than any other scholar attributes their assimilation to an inherent similarity between Confucian and Judaic traditions, which led the Jews to lose their sense of people "called apart" (*am segulah*):

> While some have attributed the reasons for Jewish assimilation into Chinese society to isolation from the rest of the Jewish world since the Ming dynasty (1368–1644), if not before, or the lack of persecution by the Chinese government, others have posited that their assimilation was due, rather, to the fact that the Jews took and passed the Chinese civil service exam in disproportionate numbers to their population, leading to their being assigned cities other than their own, to the Confucianization of intellectuals, intermarriage in their newly adopted towns and the acculturation of the Kaifeng Jewish community which was still under the influence of these Jewish Confucians.... [It was] the Chinese educational system ... [and its similarity to] the educational values held by Jews at their time of entry into China and through the time they were most likely cut off from the rest of world Jewry, [which] were

so similar to those held by the Chinese at the time that it could not have done otherwise than attract them [to the Chinese civil service]. . . . [B]oth people's educational values, in particular the perceived link between the cultivation of individual and communal ethics . . . and national survival . . . [as well as] similarities between Talmudic and Confucian methods of teaching and learning . . . led to their inevitable participation and success in the civil service exam, with the resultant assimilation into Chinese society.[56]

Living in such a tolerant culture with values perceived as similar, if not identical, to their own, Kaifeng Jews gradually neglected Judaic traditions, especially as their best and brightest studied Confucian classics for the civil service examinations, a process highlighted in Abraham's analysis. As Leslie observed, synagogue inscriptions and banners became more Confucian than Judaic: "The terminology of the Chinese inscriptions from the synagogue is highly Confucian, with a few touches of Taoism. The ideas expressed are sometimes Jewish in Confucian garb, but more often Confucian per se. We hardly ever find passages from the Jewish Law translated into Chinese."[57]

The Judaisms of Cochin and Kaifeng were both similar and different in their relationship to their local religious environments, Hindu and Confucian. They were similar in the way they adapted local ritual practices into their *minhagim*. In Cochin, it was the ascetical and noble symbols of Kerala's Hinduisms that found their way into Judaic practices—Passover and Simchat Torah in particular. In Kaifeng, it was the foregrounding of Judaic "ancestor worship"—*yizkor* and death anniversaries. Neither of these sets of ritual acculturation were problematic.

But they were also very different, for several reasons. While both Judaisms incorporated gifts from the local nobility into their synagogues, in Cochin these gifts were essentially Judaic (Torah crowns, carpets used for the *duchen* rite, and so on, with the notable exception of the copper plates, which are religiously neutral), in Kaifeng these gifts were Confucian (incense holders, steles, and painted boards emblazoned with other-than-Judaic slogans).

These displays reflected differing ideational and social realities. At the ideational level, the Cochin Jews never went so far as to identify their religious ideas with Hindu ideas, despite the great respect and gratitude that characterized their view of their neighbors' religions. For example, in their indigenous literature Cochini authors tended to emphasize Judaism's distinctiveness from the Hinduism, Islam, and Christianity of their neighbors.[58] In the inscriptions of the Kaifeng Jews, it was similarities with Confucianism, Taoism, and Buddhism that were given prominence.

At the social level, we are confronted with the profound differences in the societies in and around Kaifeng and Cochin. First, however, one vitally important similarity in these otherwise disparate cultures must be emphasized: Both Chinese and Indian cultures were tolerant in the extreme; the Jews of Kaifeng and the Jews of Cochin never experienced anti-Semitism, making them unique among the world's Jews; and the Jews of both China and India enjoyed freedom of religion among other freedoms and prospered in the security of these noble cultures.

As Abraham emphasized in her doctoral dissertation, leading Kaifeng Jews entered the Chinese civil service. To do so, they neglected Judaic learning for the Confucian classics, which were the basis of the civil service examination. The very openness of the civil service to foreigners was the key factor in Jewish assimilation and the demise of Chinese Jewry.

In traditional, hierarchical India, however, such assimilation was never an option. Traditional Indian society was a complex system of localized and caste-bound cultures that interacted through the principle of hierarchy.[59] The much-vaunted Hindu "tolerance," a term that does not do justice to the actual experience of Jews there, is in many senses the antithesis of Chinese "tolerance"—or, for that matter, of the secular–liberal modern version of "tolerance" found in the West and Westernized worlds. Traditional Hindu "tolerance" does not posit a universal culture, a universal religion, or a universal human nature to which all aspirants for success in a society must adhere and conform. Rather, the hierarchical nature of traditional India creates the societal space for human diversity, a space that has accommodated wave after wave of refugees—first Jews, and later Nestorian Christians, then Zoroastrians, and most recently Tibetans. China, too, welcomed foreigners, and foreign enclaves took pride in their sinicization. But sinicization proved fatal to the Jewish communities who embraced the opportunities it afforded. In India, success and status were more matters of fidelity to one's own tradition than mastery of another's. And therein lies the essential divergence between the Judaisms of Cochin and Kaifeng.

Notes

A version of this paper was published in *Numen* 42 (1995), pp. 110–40, and is reprinted here with permission.

1. The clearest framework for the comparative study of minority Jewish communities was offered by Stephen Sharot, "Minority Situation and Religious Acculturation: A Comparative Analysis of Jewish Communities," *Comparative Studies in Society and History* 16 (1974), pp. 329–54.

2. Rabbi Abraham Chill, *The Minhagim: The Customs and Ceremonies of Judaism, Their Origins and Rationale* (New York: Sepher-Hermon Press, 1979), p. vii.

3. See Barbara C. Johnson, " 'For Any Good Occasion We Call Them': Commu-

nity Parties and Cultural Continuity Among the Cochin Paradesi Jews of Israel," in *Studies of Indian-Jewish Identity,* ed. Nathan Katz (Ann Arbor: Association for Asian Studies Monographs Series; and New Delhi: Manohar, 1994).

4. So the Kaifeng Jew, *Ai* Tien, reported to the Jesuit Matteo Ricci. See James Finn, "The Jews in China: Their Synagogue, Their Scriptures, Their History," in *Jews in Old China: Some Western Views,* ed. Hyman Kublin (New York: Paragon, 1971 [1843]), p. 11.

5. Cf. Barbara C. Johnson, "Cochin Jews and Kaifeng Jews: Some Thoughts on Caste, Clan, 'Communities' and Conversion" (paper presented at a conference on Jewish Diasporas in China: Comparative and Historical Perspectives, Harvard University, August 16–18, 1992), p. 2. See also chapter I.C.2 in this volume: "The threat to survival . . . is . . . loss of Indianess through assimilation into Israeli culture."

6. P.J. Thomas, "The South Indian Tradition of the Apostle Thomas," *Journal of the Royal Asiatic Society of Great Britain and Ireland* (1924), p. 214.

7. Lt. M.J. Rowlandson, trans., *Tohfut-ul-mujahideen, an Historical Work in the Arabic Language,* by Zain al-Din (London: Oriental Translation Fund, 1833).

8. We are using the terms "sacred space" and "sacred time" as first suggested by Mircea Eliade in *The Sacred and the Profane: The Nature of Religion* (New York: Harcourt, Brace & World, 1959).

9. At different times, the Cochin Jews narrated alternative origin legends. For example, a couple of centuries back when Europe was in search of lost tribes, they claimed to be a lost tribe. Some of their Malayalam-language folk songs indicate a Persian origin, and at times Yemen was proclaimed their ancestral home. Today's version claims a dual ancestry from Jerusalem and Cranganore; the reasons for these narrative shifts are explored in Nathan Katz and Ellen S. Goldberg, *The Last Jews of Cochin: Jewish Identity in Hindu India* (Columbia: University of South Carolina Press, 1993).

10. This analysis of the Cochin Jews' origin legends follows upon the work of Barbara C. Johnson, "The Emperor's Welcome: Reconsiderations of an Origin Theme in Cochin Jewish Folklore," in *The Jews of India,* ed. Thomas A. Timberg (New Delhi: Vikas, 1986), pp. 161–76.

11. The meaning of Cranganore for the Cochin Jews is explored in Barbara C. Johnson, "Shingli or Cranganore in the Traditions of the Cochin Jews of India, with an Appendix on the Cochin Jewish Chronicles" (M.A. thesis, Smith College, 1975).

12. See Johnson, "Cochin Jews and Kaifeng Jews," p. 3. See also chapter I.C.2 in this volume.

13. Similarly, Knani Christians narrate how the "Cheraman Perumal" king who welcomed the Christian missionary who founded their community, Thomas of Cana in A.D. 345, converted to Christianity and made pilgrimage to the tomb of St. Thomas the Apostle in Mylapore, Madras. There he died and was buried alongside the apostle. "It seems that Chereman Perumal is a good empty name to fill with whatever events satisfy the audience of the faithful. He legitimates one or another foreign religion in India by welcoming its proselytes and himself becoming a convert in the end." Richard Michael Swiderski, *Blood Weddings: The Knanaya Christians of Kerala* (Madras: New Era Publishers, 1988), p. 64.

14. William Logan, *Malabar* (Trivandrum: Charithram Publications, 1981), vol. 1, p. 265.

15. M.G.S. Narayanan, *Cultural Symbiosis in Kerala* (Trivandrum: Kerala Historical Society, 1972), p. ix.

16. Logan, *Malabar,* p. 269.

17. Narayanan, *Cultural Symbiosis in Kerala,* pp. 38–42.

18. See Johnson, "Cochin Jews and Kaifeng Jews," [pp. 3, 4]. See also chapter I.C.2 in this volume.

19. Finn, "The Jews in China," p. 42; see also Edward I. Ezra and Arthur Sopher, "Chinese Jews," in Kublin, ed., *Jews in Old China,* p. 222.
20. Donald D. Leslie, *The Survival of the Chinese Jews: The Jewish Community of Kaifeng* (Leiden: E.J. Brill, 1972), p. 3.
21. Ibid., p. 18.
22. S.M. Perlmann, "The History of the Jews in China," in Kublin, ed., *Jews in Old China,* p. 125.
23. Leslie, *The Survival of the Chinese Jews,* p. 22.
24. Ibid., pp. 22–23.
25. Marcus N. Adler, "Chinese Jews: A Lecture," in Kublin, ed., *Jews in Old China,* p. 97.
26. Cochin's leading Jewish family, the Koders, were still meeting and dining on palm leaves with the maharajah in 1989.
27. Finn, "The Jews in China," p. 68.
28. Leslie, *The Survival of the Chinese Jews,* p. 40.
29. Finn, "The Jews in China," p. 62.
30. Perlmann, "The History of the Jews in China," p. 129.
31. Clifford Geertz, *Negara: The Theatre State in Nineteenth-Century Bali* (Princeton: Princeton University Press, 1980), p. 25.
32. Nathan Katz and Ellen S. Goldberg, "The Ritual Enactments of the Cochin Jews: The Powers of Purity and Nobility," *Journal of Ritual Studies* 4, no. 2 (summer 1990), pp. 200–201.
33. Chill, *The Minhagim,* p. xx.
34. Nathan Katz and Ellen S. Goldberg, "Asceticism and Caste in the Passover Observances of the Cochin Jews," *Journal of the American Academy of Religion* 57, no. 1 (1989), pp. 53–82.
35. Katz and Goldberg, "The Ritual Enactments of the Cochin Jews," p. 202.
36. Ibid., p. 230.
37. Ibid., p. 231.
38. Cf. Shirley B. Isenberg, "The Kaifeng Jews and India's Bene Israel: Different Paths" (paper presented at a conference on Jewish Diasporas in China: Comparative and Historical Perspectives, Harvard University, August 16–18, 1992), p. 5. See also chapter I.C.1 in this volume.
39. Leslie, *The Survival of the Chinese Jews,* p. 81.
40. Finn, "The Jews in China," pp. 73–74.
41. Perlmann, "The History of the Jews in China," p. 177. Wendy Abraham notes that the form of ancestral sacrifice described in the stele is identical to that prescribed in the Confucian classic, *The Doctrine of the Mean.* Wendy Abraham, "The Role of Confucian and Jewish Educational Values in the Assimilation of the Chinese Jews of Kaifeng, Supplemented by Western Observer Accounts, 1605–1985" (Ed.D. dissertation, Columbia University Teachers College, 1989), p. 55.
42. Adler, "Chinese Jews: A Lecture," p. 104.
43. Perlmann, "The History of the Jews in China," p. 129.
44. Leslie, *The Survival of the Chinese Jews,* p. 88.
45. Ibid., p. 101.
46. Finn, "The Jews in China," p. 29. Unfortunately, Finn gives no evidence that Jews used their Torah for divination, as do Confucians with the *I Ching* (Yi jing). One wonders about the techniques employed.
47. Perlmann, "The History of the Jews in China," pp. 182–83.
48. Leslie, *The Survival of the Chinese Jews,* p. 98.
49. This principle of Judaic "civicness" was first articulated in Babylonia in the third

century A.D. by Mar Samuel of Nehardea, who ruled that "the law of the ruling authority (*malkhuta*) is the law." It was restated by the twelfth-century French authority Rabbi Samuel ben Meir (Rashba), who opined, "All the levies and taxes and legal procedures enacted by kings in their kingdoms are binding as law (*dina*)." See David Novak, *Jewish-Christian Dialogue: A Jewish Justification* (New York: Oxford University Press, 1989), pp. 42–43.

    50. Perlmann, "The History of the Jews in China," p. 183.
    51. Leslie, *The Survival of the Chinese Jews*, p. 101.
    52. Ezra and Sopher, "Chinese Jews," p. 245.
    53. Leslie, *The Survival of the Chinese Jews*, p. 102.
    54. We employ Geertz's understanding of a religious symbol as "model of/for" to describe the process by which a religious symbolization simultaneously reflects empirical realities and shapes those realities. Clifford Geertz, "Religion as a Cultural System," in *The Religious Situation* (Boston: Beacon Press, 1968–69), vol. 2, pp. 639–88. Similarly, the founder of the social-scientific approach to the study of religion, Emile Durkheim, held that we misunderstand religious ideals (or symbols) if we separate those ideals from the real, empirical world. Rather, Durkheim argued, the "ideal" and the "real" are mutually determinative. Emile Durkheim, "The False Dichotomy of the Real and the Ideal," in *The Elementary Forms of the Religious Life* (New York: Macmillan, 1961), pp. 469–72, 474–79.

    55. Perlmann, "The History of the Jews in China," p. 197.
    56. Abraham, "Confucian and Jewish Educational Values," pp. i–ii.
    57. Leslie, *The Survival of the Chinese Jews*, p. 102.
    58. See, for example, the analysis of the sacred calendars of Judaism, Hinduism, Islam, and Christianity by David Rahabi, *Hasefer David Rahabi* (Amsterdam: Proops, 1791).
    59. See Louis Dumont, *Homo Hierarchicus: The Caste System and Its Implications* (Chicago and London: University of Chicago Press, 1980).

Part II

Nineteenth-Century Baghdadi and Ashkenazi Experiences in India, China, and Japan

Part II

Chapter II. A

Baghdadi Jews in India and China in the Nineteenth Century: A Comparison of Economic Roles

Joan G. Roland

India's Bene Israel and Cochin Jews and China's Kaifeng Jews were long-established communities whose origins and subsequent history have challenged scholars. Both India and China, however, were also host to a more recently arrived Jewish community, the Iraqis, or Baghdadis, who, as members of an ancient trading diaspora, headed east for the new entrepôts established by European commerce in India, China, Singapore, Burma, and Japan. This chapter explores the parallels and differences, as well as the interconnections, between the economic activities in India and China of this successful trading community, which contributed so greatly to the commercial development of Asia in the nineteenth century.

In the nineteenth century, when Jews from Eastern and Central Europe were migrating westward, Jews from that part of the Ottoman empire that is now Iraq began migrating eastward to Asia and Australia.[1] A decline in commerce during a series of revolutions and political harassment threatened their economic position. The port of Basra on the Persian Gulf had been a trading center of the British East India Company from 1760 onward, and many Jews from Basra and Baghdad who had already played an important role in the English commerce in the region gradually moved on to India, settling first in the port of Surat, 165 miles north of Bombay on the western coast. Referring originally to Jews who came from the area between the Tigris and Euphrates rivers, for centuries a center of Jewish learning and culture, the term *Baghdadi* or *Iraqi* soon came to include as well Jews from Syria and other parts of the Ottoman empire, Aden, and Yemen, all of whom were Arabic-speaking, and even Jews from Persia and Afghanistan, who were not. Referring more to their pronunciation of Hebrew and religious liturgy, than to their geographic origin, they often considered themselves Sephardim.[2]

As the British presidencies (major administrative subdivisions) of Calcutta and Bombay developed, however, Surat lost its preponderant position as a port and the Jewish merchants began to look for new commercial opportunities. Indians could take greater advantage of the growing trade and commerce of the eighteenth century in Bombay than they could in Calcutta, where the British monopolized the production and export trade to London of jute, tea, and indigo. But Indians could participate in Bombay's cotton and opium trade, which, heading primarily eastward, was not affected by the British monopoly. Encouraged by the British to go to India to expand commerce, leading Baghdadi families such as the Eliases, Kadoories, Abrahams, Hardoons, Ezras, Solomons, and Gubbays became wealthy merchants or acted as middlemen for the large cotton-, jute-, and tobacco-processing plants. Many of these Baghdadis became British citizens and were very loyal to Britain. Some became leaders of Asian industry, banking, trade, and real estate. Indeed, Timberg has suggested that these Baghdadi communities can be looked at from three perspectives: as units in the Baghdadi diaspora extending from London to Shanghai, as ancillaries to the British as commercial pioneers, and as units in an integrated Indian trading system.[3]

The most prominent family by far was the Sassoons, with whom the other leading families intermarried. A scion of a family that had long held the position of chief treasurer to the governor of Baghdad, but whose political fortunes had waned, David Sassoon (1792–1864) had escaped the oppression of Daud Pasha (governor of Baghdad, 1817–31), landing in Bombay in 1832. The economic empire that the Sassoons eventually established, with centers in Bombay, Calcutta, Rangoon, Hong Kong, Shanghai, Singapore, and elsewhere, and their great charitable enterprises earned for them the title of "Rothschilds of the East." The history of the Iraqi Jewish community in India and China is closely connected with that of the house of Sassoon.

David Sassoon entered the import–export arena of Bombay, then dominated by wealthy Parsis and English merchant houses. He began by exporting English textiles from Bombay to Persia, Iraq, and nearby lands, and importing products and textiles of these countries to be resold to the British in India. His familiarity with local countries, conditions, and languages, his reliable Jewish correspondents in all centers, and his firm's reputation for absolute integrity soon made his business one of the largest operating in the region. He gradually extended into Central Asia and southern China, trading in Bombay yarn, English piece-goods, and opium. By the next decade, he had purchased much real estate. Sir Bartle Frere, the governor of Bombay, described him as "the first of our non-European merchants in wealth and respectability."[4] David Sassoon was also an observant Orthodox Jew. Initially, all the firm's accounts and correspondence were in Judaeo–Arabic script. Business stopped daily at the appropriate times for Jewish prayer, and, in the early days at least, offices, branches, and workshops closed on Saturday as well as on Sunday, the official day of rest.

Word spread among the poorer Jews in Baghdad and even in Aleppo and Damascus that employment was available in the firm of David Sassoon and Company in Bombay. Sassoon not only arranged food, housing, and medical care for the new arrivals but established a school to educate their children where, in addition to the languages and basic arithmetic they would need to hold jobs, the children also studied the rudiments of their faith, including ritual slaughter of animals, so that they could eat meat if they were sent to places where there was no established Jewish community.[5] The Sassoons also established cemeteries and synagogues.

David Sassoon's philanthropy was not limited to his coreligionists. He also contributed enormously to the development of Bombay, financing the Sassoon Reformatory and Industrial Institution for Juvenile Offenders, the Sassoon Mechanics Institute, an illuminated clock-tower for the Victoria and Albert Museum, and a marble statue of the prince consort, with a Hebrew inscription.

After David Sassoon's death, his eldest son, Abdullah, who also called himself Albert, assumed the management of the firm and became a major force in developing the textile industry in Bombay. He opened a series of cotton mills that, along with Parsi enterprise, helped revolutionize the weaving industry in India and enabled Bombay to grow, in the second half of the nineteenth century, into an important manufacturing city.[6] He promoted and financed the construction of the first wet dock in Bombay, still known as the Sassoon dock, which greatly stimulated the city's commercial growth. Following in his father's philanthropic footsteps, Albert-Abdullah contributed toward the reconstruction of Elphinstone High School and financed many scholarships, becoming a close adviser to the government on educational and building projects. He also became a leading member of the Chamber of Commerce and a member of the Bombay Legislative Council from 1868 to 1872. His contacts with Persia and China were helpful to the British, who were concerned about Russian ambitions in Persia and Central Asia. In 1872, Albert Sassoon was knighted.[7]

Jealous of the assumption of leadership by Albert-Abdullah, his next younger brother, Elias, resigned from the parent firm and established a rival company to be known as E.D. Sassoon and Company. The original firm,

David Sassoon and Company (variously known as David Sassoon and Sons or David Sassoon, Sons, and Company), continued to act as general merchants; the new firm became involved mainly in banking and property and ultimately became more prosperous. While the decisions for David Sassoon and Company were made increasingly by the branches of the family settled in London, those for E.D. Sassoon continued to be made in Bombay.

At Elias Sassoon's death, the E.D. Sassoon firm was taken over by his son Jacob, who established new mills and further expanded the cotton industry. In 1880, Jacob Sassoon actively recruited workers from Baghdad, promising them the usual benefits and facilities until, at one point, the mills of his firm employed fifteen thousand people (only a small fraction of whom were Jews). He was soon the largest single employer of factory labor in and around Bombay. "In the history of the cotton textile industry in western India, the name of Jacob Sassoon stands out more prominently than that of any other single individual, not excepting even his Parsee rival Jamsetji Tata."[8] His philanthropy also extended beyond his own community, throughout the empire. In recognition of his service to the development of India, Jacob Sassoon was knighted in 1909. By the end of the nineteenth century, the two Sassoon firms represented the largest single conglomeration of mills in India. After 1891, when a heavier excise was placed on Indian cotton and several Bombay mill owners had to close down, the Sassoons were among the few to survive. And yet, as Jackson has pointed out, the Sassoons were merchants rather than industrialists. In India, the Tatas displayed more enterprise and branched out into real estate, chemicals, and cement, and eventually created an enormous hydroelectric generating plant in Jamshedpur.[9]

When David Sassoon arrived in Bombay in 1832, nearly one-third of the Bombay presidency's trade came from the export of opium. Eventually, the East India Company ceased transporting opium but gave shipping licenses to British and Parsi merchants and a few new exporting firms like the Sassoons. In Calcutta, Jews predominated in the opium trade. According to Musleah, in April 1884, of a total of 3,763 chests of opium shipped to China, 2,918 belonged to Jews: 1,040 to David Sassoon and a total of 1,878 to Calcutta merchants. The Calcutta Jews apparently controlled enough of the opium trade to depress the market by boycotting the government auctions of the raw product and then buying it up when prices had declined. Their only real competitors were the Marwaris, who had migrated to Calcutta from western India.[10]

Some Calcutta Jews exported indigo, silk, woolens, and cotton products; others imported goods from Europe. There were small independent merchants and white-collar workers with jobs in government agencies and commercial firms. The Hebrew–Arabic newspapers published in Calcutta contained shipping and fiscal information as well as reports of local and foreign market conditions.[11]

By the end of the nineteenth century, the Jewish community in Calcutta numbered more than eighteen hundred. Jews had moved into the stock exchange and become large urban landowners. Like their European counterparts in that city, large Jewish firms such as those of B.N. Elias, S. Manasseh, E. Meyer, A.M. Shellim, and M.A. Sassoon developed international networks engaged in shipping jute and cloth. The Ezras, having made a fortune in the opium trade and having intermarried with the Sassoons, became the most important Jewish family in Calcutta. Timberg points out that much of the history of the Baghdadi Jewish community revolves around acceptance of and opposition to this family dominance. When David Joseph Ezra died in 1882, he was one of the leading property owners in Calcutta, and his descendants increased his holdings. Musleah notes that, although Armenians were also buying land, European businessmen were not, except for European companies that bought buildings for their employees. Individual Europeans apparently did not intend to stay in India and therefore did not invest in land. Whereas Bombay Baghdadis faced competition from the Parsis, the Calcutta Baghdadis faced competition, at least in certain fields such as insurance and jute, from the Armenians.[12] Initially making a fortune in trading and banking, David Sassoon soon capitalized on the expansion of the Indian and Chinese markets in the latter part of the nineteenth century, although Bombay remained the center of the Sassoon empire. Like the Rothschilds in Europe, he placed his many sons as heads of newly established branches.[13]

The 1842 Anglo-Chinese Treaty of Nanjing, which opened up the five ports in China and guaranteed extraterritorial privileges for foreigners, enticed Baghdadi Jews and some Parsis from Bombay to follow British and American traders already settled in Canton (Guangzhou), Shanghai, Tianjin, Ningbo, and Hong Kong.[14] The early lead was taken by the Sassoons: David Sassoon's second son, Elias, arrived in China in 1844. Roth sees this as a turning point in the history of David Sassoon's business.[15] Elias first operated out of Canton, financing shipments and providing small-scale merchant banking facilities to others, while sending his own goods up the coast. He left a deputy to manage the branch in Canton and moved to Hong Kong (increasingly important since its transfer to the British), where some old ships' hulks near the river mouth had been converted to warehouses for the profitable opium trade.[16] Although the Sassoons helped develop the new port of Hong Kong, Elias, like other merchants, soon found Shanghai more favorable for a larger volume of China trade and established his base there in 1850, at which time there were fewer than a hundred foreign residents. Kranzler suggests that Elias, who traveled continually between branches, may have been the first Jew to reach Shanghai, but that the first permanent settlers were probably three company assistants.[17] Shanghai now became a major center of Sassoon operations, second only to Bombay. Parsi firms remained prominent in Canton, especially in the opium trade, into the late 1850s.[18]

Reluctant to confine himself to the risky and competitive opium trade, Elias Sassoon began to import metals, muslin, and cotton, while extending the family spice trade with the East Indies. He decided to buy or build warehouses rather than rent. By 1855, David Sassoon and Sons was operating along the entire China coast, drawing from it silk, nankeen, tea, hides, and skins—cargo that opium shippers needed for the return trip to India. The Sassoons now rivaled the British firm of Jardine-Matheson, which, similarly operating in England, India, and China, had also diversified into industry and real estate and kept the firm under family control. By the 1860s, the Parsis, who thought that investment in Bombay industry offered greater profitability and security, were ready to abandon opium even at the Indian end to Baghdadi firms. During the last quarter of the nineteenth century, the better English houses also withdrew from the opium trade, leaving it increasingly in the hands of the Jews. Peh-t'i Wei suggests that it was speculation at Bombay by David Sassoon and Sons that reduced the opium profit and led Jardine to give up trading in opium and to diversify.[19]

Before World War I, the Sephardic community in Shanghai consisted of between five hundred and seven hundred people, not all of whom were so wealthy as the leading families. (In Hong Kong there were sixty Sephardic Jews in 1882). Kranzler observes that the majority were of the lower socio-economic class of the non-Chinese in Shanghai. They were the clerks and other workers in the businesses of their wealthier coreligionists. David Sassoon and his oldest son, Albert-Abdullah, recruited office managers, clerks, and warehouse men from Baghdad and Bombay for the Sassoon offices in China. A similar situation prevailed in India, where there were perhaps forty "merchant prince" families among a community, in Bombay and Calcutta, of fewer than five thousand Baghdadis, at its peak.[20] Early on, the Sassoons established cemeteries, synagogues, and a school to serve the Jewish community that was growing in Shanghai, mainly in the employ of its establishments. As in India, however, the children of the wealthy were generally sent to the best English schools.[21] The flexibility and diversification of David Sassoon and Sons distinguished them from larger and more established China traders. In addition to their involvement in shipping, they became brokers or bankers, providing capital and insurance to smaller traders, and acted as commission agents, buying and selling cargoes for others. Their need to construct warehouses led them into real estate trading, speculating in property in Hong Kong and elsewhere.[22]

Elias remained in China from approximately 1844 to 1853, to be replaced temporarily by Albert-Abdullah. In fact, all the Sassoon sons had to serve their stint in China, usually without their wives. According to Roth, the most lucrative part of the trade from India to China and beyond and, later on, much of the direct trade from England to the Far East came into the hands of David Sassoon, Sons, and Company. Their Bombay base was perfectly suited to this. They had a practical monopoly on the importing of opium, fabrics, and cotton yarn. The China trade raised the house to the very first rank in British India. Elias bought shares in the China Steam Navigation Company and also sites on the Shanghai mudflats at very low prices. He invested in housing estates in the Chinese part of Shanghai to accommodate the Chinese laborers who came into Shanghai by 1855.[23] In the 1860s an international group of merchants established the Hong Kong and Shanghai Banking Corporation as a central banking unit in order to finance trade and stabilize business after the financial collapse provoked by the Taiping Rebellion. [As noted in Wendy Abraham's chapter in this volume, the Taiping was the most severe of several rebellions that convulsed China between 1850 and 1873, resulting in from twenty to thirty million deaths and in social disintegration unparalleled in world history. –Ed.] Arthur Sassoon, who was to accumulate a fortune in eight years in Hong Kong, was an original member of the Hong Kong bank's Board.[24] In 1869, a convention that would grant China additional duties on imported opium and exported silk, in exchange for which the British would receive certain commercial concessions, generated strong protests among the opium merchants. "Sassoon and Co. of Bombay, the largest dealers in the Malwa drug, protested against the impost as encouraging opium production in China."[25] The opium convention was rejected.

When Elias resigned from David Sassoon and Sons in 1867 and established his rival firm, E.D. Sassoon and Company, he opened offices in Bombay and Shanghai. At first he limited himself to trading in dried fruits, nankeen, metals, tea, Chinese gold, silk, spices, and camphor, and later in cotton. He also developed his property holdings in China. He too sent his sons to serve in China. His eldest son, Jacob, bought up more building sites in Shanghai, including some on the Bund, and was soon viewed as a commercial genius. By 1878, E.D. Sassoon and Company was competing in the opium and Indian yarn trade and investing heavily in Shanghai real estate.[26]

Rising land values in the treaty ports in the 1870s led David Sassoon and Sons to increase their investments in land. Their warehouses were full—

with opium, cotton goods, silks, spices, tea, and metals. Later, when opium sales declined, they earned more money from silver, sugar, and dyes. The company was able to hire numerous junk masters along the China coast and to charter fleets of tramp steamers. By 1880, Solomon D. Sassoon of David Sassoon and Sons was converting his property in Shanghai and Hong Kong into bungalows, shops, and apartments, which brought in high rentals.[27]

Some Baghdadi Jews who began their careers in Shanghai as employees of the Sassoons later established their own firms, and a few soon amassed fortunes for themselves.[28] One name that was eventually to eclipse even that of Sassoon in China was that of Hardoon. The Hardoons had also arrived in India from Baghdad and worked in the Sassoon firm. One of them, Silas A. Hardoon (1851?–1931), was extremely capable and took on more and more responsibilities. In the early 1870s, while in his late twenties, he was sent to Hong Kong as an adviser to David Sassoon's youngest son, Frederick, who was to oversee the business there. Hardoon was soon transferred to Shanghai, leaving Frederick to manage the Hong Kong branch. Frederick was appointed by the queen as an unofficial member of the Hong Kong Legislative Council in 1884 and was also a director of the Bank of China and Japan.[29]

Starting out in Shanghai as a clerk, Silas Hardoon soon became manager of the branch, a rare accomplishment for someone outside the Sassoon family. He tried to persuade David's son Solomon to move more heavily into cotton, as the Tatas and E.D. Sassoons were doing, rather than continue to deal in opium and other merchandise at declining profits. In 1886, Hardoon resigned from David Sassoon and Sons and after a brief, probably unsuccessful attempt to go into business for himself, joined E.D. Sassoon as their branch manager in Shanghai.[30] E.D. Sassoon's son Jacob, recognizing the economic competition that Japan might offer in both the Chinese and Indian markets, decided to produce higher-quality goods. His firm soon increased its lead over David Sassoon and Sons in cotton manufacturing. Jacob also encouraged Hardoon to expand the firm's property holdings in the Chinese quarter of Shanghai. At the same time, Hardoon bought lots for himself, whose rents he then reinvested in other property and public utilities. He was also involved in the opium trade. In 1911, Hardoon left E.D. Sassoon and founded his own company.[31]

A practicing Jew who had built the beautiful Beth Aharon Synagogue in Shanghai in 1927, Hardoon also was interested in Buddhism and thus had rare access to prominent Chinese merchants. He became a very wealthy man and served as an elected member of the Municipal Council of the French Concession from 1892 to 1901 and of that of the International Settlement from 1900 to 1903.[32] He contributed a great deal to the International Settlement in Shanghai, where a street was named for him, and to Chinese institutions and civic welfare in general.

Hardoon, who had married a Eurasian, *Luo* Jialing, built an elaborate garden on Bubbling Well Road that he named after her. Although she had probably converted to Judaism, Luo Jialing eventually became a devoted Buddhist and used her husband's money to keep a Buddhist scholar in residence editing the Buddhist canon. Hardoon's estate contained retreats for Buddhist nuns and monks, and his wife later sheltered revolutionaries there.[33] Hardoon bought Chinese paintings and manuscripts and in 1914 started a Buddhist university. At his funeral in 1931, he was buried with both Jewish and Buddhist rites. Supposedly the richest man "East of Suez," Hardoon left his huge fortune, mostly in land and property, to his wife.[34] His will (which had also included bequests for the translation into Chinese of the Koran and the Old Testament) was contested by his cousin and this led to a drawn-out court case turning on the questions of whether Hardoon was a citizen of Iraq or of China, whose law should be followed, and what foreign rights were in China. The case was eventually decided in favor of Mrs. Hardoon in 1937.[35]

Another employee of David Sassoon and Sons who was to do extremely well was (Sir) Elly Kadoorie (1867–1944), who was born in Baghdad and arrived in Shanghai via Bombay in 1880. He too soon left the Sassoon firm and started his own business, E.S. Kadoorie and Company, operating in Hong Kong and Shanghai. He eventually amassed a fortune in merchant banking, real estate, hotels, utilities, and rubber. His home on Bubbling Well Road, finished in the 1920s, was one of the most magnificent mansions in Shanghai.[36] His public service earned him a number of high honors from England, France, and China, including Knight Commander of the British Empire and Commandeur de la Légion d'Honneur. He and his brother Sir Ellis (1865–1922), who settled in Hong Kong and became a director of the Hong Kong Hotel Company, followed in the footsteps of their father, Salih Kadoorie, a well-known philanthropist in Baghdad. Contributing to both Jewish and non-Jewish institutions, they founded schools (including an endowed chair in physics at Hong Kong University and the first manual arts school for Chinese) and hospitals all over the world. Sir Elly's sons, Lawrence and Horace (who, as Lord Kadoorie, became the first man from Hong Kong to sit in the House of Lords), continued their father's widespread business activities in Hong Kong. The Kadoories, unlike the Sassoons, were ardent Zionists beginning in the early twentieth century.[37]

The Baghdadi Jews' passion for horse-racing was pursued in both India and China. In China, horse-racing was a foreign sport, foreigners having organized races starting in 1844, when they first arrived in Shanghai, and thus the racecourse lay in the center of the International Settlement. Chinese were excluded from foreign race clubs and eventually started their own, in 1911. According to Sergeant, the Shanghai races became an integral part of Shanghai business life and the ideal place for Shanghai's prominent families to display their wealth and compete for prestige. Business rivalries extended to the races. In the twentieth century, Sir Victor Sassoon, the nephew of Sir Jacob and the heir to the E.D. Sassoon fortune, and the Ezra brothers (grandsons of Isaac Ezra, an opium trader and property tycoon) were among the prominent racehorse owners.[38]

Although by the 1890s the two rival Sassoon firms were among the leading traders, shippers, and property owners in Shanghai, both worried about potential competition in China not only from Japan but also from Russia and Germany. Sir Albert-Abdullah of David Sassoon and Sons wanted to lend China money for railways and other enterprises in return for concessions, but other Sassoon brothers did not want to spend additional capital in China (or anywhere else) because of losses in silver and depreciation in their stocks and shares. Instead, they reduced their staff in Hong Kong and Shanghai.[39]

After the Japanese victory in the 1894–95 Sino–Japanese war, a treaty of commerce allowing the Japanese to manufacture goods in China and Japan soon undercut both English millowners and exporters such as the Sassoons. But the treaty also granted other foreigners licenses to establish industries, and the Sassoon firms had the facilities to take advantage of this provision. They quickly established spinning and weaving plants and rice, paper, and flour mills. Thus they made up for their losses in opium and cotton exports. Hardoon engineered E.D. Sassoon's expansion of its Shanghai plants. In 1901, David Sassoon and Company decided to meet the new competition in both India and China, especially from Japan, by incorporating as a new private limited company, public issue.[40]

Between the 1850s and 1920s, the Sephardic Jews of Shanghai, and the Sassoons in particular, were sporadically involved in efforts to contact and revive the Kaifeng Jewish community. Although they formed occasional committees to help, they could not do much to bring the Kaifeng Jews to Shanghai or to raise the funds to rebuild the synagogue. They failed in their attempts to get help from European and American Jews, who were more concerned with the plight of their coreligionists in Russia and Eastern Europe. A leading Baghdadi, N.E.B. Ezra, the editor for many years of *Israel's Messenger,* a pro-Zionist newspaper, later blamed the lack of unity, foresight, and leadership in his own community for the failure to save the Kaifeng Jews.[41]

In both India and China, the Baghdadi Jews, especially the Sassoons and

Ezras in India and the Kadoories and Hardoons in China, were generous not only to their own community but also to general education and civic and communal welfare.[42] Although the Baghdadi Jews in the nineteenth century were usually not involved in Indian or Chinese politics per se, they were active in public affairs. In Calcutta they were named as honorary magistrates. Leading members of the community were invited to the viceroy's levees and celebrations and helped to organize some of the latter. They were appointed sheriffs of Calcutta and served as municipal councilors in that city. In Bombay, the Jews played an even larger role. The government of Bombay offered David Sassoon many public appointments, but he accepted only that of justice of the peace. His son, Albert-Abdullah, was a member of the Bombay Legislative Council. In the twentieth century, two Baghdadi Jews, Sir Sassoon J. David (whose son, Sir Percival David, became a well-known collector of Chinese art) and Meyer Nissim would become head of the Bombay Municipal Corporation, that is, mayor of Bombay.[43] In Shanghai, a director of David Sassoon and Company always served as an honorary member of the Shanghai Municipal Council. Moses Ezra was the second mayor of the French Concession and also a member of the Municipal Council of the International Settlement. A street was named for him in downtown Shanghai.[44] The Baghdadi Sir Mathew Nathan (1862–1939) served from 1904 to 1907 as Hong Kong's only Jewish governor. He tried to improve Chinese–American relations, strained over America's exclusion of Chinese immigrants. The main thoroughfare in Kowloon Peninsula is called Nathan Road in his honor.[45]

Baghdadi Jews in India and China were also involved in broader Jewish affairs. In the 1880s, they became active in the branch of the Anglo–Jewish Association formed in Bombay by the Bene Israel. By 1898 there was a branch of the Anglo–Jewish Association in Shanghai. Although the upper crust of the Baghdadis in India remained aloof from Zionism in the late nineteenth and early twentieth centuries, the Shanghai Jewish community was represented at the sixth Zionist Congress at Basle, Switzerland, in 1903.[46]

Baghdadi Jews generally confined their interests to trade, finance, and industry; relatively few entered the professions. And yet, some played an important role in the development of a Jewish press in Asia. N.E.B. Ezra, the indefatigable editor of the influential *Israel's Messenger* of Shanghai from 1904 until his death in 1936, was the uncle of Benjamin, Joseph, and David Sargon of Bombay, who edited that city's *Jewish Tribune* (initially known as the *Jewish Advocate*) in the 1930s. The Sargon brothers—born of a Cochini Jewish father and Iraqi mother—had grown up in Bombay reading *Israel's Messenger* and had assimilated their uncle's concepts of journalism. Their own paper was of a much higher professional standard than that of previous Jewish newspapers in Bombay. N.E.B. Ezra and the Sargons were ardent Zionists, and their newspapers were organs of the Zionist organizations.

Conclusion

There is no doubt that the Baghdadi Jews helped Bombay, Calcutta, Shanghai, and Hong Kong develop into some of the greatest import and export and financial centers of the world. Yet their role as intermediaries, almost ancillaries of the British, needs to be stressed. Their social lives revolved around their own communal institutions; they did not truly integrate into Chinese and Indian life. Timberg has pointed out that, in Calcutta, the Baghdadi community originally formed part of the "graytown," a group of Armenians, Portuguese, and Greeks who stood, often geographically and sometimes socially, between the "blacktown" where the Indians lived and the "whitetown" of the Europeans. He suggests that their commercial success was related to their marginally "privileged" position vis-à-vis the bulk of the population.[47] Eventually, the role of economic intermediary was filled by indigenous groups such as Parsis, Marwaris, Bengalis, and Gujaratis, who, like the Jews earlier, combined their English education with commercial skills.[48] In Shanghai and Hong Kong, too, although the economic role played by the Sassoons, Hardoons, and Kadoories was enormous and, in the nineteenth century at least, was challenged mainly by British rather than indigenous competition, socially the Jews were never quite accepted by the British. Hardoon, in fact, seemed more interested in becoming integrated into the Chinese, rather than the European, society of Shanghai. Although there has been some secondary discussion of Baghdadi acculturation in Calcutta, their acculturation in China, especially through their association with wealthy Chinese comprador families, needs further study.[49]

The Baghdadi Jews, although constituting small communities in India and China, were part of an international network of family and ethnic ties. Concerned mainly with business, they played an important role in both Asian colonial history and British imperial expansion. Trading was their key activity in both countries, but it was supplemented by industrial development, real estate investment, and banking. Much research remains to be done, however, to bring these Iraqi diaspora experiences into comparative focus. There is a dearth of materials on the economic role of these Baghdadi Jews. Although books have been written on the Calcutta community, very little has appeared on the Bombay Baghdadis. For the latter half of the nineteenth and early twentieth centuries there are no communal records for Bombay and no journalism to speak of. A careful search through the *Times of India* might yield more data. For China, the financial affairs of the Sassoon companies and the political implications of their loans to various governments need to be investigated.[50]

In summation, Baghdadi Jews played a vital role in the economic expansion of many Indian and Chinese port cities. In both societies they are also distinct for their vast financial contributions to Jewish causes as well as to general educational, civic, and communal welfare.

Notes

I am grateful to the University Press of New England for permission to reproduce material that appeared in slightly different form on pp. 15–19, and 241 in my *Jews in British India: Identity in a Colonial Era*, © 1989 by the Trustees of Brandeis University.

1. See Thomas A. Timberg, "The Jews in Calcutta," in *Jews in India*, ed. Timberg (New York: Advent, 1986), p. 28.

2. David Kranzler, *Japanese, Nazis & Jews: The Jewish Refugee Community of Shanghai, 1938–1945* (New York: Yeshiva University Press, 1976), p. 45.

3. Ibid., pp. 48, 52; Thomas A. Timberg, "Baghdadi Jews in Indian Port Cities," in Timberg, ed., *Jews in India*, pp. 274–75. See also Walter J. Fischel, "The Immigration of 'Arabian Jews' to India in the Eighteenth Century," *Proceedings of the American Academy for Jewish Research* 33 (1965), pp. 1–20; and Walter J. Fischel, "Bombay in Jewish History in the Light of New Documents from the Indian Archives," *Proceedings of the American Academy for Jewish Research* 38–39 (1972), pp. 131–38.

4. Christine Dobbin, *Urban Leadership in Western India: Politics and Communities in Bombay City, 1840–1885* (London: Oxford University Press, 1972), p. 16; Cecil Roth, *The Sassoon Dynasty* (London: Robert Hale, 1941), pp. 44–48, 50.

5. Roth, *Sassoon Dynasty*, pp. 60–61; Stanley Jackson, *The Sassoons* (New York: E.P. Dutton, 1968), p. 33.

6. On the development of the Bombay cotton industry, see Morris David Morris, *The Emergence of an Industrial Labor Force in India: A Study of the Bombay Cotton Mills, 1854–1942* (Berkeley: University of California Press, 1965), chap. 3.

7. Roth, *Sassoon Dynasty*, pp. 76, 80–81, 86–87; Jackson, *Sassoons*, pp. 47, 52–53.

8. Roth, *Sassoon Dynasty*, p. 102; See also Jackson, *Sassoons*, pp. 48, 59, 62–66, 99. E.D. Sassoon was registered as an Indian firm, David Sassoon and Company as a British firm. In 1886, however, the Sassoon Mills were exclusively under Parsi management. See Sorabji M. Rutnagur, ed., *Bombay Industries: The Cotton Mills* (Bombay: Indian Textile Journal, 1927), p. 314.

9. Timberg, "Baghdadi Jews," p. 274; Jackson, *Sassoons*, pp. 100–103.

10. Ezekiel M. Musleah, *On the Banks of the Ganges: The Sojourn of Jews in Calcutta* (North Quincy, MA: Christopher Publishing House, 1975), pp. 46–48, 456–57 n. 2; Jackson, *Sassoons*, pp. 22–23.

11. Musleah, *Banks*, pp. 53–54.

12. David S. Sassoon, *History of the Jews of Baghdad* (Letchworth: S.D. Sassoon, 1949), pp. 203, 298–309; See also Isaac Abraham, *Origin and History of the Calcutta Jews* (Calcutta: Daw Sen, 1970), p. 14; Timberg, "Jews of Calcutta," pp. 29–30, 33–34, 36; Musleah, *Banks*, p. 54.

13. Kranzler, *Japanese*, p. 46; Jackson, *Sassoons*, pp. 22–27; Roth, *Sassoon Dynasty*, chap. 2.

14. Dennis A. Leventhal, *The Jewish Community of Hong Kong: An Introduction* (Hong Kong: Jewish Historical Society of Hong Kong, 1985), p. 2. See also his "Environmental Interactions of the Jews of Hong Kong," chapter III.A.I in this volume.

15. Roth, *Sassoon Dynasty*, p. 47. There is a book in Chinese on the Sassoons: Zhang Zhongli and Chen Zengnian, *Shasun jituan zai jiu Zhongguo* (The Sassoon Group in Old China) (Beijing: Renmin chubanshe, 1985).

16. Jackson, *Sassoons*, p. 23.

17. Kranzler, *Japanese*, p. 47; Mendel Brown, "The Jews of Modern China," *Jewish Monthly* 3 (June 1949), p. 160; "Almoni" (pseud., probably for Reuben Abraham), "A Short Account of the Sephardic Jewish Community in Shanghai," *Le Judaisme Sephardi* (London) n.s., 13 (January 1957), p. 605. "D. Sassoon and Sons" was listed as one of Shanghai's foreign residents in the *North China Herald*, August 3, 1850, p. 2.

18. Roth, *Sassoon Dynasty*, 48. See also Rhoads Murphey, *The Outsiders: The Western Experience in India and China* (Ann Arbor: University of Michigan Press, Michigan Studies on China, 1977), p. 85.

19. Betty Peh-t'i Wei, *Shanghai: Crucible of Modern China* (Hong Kong, New York: Oxford University Press: 1987), p. 113. See also Jackson, *Sassoons*, p. 24; Murphey, *Outsiders*, p. 85; David Owen, *British Opium Policy in China and India* (New Haven: Yale University Press, 1934; repr. Archon, 1968), pp. 259–60. For an interesting comparison of the Sassoons and Jardine Matheson, see Harriet Sergeant, *Shanghai* (New York: Crown, 1990), pp. 129–30.

20. Timberg, "Baghdadi Jews," p. 274; Kranzler, *Japanese*, pp. 47, 51–52; Jackson, *Sassoons*, p. 27; "Hong Kong," *Encyclopaedia Judaica* (New York: Macmillan, 1971).

21. Timberg, "Baghdadi Jews," p. 276. For the religious life of the Baghdadi community in Shanghai, see Kranzler, *Japanese*, pp. 48–51; and Roth, *Sassoon Dynasty*, pp. 49–50.

22. Jackson, *Sassoons*, pp. 24, 26, 27–2; Wei, *Shanghai*, p. 106. On the Sassoons' early involvement in Nagasaki commercial lots, see Lane Earns, "The Shanghai/Nagasaki Judaic Connection, 1859–1924" (paper presented at a conference on Jewish Diasporas in China: Comparative and Historical Perspectives, Harvard University, August 16–18, 1992), pp. 5–6. See also chapter II.B in this volume.

23. Jackson, *Sassoons*, pp. 27–29; Roth, *Sassoon Dynasty*, p. 49.

24. Jackson, *Sassoons*, pp. 42–43; Sergeant, *Shanghai*, p. 166. See also Frank H.H. King, *The History of the Hong Kong and Shanghai Banking Corporation* (Cambridge: Harvard University Press, 1988).

25. Owen, *British Opium Policy*, p. 247.

26. Jackson, *Sassoons*, pp. 51–52, 57.

27. Ibid., pp. 58, 64.

28. Kranzler, *Japanese*, p. 48.

29. *Jewish Chronicle* (London), March 14, 1884, p. 9; Roth, *Sassoon Dynasty*, pp. 167, 184; Jackson, *Sassoons*, pp. 57–58.

30. Jackson, *Sassoons*, pp. 64, 66. On Hardoon, especially in the twentieth century, see Chiara Betta, chapter III.C.1 in this volume. Works in Chinese include *Xu* Zhucheng, *Unofficial Biography of Hardoon* (Shanghai: Shanghai Culture Publishing Company, 1983); and two novels: Shen Ji, *Big Shot* and *The Inside Story of an Influential and Rich Clan* (Liberation Daily, 1990), as cited by *Xu* Xin, "Chinese Research on Jewish Diaspo-

ras in China" (paper presented at a conference on Jewish Diasporas in China: Comparative and Historical Perspectives, Harvard University, August 16–18, 1992), pp. 5, 6, 9.

31. Jackson, *Sassoons,* p. 100; Betta, "Hardoon," p. 1.

32. Roth, *Sassoon Dynasty,* p. 100; Betta, "Hardoon," p. 1.

33. Betta questions whether *Luo* Jialing ever converted to Judaism; see Betta, "Hardoon," pp. 2–5. See also Wei, *Shanghai,* pp. 90, 179; and *Pan* Ling, *In Search of Old Shanghai,* pp. 71–75.

34. "The Passing of Shanghai's Largest Land-Owner," *China Weekly Review,* June 27, 1931, p. 126.

35. Roth, *Sassoon Dynasty,* p. 100; "Hardoon," *Universal Jewish Encyclopedia* (New York: Universal Jewish Encyclopedia, Inc., 1948); Sergeant, *Shanghai,* pp. 127–29; Jackson, *Sassoons,* p. 100; Kranzler, *Japanese,* pp. 55–56.

36. "Kadoorie," *Universal Jewish Encyclopedia.* "Kadoorie." Sergeant has an interesting description of this home (*Shanghai,* pp. 124–27).

37. "Kadoorie," *Encyclopaedia Judaica;* Josef Zeitin, "The Shanghai Jewish Community," *Jewish Life* 41 (October 1973): 56–57; Wei, *Shanghai,* p. 96. See also Lawrence Kadoorie, "The Kadoorie Memoir," *Sino-Judaic Studies: Whence and Whither* (Hong Kong: Hong Kong Jewish Chronicle, 1985), pp. 83–89. In Chinese there is *Pan* Guang, "With Lord Lawrence Kadoorie," *International Outlook* 12 (1990), cited by Xu, "Chinese Research," (paper presented at a conference on Jewish Diasporas in China: Comparative and Historical Perspectives, Harvard University, August 16–18, 1992, p. 6.

38. Sergeant, *Shanghai,* pp. 106–7.

39. Jackson, *Sassoons,* p. 103.

40. Jackson, *Sassoons,* pp. 107, 119; Roth, *Sassoon Dynasty,* p. 93.

41. Michael Pollak, *Mandarins, Jews, and Missionaries: The Jewish Experience in the Chinese Empire* (Philadelphia: Jewish Publication Society, 1980), pp. 175–216, *passim,* 225; Hyman Kublin, ed., *Jews in Old China: Some Western Views* (New York: Paragon, 1971), pp. xviii–xix, 116–117; William C. White, *Chinese Jews: A Compilation of Matters Relating to the Jews of K'ai-fêng Fu* (New York: Paragon, 1966), vol. 1, pp. 152 ff.; Kranzler, *Japanese,* pp. 54–55.

42. Roth, *Sassoon Dynasty,* p. 65; Kranzler, *Japanese,* p. 55.

43. Sassoon J. David, Bart. (1849–1926), was a member of the large interrelated family of the Sassoons and Ezras. He made his money in the cotton industry and in 1905 was chairman of the Bombay Millowners' Association and president of the Central Bank of India (Rutnagur, *Bombay Industries,* p. 705).

44. Jackson, *Sassoons,* p. 214; Kranzler, *Japanese,* p. 55; Zeitin, *Shanghai Jewish Community,* p. 56.

45. Leventhal, *Jewish Community,* p. 2. See also *Israel's Messenger* 2 (September 22, 1905), p. 21.

46. Herman Dicker, *Wanderers and Settlers in the Far East: A Century of Jewish Life in China and Japan* (New York: Twayne, 1962), p. 67. For the development of Zionism in Shanghai, see issues of *Israel's Messenger* from 1904 to 1910 as well as chapters by *Pan* Guang and *Maruyama* Naoki published in this volume.

47. Timberg, "Jews of Calcutta," p. 38.

48. Timberg, "Baghdadi Jews," pp. 277–78.

49. Betta, "Hardoon," p. 6; Leventhal, "Environmental Interactions," pp. 10–12. Cf. Musleah, *Banks of the Ganges, passim;* and Esmond D. Ezra, *Turning Back the Pages: A Chronicle of Calcutta Jewry* (London: Brookside Press, 1986). Xu, "Chinese Research," pp. 5, 6, mentions some recent works in Chinese dealing with the Baghdadi Jews: *Tang* Peiji, "Lishi zhimi: Shanghai youtairen yanjiu zhiyi" (A Mystery in History:

A Study of Jews in Shanghai), *Tongji daxue xuebao, renwen sheken ban* (Tongji University Journal, Social and Humanity edition), no. 2 (1991); and *Wang* Qingyu, "Jiu Shanghai de youtairen" (Jews in Old Shanghai), *Shanghai shehui kexueyuan xueshu jikan* (Academic Quarterly of Shanghai Academy of Social Sciences), no. 2 (1987) pp. 165–72.

50. See King, *Hong Kong and Shanghai Banking,* vol. 3, p. 409.

Chapter II.B

The Shanghai–Nagasaki Judaic Connection, 1859–1924

Lane Earns

The study of the Jewish community in Shanghai in the late nineteenth and early twentieth centuries should not be confined to the Chinese mainland but should include an examination of East Asian ports linked by water boundaries.[1] An obvious comparison is with the Japanese treaty port of Nagasaki. Shanghai and Nagasaki face each other across a mere five hundred miles of the East China Sea; in fact, they are considerably closer to each other than they are to their respective capital cities of Beijing and Tokyo. In addition, Shanghai and Nagasaki were opened to Western trade and settlement only sixteen years apart.

Among the many links between the two port cities was a small yet active Jewish merchant community. While the growth of the two Jewish communities roughly paralleled each other over the course of the last half of the nineteenth century, in the first quarter of the twentieth century their paths diverged. Whereas the Shanghai Jewish population continued to swell, the number of Jews in Nagasaki steadily declined after the 1905 Russo–Japanese war, until by 1924 there were not even enough Jews in town to keep the local synagogue open.

The foreign settlement at Shanghai was officially opened on November 17, 1843, in the aftermath of the Opium War and the resulting Treaty of Nanjing.[2] Foreign settlement was slow in the beginning, but Jewish influence was present early on in the person of Elias D. Sassoon of Sassoon and Company. Elias was the second son of David Sassoon, the Baghdad native who had established his famous merchant house headquarters in Bombay in 1833.[3] David sent Elias to China in 1844, and by 1850 Shanghai had become the headquarters of the Sassoon Chinese operations.[4] The inaugural issue of Shanghai's English-language newspaper, *North China Herald,* dated August 3, 1850, listed Abraham, M.S. Mooshee, and J. Reuben of "D. Sassoon and Sons" among the city's foreign residents.[5] Sassoon and Sons, which would soon become one of the most important business operations in town, traded primarily in Indian cotton, opium, tea, and silk in these early years.

The Jews who made their way to Shanghai at this time were predominantly Sephardic Jews from Baghdad and Bombay who came to work as clerks for Sassoon and Sons. While many continued to work for the Sassoons for years to come, others later left the company to establish their own firms. Most remained in Shanghai, although some were either transferred or left of their own volition for other treaty ports in East Asia.

The Jews of mid-nineteenth-century Shanghai were closely bound together through birthplace, employment, marriage, and religious beliefs; but formal social and religious institutions were slow to develop. In the early years, what social and religious leadership there was came from the Sassoons. They provided for basic religious needs at work and in 1862 donated a cemetery to the Jewish community.[6] The Baghdadi community began to rent buildings for religious worship by the 1870s, but religious organization did not begin in earnest until the meeting of Beth El Synagogue subscribers in 1887. A more Orthodox element of the community broke away to form a second synagogue, called Sheerith Israel, in 1900.[7] An afternoon Jewish school was constructed in late 1902, and in April of the following year the Shanghai Zionist Association was established.[8] This was followed in February 1904 by the founding of the Jewish Benevolent Fund and in April of the biweekly newspaper *Israel's Messenger.*[9]

The Baghdadi community in Shanghai reached its peak in the 1920s, when its 500 to 700 strong population witnessed the construction of two new synagogues. Ohel Rachel, the successor to Beth El, was built with the support of funds from the estate of Sir Jacob Sassoon, the son of Elias; and Beth Aharon, the successor to Sheerith Israel, was constructed with money donated by Silas A. Hardoon, a wealthy merchant who originally started out with David Sassoon and Sons, and later worked for E. D. Sassoon and Company before going into business for himself in 1911.[10]

The great Baghdadi merchants of Shanghai supported not only strictly Jewish projects but those of the Shanghai foreign community as a whole. As Kranzler notes, "They . . . contributed more than their share to civic, communal and charitable causes."[11] Representatives of the Sassoon and Hardoon companies also frequently served as members of the various municipal councils in Shanghai.

Joining the Baghdadi Jews in Shanghai in the final decade of the nineteenth century were Ashkenazi Jewish refugees from Russia. The Ashkenazi Jews—most of whom came via Harbin—were not so economically successful as their Baghdadi counterparts and quite often worked in small provision shops or bars in the poorer sections of town. Until 1902 those who worshiped went to the Baghdadi synagogues, but in that year they organized their own congregation. This was followed by the 1907 construction of an Ashkenazi place of worship, the Oihel Moishe Synagogue.[12] By the 1920s the Ashkenazi community in Shanghai had grown to approximately 1,000 and had even appointed its own rabbi.

The Baghdadi and Ashkenazi merchant community of Shanghai, which had begun in 1850 with the arrival of Elias Sassoon, had grown to a population of 1,700 by the mid-1920s. The community maintained three synagogues (two Baghdadi and one Ashkenazi), a school, two cemeteries, and a variety of social organizations. While most of the Jews came from Iraq, India, or Russia, others had emigrated from Eastern Europe or as far away as France, Germany, and Italy.

When the foreign settlement officially opened at Nagasaki, Japan, on July 1, 1859, the Shanghai foreign settlement just across the East China Sea served in many ways as a model for Western trade and governance. Foreign firms with offices in Shanghai took advantage of their trading experience in East Asia and their geographic proximity to Japan to open branch offices in Nagasaki. Many of the government and social institutions previously established in Shanghai were also instituted in its Japanese counterpart. While this can be said of Western practices in general, it can also be specifically applied to the Jewish communities of the two treaty port towns, as the more established Shanghai colony often served as elder brother to the smaller Jewish settlement of Nagasaki.

One of the first Shanghai trading firms to dispatch a ship to Nagasaki was D. Sassoon and Sons, which sent a cargo of sundries in February 1859—six months before the official opening of the port.[13] Sassoon and Sons was also on the initial waiting list for prime waterfront commercial lots in October 1860—just as it had been in the early days of the foreign settlement in Shanghai. Applying for waterfront lot number four was M. Ezekiel, in the name of Sassoon and Sons.[14] Unlike the situation at Shanghai, however, Sassoon and Sons decided not to station a direct representative in Nagasaki but, instead, work through general commission agents from other firms in town. The agent initially chosen was Kenneth R. MacKenzie of Jardine-Matheson; but upon his return to China in May 1861 the affairs of Sassoon and Sons in Nagasaki were conducted by Thomas Glover, a young Scottish merchant-adventurer who would go on to become the most famous Western merchant in Nagasaki.[15] The decision by Sassoon and Sons not to operate a branch office in Nagasaki probably stemmed from the realization that

Yokohama would soon overtake Nagasaki as the major port of foreign trade in Japan.

The departure of Sassoon and Sons from Nagasaki meant that there would not be a sudden influx of Jewish merchants as there had been earlier in Shanghai, but in the first decades there were always a few Jewish merchants in town. One such person was the Jewish-American Elias Tolman, who was on the October 1860 list of U.S. citizens desiring to rent commercial lots.[16]

In addition to land and court records, early Jews in Nagasaki could also be identified through examination of the foreign cemeteries in town. The first recorded Jewish burial in Nagasaki was that of an American sailor, Solomon Keeler, who died in the opening decade of the foreign settlement and was buried at Inasa International Cemetery.[17]

By the time that Jewish merchants from Eastern Europe and Russia began to make their way to Nagasaki from Shanghai and Harbin in the 1870s, the old foreign settlement was full and they were forced to settle in Umegasaki, the newest and least desirable area of foreign residence, or along Sagarimatsu Creek, the foreign bar district of town and the dirtiest and most dangerous part of the settlement. Most of these Jewish merchants, like their Ashkenazi counterparts in Shanghai, operated bars and inns, provisions stores, or tailor shops.

Jewish merchants in Nagasaki during the 1870s and early 1880s had no organized social or religious institutions—not even a large business to look after their needs as the Jews in Shanghai had in Sassoon & Sons. Leadership in the early Nagasaki Jewish community was shared by the merchants Haskel Goldenberg and Samuel Goldman.[18] Other Jewish merchants of the day included Giuseppe Schiller, R. Abraham, Ernestine Grunberg, William Hoffman, A. Naftaly, J. Steinberg, J. Soloman, and Tobias Saphir. They operated establishments with names like "Garibaldi Inn," "Snugger Inn," "City of Hamburg Inn," "Britannia Inn," "Oriental Tavern," "British Queen," "Albion Inn," "Globe Tavern," "Prince of Wales Saloon," and "Temple Bar Inn."[19]

The situation began to change in the 1880s, however, with the arrival of two important Jewish families—the Lessners and the Messes (Ginsburg). The Lessner family, which came from Constantinople, consisted of Leb (Leo) and his wife, Hannah, one daughter and a son, Sigmund. Leb Lessner, an Austrian national, became the spiritual leader of the Jewish community in town; Hannah was a native of Russia. Sigmund, who was born in Bukovina, initially operated a tavern called the "Traveler's Inn" at no. 16 Umegasaki. In September 1887 he married Sophie Feuer at the Lessner family residence.[20] The couple never had any children of their own, although they adopted a son and daughter in 1893.[21] Sigmund's sister later married Jacob Lyons, a prominent French resident of Yokohama.

M.A. Ginsburg was a native of Odessa who changed his name from Mess and fled Russia to avoid arrest for military desertion. By the mid-1870s he had made his way to Yokohama, where he later founded his own provisions company. Ginsburg made frequent business trips to Nagasaki over the course of the next decade, before establishing his headquarters there at no. 50 Oura. He was joined in Nagasaki by his brothers, Marcus and Nathan Mess. Marcus began as an employee of Ginsburg and Company in 1883, and ten years later became a partner in the firm. Nathan opened a successful curio shop at no. 10 Umegasaki in October 1887.

By the late 1880s Ginsburg found himself in the position of being able to aid the Russian government in acquiring coal for its Far Eastern Squadron after it had run short because of an argument over supply with the Japanese government. In the aftermath of this good deed, he confessed his identity and petitioned Tsar Alexander III for a pardon. According to a local Nagasaki newspaper, "Ginsburg not only received the Imperial pardon, but the thanks of the Czar, a monetary reward, a decoration, and the right of trading in Russia."[22] In 1896 Ginsburg was decorated by the Russian government with the Third Class Order of Stanislav for important services rendered to the Russian naval squadron.[23]

The Jewish community in Nagasaki continued to grow and prosper during the 1890s. Much of this prosperity was tied to servicing the Russian Far Eastern Fleet, stationed at the port during the winter months (the port at Vladivostok froze over in the winter and could not be used). One result of the growth was the need for a Jewish cemetery. In 1886 a German-Jewish sailor and the infant son of Samuel Goldman were buried in an addition to the international cemetery at Oura, but soon after this cemetery became full and was closed.[24] A large new international cemetery was then opened across town at Urakami (Sakamoto) in 1888. In July 1892 Ginsburg purchased lots twelve to twenty-six and Nathan Mess bought lots twenty-seven to thirty just within the front gate at Sakamoto, to be used as a Jewish cemetery.[25] As was the case in Shanghai, the Jewish cemetery was a result of donations by certain rich merchants, not the joint effort of the Jewish community.

Another sign of the increased size and prosperity of the Jewish community in Nagasaki was the establishment on September 3, 1896, of the synagogue Beth Israel at no. 11 Umegasaki by Haskel Goldenberg, with the cooperation of Sigmund Lessner.[26] Leb Lessner was appointed gabbai of the new synagogue.[27]

All the while, Sigmund Lessner's business continued to flourish, and by 1899 he had provision stores at nos. 6, 9, and 10 Umegasaki. As was the case in Shanghai, increased prosperity at this time led to the development of a Jewish Benevolent Association (1901) and an Anglo–Jewish Association (1902) in Nagasaki. As the uncontested social leader of the Jewish community, Sigmund Lessner was named president of both organizations. In his capacity as head of the Nagasaki Jewish Benevolent Association, Lessner organized annual Fancy Dress Balls to raise funds for charity, and served as spokesperson for the twenty-three Jewish tavern ("grog shop") owners in town who belonged to the organization. The bar owners were under constant attack from the local English-language newspaper editor to clean up the area (both physically and spiritually) along Sagarimatsu Creek, and Lessner often was forced to come to their defense.[28] Lessner also led the fund drive (which included appeals to the Jewish community in Shanghai) to open a new Jewish cemetery across the street from the old one at Sakamoto after it too had become full.

As the year 1903 opened, the Jewish community of Nagasaki had grown to about 100 residents, and its two leaders, Sigmund Lessner and M.A. Ginsburg, had every right to feel that the future would be bright. In January, Ginsburg took over the Agency of the Russian Volunteer Fleet, which made him provisioner for practically all Russian shipping in East Asia.[29] In July, Lessner left for a six-month pleasure trip to Europe and the United States— his first venture back to Europe since his arrival in Nagasaki seventeen years earlier.[30] By the end of the year, however, prospects were not so optimistic, as war between Japan and Russia was on the horizon.

Hostilities between Japan and Russia broke out in February 1904. The resulting war marked the beginning of the end of the Jewish community in Nagasaki. Most of the Jewish merchants in town were Russian, and even those who were not dependent in large part on servicing the Russian community in town and Russian shipping in East Asia.

The hardest hit was the firm of Ginsburg & Company. Both M.A. Ginsburg and Marcus Mess left Nagasaki for St. Petersburg in September 1903 and never returned.[31] Ginsburg and Company maintained an office in Nagasaki until March 1909, when the departure of J.M. Hornstein signified the official closing of the firm's local agency.[32]

Because he possessed Austrian citizenship, Sigmund Lessner was less affected by the war. His business once again began to prosper after the war, as a new wave of Russian immigrants made its way to Nagasaki in the wake of the 1905 revolution in Russia. Lessner added auctioneering to his wholesale and retail provisions business after the war, and continued to acquire property within the confines of the old foreign settlement.[33] This included the purchase of a large private residence at no. 16 Naminohira, overlooking the entrance to the harbor. Lessner also revived the annual Jewish Benevolent Association Fancy Dress Balls in 1907 and 1908, but with the steady decline of the Jewish population in town, these too had to be abandoned.

By the outbreak of World War I most members of the Jewish community of Nagasaki had moved on to the more thriving East Asian ports of Yokohama or Shanghai. The serious decline in the number of Jews in Nagasaki was reflected in the fact that only four Jewish residents were buried in the large addition to the Jewish cemetery at Urakami that Lessner had helped establish—and none after 1911.34 Those who did remain behind were primarily tavern owners in the foreign bar district along Sagarimatsu Creek.[35]

Although Sigmund Lessner had weathered all previous hardships, World War I precipitated a series of events that were beyond his control. Like all other Jews who desired residence within the foreign settlement at Nagasaki from 1859 to 1899, Lessner had to declare himself under the protection of a foreign consulate. Some Jews chose Russian citizenship, while others were under the jurisdiction of the American, British, French, or German consulates. Sigmund Lessner had obtained Austrian citizenship through his father, and while this helped him in the Russo–Japanese war, it proved to be a terrible burden during World War One.

On April 26, 1916, the British government prohibited trade with enemy subjects in a document entitled "Trading with the Enemy" (Statutory List) Proclamation, 1916, no. 2. The list, as it applied to Japan, was published in the May 16, 1916, issue of the *Nagasaki Press*. Of the names on the original list, only two were from Nagasaki, a German who had died earlier in the year, and the Austrian citizen Sigmund Lessner. The Japanese government proceeded to devise a similar list of its own. While Lessner's name was dropped from the British Black List in February 1917,[36] it remained on the Japanese list and his business operations were suspended. In December of the same year, Lessner and a Mr. Cohn, possibly Abraham Cohn, were both fined by the Japanese government over a misunderstanding involving the sale of land to French Catholic sisters in town.[37] Lessner's adopted son, Percy, who had been living abroad for years, tried to come back to Nagasaki with his wife in July 1917, but was quickly deported by Japanese officials as an enemy subject.[38]

While life during the war was very difficult for the Lessners, the synagogue at Umegasaki continued to operate. This can be seen in an ad for Yom Kippur services carried by the English-language newspaper in 1918.[39]

In June 1919 all black lists in Japan were suspended, but within a matter of days an Enemy Property Act was promulgated. On July 3 enemy subjects residing in Nagasaki (including Lessner) were ordered to report to the prefectural government offices and directed to submit an inventory of their possessions.[40] While some of his property was confiscated by the Japanese government, Lessner was eventually allowed to resume his business operations.

A local newspaper account commented that he was "looking forward with pleasure to some years of active business life before retirement."[41]

This was not to be, however, as Sigmund Lessner died of heart failure after completing the walk from his house to his office on a February afternoon in 1920. His sudden death at the age of sixty shocked the foreign community of Nagasaki. Lessner's contributions to the community were described in the local English-language newspaper as follows:

> Mr. Lessner took a very active interest in all local affairs and his business ability and shrewd common sense were always at the service of the community and his many friends. Nominally an enemy subject during the war, he remained on terms of closest friendship with Allied residents and generously contributed to war charities. He was ever ready to help those in distress and local institutions lost a warm-hearted friend. For many years he has been head of the Jewish community, but his purse knew no religious distinctions.[42]

Sigmund Lessner's funeral service was conducted by Mr. Cohn, possibly Abraham Cohn, at the Beth-El Synagogue at Umegasaki, which Lessner had helped build, and he was buried next to his parents in the Jewish section of the cemetery that he had helped maintain over the years through generous contributions. The *Nagasaki Press* said of the funeral: "The entire foreign community was represented, including all nationalities and the business and missionary sections, for no man was more generally known and respected than the deceased."[43] Later a bust (the only one in the international cemeteries) of Lessner was constructed atop the tombstone of the man who was known far and wide for his love of children.[44]

With the death of Sigmund Lessner, his widow, Sophie, became the matriarch of the ever-dwindling Jewish community in Nagasaki. The woman who used to walk her husband home from work every evening was so grieved by her husband's death that she could not attend the funeral services. Her life was shattered even further when some of her property was confiscated as enemy property and sold at government auction within a month of her husband's passing.[45] More property (including the family residence) was confiscated and sold at auction the following September.[46]

Sophie Lessner did not let misfortune deter her, however, as by March 1921 she was operating an auction house along Sagarimatsu Creek. In spite of deteriorating health, she continued to conduct business until July 4, 1923, when she left Nagasaki for Shanghai in order to receive treatment from specialists for diabetes.[47] She entered the French Hospital in Shanghai on July 7, slipped into unconsciousness the following morning, and died on the ninth. Rather than return her body to Nagasaki for burial next to her husband, Sophie's adopted son Percy, who was residing at the time in Shanghai, had her interred at the Jewish cemetery on Baikal Road in Shanghai.[48]

For all practical purposes, the death of Sophie Lessner marked the end of the Jewish community in Nagasaki. The large wave of Russian Jews that made its way to Shanghai and Yokohama after World War I and the Russian revolution did not reach Nagasaki, because business opportunities in the Kyushu port were limited and there were no longer families like the Lessners to assist new immigrants and hold the Jewish community together.

The connection between the Jewish communities in Shanghai and Nagasaki that had begun in 1859, however, remained close to the end. Not only did Sophie Lessner die in Shanghai, but the last person buried in the Jewish section of Nagasaki's international cemetery (in 1922) was a commission agent from Shanghai who had come to a neighboring spa in a failed attempt to recover his health.[49]

In late 1923 the final curtain began to descend on the Jewish presence in Nagasaki. With Mrs. Lessner's death and the departure of practically the entire Jewish population from the port city, some ex-residents who were at the time living in Shanghai decided to empower the Shanghai Zionist Association and the Oihel Moishe Synagogue to dispose of the Beth-El Synagogue in Nagasaki.[50] Acting upon instructions from these groups, the Japanese government in Nagasaki auctioned off the property and building and sent a check for $2,618 to N.E.B. Ezra of the Zionist Association in Shanghai.[51]

The close ties between the Jewish communities in Shanghai and Nagasaki are reflected in the fact that, when the time came to end the Jewish presence in the latter port, the Jewish population disregarded national boundaries and turned to Shanghai for assistance. Instead of looking for help from Jewish communities in Japan at Yokohama and Kobe, the remaining Jews in Nagasaki turned to compatriots with closer historical bonds, even though they lived in a different country.

The Shanghai–Nagasaki Judaic connection in the late nineteenth and early twentieth centuries reinforces the notion that, when studying the treaty ports of East Asia of this period, it is essential to examine them as part of a larger network that transcends national boundaries. This is especially true when one considers the fact that many of the Jews who came to East Asia were originally stateless peoples to whom nationality meant less than shared religious and cultural values.

Notes

1. Important East Asian ports outside China included such cities as Yokohama, Pusan, Vladivostok, Hakodate, Kobe, and Nagasaki.
2. John K. Fairbank, *Trade and Diplomacy on the China Coast: The Opening of the Treaty Ports, 1842–1854* (Cambridge, MA: Harvard University Press, 1953), p. 155.
3. Joan G. Roland, *Jews in British India: Identity in a Colonial Era* (Hanover and London: University Press of New England, 1989), p. 16. In a paper entitled "Baghdadi Jews in India and China: A Comparison of Economic Roles," Roland states that in 1867 Elias, jealous of his older brother's assumption as head of the family's business operations in Bombay upon their father's death, "resigned from the parent firm and established a rival company to be known as E. D. Sassoon and Company. The original firm, David Sassoon and Company, continued to act as general merchants; the new firm became involved mainly in banking and property and ultimately became more prosperous" (pp. 4–5). Paper presented at a conference on Jewish Diasporas in China: Comparative and Historical Perspectives, Harvard University, August 16–18, 1992.
4. James V. Davidson, in his 1964 account *Yellow Creek: The Story of Shanghai* (Philadelphia: Dufour, 1964), asserts that David Sassoon opened a branch office in Shanghai in 1845 (p. 35), a claim I have not been able to confirm.
5. *North China Herald*, August 3, 1850, p. 1.
6. David Kranzler, *Japanese, Nazis, and Jews: The Jewish Refugee Community of Shanghai, 1938–1945* (New York: Yeshiva University Press, 1976), p. 48.
7. Ibid., p. 49.
8. N.E.B. Ezra, "Shanghai," in *The Jewish Encyclopedia* (New York and London: Funk and Wagnalls, 1905), vol. 9, p. 232.
9. Ibid. The driving force behind both the Zionist Association and the newspaper was N.E.B. Ezra. Ezra was the editor of *Israel's Messenger* from its founding in 1904 until his death in 1936. For more information on Ezra and his relationship to the Zionist movement, see chapter III.D.1 in this volume by *Maruyama* Naoki.
10. Kranzler, *Japanese,* p. 49. For more information on Hardoon, see chapter III.C.1 in this volume by Chiara Betta.
11. Kranzler, *Japanese,* p. 55.
12. Ibid., p. 60.
13. According to the *North China Herald,* February 19, 1859, Sassoon & Sons dispatched the British ship *Henry Ellis* on February 13.
14. Montegue Paske-Smith, *Western Barbarians in Japan and Formosa in Tokugawa Days, 1603–1868* (New York: Paragon, 1968), facing p. 234. Sassoon and Sons followed only Dent and Company, Jardine-Matheson & Company, and Walsh and Company, all three of which had representatives serving as foreign consuls in Nagasaki for Portugal, France, and the United States, respectively, and thus were given first priority in lot selection.
15. Shinya *Sugiyama,* "Thomas B. Glover: A British Merchant in Japan, 1861–70," *Business History* 26, no. 2 (1984), p. 117.
16. John G. Walsh, U.S. consul to Nagasaki to the secretary of state, October 3, 1860. "Record of the Original Allotment of Land in the Foreign Quarter at the Port of Nagasaki, Japan" contained in the *Records of the United States Consulate at Nagasaki, Japan, 1859–1941* (Record Group 84), National Archives, Washington D.C.
17. Lane Earns and Brian Burke-Gaffney, *Across the Gulf of Time: The International Cemeteries of Nagasaki* (Nagasaki: Nagasaki Bunkensha, 1991), p. 153.
18. Goldenberg was a native of Galatz, Romania, who came to Nagasaki in the mid-1870s and operated a series of successful taverns and inns. He married a Japanese

woman named Ide Kita in October 1894 and saw his wife and three children embrace Judaism before his death in 1898. For further details concerning Goldenberg, see Lane Earns, "Life at the Bottom of the Hill: A Jewish-Japanese Family in the Nagasaki Foreign Settlement," *Crossroads: A Journal of Nagasaki History and Culture,* no. 2 (1994), pp. 79–90. Goldman was an Austrian national who at different times was a storekeeper and a tavern proprietor. He died in Alexandria in early 1889, after having left Nagasaki the previous year because of ill health. His wife, child, and sister all died and were buried in Nagasaki.

19. The names of the various Jewish merchants and the hotels and taverns they operated are found in *The Nagasaki Directory,* an annual listing of foreign residents in Nagasaki printed in Hong Kong. The directory began in 1865 and continued, in one form or another, until 1941.

20. *Rising Sun and Nagasaki Express* (Nagasaki), September 7, 1887, p. 2.

21. The adoption of their son in 1893 occurred under rather unusual circumstances. Sigmund Lessner was informed by a passenger who had arrived in Nagasaki by ship from Shanghai that a Japanese woman had also been on board accompanied by three European boys—one of whom appeared to be Jewish. Lessner combed the city and found the woman and children. The woman claimed that she had bought the children three years earlier, but her story proved inconsistent when questioned by authorities as to where and from whom she had purchased them (*Rising Sun and Nagasaki Express,* August 23, 1893, p. 3). Upon further investigation, the woman agreed to relinquish her claim to the Jewish child for a price—originally $300, but later agreed upon at $10. Under a court ruling, Lessner agreed to support the child, named Pessi Abramovich, for one year, while a search was conducted for his father. If after that time the father could not be located, or it was determined that he did not want the child, Lessner would adopt Pessi as his son (*Rising Sun and Nagasaki Express,* September 20; 1893, pp. 2–3). Pessi (Percy) was adopted by the Lessners the following year and raised in Nagasaki before moving on to Shanghai as an adult to conduct business. I would like to thank Brian Burke-Gaffney of Nagasaki for information regarding this incident.

22. *Nagasaki Press* (Nagasaki), January 27, 1905, p. 2.

23. *Rising Sun and Nagasaki Express,* May 13, 1896, p. 2.

24. Earns and Burke-Gaffney, *Across the Gulf of Time,* p. 159.

25. Contained in *Raikan* (Official Correspondence), July 28, 1892. Original handwritten correspondence between Western consulates and Japanese government officials in Nagasaki from 1860 to 1905, held in the local history section of the Nagasaki Prefectural Library.

26. *Nagasaki Shipping List* (Nagasaki), September 4, 1896, p. 2.

27. A gabbai is a synagogue officer, usually treasurer.

28. For an example of an attack on the Jewish tavern owners, see *Nagasaki Press,* November 7, 1902, p. 2.

29. Ibid., January 13, 1903, p. 2.

30. Ibid., July 20, 1903, p. 2.

31. Ginsburg went on to become an influential banker in Russia. Marcus Mess died in St. Petersburg in January 1909, leaving behind a wife and five children (*Nagasaki Press,* January 23, 1909, p. 2).

32. *Nagasaki Press,* March 13, 1909, p. 2.

33. The foreign settlement at Nagasaki was officially closed in 1899, but the number of foreigners living in the town continued to swell until the Russo–Japanese War. Most chose to retain their residences within the confines of the former settlement.

34. For a record of Jewish residents buried in the addition, see Earns and Burke-Gaffney, *Across the Gulf of Time,* p. 265.

35. In February 1910 one of these tavern owners, Moses Fuxman, the proprietor of the "Oriental Bar," was arrested for possession of counterfeit money (*Nagasaki Press,* February 19, 1910, p. 2). In 1913 a fire that began in the "Navy Club Hotel" occupied by one Abram Greenberg destroyed three surrounding buildings owned by the Japanese widow of Haskel Goldenberg (*Nagasaki Press,* September 26, 1913, p. 2).

36. *Nagasaki Press,* February 9, 1917, p. 2.
37. Ibid., December 14, 1917, p. 2.
38. Ibid., July 22, 1917, p. 2.
39. Ibid., September 15, 1918, p. 1.
40. Ibid., July 5, 1919, p. 2.
41. Ibid., February 25, 1920, p. 2.
42. Ibid.
43. Ibid., February 26, 1920, p. 2.
44. Lessner's obituary in *Nagasaki Press* remarked: "In him the little ones of the community have lost a great-hearted friend, and many who have left Nagasaki will hear with sadness of his passing. In past days his Christmas show was one of the sights of Nagasaki and to the children who went to look at the toys he was very generous and the personification of the Spirit of Christmas." One of the children who was sorry indeed to hear of Lessner's death was thirteen-year-old Geraldine Walvoord, the daughter of a Reformed Church missionary who had departed Nagasaki three months earlier in the aftermath of the sudden passing of her own father. Geraldine, who today is ninety years old and lives in Holland, Michigan, still cherishes a wooden-covered book of dried flowers entitled *Flowers of the Holy Land* given to her by Lessner. The book, presented by Lessner on June 12, 1918, includes the handwritten inscription "To my little friend, Miss Geraldine Walvoord, With Love, S.D. Lessner."
45. *Nagasaki Press,* March 20, 1920, p. 2.
46. Ibid., September 3, 1920, p. 2.
47. Ibid., July 15, 1923, p. 2. It was not uncommon for members of the Jewish community in Nagasaki to travel to Shanghai for special services. Herman Dicker, in *Wanderers and Settlers in the Far East: A Century of Jewish Life in China and Japan* (New York: Twayne, 1962), notes that a Jewish couple from Nagasaki had to take their son to Shanghai in 1904 to have a bris (*brit milah*) performed because there was no qualified circumciser in Nagasaki (p. 162).
48. *Nagasaki Press,* July 15, 1923, p. 2; and *North China Herald,* July 14, 1923, p. 108.
49. See Earns and Burke-Gaffney, *Across the Gulf of Time,* p. 265, for an account of the death of Robert Roth.
50. *Nagasaki Press,* September 21, 1924, p. 2.
51. While the sale of the synagogue in Nagasaki marks the symbolic end of the Jewish community in Nagasaki, a few Jews still remained in town. One was Abraham Cohn, a Romanian Jew who had lived in Nagasaki since 1914. He later moved to Shanghai, where he became an important member of the Jewish community during the Japanese occupation of the city (Marvin Tokayer and Mary Swartz, *The Fugu Plan: The Untold Story of the Japanese and the Jews During World War II* [New York and London: Paddington Press, 1979], p. 227).

Part III

Twentieth-Century Baghdadi and Ashkenazi Experiences

A. Urban Profiles: Hong Kong

Chapter III.A.1

Environmental Interactions of the Jews of Hong Kong

Dennis A. Leventhal

On January 26, 1841, the British Navy planted a flag on Hong Kong Island. Until then, Hong Kong had been virtually a historical irrelevancy. The nearby mainland and surrounding islands hold some "digs" evincing inhabitants of various Chinese dynasties, such as the Ming, Song, and Han, and even the Neolithic period. But despite the extensive maritime activity of the Southern Song and early Ming, and the flood of coastal pirates coming out of Ashikaga Japan, "Fragrant Harbor" (the literal translation of "Hong Kong") apparently had never developed into anything much more than a minor anchorage and careenage for fishermen and smugglers throughout the long course of Chinese imperial history. However, it did serve as a neutral point of contact with the outside world, and it is that aspect that held a potential subsequently realized for developing East–West relationships.[1]

When the Treaty of Nanjing in 1842 added Hong Kong to Britain's mercantile/colonial network, it became a staging point for trade with the treaty ports of the China coast. It evolved slowly during the nineteenth and early twentieth centuries, and then exploded into a major entrepôt with the post–World War II boom in East Asia, fueled further by the opening of the China trade in the late 1970s.[2]

Jewry in Hong Kong followed a similar evolution. Jews were among the first settlers in the 1840s, and a Jewish community life began to develop from the mid-1850s.[3] This early community consisted primarily of Baghdadi commercial pioneers whose families had migrated under the protecting wings of British imperial expansion from the Middle East, through India, and from there on to the China coast and Japan. The prime focus of their activities in Hong Kong was management of their commercial links (primarily in general trading) with the Chinese treaty ports.

These merchants of Baghdadi origin can be characterized as international family networks, with intermarriages almost as important as capital for the generation of business. Their paternalistic leaders assumed responsibility for organizing Jewish community life wherever they settled. In Hong Kong. this resulted in the establishment of a Jewish cemetery in 1858, and the construction of Hong Kong's first and only synagogue building, Ohel Leah, in 1901–2. As Jewish community leaders, they also donated both funds and land to the Jewish community in the form of a trust (dated April 13, 1903), which remains today a prime support for the maintenance of Jewish community property and religious activities.[4]

While some European Jews, primarily from France, also settled in Hong Kong and established new specialty businesses such as retailing,[5] the core of the community remained Baghdadi. Even as late as 1925, when the community's first cantor was imported from Baghdad, the primary language of the majority of the community was still Arabic.[6]

Estimating the size of this community in its earlier stages is problematical because of the lack of adequate internal records. We know the names of the leading families—Sassoon, Kadoorie, Somech, Sopher, Gubbay, and others; but we do not know the numbers of relatives and family retainers who formed the backbone of their business infrastructure.[7] While a 1914 publication describes Ohel Leah Synagogue as having "accommodation for about 500 persons," a 1933 publication states the community consisted of between fifty and seventy-five families, and a 1936 publication puts the Jewish population at around one hundred persons.[8]

In both 1937 and the immediate post–World War II period, influxes of Jewish refugees from the China mainland, primarily from Shanghai, placed a strain on the resources of the local Hong Kong community. However, these were transient phenomena, and most of these refugees eventually moved on to such places as North America, Australia, and Israel within a relatively short time.[9]

It was the post–World War II boom in Asian trade, and the opening of the China trade in particular, that led to a dramatic increase in Hong Kong's Jewish population, as well as fundamental changes in the demographic and religious character of the community. In 1989, there were 384 voting members of Ohel Leah Synagogue/Jewish Recreation Club of Hong Kong (OLS/JRC), with some 80 children from these families registered in the community's various educational and social programs. A 1989 questionnaire-survey of this membership, which achieved a 39 percent return, revealed a profile of nationality groupings as follows: 39 percent American,

27 percent British, 17 percent Israeli, and 17 percent other. Of these respondents, 71 percent indicated Ashkenazi identification.[10]

This demographic change was reflected in Ohel Leah services, which had begun to follow the Ashkenazi form. Also in 1989, a small number of Syrian Jews established their own separate minyan (quorum for prayer services) and imported their own rabbi, and the Lubavitch Hasidic movement established a Chabad House and picked up a small following. In that same year, the United Jewish Congregation of Hong Kong, the first organized Reform-Liberal group, was founded.[11] Today, these groups together have a constituency of approximately six hundred families. The total of unaffiliated Jewish residents of Hong Kong, however, is unknown. Subjective "guestimates" range from two thousand to four thousand.

As further indication of these fundamental changes, it should be noted that, whereas the vast majority of the pre–World War II Jewish population were descendants of the families and associates of the nineteenth-century Baghdadi commercial pioneers (that is, were virtually lifetime residents), the 1989 survey indicated that some 55 percent of the population at that time had lived in Hong Kong for four years or less and only 14 percent indicated Hong Kong residency for more than twenty years.[12]

Economic Activities

Very little work has been done on specifically Jewish economic activities in Hong Kong. Of the early Baghdadi merchant houses, only the Sassoons seem to have been the subject of focused published study.[13] Lord Kadoorie's anecdotal memoir dated 1979 provides some personalized insights to the nature of Jewish commercial activities on the China coast and their familial links within the rubric of the British empire during the late nineteenth and early twentieth centuries.[14] However, that these commercial pioneers helped build Hong Kong's basic economic infrastructure is evinced by their part in establishing the Hong Kong and Shanghai Banking Corporation and their continuous membership on its board of directors during its early years.[15]

The immense contribution of the Kadoorie family to the post–World War II economic success story of Hong Kong is documented in various publications.[16] Their business activities concentrated in Hong Kong & Shanghai Hotels Ltd. (i.e., the Peninsula Group), China Light and Power Company (which is a major investor in the Daya Bay nuclear power facility), the Peak Tram Company, and others.[17] Their many philanthropic activities have been geared primarily to bringing economic "self-help" education to the local Hong Kong Chinese population.[18] In addition to the world-famous Kadoorie

Agricultural Aid Association Experimental and Extension Farm in Hong Kong, the Kadoories established schools and hospitals in Hong Kong, China, India, Nepal, and the Middle East.

During the nineteenth and early twentieth centuries, local Baghdadi mercantile activities can be seen as part of an international network of family and ethnic ties that placed itself within different cultural environments, maintained a degree of cultural isolation, and focused its commercial efforts on "niche" activities not readily accessible to the people of its various cultural environments. This analytical paradigm, that is, the "trading diaspora," is explored in Philip D. Curtin's *Cross-Cultural Trade in World History* (New York: Cambridge University Press, 1984), and could be a useful analytical tool when more detailed information about early Jewish economic activities in Hong Kong and other East Asian locations is uncovered. However, because of increasing links with Hong Kong's governing British bureaucracy, and positive responses to the challenges of Hong Kong's changing regional economic role, local established Jewish economic activity gradually became part and parcel of the basic economic infrastructure of Hong Kong itself as a modern manufacturing and financial center.

The expansion of China trade after the signing of the 1972 Shanghai Communiqué, in which China and the United States announced their intention to work toward normalization of diplomatic relations, led to a large influx of American investment and businessmen. Hong Kong's population began to include Jews involved in a much wider range of economic activities, as shown in the 1989 survey referred to above. Specifically, among the respondents, 24 percent stated they were involved in trading or retailing; 23 percent in service industries, for example, banking, finance, transportation, and insurance; 18 percent in various professions, such as law, education, medicine, and art; 14 percent in manufacturing; and 2 percent in government. Furthermore, 62.5 percent of the female respondents indicated being engaged in business or professional activities. Of those directly involved with China, 73.6 percent began that involvement *after* the Shanghai Communiqué was signed.[19]

The question of what would follow the 1997 handover to Chinese Mainland control is of concern to Hong Kong's Jewish community as well as other resident groups. The 1989 survey indicated that 77 percent of the respondents believed that they would leave Hong Kong before 1999. It should be noted, however, that we cannot link this response directly to the 1997 issue. Because many of the respondents came to Hong Kong as employees of large multinational corporations, many of them will leave because of normal corporate rotations for "international" staff.[20] Thus, this percentage needs to be correlated with the historical annual turnover in OLS/JRC membership to permit any meaningful interpretative extrapolation. It is also easy to generalize by saying that, since the local Jewish community is here primarily to enjoy the economic freedoms of a constitutionally laissez-faire economic system, if the People's Republic of China's post-1997 Special Administrative Region (SAR) government in Hong Kong changed that system sufficiently to affect adversely Jewish economic interests, an exodus is possible.

Of real significance, however, is a major project, begun physically in 1990, in which the property of the Jewish Community Trust is undergoing redevelopment. The end result will include repair and renovation of Ohel Leah Synagogue, construction of new and greatly expanded facilities for the religious school and club, and residential facilities that will provide enhanced regular income for the Trust. "Given the published concerns about the forthcoming re-unification of Hong Kong with the People's Republic of China in 1997, these developmental activities demonstrate remarkable confidence in the future of Hong Kong, and the Chinese government's promise of continued religious freedom."[21]

Acculturation and Assimilation

Discussing acculturation and assimilation within the context of Hong Kong is a bit complex. Created by British colonial bureaucrats and merchants, Hong Kong developed an ever-increasing Chinese population responding to the demand for labor and attracted foreign merchants who saw the British flag as an umbrella of security for their activities. The resultant demographic uniqueness of Hong Kong must be understood before looking at the place of Jews within the local society.

A local government report dated 1845 gave a breakdown of the total population of 23,817 as follows:

Europeans	595
Indian	362
Chinese in brick buildings	7,460
Chinese in boats	3,600
Laborers	10,000
Visitors	300
Chinese in the employ of Europeans	1,500[22]

In 1859, the total population grew to 86,941, of which 98 percent were Chinese. By 1865, the total was 125,504, with Europeans numbering

2,034. By 1898, the total was 254,400, of which 6 percent were British and other foreigners. In 1925, Chinese constituted 97 percent of a population of 725,100. At the end of World War II, Hong Kong's total population reached 1,600,000.[23]

In 1992, with a total population of some 5.8 million (roughly comparable to the population of Switzerland), Hong Kong's foreign population has increased to the point where the total number of resident American nationals just about matches the *entire* population of Hong Kong in 1845.[24] The proportion of foreigners to Chinese has not changed appreciably over the years. The "mix" among the foreign residents themselves has undergone considerable change.

The mix among the Chinese themselves has changed, also. The earlier, pre–World War II Chinese population was primarily Cantonese, with Hakka, Shantou, and Jiuzhou minorities. After the Communist takeover in 1949, a large influx of Shanghainese provided a new social element, along with a new source of entrepreneurial talent. Following the establishment of China's "Open Door" policy, which began the country's reintegration into the world economic community, there has been an appreciable inflow of Chinese from various other provinces, many of whom are involved with Beijing's increasing investments and other business interests in Hong Kong.

As noted above, the "mix" among Hong Kong's Jewish population has also changed dramatically, that is, the predominantly Baghdadi plus West European Jewish population of pre–World War II Hong Kong has changed to a predominantly American, British, and Israeli "mix."

The interests, concerns, and social structures, networks of political and economic relationships, and "international" orientation of the foreign elements have always diverged considerably from those of the local Chinese population. The Jewish population tended to hold "international" perspectives similar to those of the other foreigners, in an environment that was relatively comfortable with a cultural plurality reinforced by the sense of class distinctions of the British colonial overlords.

The maintenance of social distinctions within the foreign community of Hong Kong is reflected by its long tradition of club-centered social life. As of 1998, this "dot on the map" still has such "exclusive" clubs as Royal Hong Kong Yacht Club, Royal Hong Kong Jockey Club, Hong Kong Club, Ladies Recreation Club, and many others, including clubs for various ethnic and national groupings, such as Americans, Indians, and Pakistanis.

The Jewish Recreation Club of Hong Kong was built in 1905, a gift from the Kadoorie family. It quickly became the social center of the Jewish community. A description of this club, published in 1925, reflects a picture of a Jewish society very much in tune with the lifestyle of Hong Kong's British colonial rulers:

> This [club] was equipped with something of the comfort characteristic of a social or political club in the West End of London. There was a large and tastefully furnished room with a grand piano, which could serve as drawing-room, concert hall and lecture theatre; there was a billiard room that was seldom neglected, and a bar presided over by a white-jacketed Chinese mixer who could dispense any cocktail you chose.[25]

This image of affinity to British culture is further colored by a roll call of some of the Jews who were an integral part of the British establishment. Some Jewish community leaders were recipients of knighthoods and patents of nobility from the British crown, such as Sir Elly Kadoorie, Sir Ellis Kadoorie, Sir Horace Kadoorie, and Lord Lawrence Kadoorie. Some appointed governmental leaders of Hong Kong were also Jewish, for example, Sir Matthew Nathan (governor of Hong Kong from 1904 to 1907), and Sir Piers Jacobs (finance secretary during the late 1980s and early 1990s). Distinctly Jewish names can be found on the role of Past Masters of an English Masonic Lodge in Hong Kong.[26]

Nevertheless, the very existence of a "Jewish" club, that is, for Jews only, in conjunction with the synagogue as the center of Jewish community life, makes it clear that a degree of ethnic and religious integrity was maintained by this community. The current situation, a product of the dramatic demographic changes mentioned above, presents an interesting picture. The respondents to the 1989 survey, all members of Ohel Leah Synagogue, include people from thirty-three different countries of birth. Of these, 73 percent know more than one language, and 43 percent know more than two languages.[27] Collectively, the respondents are speakers of twenty-three different languages. Religious-philosophical affiliations and perspectives run the full gamut from Hasidic to mainstream Orthodox to secular-humanist.[28] In short, Hong Kong now presents a Jewish cultural collage that can be seen as a microcosm of world Jewry. This microcosm is further reflected by the nature of its internal conflicts between Orthodox and Reform, Orthodox and Trustees, and Orthodox and Orthodox.[29]

The community's relationship with the majority Chinese population needs much more research. We have no data on the numbers of Chinese employed by Jewish-owned companies throughout Hong Kong's history. The early Jewish merchant houses employed compradors, or ethnic Chinese agents in charge of Chinese employees, in the same fashion as did other foreign businesses.[30] But we have as yet little detailed information on this aspect of commercial relationships with the local population.[31] It is known that the early Jewish "patriarchs" shared their wealth with the Chinese through philanthropic activities. For example, Sir Ellis Kadoorie established a number of nondenominational schools in Hong Kong, Guangzhou, and Shanghai to "provide Chinese students with a background in English so as to assist them in obtaining work with the foreign firms set up in this part of the world."[32]

The 1989 community profile survey points to some more definable aspects of Jewish relationships with the Chinese environment. Five percent of the respondents indicated having been born in China and 3 percent in Hong Kong itself. Eleven percent indicated that their parents have lived in China and 9 percent in Hong Kong.[33]

Three percent indicated that their primary or native language is Cantonese, in particular Chinese women who have converted to Judaism as a result of marriage.[34] Of those who have learned Chinese as a second language, 9 percent of the survey respondents know Mandarin and 7 percent know Cantonese.[35]

No statistics exist on assimilation in Hong Kong. Most Jewish children go to college overseas in North America, Europe, or Australia. Some of the high school–age children go to boarding schools abroad. This present-day practice apparently conforms to a traditional pattern of the earlier residents of Hong Kong. Even the local patriarch, Lord Kadoorie, received his advanced education overseas.[36] Since most of these children make their way in life in their "home" countries, any input they may make to the statistics of assimilation would most probably occur in those countries. However, anecdotal evidence suggests that the younger members of families who have made a lifetime commitment to Hong Kong as their home return to Hong Kong after advanced education abroad and reconnect with local Jewish organizations. It remains to be seen if this trend will endure well after Hong Kong's 1997 handover to the People's Republic.

Jewish schooling, generally considered an important facet of defense against assimilation, has never been very strong in Hong Kong. A 1914 report states that there was no religious school at that time.[37] A 1936 report states that a small school had been started "some time ago," but was closed "owing to the lack of interest in parents in sending their children to it to learn Hebrew."[38] Current educational programs are evolving to meet the changing needs of a changing community. The Ezekiel Abraham School is a Sunday school (with some midweek classes) for five- to thirteen-year-olds. With a 1991/92 enrollment of approximately eighty children, it offers instruction in the Hebrew language and Jewish history, culture, and religious observances. The Lubavitch Hasidic movement has a small nursery school. A modest teen social program has begun, and adult education courses have been available for the past several years.

The most striking manifestation of new educational efforts is the Carmel School. Throughout the history of the Hong Kong Jewish community, because of the relatively small number of Jewish children, no attempt was ever made to set up a Jewish day school. However, in 1991/92, the Carmel School for preschoolers was established as a day school with an enrollment of thirty children in the three- to four-year-old range. For the 1992/93 year, there were fifty-seven applications for preschool enrollment as of May 1992 and twelve applications for a Primary One class. If the demand warranted, it was intended to expand up through the primary grades in a gradual, step-by-step manner.

Antisemitism

"There is no antisemitism in Hong Kong."[39] This has been stated many times and, on the surface, would seem to be true. None of the pre–World War II published reports on Hong Kong Jewry mentions the existence of antisemitism. In fact, two of them comment positively on its absence. One states, "The Jews of China are held in the highest esteem by the foreign population and by the Chinese people."[40]

The 1989 survey found that 83 percent of the respondents held the opinion that the surrounding non-Jewish environment was fundamentally "neutral" toward Jews, that is, "the local people are unconcerned about, or ignorant of, Jewish affairs and people." Another 15 percent felt the environment is "philosemitic," that is, "has respect and regard for Jewish culture and Jewish people."[41]

The standard rationale for this delightful phenomenon is that Jewish presence on the China coast has been marked by small numbers and noteworthy entrepreneurial and philanthropic achievements, within a context that is generally devoid of Christian mental baggage and holds many cultural values and traits similar to those of traditional Jewish culture. However, the cultural similarities between Chinese and Jew are of less real significance than the much greater cultural differences.[42] Balanced and accurate knowledge of Jewish history and culture is not now, and has never been, available to the Chinese people as part of their regular education. There is also much anecdotal evidence that the vast majority of the Chinese lack understanding of the distinctions between the State of Israel and Judaism/Jews. I am therefore forced to the conclusion that one may not necessarily assume unlimited continuity of the status quo in terms of the absence of antisemitism. The upsurge in the 1990s in Japanese literary antisemitism adequately demonstrates the possibility of this phenomenon appearing in a non-Christian, non-Muslim, Asian cultural framework.

There has been one recent case of antisemitic libel stemming from a Chinese. In April 1991, the *Hong Kong Daily News,* a local Chinese-language newspaper, published an article, under the pseudonym of "Ah Wei," entitled "The Jews' Deep-Rooted Bad Habits: The Bad Nature of the Jews." This article was a potpourri of defamatory remarks derived from standard antisemitic literature. It made such statements as "Why have these people (the Jews) been cursed by God to wander the world forever?" "Who was it that betrayed Jesus? You just think about it"; "Everywhere (they go) they make money and cheat people, yet they keep themselves aloof and have never thought of giving something back to society. Is this reasonable?" "Some of America's congressmen are financially supported behind the scenes by Jews"; "(Jews) are heartless, rich, cruel and ruthless warmongers, a selfish and avaricious race"; "They (the Jews) are united in oppressing and harming weak peoples"; and "They (the Jews) are a calamity for humanity."

The Jewish community responded to this by sending a deputation to the office of the editor of the offending newspaper presenting a letter of protest for allowing such an article to be printed and requesting a commitment not to allow such incitement to racial hatred to occur again. The written response from the newspaper's general manager demonstrated a total lack of understanding of the potential dangers of articles of this nature. It asserted that Ah Wei's article was protected by an editorial policy "in line with the tradition of speech freedom." It claimed that the paper did "not hold any prejudicial stand on sensitive issues such as those relating to racial matters" and that their editorial policy did not "bar us (the editors) from making fair comments on matters of public interest."[43] In planning a suitable reply, the Jewish group discovered that Hong Kong has no statute prohibiting incitement to racial violence.

While this was a one-time occurrence,[44] the local English-language press maintains a low-grade anti-Israel stance. However, this may not be conscious editorial policy because most of their published stories relating to Israel are taken from the wire services, rather than being original work by their own reporters. Thus, the biases in reporting seem to stem from the writers for the Western wire services. It should be noted that, whenever Israel appears prominently in the news in an adverse light, it usually stimulates a spate of "negative" letters to the press or adverse editorials.

That some expatriate residents of Hong Kong have brought anti-Jewish prejudice with them to Hong Kong was in evidence during the 1987–88 public controversy over the plan for redevelopment of Jewish Trust property. The controversy arose over the question of whether the old synagogue building would be replaced or repaired and renovated, and led to non-Jewish authorities' and individuals' trying to control the course of events in this matter. It became an occasion for some non-Jews to make calumnious accusations in the local English-language press against the Trustees of Ohel Leah Synagogue in particular and Jews in general.[45]

American Jews (with children) in Hong Kong have to face a unique situation. The only school in Hong Kong with an American curriculum is the Hong Kong International School (HKIS). While its academic standards are high, for curious historical reasons it is owned by the Missouri State Lutheran Synod. As a result, the formal statement of its "mission and character" includes the following:

> Hong Kong International School lives with a paradox: its foundation is the Christian Gospel, yet it serves a community which is religiously plural. In response, HKIS expresses its Christian commitment formally, through such activities as religious instruction and chapel programs, as well as informally through relationships choosing to expose students to the teachings and example of Christ *while maintaining respect for students' personal beliefs* (italics added).[46]

The reality behind this statement of principle has been observed by this writer by virtue of his having put two children through this school, beginning with kindergarten. It has been observed, for example, that while the general academic caliber of its teachers is high, priority in hiring goes to candidates with a strong sense of "Christian mission." As a result, there have been, and continue to be, regular incidences of "heavy" Christian proselytizing by individual teachers at every grade level.

Contrary to the practices of most other private Christian schools worldwide, which allow non-Christian students to choose freely whether or not to take religion courses, HKIS makes religion classes and chapel attendance mandatory for all elementary and junior high students. Furthermore, high school students must take a minimum of one religion course for each year in attendance in order to graduate. While this latter is in theory an "elective," the range and nature of religion courses offered ensures that a majority of the courses will of necessity be wholly Christian in content or interpretive perspective.

As a result of close and continuous monitoring of course content, individual teacher approaches, and "required reading" materials (much of which retains the anti-Jewish biases of Christian thought documented and analyzed in Rosemary Ruether, *Faith and Fratricide: The Theological Roots of Anti-Semitism* [New York: Seabury Press, 1974]), this writer is convinced that the last portion of the above "mission statement" is "honored more in the breach." Although most of the negative effects of this can be dealt with in a low-key fashion by sensitive and knowledgeable monitoring and response by parents, it remains an uncomfortable situation for American Jewish parents, especially since they have virtually no other local option for obtaining a high quality, American-style education for their children.

The incidents and situations reported above will naturally seem quite mild, even negligible, in comparison with antisemitic manifestations in other places in the world. They are cited here only to characterize and highlight the relative absence of this psychosocial obscenity in Hong Kong and, on the other hand, to suggest that there is sufficient reason to caution against complacency. In sum, given the fundamental absence of antisemitism amongst the general populace, Hong Kong continues to offer a comfortable environment for Jewish life.

Conclusion

It is obvious that much more research is needed before the full impact of Jewish economic activity on Hong Kong's development can be assessed. At present, we do not even have a historical roster of Jewish-owned companies, numbers of employees, and nature and volumes of business, a basic starting point for such analysis.

What is clear, however, is that Jewish life in Hong Kong has paralleled the evolution of Hong Kong itself, and is directly linked to the fate of Hong Kong under the post-1997 SAR government. If Hong Kong's position as a major entrepôt and a major financial center can be maintained, the extraordinary growth following the signing of the Shanghai Communiqué will not be lost and will experience positive continuation, with a corresponding effect on the life and health of the Jewish community. If Hong Kong reverts to a backwater of history as a result of policies that place Beijing's immediate political concerns over economic realities, Jewish life in Hong Kong will fade away in corresponding fashion.

At present, the Jewish community has a positive attitude toward the future. Its numbers are increasing, it has begun a major facilities redevelopment program, and there now exists a wider range of facilities for Jewish self-expression than ever before in Hong Kong's history.

Jewish life in Hong Kong offers some interesting areas of research. The earlier phase of Baghdadi commercial pioneers presents the potential of a valuable case study in trade diaspora relationships and the nature of their functioning. The rapid growth of the Jewish community in the years since the Shanghai Communiqué was signed can be studied as a facet of Hong Kong's role in the expansion of the China trade. The increasing complexity of internal community relationships in recent years offers a social laboratory for the study of Jewish intracommunal problems. And the full extent and effects of Jewish contributions to the evolution of Hong Kong itself have yet to be documented and analyzed.

The Hong Kong experience could turn out to be a short-lived phase in the long history of the Jewish Diaspora. It could also prove to be an important staging area for positive cross-cultural exchanges between the Chinese and Jewish peoples well into the twenty-first century. In either case, the Jewish experience in Hong Kong forms a significant part of modern Diaspora history by virtue of its having been, and being, a proactive foothold in East Asia.

Notes

1. See S. Jackson, *The Sassoons* (New York: E.P. Dutton, 1968), p. 23.
2. G.B. Endacott, *A History of Hong Kong* (Hong Kong: Oxford University Press, 1964), is a standard historical survey, with major emphasis on local government policies and problems.
3. The Sassoon family, which had "already established a merchant house in Canton and Macau," was among the first Hong Kong settlers. N. Careem and M.A. Hopper, "The Legendary Name of Kadoorie," *Kaleidoscope*, 3, no. 9 (1976), p. 8.
4. See Lord Lawrence Kadoorie, *Review of Community Affairs* (Hong Kong: Private publication of the Incorporated Trustees of the Jewish Community of Hong Kong, 1986), p. 3.
5. "Prominent amongst them was the family who established Sennet Freres, the leading Jewelers here for many years" (ibid.).
6. Dennis A. Leventhal, *The Jewish Community of Hong Kong: An Introduction* (Hong Kong: Jewish Historical Society of Hong Kong, 1985; rev. 1988), p. 6.
7. Lord Lawrence Kadoorie, "The Kadoorie Memoir," *Sino-Judaic Studies: Whence and Whither* (Hong Kong: Hong Kong Jewish Chronicle, 1985), p. 83 (hereafter, cited as "Kadoorie Memoir").
8. Paula R. Sandfelder, "Some Views of Hong Kong's Jewish Community from the Past," *Faces of the Jewish Experience in China,* ed. Dennis A. Leventhal and Mary W. Leventhal (Hong Kong: Hong Kong Jewish Chronicle, 1990), pp. 21, 22.
9. One potential avenue of demographic research still relatively untouched is Hong Kong's Jewish cemetery. Containing more than three hundred graves, it has never been surveyed to provide base data for further research into the fundamental question of who came to Hong Kong, when, from where, and to do what. It could readily be compared with contemporaneous Jewish cemeteries of about the same size and in excellent condition in Yokohama and Kobe.
10. Dennis A. Leventhal and Mary W. Leventhal, "Profile of Hong Kong's Ohel Leah Synagogue/Jewish Recreation Club Community: A Survey Report," in *Faces of the Jewish Experience in China,* pp. 30, 33 (hereafter, cited as "Profile").
11. Ibid., pp. 3–6.
12. Ibid., p. 38.
13. Jackson, *Sassoons.* **Chan** Sui-jeung, of the University of Hong Kong, has reported that his investigations utilizing Hong Kong's Government Information Service,

which stores local newspapers and other materials, have not uncovered any materials relevant to this area of research.

14. "Kadoorie Memoir," pp. 83–86.

15. Frank H.K. King, *The History of the Hongkong and Shanghai Banking Corporation*, 4 vols., (Cambridge: Cambridge University Press, 1987–91); and Jackson, *Sassoons*, pp. 42–43, 101.

16. For example, see Nigel Cameron, *Power: The Story of China Light* (Hong Kong: Oxford University Press, 1982); and Anthony Lawrence, *Magic Carpets: The Tai Ping Story* (Hong Kong: Tai Ping Carpets, 1987).

17. For example, the Kadoories established Hong Kong's first textile factory, the Nanyang Cotton Mill Ltd., in cooperation with Y.C. *Wang* and H.S. *Yang*, two post–World War II immigrants from Shanghai. Interview with Lord Lawrence Kadoorie, May 19, 1992.

18. For example, see W.J. Blackie, *Kadoorie Agricultural Aid Association, 1951–1971* (Hong Kong: Libra Press, 1972).

19. "Profile," pp. 29, 43–44.

20. The transient nature of Hong Kong's "international" population is a well-noted phenomenon. Speaking of foreign community life in pre–World War II Hong Kong, Lord Kadoorie stated that "if Shanghai can be seen as a residence, Hong Kong must be viewed as a hotel." Interview, May 19, 1992.

21. "Profile," p. 6.

22. Endacott, *History*, p. 65.

23. Ibid., pp. 116, 252, 289, 310.

24. According to Hong Kong Immigration Department statistics, as of April 30, 1992, the ten largest resident expatriate groups are as follows: Filipinos, 81,000; Americans, 23,000; British, 18,000; Indians, 18,000; Thai, 18,000; Canadians, 16,000; Australians, 14,000; Japanese, 13,000; Malaysians, 12,000; and Portuguese, 9,000. See *South China Morning Post*, June 22, 1992, p. 3.

25. I. Cohen, *The Journal of a Jewish Traveller* (London: John Lane, 1925), p. 116, quoted in Sandfelder, "Some," p. 16.

26. List of Past Masters of Perseverance Lodge of Hong Kong, No. 1165, F. & A.M. (English Constitution) includes such names as C.C. Cohen (1868), H.A. Cohen (1870), and A. Levy (1871–72).

27. "Profile," pp. 28–29, 36–37, and 41–42.

28. Ibid., pp. 34–35, 51–52.

29. A March 1992 controversy erupted over who is entitled to be buried in the Jewish Cemetery of Hong Kong. This is a Hong Kong scenario of the Orthodox assertion of authority on the "Who is a Jew?" question.

30. By the mid-nineteenth century the comprador, or compradore, was a Chinese merchant employed on contract to handle all the Chinese side of a foreign firm's activities, especially laborers and local business transactions. Compradors evolved into a class of entrepreneurs inextricably tied with the treaty ports. Thus, just as the Hotung family's businesses stemmed from a compradorship with Jardines, prominent Hong Kong businessman Stanley Ho's ancestors include a comprador serving the Sassoons. On the pre–Nanjing Treaty (1842) origins of compradors, see *Hao* Yen-ping, *The Comprador in Nineteenth Century China* (Cambridge, MA: Harvard University Press, 1970).

31. A new effort to dig into these relationships is explored in Motono Eiichi, "A Study of the Legal Status of the Compradores During the 1880s with Special Reference to the Three Civil Cases Between David Sassoon Sons & Co. and Their Compradores, 1884–1887," *Acta Asiatica: Bulletin of the Institute of Eastern Culture* (Tokyo), no. 62 (1992), pp. 44–70.

32. "Kadoorie Memoir," p. 89.
33. "Profile," pp. 39–40.
34. Ibid., p. 41. Intermarriage is not the only route by which Chinese have become Jews. Aside from the "Kaifeng story," my own two children are Chinese, adopted almost at birth and duly converted in accordance with *halacha,* or Jewish religious law. The oldest, our *lao-da,* graduated Brandeis University in 1996. The story of another family that added to our "Chinese Jewish" population by adoption is found in Avraham Schwartzbaum, *The Bamboo Cradle: A Jewish Father's Story* (New York: Feldheim, 1988).
35. "Profile," p. 42.
36. "Kadoorie Memoir," pp. 86, 88.
37. Joseph Krauskopf, "A Rabbi's Pilgrimage in the Orient," *Our Pulpit Sunday Discourse Delivered in Temple Keneseth Israel* (Philadelphia) 27, no. 17 (March 18, 1914), pp. 80–81; quoted in Sandfelder, "Some," p. 12.
38. W. Buchler, "The Jews of Hong Kong," *B'nai B'rith Magazine* (Cincinnati) 46, no. 2 (November 1931), pp. 56–57; quoted in Sandfelder, "Some," p. 22.
39. The hyphenated form of the word "anti-Semitism" suggests linguistically an opposition to "Semites." Since not all Semites are Jews, and not all Jews are Semites, I believe this word should not be hyphenated so as to stand as a distinct reference to a particular sociopsychological phenomenon. It is well known that this term was coined in the 1870s to denote the pseudo-scientific attempt to justify irrational hatred of Jews and Judaism. In this practice I follow Robert S. Wistrich, *Antisemitism: The Longest Hatred* (New York: Pantheon Books, 1991); Dennis Prager and Joseph Telushkin, *Why the Jews: The Reason for Antisemitism* (New York: Simon and Schuster, 1983); *Antisemitism World Report 1992* (London: Institute of Jewish Affairs, 1992); Bernet Litvinoff, *The Burning Bush: Antisemitism and World History* (London: W. Collins Sons & Co., 1988); and others.
40. Sandfelder, "Some," p. 25.
41. "Profile," p. 52.
42. See *Wang* Gung-wu, "Cultural Perceptions: Self and Others," in *The Jews and Asia: Old Societies and New Images, Proceedings of the Second Asian-Jewish Colloquium Held By the Asia Pacific Jewish Association* (Hong Kong, March 1987) (Melbourne, Queensland: Asia Pacific Jewish Association, 1989), pp. 30–33.
43. Letter from K.C. Lung, general manager and deputy publisher, *Hong Kong Daily News Ltd.,* to Dennis A. Leventhal, Chairman, Jewish Historical Society of Hong Kong, ref. no. KO24–6/91, dated June 27, 1991.
44. This can only be assumed since neither the Hong Kong Jewish community nor the Israeli consulate general in Hong Kong maintains a professional media-monitoring program to cover the local Chinese-language press.
45. A few examples suffice to demonstrate the nature of these published statements:
(a) "Mr. Bill Meacham, a member of the Antiquities Advisory Board, has accused Lord Kadoorie and his fellow trustees of selling the Jewish community's birthright to Swire Properties, which wants to destroy the synagogue and build on the site." Kath Southam, *Sunday Morning Post,* December 6, 1987, p. 7.
(b) "Many people in Hong Kong . . . feel powerless in the face of the onslaught of Lord Kadoorie and his well-organized supporters. . . . Others in the community are deprived of their place of worship because of Lord Kadoorie's blind determination to extract from the site a maximum commercial return." Open letter to the governor of Hong Kong from William Meacham, *South China Morning Post,* December 26, 1987, p. 8.
(c) "It is not the first time in Jewish history that sacrifices were made to Mammon. . . . The synagogue's future is an issue involving a lot of money . . . a big temptation. . . .

Anti-Arab and anti-German sentiments have been well maintained and perpetuated mainly by efforts of the Jewish race." Ivan Lau, Sally Lin, and John S.M. Leung, Letter to the editor, *Hong Kong Standard,* January 6, 1988.

(d) "'The saga of the Ohel Leah is beginning to look like a crucifixion . . . ,' (Bill Meacham) said." Nigel Rosser, *South China Morning Post,* May 23, 1988.

It should be noted that the controversial aspects of the redevelopment program were ultimately resolved by, and from within the resources of, the Jewish community itself. Outside, that is, non-Jewish, attempts to control these Jewish decisions about local Jewish destiny were finally warded off. Absurd attacks such as those referred to here above eventually disappeared from the press.

46. *Hong Kong International School: Academic Program Booklet, 92–93,* p. 1.

B. Urban Profiles: Harbin

Chapter III.B.1

The Construction of the Chinese Eastern Railway and the Origin of the Harbin Jewish Community, 1898–1931

Zvia Shickman-Bowman

Jewish settlers were attracted to Manchuria in general and to Harbin in particular because of the more tolerant tsarist Russian policy toward the Jews in this region.[1]

Tsarist Russia began to plan expansion into Manchuria toward the end of the nineteenth century. In 1860 the Treaty of Beijing had given Russia the north bank of the Amur "from the river Gorbitsa to the Sea of Okhotsk," as well as the Maritime Province with the valuable port of Vladivostok at its farthest extremity. Before 1895 there had been only a few Russian settlers and visitors to Manchuria while Western businessmen and missionaries were already well established at the treaty port of Niuzhuang, Mukden (Shenyang), and Jilin (Kirin).[2] But by 1895 official, military, and business circles in Russia thought that the time was ripe for the Russian empire to expand into Manchuria.

The tsarist government was afraid that Manchuria would fall under Japanese influence. China's army and navy were destroyed in the Sino–Japanese war of 1894–95. In the 1895 Treaty of Shimonoseki China recognized the independence of Korea and ceded Formosa (today's Taiwan), the Pescadore islands, and the Liaodong Peninsula to Japan.[3] Moreover, China was to pay an indemnity of 200 million taels and to open four more ports to foreign commerce.

China's weakness and backwardness, clearly revealed by its defeat, caused most European powers including tsarist Russia to demand more political and economic concessions. Since tsarist Russia wanted to establish its sphere of influence in Manchuria, it persuaded Germany and France to join in its efforts to force the Japanese to return the Liaodong Peninsula to China in consideration of a further indemnity of 30 million taels.[4] The peninsula was eventually leased to Russia in 1898. The Chinese government had belatedly realized that it had to develop its industry, modernize its army, and develop its railway system. In 1896 the Chinese foreign minister *Li* Hongzhang, negotiated a secret treaty with Russia. In return for a defensive alliance for fifteen years, China granted Russia a concession to build and operate the Chinese Eastern Railway (CER) across northern Manchuria in a straight course from Chita to Vladivostok. This railroad was to be managed by a private corporation.[5]

The actual contract for construction and operation of the CER was signed in Berlin on September 8, 1896, by China's envoy to Russia and Germany, *Shu* Jingcheng, the president of the Russo–Chinese Bank, Prince E. Ukhtomsky, and its managing director, A. Rotstein. The contract gave the company a free hand to administer an extraterritorial zone (*polasa otchuzhdenia*) about a thousand miles long and fifteen miles wide in the vicinity of the line and to exploit the natural riches of this area. The railway was to revert to China after eighty years or could be purchased by it from the partnership after thirty-six years.[6]

However, this clause did not worry the Russian government since it hoped to dominate completely, if not actually acquire, all of Manchuria within thirty-six years.[7]

A vast army of Chinese coolies, estimated at 60,000 to 200,000, was hired mainly in Shandong province to work alongside the Russian laborers on the construction of the CER.[8] Despite the difficult terrain, harsh climatic conditions (hot, humid summers and bitterly cold winters), and the destruction of part of the line during the Boxer uprising of 1900, by July 1, 1903, the railroad was ready for use.[9] The finished line ran from Manzhouli in the west to Pogranichnaia (Suifenhe) in the east and from the newly built town of Harbin to Port Arthur in the south, covering more than 1,600 miles.[10] It linked the Trans-Siberian line with Vladivostok, finally giving the Russian empire a relatively quick access to Sea of Japan and ultimately to the Pacific Ocean. According to Russian accounts, the total cost of construction of the railway amounted to US$223,332,502, including the cost of the South Manchurian branch and the expenses caused by the Boxer Rebellion.[11]

Despite the hidden resentment the Chinese population must have felt toward the Russian colonizers, the Chinese tolerated them because of the enormous economic benefits that came in the wake of the construction of the CER. Before the CER construction began, the vast territory of Manchuria—390,000 square miles—was still largely wild and underpopulated, especially in the two northern provinces of Jilin and Heilongjiang.[12] The very construction of the railroad attracted enormous funds and large numbers of workers to Manchuria. Russian engineers, laborers, guards, merchants, and clerks came to Manchuria to provide track material, food, piece goods, and manufactured articles.[13]

These settlers started forming Russian enclaves along the CER. The railway also enabled hundreds of thousands of land-starved Chinese peasants and petty traders (mainly from Shandong province) to settle in Manchuria.[14] Its fertile plains and valleys attracted tens of thousands of Korean and later Japanese farmers and traders to settle there.[15] They cleared vast tracts of virgin land and started growing millet, barley, and sorghum for local consumption and wheat to satisfy the growing Russian demand. The Manchurian climate and soil were particularly suitable for growing soybeans. Soybean oil and cakes found a Russian, Japanese, and, later, European market. Thus besides passengers, the CER soon started carrying millions of tons of grain, soybeans, bean cake and oil, firewood, coal, timber, iron, sand, and livestock from Manchuria to Russia (and via Vladivostok to European markets), Japan, and South China. The railway imported manufactured goods, wines, vodka, tobacco, sugar, porcelain, iron, steel, medicine, and fresh produce unavailable in Manchuria.[16] While tsarist Russia's aim was to exploit Manchuria's rich resources and to annex it in the long run, China benefited by acquiring a railway system that assisted its economic life and trade.

Before the arrival of Russian engineers and builders in 1898, Harbin was a tiny hamlet of a few mud-brick huts surrounded by fields. However, its excellent location at the intersection of the Sungari River and the CER lines from Manzhouli to Vladivostok, Shenyang, Dalian, and Port Arthur made it a natural choice as the future administrative center of the CER.[17]

Once the constructors of the railroad decided to establish their regular residence in Harbin, tens of thousand Russian and Chinese workers began building a town on the right bank of the Sungari River. By the turn of the century, Harbin had three neighborhoods: "Old Harbin"—old adobe huts built around an abandoned spirits factory, in which the first surveyors lived; the Pristan (Pier) area by the river; and the Novyi Gorod (New Town) above the river. One liberal-minded Russian volunteer medic who was stationed in Harbin during the Russo–Japanese war of 1904–5 described the town in the following unflattering terms:

> Old Harbin at that time consisted either of luxurious villas of the engineers, or mud huts. Only 10% of the population lived there. Pristan, the business quarter by the river, was full of Chinese petty traders and workers of all kinds, who slept in the surrounding settlements. It contained shops, baths,

Chinese theatres, inns, industrial enterprises (mostly steam flour mills), eating shops, and Chinese eating stalls, all crammed into a very small space, in a low basin, at one time a channel of the Sungari. This part of the town is revolting, [declared the volunteer medic], here is concentrated all that is worst of Russian and Chinese civilization.... There is not the slightest hint of any sanitary arrangements; in rainy weather impenetrable mud, in which one could easily drown, and in dry [winter and summer] a revolting, choking, stinking yellow dust. And yet almost 1/3rd of the Harbin population lives here, and masses of Chinese come in to work every day. The aristocratic part of the town, New Harbin, is much more attractive. Here there are attempts to pave some of the streets, and wooden pavements are to be found in places. In the centre two and three storied houses are to be seen, the wooden buildings of the railway employees are very elegant, surrounded with verandahs and balconies, concealed from the public gaze by fast growing greenery. Many public buildings are striking in their luxury.... But all real town organization is in the future, here too is impenetrable mud in the rainy seasons, terrible revolting dust winter and summer; insanitary condition of the streets, stench and filth.[18]

Why did this small, dusty town not very different from a new prairie town in the Wild West of America attract hundreds and later thousands of Russian Jews? Paradoxically, Jewish settlers found more freedom in the late imperial Russian town of Harbin built in the wilderness of Manchuria than in Russia proper. The years 1882 to 1905 were marked by an official policy of discrimination against and russification of Poles, Armenians, Latvians, Lithuanians, Georgians, Tatars, and Jews. Even Russian sectarians like Duhobors ("fighters by the Spirit"), Old Believers, and Mennonites were regarded as subversive elements and were subjected to constant police surveillance and harassment.[19]

Russia's 5 to 6 million Jews were mainly confined to "the Pale of Settlement"—the border region stretching from the Baltic to the Black Sea. An imperial decree of 1882 had forbidden them to live outside towns or large villages and canceled the right of Jewish soldiers to remain outside the Pale after their military service was finished, as they had done since 1867. In 1891 large numbers of Jewish merchants and artisans were expelled from Moscow and only Jewish merchants of the First Guild were allowed to settle outside the Pale. Jews were barred from participating in municipal self-government.

Furthermore, Jews were restricted in their choice of occupation. The Ministry of War limited the proportion of Jews serving as military doctors or orderlies to 5 percent of army medical personnel. A decree of 1887 introduced numerous clauses for Jews at universities and secondary schools: Jewish pupils were not to exceed 10 percent of all pupils in the Pale, 5 percent in the provinces outside it, or 3 percent in St. Petersburg or

Moscow. The spirits monopoly that was introduced in 1894 robbed many rural Jews of their livelihood since they could not renew their licenses to sell spirits. In 1899 Jews were banned from establishing new Jewish settlements east of the Ural mountains. All these restrictions, coupled with periodical bloody pogroms in major cities like Kiev, Odessa, and Kishinev and in the Pale, drove approximately 2 million Jews to America, England, Latin America, and elsewhere in the West.[20]

These restrictions did not apply in faraway Manchuria. The influential minister of finance, Sergei Witte, wanted to attract capable settlers to the region. During his 1902 visit to Manchuria, he was disgusted by the poor quality of the Russian settlers who went there and decided not to aid them in the future. He advised, at a 1903 St. Petersburg conference on migration, that only traders and retired soldiers and railway guards should be accepted as settlers.[21] Witte and his successor, Prince Vladimir Kokovtzov, recognized the sharp business acumen of Jews and other minorities and thus welcomed them to settle in Manchuria in order to speed up its development.

The first Jewish settlers in Manchuria came from Siberia. Many were descendants of soldiers conscripted by Nicholas II.[22] A hardy and free-spirited lot, they were not deterred by the harsh climate of Manchuria or the primitive living conditions of the CER builders. While employment on the CER was not open to Jews, they were allowed to supply Russian engineers with building materials and builders and workers with goods and food.[23] Starting with a handful in 1898, by 1903 the Jewish population grew to five hundred. While there were pockets of Jewish settlement all along the CER line in Manzhouli, Hailar, Shenyang, and Qiqihar, their largest concentration was in Harbin.[24]

On February 16, 1903, they established the Jewish minority (*natsional'naia*) community, hereafter referred to as "the community." Its elected spiritual directorate (*dukhovnoe pravlenie*) received police approval. Rabbi Shevel Levin, who had served in Omsk and Chita in Siberia, arrived in Harbin in August 1904.[25]

After the Russian defeat in the Russo–Japanese war in 1905, many demobilized Jewish soldiers settled in Harbin and were soon joined by their families plus thousands of refugees fleeing pogroms in Odessa, Kishinev, and other towns and villages. The Bolshevik Revolution of 1917 and subsequent Russian civil war caused a flood of refugees, both Russian and Jewish, to escape to the relative safety of Harbin, Tianjin, and Shanghai. By January 1919 the community numbered more than ten thousand people and at its peak in the 1920s it numbered about fifteen thousand.[26]

In 1922, Russians comprised 120,000 of Harbin's 485,000 inhabitants. Chinese numbered 300,000, followed by 34,000 Koreans and 5,000 Japanese. There were also some other minorities (Armenians, Georgians, Baltic Germans, and Poles) in the city.[27] Despite the fact that the Jews constituted only about 3 percent of the general population of Harbin, they played a prominent part in the business and public spheres. Among the most successful Jewish firms were the following.

The Company of the Descendants of Leontii Skidelsky

The company was founded in 1891 by Leontii S. Skidelsky. He constructed many buildings along the Trans-Siberian Railway between Khabarovsk and Vladivostok. After establishing himself in the Ussuri region, Skidelsky branched out into northern Manchuria. In 1903, when the CER was completed, Skidelsky purchased five (later six) forest concessions from the Chinese government and became the CER's main supplier of timber.

Skidelsky supplied the CER with coal between 1910 and 1913. Leontii passed away in 1916 and the control of the firm passed to his sons, Solomon and Semion. With the cooperation of the local Chinese government, Solomon established the Mulin Coal Company along the Mulin (Muren) River. Its coal was of high quality. Solomon and Semion also operated a large flour mill in the Fujiadian suburb of Harbin and played a prominent part in Harbin's stock exchange and banks. In 1921 they built the first Talmud Torah [Jewish parochial school] in Harbin and contributed generously to local committees for the poor and orphaned, both Jewish and Chinese.[28]

The English-Chinese Eastern Trading Co. Ltd. of Roman Kabalkin

Roman Kabalkin (1850–1933) was another prominent Harbin Jew. He was already a successful trader and exporter of grain in Russia before settling down in Harbin in 1906. He started exporting Manchurian grown grain and soybeans to Europe via the CER. In 1909 Kabalkin established his own soy bean exporting firm in London by attracting British investors and named it "The English-Chinese Eastern Company." By 1914 Kabalkin had opened a large oil factory in "Old Harbin"—the first to be equipped with the latest European machinery. The factory filtered soybean oil, refined for salads under the brand name Acetco and pressed soybean cakes for cattle. His high-quality refined soybean oil was exported to the United States.

Kabalkin was active in the Harbin Stock Exchange and other business bodies. An ardent Zionist, he was one of the organizers of the "Mizrach Ha'rahok" (The Far East) Palestine Society in Harbin and spent the last ten years of his life in Tel Aviv.[29]

S. Soskin and Co. Ltd.

Semion Soskin was born in 1880 to a wealthy grain merchant in the town of Kerch in the Crimea. Sent by his father to Harbin in 1902 because of his laziness and womanizing, by the end of 1903 he was already heading a timber business. He made his fortune during the Russo–Japanese War building three public baths, two food stores with cold rooms, and a flour mill for the Russian army. Realizing that the army would need huge amounts of wheat, sorghum, millet, and soybeans, Semion also became a major supplier of these.

Despite his youth, his astute business acumen helped him become one of the richest traders in Harbin by the end of the Russo–Japanese War. Soon, his whole family joined him in Harbin as the result of the violent pogroms against the Jews sparked by the Russian defeat in the war.

Semion and his brother Isaac established a successful firm that exported wheat and soybeans, soybean oil, and soybean cakes to Europe, Japan, and South China. By 1923 their firm exported nearly 250,000 kgs of wheat, soybeans, and oil, more than a quarter of the CER's total annual export.

S. Soskin and Company invested more than 40 million gold rubles in Manchuria. Between 1920 and 1923 the company paid the CER 10 million gold rubles in transportation fees. The company also contributed up to 50,000 rubles a year to charity.[30]

Sugar-refining Factories Owned by L. Zickman and A. Kagan

Lev Zickman, who hailed from the Ukraine and worked as a traveling salesman in Siberia, was among the pioneers in the Manchurian sugar beet trade. The first sugar beet processing plant at Ashihe, about twenty-five miles southeast of Harbin, was founded by a group of Polish industrialists in 1907. They taught local farmers how to cultivate sugar beets. Later three more plants opened in Manchuria, and all four flourished because of the high price of sugar during World War I.

After the war, imported cane sugar from Southeast Asia started reaching the Manchurian market. This competition forced down the price of local sugar. In addition, Manchuria was badly affected by the postwar worldwide depression. These two factors forced the gradual closure of all the local sugar plants.[31] The Ashihe plant, which Zickman had taken over, lasted longest. In 1927–28 Zickman sold it to the American Trading and Milling Company.

In 1926, A.I. Kagan, a wealthy grain merchant, purchased a sugar factory in Ashihe from French Limited Company, headquartered in Warsaw. He modernized it and added many new machines for the production of soft Chinese sugar and hard cube sugar and sugarcones. Despite his large investments in the factory, Kagan went bankrupt in 1929.[32]

The Flour Mills

Bread is the carbohydrate staple of the Russian diet, and many flour mills were established in Manchuria with the influx of the Russian soldiers during the Russo–Japanese War. At least five Manchurian flour mills belonged to Jews:

a. Bonner and Mindalevich's mill could grind 48,000 kgs of flour a day.
b. Drizin and Patushinsky's mill had the same capacity.
c. L. Skidelsky's flour mill could grind up to 19,000 kgs a day.
d. A. Kagan owned a flour mill and a macaroni factory.
e. The Soskin brothers owned flour mills and supervised the operation of Russian-owned mills.

Most flour mills were located in Fujiadian. During World War I, food shortages boosted demand for product from flour milling firms in Manchuria. Many mills now were owned by Chinese. The Bolshevik revolution of 1917, the ensuing civil war, which caused the collapse of the Russian ruble, and the postwar depression all contributed to the decline of the flour-grinding industry. By 1923 half the flour mills in Harbin were bankrupt. While oil mills were also affected by the depression, they managed to make a gradual revival and soon took over as the main agricultural industry in North Manchuria.[33]

Fur Trading Firms

Manchuria's vast forests were home to many animals, including tigers, bears, sables, squirrels, otters, beavers, and marmots. As a result of the successful development of cattle breeding, many Chinese farmers and Mongolian cattlemen also had big herds of sheep, cattle, horses, and ponies.

Harbin was the principal northern Manchurian center for the collection and distribution of furs and skins, while Shenyang was the principal center in the south. Around December of each year foreign buyers would come to Harbin and Shenyang to buy the above-mentioned skins plus those of dogs and ponies.

The Jewish fur traders included B. Goldman, the Brenner brothers, Gold,

Gutbezahl, Zondovich, and Ullman. Some traders, like Lev Jacobsohn, had offices both in Harbin and Tianjin. Others worked for American-Jewish firms such as M. Bernstein and Sons, which was based in New York but had branches in China and Japan.

Most skins and furs were exported to America. The New York stock market crash of 1929 and the ensuing Depression in America adversely influenced the fur market in China.[34]

Jewish Banks and the Stock Exchange

Harbin had two Jewish banks: the Far Eastern Jewish Bank of Commerce, established in 1922, and the Jewish People's Bank, founded a year later.[35] Both banks were located in the Pristan area but served different customers. The Bank of Commerce was founded by established businessmen, like Isaac Soskin, Solomon Skidelsky, and Jacob Kabalkin. It was headed by Jacob Frizer and aimed to assist the more established Jewish businessmen. The Jewish People's Bank, on the other hand, was founded by small traders and was meant to serve working men and women. Many of them turned to the bank to secure a loan in order to start their own business.

The established Jewish businessmen also played a prominent role on the Harbin Stock Exchange. In 1924 Jacob Kabalkin was elected as the president of the Stock Exchange Committee.[36] Isaac Soskin and Leontii Skidelsky were members of the board. Kabalkin was re-elected in 1928, while Isaac Soskin became one of the vice-presidents. Solomon Skidelsky became a member of the board that year. Jacob Kabalkin served as the president of the Stock Exchange committee until 1934, when he was forced by the Japanese to resign. The Japanese took over many business enterprises in Harbin, including the grain exchange.[37]

Jews also played an active role in municipal affairs. When municipal self-government was instituted in 1908, ten out of forty electors were Jewish. Two, Evsei Dobisov and Isaac Fride, were among four later selected to serve on the town council. While the Jews constituted only a small minority of the general population of Harbin, they generated work for the local Chinese population and poured millions of rubles, and later yen, into Manchuria.

Communal Institutions

The community helped many thousands of Jewish refugees fleeing a Russia ravaged by its 1918–24 civil war. It was a warm and caring community that stressed Jewish education, mutual aid, and care for the sick and elderly. It represented a whole spectrum of political ideology—from Zionism to Orthodoxy and from communism to anticommunism.

The Harbin Jewish community was governed by an Executive Council consisting of no fewer than eleven members. They were elected for a two-year period by the members of the community. All Jews from the age of twenty could be members of the community upon paying an annual fee of two local dollars. Members of the council elected a chairman, a vice-chairman, a secretary, and a treasurer from the eleven-member council. Members of the Council formed special committees (educational, refugees, economic, financial) that were charged with running communal affairs.

Besides the communal work done by the members of the council, much help to the old and needy was offered by the different charitable organizations. The Jewish Ladies' Charitable Society started operating in 1907. Its aim was to help the poor and the ailing in the community. It helped pay rent, provide meals, pay school fees, and repay the loans taken out by poor Jewish workers from societies like Gmilut-Chesed and Ezra.[38]

The Jewish Free Kitchen was officially established in 1918. Located in a two-story brick house built by Joseph Rabinovich on Artilleriiskaia Street, it provided free meals to elderly Jews, to the chronically ill, and all the poor of the community. In the twenty years of its existence, from 1918 to 1938, the Free Kitchen provided the poor with more than a million free lunches.[39] Gmilut-Chesed, founded in 1916, and Ezra, founded in 1924, provided the needy Jews of Harbin with interest-free loans. Their capital consisted of monthly fees, donations, subsidies paid by different communal organizations, and the proceeds of plays and charity concerts. Both societies granted thousands of grants and helped many Jews set up their own businesses.[40]

Mishmeret Cholim (Sick Fund) provided free medical care to the poor along the CER line. It was founded in 1920 by Dr. Abraham I. Kaufman and a few other prominent citizens of Harbin. At first it operated from two little rooms until the community raised enough money to build a spacious hospital on a lot donated by a rich widow, E. Naftalina-Yoffe. The new hospital was opened in 1933 and provided excellent medical care, as well as dental care, again free, for poor patients.[41]

Moshav Zkenim (Home for the Aged) was founded in 1920. The building was donated by J.A. and S.M. Rabinovich and housed from twenty to twenty-five elderly and sick Jews who had no relatives in Harbin or whose relatives could not afford to take care of them. The home was funded by donations, collections, and payment of membership fees.[42]

The above typifies the wide-reaching scope of the institutions and activities of this vibrant community, which also included Jewish organizations such as Betar and the Women's International Zionist Organization. A picture emerges of a community with such dynamic leaders as Aharon Kiselev, rabbi from 1913 until his death in 1949, and Dr. Kaufman. Kaufman came to Harbin in 1912 as a doctor but quickly became the leader of the community. Besides heading the Jewish Hospital, he delivered lectures on Jewish history, poetry, and philosophy, edited and contributed to the newspaper *Evreiskaia zhizn'* (Jewish Life), and headed the National Jewish Council and the Far Eastern Jewish Conferences.

The year 1931 marked the zenith of the community. The ensuing Japanese occupation and economic domination of Manchuria caused most of the community to seek calmer waters in Tianjin and Shanghai. By 1937 the community had declined from fifteen thousand to three thousand people, signaling the disintegration of this enclave of Jewish life.[43] The Jewish community of Harbin was not interested in integrating with the local Chinese population. Very few Jews spoke Chinese or showed interest in Chinese culture. Their Chinese servants and business associates mostly spoke some Russian but displayed no anti-Semitism. Jews were spared the institutional anti-Semitism that plagued their brethren in the Russian empire. While anti-Semitic attacks in the White Russian press and occasional physical and verbal abuse of Jews by White Russians were not uncommon, on the whole the Jews enjoyed a peaceful existence. In the short period of thirty years, the Jews of Harbin had succeeded in establishing a thriving, economically successful community.

Notes

1. I am writing a history of the Jewish community of Harbin from 1898 to 1958. Most of the source material quoted in this paper is located in the National and University Library at the Hebrew University of Jerusalem as well as in Jerusalem's Archives of the Jewish Agency and Central Zionist Archives. Metzudat Ze'ev, the Zionist-Revisionist archive and museum in Tel Aviv, also houses memorabilia pertaining to Betar activities in China.

I have a personal interest in the history of the Harbin Jewish community because my late grandparents, Avraham and Sophie Shickman, came to Harbin as a young couple after the 1905 pogroms in their native Odessa. My father, Isaac Shickman (1908–1988), and my aunt, Fruma Shickman-Yormark (1910–), were born in an adobe house on Konnaya Street. My father was sent to schools in Tianjin, and the family subsequently moved there. In 1968 we emigrated to Israel, where my mother became a lecturer in Chinese at the Hebrew University.

The question of why the Harbin Jews maintained such limited contacts with the Chinese is dealt with in my forthcoming book. It is also dealt with in chapter III.B.2 by Boris Bresler in this volume. The story of the community's displacement under the Japanese occupation is beyond the scope of this article.

2. Rosemary K.I. Quested, *"Matey" Imperialists? The Tsarist Russians in Manchuria 1895–1917* (Hong Kong: University of Hong Kong Press, 1982), p. 8.

3. William Langer, comp. and ed., *An Encyclopaedia of World History*, 4th ed. (London: George G. Harrap, 1968), p. 913.

4. Ibid. See also Herman Dicker, *Wanderers and Settlers in the Far East: A Century of Jewish Life in China and Japan* (New York: Twayne, 1962), pp. 17–18.

5. Tang Sheng-hao, *Russian and Soviet Policy in Manchuria and Outer Mongolia, 1911–31* (Durham, NC: Duke University Press, 1959), p. 47.
6. Ibid.; also Quested, *"Matey" Imperialists*, p. 22.
7. Paul H. Clyde, *International Rivalries in Manchuria, 1689–1922* (New York: Octagon Books, 1966), p. 60.
8. Ibid., p. 26.
9. Ramon H. Myers, ed., *North Manchuria and the Chinese Eastern Railway* (Harbin: C.E.R. Printing Office, 1924, repr. New York: Garland, p. 36.
10. Ibid., p. 36.
11. Ibid., p. 37.
12. Quested quotes a Russian estimate from 1894 that there were 400,000 people in Heilongjiang and 626,000 in Jilin. See Quested, *"Matey" Imperialists*, p. 9. A contemporary CER-commissioned survey estimated the population of these two provinces at 2 million people. See Myers, *North*, p. 11.
13. Ibid., p. 270. See also John J. Stephan, *The Russian Fascists* (London: Hamish Hamilton, 1978), pp. 37–40.
14. Ibid., p. 37.
15. Stephan, *Russian*, p. 40, gives the number of Koreans in Harbin in the 1920s as 34,000 and Japanese at 5,000.
16. *K.V.Zh.D. statisticheskii ezhegodnik, 1923* (CER Statistical Yearbook, 1923) (Harbin: CER Press, 1923). See also Quested, *"Matey" Imperialists*, p. 217.
17. Stephan, *Russian*, p. 40.
18. Quested, *"Matey" Imperialists*, pp. 129–130.
19. According to the census of 1897, Russians and White Russians numbered 61,550,000 and formed 49 percent of the total population, followed by 22,400,000 Ukrainians (17.8 percent); 7,900,000 Poles (6.3 percent); 5,000,000 Jews (4 percent); 1,350,000 Georgians (1 percent) and 1,150,000 Armenians (0.9 percent). Hugh Seton-Watson, *The Decline of Imperial Russia, 1855–1914* (London: Methuen, 1952), pp. 28–34.
20. Ibid., pp. 158–59.
21. Quested, *"Matey" Imperialists*, p. 103.
22. Jewish adolescents, especially orphans, were conscripted at a young age into the Russian Army by a decree of Tsar Nicholas II. Those who were hardy enough to serve out the full term of twenty-five years were then granted the privilege to live anywhere in the Russian empire. Many chose to settle in Siberia, where there were fewer restrictions.
23. David Wolff, "To the Harbin Station: City Building in Russian Manchuria, 1898–1914" (Ph.D. dissertation, History, University of California at Berkeley, 1991), p. 197; also Quested, *"Matey" Imperialists*, pp. 266, 364 n. 7.
24. There were restrictions on Russian Jews residing in Port Arthur. Only Jews who were baptized and those of high status were permitted. Quested, *"Matey" Imperialists*, p. 109.
25. Wolff, "Harbin," p. 187, erroneously gives the initial "W" for his name.
26. These statistics are taken from *Evreiskaia zhizn'*, nos. 1–2, January 14, 1938, and nos. 3–4, January 27, 1938, and *Sibir Palestina* (Harbin), no. 4, January 27, 1922.
27. Stephan, *Russian*, p. 40.
28. *Manchuria Monitor*, nos. 5–7 (1925).
29. All the facts on Kabalkin are taken from *Sputnik komersanta yezhegodnik* (Annual Commercial Guide) (Harbin: no publisher, 1926), pp. 107, 374–75.
30. See *Bulletin museia o-va izuchenia Manchurskogo Kraiia i dzhubileinoi vistavki K.V.Zh.D.* (Bulletin of the Museum of the Society for the Study of Manchuria and Jubilee Exhibition of the CER) (Harbin, no publisher, 1923), pp. 41–43; and *Manchuria Monitor*, no. 8 (1926), p. 28.

31. *Economicheskii vestnik Manchurii* (Manchuria Economic Monitor) (Harbin), nos. 25–26 (1926). According to Zickman's nephew, Gregory Grossman, Zickman moved to Harbin in 1916 and purchased the Ashihe mill around 1930 from the U.S. National City Bank, which had foreclosed on the property following bankruptcy under Kagan. In 1934 Zickman sold the mill to a newly formed corporation in which he was a major stock holder. (Gregory Grossman, letter to the author, September 9, 1992.) Grossman's information is at variance with the published source.

32. *Manchuria Monitor*, no.11 (1926).
33. *Economicheskii vestnik*, vol. 1 (January 28, 1923), p. 27.
34. *Manchuria Monitor*, no. 11 (June 1, 1931).
35. *Harbin's Trade & Industry Guide* (Harbin), pp. 381–82.
36. *Economic Harbin Herald*, nos. 47–48 (1924), pp. 25–26.
37. Dicker, *Wanderers*, p. 23.
38. See *Casoviy otchet damskogo evreiskogo blagotvoritelnogo o-va v Harbine za 1935 god* (Annual Report of the Jewish Ladies' Charitable Society in Harbin for 1935) (Harbin: privately published, 1935).
39. See *Evreiskaya besplatnaia i deschevaia stolovaia* (Jewish Free and Cheap Kitchen) (Harbin: privately published, 1935).
40. See *Jewish Life*, no. 45 (November 21, 1926) and *Sibir Palestina*, no. 6 (February 6, 1925).
41. See *Ustav obschestva popechenia o bednich bolnich evreiiach goroda Harbina "Mishmeret Cholim"* (Sick Fund for the Poor Jews of Harbin) (Harbin: J. Ellenberg Printing House, 1926).
42. See *otchet o-va popechenia doma prestarelych evreev "Moshav Zkenim" imeni S.M. i I.A. Rabinovich za 1935 god* (Annual Report of the Care-Taking Society for the Old Age Home Named After S.M. and I.A. Rabinovich for 1935) (Harbin: 1935).
43. *Evreiskaya zhizn'*, nos. 51–52 (December 29, 1937).

Chapter III.B.2

Harbin's Jewish Community, 1898–1958: Politics, Prosperity, and Adversity

Boris Bresler

The existence of Russian Jewish communities in China covers a relatively short period of time, only sixty years (1898–1958). During this time the communities went through two world wars (1914–18 and 1939–45); two major local wars (Russo–Japanese, 1904–05, and Sino–Japanese, 1937–45); the Chinese revolution (1911) abolishing imperial rule; two local conflicts (Sino–Soviet in 1929 and Sino–Japanese in 1931); and two revolutions involving civil wars (Russian, 1917–20, and Chinese, in 1946–49). During this period the Harbin community lived under five different political authorities: Russian (tsarist, 1898–1917), local warlord *Zhang* Zuolin (Chang Tsolin) (1917–31), Japanese (Manchukuo, 1931–45), Soviet army (1945–47), and the People's Republic of China (PRC) (since 1949). These turbulent political events and diverse local administrations shaped the rise, growth, and fall of Russian Jewish communities in China.

From a historical perspective, the internal political conflicts within the communities are equally significant. The struggle between secular groups and Orthodoxy, between Zionists and Socialists, and the Jewish confrontation with anti-Semitic Russian extremist elements, are all part of the history of the Harbin Jewish community.

Established in 1903, it was the first Russian Jewish community in China and for almost a quarter century served as a haven for Jews escaping eastward from Russia, during both the tsarist and the Soviet regimes. At its zenith, Harbin was the cultural center of all Russian Jewish life in China. Also, it was the city from which many thousands of Russian Jews dispersed elsewhere. Even in its decline, Harbin served as a base for the Far East Jewish National Council, recognized by the Japanese and Manchukuo authorities as the representative body of all the Jews in China. This background is central to understanding the history of all the Russian Jewish communities in China.

The Early Years, 1898–1916

Following the wave of pogroms in the Russian Pale of Settlement in the 1880s and the expulsion of Jewish workers from Moscow in 1891, a large number of Russian Jews left their homes in search of a better life. Some were attracted by the opportunities in Manchuria, where in 1896 Russia received a concession from China to build the Chinese Eastern Railroad (CER), an extension of the Trans-Siberian Railroad. The railroad consisted of three branches emanating from Harbin. The territory and the communities along the railroad were located within an extraterritorial zone (*polosa otchuzhdenia*), initially about fifteen hundred miles long and five miles wide; about four hundred miles of the southern branch was ceded to the Japanese in 1905 as a result of the Russo–Japanese war.

The CER was established as an independent enterprise financed through the Russian–Chinese (later Russo–Asian) Bank by the Russian government. The concession was to terminate after eighty years following the completion of the project at which time the ownership would be transferred to the Chinese government.[1] Russian laws were not automatically applicable in the zone except as mandated by the administration of the CER. The railroad administration, controlled by the Russian Ministry of Finance, was interested in rapid economic development of the new region and encouraged investors and entrepreneurs to emigrate to Manchuria. As part of this policy, Russian Jews were freed from the restrictions that made Jewish life painful in Russia proper. In Manchuria they could start a new life without changing their language or life-style.

This enlightened policy of equal opportunities for the Jews was set by the builder and first administrator of CER, Alexander I. Yugovich, a native of Odessa educated in England as a civil engineer. It was continued by his successor, General Dmitri L. Khorvat, also an engineer, who pursued his military career as a builder of railroads. The freedom granted the Jews in the "zone" was a matter of contention between the local administrators and the central government in St. Petersburg. In this contest, General Khorvat, who was a fair and pragmatic administrator, prevailed.[2]

Many of the Jewish entrepreneurs who arrived in Manchuria at the turn of the century played an important role in developing the natural resources of the region. They were followed by professionals (doctors, lawyers, architects) as well as tradesmen and merchants. Most of them were concentrated in Harbin, a new Russian town established in 1898 on the site of a small Chinese village. There is some controversy about the person who selected the site for the town. While most Russian sources identify A.I. Shidlovski, an engineer employed by CER, it now appears that M.V. Gruliov, a Jew who converted to the Russian Orthodox faith and later reached the rank of general in the Russian army, selected the site during an earlier expedition to the region.[3]

The first "steering" committee of the Harbin Jewish community was elected in 1903. In accordance with the then-current administrative regulations in Russia, it was an organization dealing with the religious and welfare needs of a given religious congregation. The main needs facing the Jewish community of about five hundred were establishing a permanent synagogue, building a cemetery, employing a rabbi and *shokhet* (ritual slaughterer of meat), baking of *matzoh* (the unleavened bread eaten during Passover), and registering marriages and births.[4]

During the 1904–5 Russo–Japanese war, the Harbin population was swelled by army personnel. The Jewish community records listed more than nine hundred Jewish soldiers stationed in the vicinity, and it is estimated that more than twenty-five thousand Jews were serving in other military units in Manchuria during the war.[5] At the end of the war, some of the demobilized Jews, impressed by the opportunities in the zone, decided to settle in Manchuria.

The pogroms in the Russian Pale of Settlement during the first decade of the 1900s, like the earlier persecutions, drove a large number of Jews to seek security and a better life elsewhere. Freedom and opportunity in Manchuria attracted many settlers, including a group from Siberia and the Maritime Provinces (the region bounded by the Ussuri and Amur rivers on the west and by the Sea of Japan on the east). In 1909 new restrictions on the right of Jews to reside in the Maritime Provinces were particularly instrumental in encouraging migration to Manchuria. These new immigrants brought with them capital and experience in developing natural resources, trade, and industry.

After Russia's entry into World War I in August 1914, Russian Jews were drafted into the army; many young Jews volunteered. But after the defeat of the Russian forces on the western front, the army ordered a massive evacuation of Jews from the western border provinces (Finland, Estonia, Latvia, Lithuania, and parts of Poland and Belorussia). Some were arrested and tried for allegedly spying on behalf of the Germans. Hundreds of thousands were evacuated, many receiving only twenty-four hours' notice.[6] Although most of these were resettled in Russia's Pale of Settlement (some in other central provinces), many also found their way to Harbin.

By 1916 the Jewish population of Harbin increased to about six thousand. The social welfare problems—dealing with the poor and the refugees—and cultural needs expanded. Special committees and organizations were established to deal with these problems. The conduct of the community affairs had no clear definition of its responsibilities. Each committee had to solicit funds independently, and there was no coordinated effort to deal with the community problems.

The Second Phase, 1917–1931

In 1917, after the February Revolution in Russia, the Kerensky government abolished all restrictions based on nationality or religion. In Harbin this was reflected in a total reorganization of the community institutions. An interim committee, elected at a general community meeting held on April 30, 1917, was charged with the task of restructuring.[7] The committee consisted of thirty-one members: thirteen Zionists, four Orthodox, two Bundists (members of a Jewish Marxist group), and twelve others representing the nonpartisan Jewish voters.[8]

Two conflicting views emerged in the committee. A secular group, including both the Zionists and the non-Zionists, favored a federation-type council that would include representatives of all community organizations, religious and secular alike, in proportion to the votes received by each. The Orthodox group favored a council restricted to dealing with religious problems only. After prolonged debates, the views of the secular group prevailed. Another conflict arose in dealing with women's right to vote. The Orthodox demanded that the new by-laws should abolish the women's right to vote, while the secular groups insisted on universal suffrage. On this issue the secular group prevailed as well.

Bitter conflicts developed within the interim committee between the Nationalist–Zionist group and the Bund representatives. The latter demanded primacy of Yiddish over Hebrew, elimination of the Palestine Committee within the council, and the exclusion of Bible studies from the Jewish school curriculum. After months of debate, the Bund representatives were defeated and resigned from the interim committee. This did not end the struggle between the Bund supporters and the Zionists allied with the "independent" segments of the community.

The internal struggles continued around such issues as the Yimaldag club (the Yiddish Musical Literary Dramatic Group), the elections of the local City Council, and the election of representatives to the Jewish All-Russia Assembly held in 1918. Some of these internal conflicts continued well into the mid-1920s.

The Bolshevik Revolution in November 1917 and the ensuing civil war was followed by massive emigration of Russia's Jewish middle class. Tens of thousands fled both European Russia and Siberia to China, and Japan via the Trans-Siberian Railroad. Many were en route to the United States and other destinations. Some found haven in China, and this resulted in further growth of the established Jewish communities.

From 1918 to 1921, while the Russian Far East was occupied by allied intervention forces representing fourteen countries, the railroad went into a decline. In 1921 control of the railroad passed to a special directorate under the leadership of B.V. Ostroumoff, who made remarkable improvements in the facilities and operation of the railroad. In 1924 an accommodation was reached with the Soviet government whereby the CER was to be administered jointly by China and the USSR. The zone lost its extraterritorial status and technically reverted to Chinese political control. Formal diplomatic relations between China and the Soviet Union were established, and Soviet administrative and technical personnel arrived in Harbin to take over the jobs heretofore held by the stateless Russian émigrés, employed in the meantime by the Ostroumoff administration. The CER effectively became a Sino–Soviet joint venture on Chinese soil.

At this point many of the residents who held old Russian passports, no longer valid, were offered the opportunity to exchange them for Soviet passports. Many accepted the offer, some in order to preserve their jobs with the CER, which now employed Soviet administrators and technical staff. Others took out Soviet passports in order not to become stateless, and some, of course, desired to become Soviet citizens because they sympathized with the revolution. The majority of the Russian Jewish community elected to become stateless émigrés. Most of the "red" and the "White" Russians lived side by side continuing social contacts and doing business with each other as usual.

In 1925, after the abrogation of the New Economic Policy (NEP) in the Soviet Union, another wave of Jewish emigration followed. Some of those arriving in Harbin were issued exit visas (which required payment of a large sum of money in foreign currency to the Soviet government) while others crossed the Soviet borders illegally.[9]

In the spring of 1929 the Chinese attempted to force the Soviet Union to give up its share of control of the CER. They raided Soviet consulates in Manchuria and alleged that they found evidence of Soviet railway officials' spreading communist propaganda against the Chinese government. A number of Russian (and Chinese) railroad executives were arrested, some were fired or expelled, and Chinese forces seized the railroad and established a special White Russian Guard Corps to ensure the security of the railroad.

The incident escalated, diplomatic relations were broken off, and by September both Soviet and Chinese troops were amassed on the border. Following some skirmishes, Soviet troops occupied portions of western Manchuria, including the key railroad town of Manzhouli, which had a substantial Jewish community. At the time, the Jewish community of Manzhouli numbered about fifteen hundred and had a splendid synagogue, Jewish school, and library. It survived the Sino–Soviet episode—but not for long. Its demise came with the Japanese occupation of Manchuria in 1932, when Jews emigrated to Harbin, Tianjin, Shanghai, and other urban centers in China.[10]

By the end of 1929 Sino–Soviet negotiations resolved the dispute by restoring the status quo ante on the railroad and in diplomatic relations. The consequences of this conflict, insofar as the Jewish communities in Manchuria were concerned, were not great, although it was the first signal of the possibility of Sino–Soviet confrontation over the Chinese anticommunist campaign. This issue dominated the concerns of the Harbin community to a far greater extent than the New York stock market crash in October 1929.

Jewish Community Life Before 1931

Most of the early Jewish pioneers seeking fortunes found them either in industry or trade. The Jewish community contributed its share to the city's growth. Jews occupied positions of responsibility and trust on the stock exchange, in the chamber of commerce, and played important roles in trade and professional associations.[11] With material success came community and cultural institutions—synagogues, a cemetery, a home for the aged, support for the sick and for the poor, schools, youth organizations, clubs, publications, dramatic productions, and lectures.

Community medical care and a home for the aged were established in 1920; the latter also provided free meals for the needy. In 1921 the Jewish Commercial Far Eastern Bank and in 1923 the Jewish People's Bank were established. A Jewish cultural club, Yimaldag, had a good Jewish library and presented lecture series (in both Russian and Yiddish), dramatic performances, as well as musical and social evenings in the club. A Yiddish Social Democratic (Menshevik) paper, *Der vayter mizrekh* (The Far East), was published during 1921–22. Lectures, recitals, special festivals, and dramatic and musical performances sponsored by various Jewish organizations were presented to the local community. Two important Zionist periodicals, *Evreiskaia zhizn'* (Jewish Life) and *Gadegel* (The Flag), were published in Russian.

Jewish cultural life flourished—mostly in Russian and, to some extent, in

Yiddish. The Jewish fare of theater, music, and lectures had to compete with an even richer program of Russian offerings. These often included the visits by the Moscow Art Theater, Moscow (Bolshoi) Opera, and top soloists from abroad.

The congregations of the two large synagogues in Harbin enjoyed the services of talented cantors. Traditional observance of Purim included a full-fledged costume ball at the Commercial Club. Donations to local charities collected at the ball were substantial: During the depression of the early 1930s, more than 8,000 yuan (equivalent to approximately US$40,000 in current dollars), was collected at one of the balls.[12]

By the end of 1920, publication of the *Sibir Palestina,* a Zionist magazine previously published in Irkutsk (Siberia), was moved to Harbin, and in January 1921 Dr. Avraham [Abram] Iosifovitch Kaufman (1886–1971), a prominent figure in the Zionist movement in the Far East and a leader of the Harbin Jewish community, took over as editor.

Shortly thereafter he started to transform the magazine from a Zionist news-oriented weekly into a sophisticated journal presenting, in addition to the Zionist news, essays on Jewish literary and public issues. Beginning in mid-1926 the magazine was published under the title of *Evreiskaia zhizn'.* In the late 1930s, as the Jewish population of Harbin was greatly reduced, the magazine encountered severe financial problems. Hoping to influence editorial policy, the Japanese authorities offered a monthly subsidy; but Kaufman refused the subsidy. A grant from Lev G. Zikman, a prominent businessman active in Jewish affairs, made publication of this magazine possible until its closure by the Japanese authorities in 1943.[13]

In 1932 a new publication appeared in Harbin. The young leaders of Vladimir Ze'ev Jabotinsky's Zionist Revisionist group Betar brought out the biweekly *Gadegel* [The Flag]. The idea of this second Zionist publication caught on quickly. Under Alexander Y. Gurvich as editor, it included segments devoted to the *Yishuv* (Jewish community in Palestine), the Diaspora, other news of international Jewry and essays by noted Zionists like Jabotinsky, Abraham Menahem Mendel Ussishkin (1863–1941), and Joseph B. Schechtman (1891–1970). Gurvich remained the editor of the magazine until his departure from Harbin in the spring of 1941. His place was taken by Simon A. Klein, who edited the magazine for about a year until it was closed by the Japanese in the spring of 1942.

The first Jewish school was established in Harbin in 1907. By 1909 it had a hundred students; classes were held in a totally inadequate small Chinese house. By 1910 the community built a splendid elementary school capable of accommodating several hundred pupils. The school was enlarged to a full high school in 1917, but seven years later the school had to close because of lack of financial support, and the building was sold to the Harbin Municipal Council.[14]

A Talmud Torah (Jewish school offering a program through elementary and junior high grades), with instruction partly in Hebrew and partly in Russian, was established in 1920 and remained open until 1950. Its program prepared the graduates for transfer to the local Russian high schools.

After the closing of the Jewish high school in 1924, most of the Jewish children studied at the Harbin Public Commercial School. All instruction was in Russian, with English (or German) and Chinese as foreign languages, and with compulsory instruction in religion for the Russian-Orthodox students. For the Jewish students release-time instruction in Jewish history and (in the senior year) in Jewish literature was compulsory.

A few Jewish students, seeking higher education, went abroad. In the 1920s Jewish students from Harbin attended Smith College, the Massachusetts Institute of Technology, and the universities of California at Berkeley, British Columbia, Paris, Liège, Bologna, and Berlin. After graduation many returned to Harbin; only a few remained abroad.

Recognition of the importance of Jewish education of the young and support for Jewish youth organizations was an early priority of the Harbin Jewish community. A number of different Jewish youth organizations were started—Techiya [Resurrection], Hechaver [the Comrade]—but they did not last more than a few years. Maccabi, one of the earliest Zionist youth organizations with a major interest in athletics, went through cycles of intermittent activity between 1921 and 1945.

A Hashomer Hatzair (Young Watchman) group was formed in the spring of 1927 in Harbin by about a dozen youngsters mostly in their teens. This group was motivated by Zionist ideals, prepared Jewish youth for pioneering (*chalutzuit*) and, unlike the movement elsewhere, was not committed to Socialist-Marxist ideology. In the spring of 1929, the leadership group split sharply along ideological lines and the large majority formed a new group, Betar (*Brit Trumpeldor,* named for a Zionist hero killed in Palestine in 1921 defending a Jewish settlement in Galilee). Within the year Hashomer ceased to exist, while Betar continued its activities from 1929 to 1945. It was dissolved at the end of World War II, when Harbin was "liberated" from Japanese control by Soviet Russian troops.

Betar was the largest Jewish youth organization in Harbin. As a Jewish youth organization, it had practically no rival. The Scout and Campfire programs had a strong national Russian orientation (there were no Jewish members in either organization), and there were no "little leagues" in sports except those associated with political organizations.

Betar's cultural activities included studying the history of Zionism (in great detail), the history of liberation movements of other nations, the history and geography of Eretz Israel, and Jewish ethics and philosophy. Classes and weekly meetings were held in the Betar clubhouse. An active athletic program included ice skating (speed skating), boxing, indoor gymnastics, ping-pong, track and field, and volleyball. Its athletes competed in many of the citywide competitions and often placed at the top, winning citywide championships. Coordinated by a sports committee, the program owed much of its success to the coach, Werner I. Tukianen, a Finn who won the respect and affection of all the Betar sportsmen in Harbin.[15]

At the beginning of the 1930s, while the Harbin community was thriving, the extremist elements of the White Russian community, primarily the Russian fascist anti-Semites under the leadership of Konstantin Rodzaevski, were becoming more vociferous. The rise of fascism in Italy and nazism in Germany provided them with strong ideological and financial support.[16] Curiously, anti-Semitism was also rife among the Soviet young toughs, members of Komsomol (Communist Youth League), working in the railroad machine shops. The groups roamed the streets, and fist fights between the Jews and their foes were common.

Jewish youths were fair game for both sides and had to learn to defend themselves as best they could (some better than others). For the Komsomol, the Jewish kids were the enemy as "dirty Yid capitalists," even though most of the Jewish families were far from rich. For the Fascists, the Jews were the enemy as "dirty Yid Communists," even though most belonged to the Zionist youth organization Betar and were frequently called "Jewish Fascists" by some of their leftist Jewish friends.

Some Betar members trained in boxing and could fight well. There were about a dozen first-class street fighters among the Betar members, and they were the "enforcers." When some of the Jewish kids were bloodied in a fight and later could identify their attackers, the "enforcers" took revenge. This greatly discouraged many of the would-be "Jew-killers."

The Japanese Occupation, 1931–1937

Following its occupation of Manchuria in 1931, Japan initiated steps to tighten political and economic control of the region. It had two principal objectives: (1) to force Soviet influence out of Manchuria and to take control of the CER and (2) to take over or at least to receive a substantial share in the businesses owned by non-Japanese (including Chinese, Russians, Jews, and Western foreigners). This meant the destruction of many Jewish businesses.

To maintain the appearance of respectability in the international community, the Japanese set up a puppet country, Manchukuo, under a Manchurian emperor. The new authorities were Japanese, but the top official was a Manchu, the last emperor of China.

The Japanese put tremendous pressure on the Soviet administration of the CER, accusing them of various subversive activities, staging public protests and marches that called for the Soviet Union to give up control of the railroad. Where the Chinese did not succeed in 1929, the Japanese did. In 1934 the Soviet Union sold its CER rights to the Japanese, and in 1935 a large group of railroad employees who were Soviet citizens were repatriated. A few Russian Jewish families with Soviet passports, attracted by the formal provisions of the new Soviet constitution, also chose to return to Russia: Most of them landed in prison camps.[17]

The Japanese, in pursuit of their policy of taking control of the economic life of the region, recruited local Russian Fascist organizations into their service. These organizations were natural allies of the Japanese partners in the German–Italian axis. The Russians in the service of the Japanese gendarmerie used unsavory means in the anti-Bolshevik and anti-Jewish campaigns, which forced many Jewish residents of Harbin to abandon their businesses and depart from the region. Part of this campaign was extortion—demanding large payments for release after false arrests for "sabotage" and other trumped-up charges. The worst part of the campaign was kidnapping and torture, with demands for large ransoms.[18] The kidnapping started in the spring of 1932, and in the following eighteen months twelve persons were kidnapped—eight of them Jews. Four of the twelve victims, all Jews, were killed or died in captivity.

The political atmosphere in Harbin changed dramatically from tolerance and respect for minorities to hate and harassment. It was a policy of the authorities from which there was no recourse. Small wonder that this motivated many in the Jewish community of Harbin to seek refuge elsewhere. In the early 1930s some families went to Palestine, some left China for the United States and other destinations, but most went to Tianjin and Shanghai. It is estimated that in 1931 some thirteen thousand Russian Jews lived in Harbin. The next few years saw a massive exodus of the Russian Jewish community. By 1935 only about five thousand Jews remained in Harbin.

Japan's War Against China, Great Britain, and the United States, 1937–1945

In 1937 the Japanese began their expansion into the rest of China. By the end of the year both Tianjin and Shanghai were occupied. The foreign concessions were not affected by the occupation, and because the Russian

Jews were concentrated in these concessions, their life was not immediately affected.

At the end of 1937, a conference of Jewish communities of the Far East established the Far East Jewish National Council. Dr. Kaufman was elected chairman of the council, which included seven representatives from Harbin, two from Mukden (Shenyang), two from Hailar, one from Dairen (Dalian), one from Tianjin, two from Qiqihar, and one from Kobe, Japan. Shanghai, Qingdao, and Manzhouli were not represented in the first group of representatives, but joined the council later.[19]

The council was established for the purpose of direct representation of Jewish interests in the Far East to the Japanese authorities—and to bypass the so-called Bureau of Russian Emigrés (BREM), which the Japanese authorities used as a means to pressure the Russian population to support their objectives.

In greeting the conference, General *Higuchi* Kuhiro, head of the Japanese Military Mission in Manchuria, declared:

> We are not uninformed about the conflicts between the Jews and other nations and their results.... Japanese people have no racial prejudice, look upon the Jewish people with friendship and stand ready to join forces with the Jews, as with all others, in the struggle for peace and well-being of humanity, and to maintain mutual cooperation and close economic ties.[20]

One of the most important contributions of this council was the representation before the Japanese authorities, which in 1942 prevented implementation of Nazi policies against the Jews of Shanghai, including about twenty thousand refugees from Nazi-occupied Europe.

Before 1941 stateless Russian Jews living in Harbin as well as in foreign settlements in Tianjin and Shanghai were better off than Soviet Jewish citizens who were exposed to the particularly nasty anti-Semitic harassment of Russian fascist mercenaries of the Japanese. When the Pacific war broke out in December 1941 after Japan bombed Pearl Harbor, the situation reversed itself. The tenuous protection of the foreign concessions was gone as their American, British, and French former owners were now at war with Japan. The Soviet Union, however, was not at war with Japan and would not declare war on Japan until 1945. Between 1941 and 1945, therefore, the Japanese in China were careful not to offend the Soviet citizens so as not to provoke an incident that might lead to war with the Soviet Union. Thus Soviet passport holders (including Jews) had a kind of protection from both Japanese intimidation and attacks by the Russian Fascists.

Postwar Years

For Jews of Harbin the years 1941 to 1945 were difficult, but the community was not threatened by any catastrophic situation. Paradoxically, when Jews everywhere celebrated the Allied victory, the situation disintegrated for the Harbin Jewish community. In Manchuria the Japanese army surrendered to the Soviet army, which quickly occupied the territory. The Japanese surrender was orderly, except in Hailar, where several Jewish families were massacred by the retreating Japanese. The author of this article knows personally one woman (now resident in Israel) whose parents and brothers were massacred.

During the Soviet occupation, the Harbin Jews lived in fear of arrest and imprisonment. Valuable community archives were destroyed to prevent their use as "incriminating" evidence by the KGB (Soviet secret police). In Harbin, within days of the Soviet occupation, the KGB began to arrest prominent citizens in the community, and—without formal charges or interrogation—shipped them to the Soviet jails and gulags (prison camps). The first group of these political prisoners included more than one thousand Russians and some thirty-five Jews.[21] Few of them survived the prison camps. Fewer still were allowed to leave the Soviet Union after their release from prison.

The Soviet army left Harbin after about one year, and the town was given over to the control of the Chinese communist armies. By 1949, the PRC government in Harbin had developed close ties with the Soviet government. The Soviet consul-general and the newly created Association of Soviet Citizens became influential, and this caused further difficulties for the Harbin Jews.

A rift between the Chinese and Soviet governments started developing in the mid-1950s, and a few years later all Soviet citizens departed from Harbin. Remnants of the Jewish community remained in Harbin throughout these years—but almost all Jews had left Harbin by 1960.

Exodus, 1946–1958

When the war ended with the Japanese surrender in August 1945, there were approximately 8,500 Russian Jews in China, about 3,500 in Shanghai, 2,500 in Tianjin, 2,000 in Harbin, and 500 in smaller communities such as Dalian and Qingdao. As noted earlier, the Japanese in Manchuria surrendered to the Soviet army. As a result, the Harbin and Dalian communities were cut off from the rest and could not access the International Refugee Organization, the Hebrew Immigrant Aid Society, the American Joint Distribution Committee, or the Palestine-based Jewish Agency (PALAMT in China). The first contact between PALAMT and the Jewish community of Harbin was made in August 1949. At that time it had a population of about 1,600, and the Dalian community numbered around 120.

During the three years (1948–51) PALAMT evacuated to Israel some 5,300 persons including 1,046 individuals from Harbin and 86 from Dalian. The story of the end of the Jewish communities in China has been summarized by Walter J. Citrin, head of the PALAMT in Hong Kong, in a June 1954 letter to the Jewish Agency executive in Jerusalem.

> It is obvious that the Communist government in China is keen to clear the country of the foreign element. However, the departure of a foreigner of any nationality, even the "politically loyal" is made difficult by many financial commitments, that is to say, that the authorities make things very difficult as long as the person who wants to leave is still in funds, and lets the person go only after making quite sure that his personal funds are exhausted. . . . There are innumerable bureaus who have to clear a person before he is given the final exit permit.
>
> As regards former Russian subjects presently holding Soviet passports, which group constitutes the majority of Jews remaining in China, there is one additional problem and that is clearance from the Soviet Citizens Association and the Soviet Consulate General. This again is connected with "voluntary contributions" which are set beyond the means of the migrants. This particular clearance is more difficult to obtain in the north of China, and particularly in Harbin. It often happens that after the exit permit is granted, it is cancelled one or two days before the intended departure of the migrant. No reason is given for such action, and the person, having liquidated his business and personal affairs, is left to sit and meditate until his final fate is decided some months later.[22]

In June 1954, 564 Jews were awaiting evacuation from China: 323 from Harbin, 167 from Shanghai, and 74 from Tianjin. Except for a handful of elderly individuals who remained and died in China, all of the above had left China by the 1960s.[23]

Acculturation, Assimilation, and Anti-Semitism

The sixty-year sojourn of Russian Jews in China witnessed very little acculturation. There are a few examples of Chinese culture influencing the pursuits of individual Russian Jews, such as Aaron Avshalomov, who composed music rooted in Chinese tradition (written in Shanghai in the 1920s and 1930s); Israel Epstein, a Jewish Maoist who stayed on in China to become editor of *China Reconstructs* magazine; and Emmanuel Pratt, who wrote the first Chinese–Hebrew dictionary (published in Jerusalem in

1995). On the lighter side, many Jewish women in China as well as in the United States accepted mah-jongg as the gambling game of choice. (In the United States there are still groups of former China residents who meet for a game of mah-jongg on a regular basis.)

These are isolated examples and do not reflect a general impact of Chinese experience on Jewish culture. Some of the reasons for this lack of acculturation are the following. The Russian Jews in China lived in colonial enclaves (Russian, English, American), not in direct contact with the Chinese culture. The most powerful mechanisms of acculturation, the requirement to learn the language of the host people, was absent: The Chinese had to learn the language of the foreigners in control, not the other way around. Thus, the Chinese spoke "fractured" languages (*pidgin* English or Russian). Jewish children attended Russian, English, American, French, German, or Jewish schools. Hardly anyone attended Chinese schools.

Also the Russian Jews in China (whose Jewish culture was already "acculturated" by the Russian experience of their parents and grandparents) viewed themselves as transient refugees. As such they had an exaggerated mission of preserving their identity and their culture as Russian Jews, and they resisted the influence of Chinese customs, art, and institutions on their life.

Finally, acculturation is a slow process, usually involving exposure of many generations to the host culture. The Russian Jews lived in China for no more than two generations: Typically only one generation was born in China. Given the colonial environment and the barriers to the cultural contacts between the Jews and the Chinese and the short duration of this Diaspora experience, acculturation would be quite unlikely.

Acculturation is an indispensable prerequisite to assimilation. In the absence of acculturation, assimilation of Russian Jews into the Chinese community was almost totally absent. There was some assimilation of Jews into the Russian community in China, but the extent of this has not been adequately documented.

Conclusion

The Harbin Jewish community was remarkable in many respects. The founders possessed an uncommon entrepreneurial spirit. Many of the Harbin pioneers from Siberia and the Maritime Provinces already had experience in the development of new territories. Others were willing to put up with many physical and social hardships in order to take advantage of the opportunities for material success.

The early Jewish pioneers made major contributions to the growth of Harbin from a barren site to a vital and prosperous city. These contributions included industrial facilities, international trade, retail businesses, community services, public buildings, and housing. From the start, Harbin Jews played an important part in the political and economic life of the city. In 1909, of the forty members of the City Council, twelve were Jews. In subsequent years Jews continued to play an important part in the economic and political life of the community. This gave the Jewish community a sense of belonging (whether conscious or subconscious).

Many leaders of the pioneering Jewish community in Harbin were well-educated, energetic, and dedicated to the preservation of Jewish national and cultural values, in particular Dr. Kaufman, who served the Jewish community for more than thirty years. The rich social and cultural life was enhanced by the hospitable attitude of the Chinese administration, which allowed, and in fact required, that the community be responsible for its own social and cultural needs.

The Harbin Jewish community from the beginning developed a strong democratic framework for the community structure, wherein the leadership of the community was elected and was accountable to its constituency.

Finally, a successful program of Jewish education of the youth and the support of Jewish youth organizations such as Betar and Maccabi developed a special sense of identity and continuity of the community that still unites the surviving second generation of ex-Harbinites worldwide.

Notes

Portions of an earlier version of this article appeared in the *Bulletin,* Igud Yotzei Sin in Israel (Association of Former Residents of China) 334 (March–April 1994), pp. 8–9; 335 (May–June 1994), pp. 10–11; 336 (August–September 1994), pp. 25–27; and 337 (October–November 1994), pp. 15–17.

The author gratefully acknowledges reviews of an earlier draft of this paper and helpful suggestions by Gregory Grossman, Peter Berton, Evsey Domar, and Leo Hanin. Editorial suggestions by Jonathan Goldstein have been particularly helpful. Any errors of omission or commission are exclusively the author's.

1. Evgenii Kh. Nilus, *Istoricheskii obzor K.V.Zh.D., 1896–1923* (Historical Survey of the CER, 1896–1923) (Harbin: K.V.Zh.D., 1923); *Polytechnic* (Sydney, Australia), no. 10 (1979). Newsletter of the Harbin Polytechnic Institute Alumni Association.

2. David Wolff, "To the Harbin Station: City Building in Russian Manchuria, 1898–1914" (Ph.D. dissertation, History, University of California at Berkeley, 1991).

3. Mikhail V. Grulyov, *Zapiski generala-evreia* (Memoirs of a Jewish General) (Paris: n.p., 1930).

4. Abram [Avraham] I. Kaufman, "Memoirs" (in Russian) (Tel Aviv) *Bulletin,* Igud Yotzei Sin in Israel (Association of Former Jewish Residents of China).

5. Gruliov, *Zapiski;* and Kaufman, "Memoirs," *passim.*

6. Oscar O. Gruzenberg, *Ocherki i rechi* (Sketches and Speeches) (New York: n.p., 1944).

7. S.I. Ravikovich, "Reorganization of the Jewish Community in Harbin, 1917," *Evreiskoie Slovo,* no. 1 (1918).
8. Kaufman, "Memoirs," *passim.*
9. Grigori I. Pasternak, and Eugene Raleigh, *To Reach This Season* (Berkeley: Judah L. Magnes Museum, 1983).
10. R. Basin, "Memories of Manzhouli (Manchuria)," *Outlook* (November–December 1981).
11. Tzvia Shickman-Bowman, "The History of the Harbin Jewish Community, 1898–1931," in chap. III.B.7 in this volume.
12. "In Spite of Depression! ... A Jewish Ball at the Komsob," *Rubezh* (Harbin) (March 1934).
13. Yaakov V. Ziskin, *Life of Jews in the Far East,* unpub. mss. in Archives of the Igud Yotzei Sin in Israel, Tel Aviv.
14. *Bulletin,* Igud Yotzei Sin in Israel, no. 326 (1992).
15. *Betar in China,* 1929–1949 (in Russian and Hebrew) (Tel Aviv: n.p., 1974).
16. John J. Stephan, *The Russian Fascists* (New York: Harper & Row, 1978); P. Balakshin, *Final v Kitaie* (The End in China) (San Francisco: Sirius, 1958).
17. Pasternak, *To Reach This Season, passim;* Abram I. Kaufman, *Lagerny vrach* (The Camp Doctor) (Tel Aviv: Am Oved, 1973).
18. Amleto Vespa, *Secret Agent of Japan* (Boston: Little, Brown, 1938).
19. Kaufman, "Memoirs," *passim.*
20. *Bulletin,* Igud Yotzei Sin in Israel, no. 296 (1988), p. 5.
21. Pasternak, *To Reach This Season, passim*; Kaufman, *Lagernyi vrach, passim.*
22. Walter J. Citrin, Chairman's Report on Activities, *Far Eastern Palestine Office of the Jewish Agency,* Shanghai, August 1948–September 1951, in the Central Zionist Archives, Jerusalem.
23. "Annual Report, Council of Jewish Community, Shanghai, 1958," Archives of Igud Yotzei Sin in Israel, Tel Aviv.

C. Occupational Profiles: Shanghai

Chapter III.C.1

Silas Aaron Hardoon and Cross-Cultural Adaptation in Shanghai

Chiara Betta

Long neglected, the history of Jewish communities in China between 1845 and 1956 has, since the mid-1980s, attracted widespread interest among academics in the West and in the People's Republic of China. Scholarly research has been especially facilitated by the consultation of previously unknown or unavailable archival sources and newspapers collections held in the People's Republic of China, the United States, Israel, and Great Britain. Ten years on, we have a much deeper understanding of Jewish presence in China, especially in Shanghai. Yet the histories of the earliest and most prominent Baghdadi[1] families and individuals who sojourned or settled in Shanghai still remain partly unexplored. Hence this brief chapter explores the life of Silas Aaron Hardoon (1851–1931), a Baghdadi Jew who started his career as a minor employee of David Sassoon and Company and who was reputed to be the richest individual in East Asia at the time of his death. Quite apart from the exceptional nature of his rags-to-riches story, he was unique among Baghdadi Jews in that he established broad ties with the Chinese sociocultural milieu.

Despite Hardoon's commercial achievements and the exceptional nature of his interaction within the Chinese environment, he remains a little-known figure mainly because of the scarcity of information on his life and the fact that the available sources are scattered and not always accessed easily. The task of any researcher is made even more arduous by the lack of contemporary accounts.[2] One of the few is that written by Hardoon's American crony Carl Crow, who described his "Oriental" friend as a tough, pungent real-estate owner often feared by his tenants for his ruthless ways. He also recollects that his display of wealth often contrasted with his spartan tastes and mused, "The desk at which he sat was one that could not be duplicated in any furniture store in America for no store would stock one so cheap."[3]

There is, in contrast, an unexpected abundance of Chinese works on Hardoon, his wife, and their landscaped Chinese garden, the Aili Garden (*Aili yuan*) also known as Hardoon Garden (*Hatong huayuan*). The majority of these writings have fictional connotations and have appeared in Shanghai from 1920s onward. From this it is clear that Hardoon's outlandish lifestyle has facilitated the remolding of his image according to the prevailing political, social, and economic moods of Chinese society. As a result, Hardoon's story has exerted a potent fascination over the past three generations of Shanghainese and of Chinese in general: the "petty urbanites" (*xiao shimin*) of the 1930s, the Chinese masses of the Maoist period, and the emerging new entrepreneurs of the 1990s.[4] As for Chinese works published in China between 1949 and the beginning of the 1980s, they have depicted Hardoon as an "exploiter" (*boxuezhe*) of the Chinese masses whose evil deeds need to be continuously exorcised through the exposure of his "bloodsucker" (*xixuegui*) behavior.[5] However, since the end of the 1980s, as a result of the gradual economic liberalization of China and the re-evaluation of Shanghai's capitalist past, Hardoon has regained a human dimension in most Chinese writings. Unfortunately, an anti-Semitic harangue, which might contribute to the spread of anti-Semitic prejudices among Chinese, has emerged in some of the most recent texts on Hardoon.[6]

The scarcity and superficiality of Western sources, together with the distorted picture of Hardoon presented by Chinese works, leaves many blank spaces, which this chapter will try to fill in. First, any exploration of Hardoon needs to consider the trade diaspora of Baghdadi Jews to India and to East Asia and the history of the early Baghdadi Jewish community in Shanghai.[7] The city was opened to foreign trade in 1843, after the signing of the Treaty of Nanjing, which marked the end of the first Opium War (1839–42). The year after, David Sassoon (1792–1865), the scion of the most eminent Jewish family in Baghdad (who had founded a flourishing commercial enterprise in Bombay in 1832) sent his second son, Elias David, to China with the aim of expanding the business interests of the family firm.[8] Elias David established a branch of David Sassoon and Company in Shanghai in 1845, and five years later three clerks of the firm were among the two hundred foreigners who had taken residence in the city.[9] By 1874, David Sassoon & Company and the competing firm of E.D. Sassoon and Company (founded by Elias David in 1867) already employed twenty Baghdadi coreligionists who constituted the core of the local Jewish community.[10] It is less known that among the early Jewish sojourners and settlers there were also merchants, petty traders, and adventurers from places such as London, Manchester, and Constantinople (Istanbul).[11] One should then add that, at the turn of the century, Russian Jews, who were mostly fleeing bloody pogroms, then started to flock to Shanghai. By the 1920s they outnumbered their coreligionists of Baghdadi origin.

The Sassoon firms in Shanghai, especially in the earliest period, not only acted as the primary employees of Baghdadi coreligionists but also took care of their religious and social needs, an encompassing role similar to that which they played in Bombay. There is hence an indisputable link between the establishment of the Sassoon firms in Shanghai and the consequent arrival of Baghdadi Jews in the city. Hence one cannot overlook that the Sassoon firms prompted a number of Baghdadi families and individuals to move to East Asia, where they often established their own business after leaving the Sassoon firms.[12] Such was the case of Silas Aaron Hardoon.

Salih Harun or Saleh Haron,[13] then Anglicized as Silas Aaron, the son of Harun or Haron (Aaron), was born in Baghdad in 1851, one of six children.[14] Five years later Harun and part of his family moved to Bombay, with the hope of finding employment at David Sassoon & Company He was, indeed, given a menial occupation by the firm and Silas Aaron (hereafter Hardoon) probably received free education at one of the schools set up by the Sassoon family.[15] Significantly, Hardoon learned to write in Judeo–Arabic, a language he used to jot down personal notes until the end of his life. In the course of his life he also learned English, which he spoke with a strong Arabic accent.[16] As an adolescent, Hardoon found employment at David Sassoon & Company and, since he was a promising youth with a remarkable business acumen, was transferred to the Hong Kong branch of the firm, probably around 1870. In 1874 he was sacked, for some unknown reasons, but was nevertheless able to secure a humble job, with the help of his friend S.J. Solomon, at the Shanghai branch of David Sassoon and Company. In the following years Hardoon made notable career advancements and was entrusted with the purchase of properties in the Shanghai foreign settlements on behalf of his employers.[17] Hardoon, however, harbored independent commercial aspirations and around 1882 left David Sassoon and Company with the intention of establishing himself as a cotton broker. Yet, according to Stanley Jackson, "Shipowners did not favour credit for a possible competitor to their better-placed clients, while local officials expected their full 'squeeze' in cash."[18] Five years later he returned to the secure fold of the Sassoon firms as manager of the Shanghai branch of E.D. Sassoon and Company. By the early 1890s, when he was appointed partner, he was managing the real estate investments and opium imports of the firm. In 1900 he also founded his own firm, the Hardoon Company, which mainly took care of his extensive property holdings. He severed his association from E.D. Sassoon and Company in 1911.[19]

According to Shanghai lore, Hardoon was a dealer of *tu*, a word carrying both the meaning of opium and land.[20] In effect, Hardoon traded in opium at least until 1918. According to one estimation, in 1907 (when the British government implemented a policy of gradual reduction of opium imports over a period of ten years) Hardoon had in store about five tons of the drug in his go-downs. In the following decade he then purchased a large amount of opium, of the apparent value of 1 million taels with funds entrusted him by Chinese officials.[21] Hardoon employed opium revenues to finance his continuous purchase of real estate in the Shanghai International Settlement, especially in the central and western districts. Like other land developers, he also used to mortgage his assets to raise funds to make further purchases. The steady increase in the value of properties in the International Settlement combined with Hardoon's exceptional business foresight were the primary reasons for Hardoon's rise as Shanghai's major individual landowner. By the time of his death in 1931, Hardoon's assets were valued at approximately 150 million yuan and consisted of about 450 *mu* of land with 1,200 buildings erected thereon.[22]

From the above, it might be inferred that Hardoon's commercial career needs to be analyzed within the commercial networks of Baghdadi coreligionists and in the light of the real estate boom in the Shanghai foreign settlements between 1890 and 1931. Yet one should not overlook that Hardoon's career was also favored by his close commercial links with prominent members of the Chinese gentry-merchant and military elite. In this regard Jackson maintains that it was Hardoon's "interest in Buddhism which gave him an intimacy with prominent Chinese merchants denied to most outside businessmen."[23] It is more precise to suggest that Hardoon came into close contact with the host milieu through his marriage to Liza Roos, mostly known by her Buddhist name *Luo* Jialing, "that is, Kavalinka, a beautiful song-bird of the Himalayas."[24] Hardoon and Luo married according to Chinese and also apparently to Jewish rites on September 26, 1886, though no *ketuba*, or Jewish religious marriage certificate, was ever found. A civil marriage was not held until August 23, 1928. It is significant to note that Baghdadi Jews rarely married outside the Jewish faith in Shanghai. In addition, marriage to a Eurasian of humble origins defied one of the strongest social taboos of treaty-port society.[25]

Luo was the daughter of *Shen* Yi, a poor Chinese woman originally of Fujian province, and of Isaac Roos, a Frenchman who might have been Jewish. Roos most probably left Shanghai when Luo was three years old, and consequently she grew up in an overwhelmingly Chinese environment on the outskirts of Shanghai. As an adult, she was deeply imbued with Chinese beliefs and identified herself as Chinese. At a local level she also saw herself as Shanghainese. Luo's Chinese identity can be especially seen in her life-style, her devotion to the Buddhist faith, and her respect of ancestor worship. She even established a Chinese lineage trust for the Chinese children she adopted, with her surname, after 1897. After 1919, the Hardoons also adopted eleven children of various backgrounds: Some were White Russians, other Russian Jews, and the rest of unknown origins. Notwithstanding Hardoon's willingness to bring them up according to the Jewish faith, they were deeply influenced by their overwhelming Chinese surroundings.[26]

It is pivotal to stress that Hardoon's marriage to a Eurasian, who strongly identified herself as Chinese, served as the social context through which he established broad ties with Chinese of all walks of life. Luo also prompted Hardoon to adopt Chinese tastes, as is shown by the fact that the couple lived in a Chinese traditional landscape garden, the Aili Garden. One should also note that the main house of the Aili Garden, where the Hardoons resided, mirrored the hybrid aspirations of the local Chinese merchant elite. In contrast, the residences of Hardoon's Baghdadi coreligionists reflected their Anglicized tastes and their aim of integrating into the Shanghai Western community.[27]

The Aili Garden was erected between 1904 and 1909 and was designed by the Buddhist monk *Huang* Zongyang (1865–1921). During the period Huang lived with the Hardoons, between 1898 and the end of 1914, he exerted the role of influential adviser on Chinese affairs to Hardoon and of spiritual guide to Luo.[28] At the beginning of the century he began to associate with Shanghai's reformist circles and was among those who established the progressive Chinese Educational Association (Zhongguo jiaoyuhui) in the spring of 1902. Huang acted as chief fundraiser to the organization since he could raise donations from his wealthy patrons. Accordingly, the following autumn, Luo contributed to the establishment of the radical Patriotic School (Aiguo xueshe) and bore all the expenses of the Patriotic Girls' School (Aiguo nüxuexiao). The latter was, at the time, one of the most modern educational institutions for Chinese women. It is hence not surprising that Luo's enlightened role was praised in a brief biographical article that appeared in the *Nübao* (Women's Journal), a publication advocating education and independence for Chinese women.[29] By the spring of 1903 Huang, like other members of the Educational Association, adopted an increasingly anti-Manchu stance, which he expressed in a number of virulent attacks published in *Subao*. Not unexpectedly the publication was forced to close in July and its two most notorious contributors, Zhang and *Zou* Rong, were tried in the Shanghai Mixed Court. They were sentenced in May 1904 to two and three years of imprisonment, respectively. As for

Huang, when the *Subao* case erupted he hid in the Aili Garden and also received financial help from Hardoon but was nevertheless forced to flee to Japan for about a year.[30]

On his return to Shanghai, Huang avoided active participation in revolutionary activities and devoted most of his time to fostering Buddhist causes. The Hardoons financed Huang's endeavors, the most distinguished of which is the reprint of the Buddhist Canons, the *Tripitaka,* between 1909 and 1913. Huang, together with other monks also contributed to the establishment of the Avatamsaka College (Huayan daxue) (the first Buddhist university in Shanghai) in the Aili Garden in September 1914. By the end of December, however, the school had moved to Hangzhou after students and dharma masters refused to kowtow to Hardoon on his birthday.[31] The request had been forwarded by *Ji* Juemi, an unscrupulous and adventurous character, who had become Luo's new favorite and soon after replaced Huang as the Hardoons' chief adviser. The relevance of this episode lies in the fact that it testifies to how Hardoon utilized symbolic rituals in his often-bizarre effort to enhance his status and social standing in the Chinese milieu.

Huang wielded a strong influence on Hardoon at least until the end of 1914. One should note that when he returned for a brief period to political activism during the 1911 Revolution, which led to the permanent downfall of the Qing dynasty, he favored Hardoon's support of the revolutionary forces in Shanghai. First, Hardoon used his economic power to secure a stable situation in Chinese Shanghai in the days that followed a successful revolutionary uprising on November 3. Hardoon, advised by Huang, financed the appointment of *Li* Xiehui, the leader of the Restoration Society (Guangfuhui), as Wusong military commissioner with the aim of avoiding a possible military confrontation between him and the newly appointed Shanghai Military Commissioner *Chen* Qimei, the local leader of the Revolutionary Alliance (Tongmenghui). Second, during November and December, Hardoon lent his secure residence to the revolutionaries, who conducted a number of meetings there. Hardoon also entertained the leading revolutionary *Sun* Yat-sen (1866–1925), an old acquaintance of Huang, on his return to Shanghai on December 25 and during a party held in the Aili Garden the following day.[32]

Hardoon's participation on the side of the revolutionaries and the Shanghai local gentry-merchant elite during the 1911 Revolution testifies that, after almost forty years spent in Shanghai, he had acquired an intimate understanding of the Chinese sociocultural and political milieu. Most important, he had learned how to master *guanxi,* networks of personal relationships that are of fundamental importance in the social behavior of

Chinese and imply reciprocity from the parties involved. Hardoon's capacity for managing complex relationships with Chinese can be especially noticed by the fact that, in the most turbulent days of 1911, he provided much-coveted shelter to Qing officials who had pragmatically turned their alliance to the Republic. As the *China Press* summarizes: "During the early revolutionary days, the Hardoon estate was the favourite refuge of generals fleeing for their lives. The militarists, it is said, would escape to Shanghai and disappear altogether until traced to the hospitable Hardoon home, where they lived as guests."[33] The most notorious refugee in the Aili Garden was the Manchu *Ruizheng,* with whom Hardoon had established commercial links around 1906. Ruizheng fled the city of Wuchang, where he held the prestigious position of governor-general of Hunan and Hubei, at the inception of the revolution on October 10. He did not pose any active resistance to the revolutionaries, and, after a few weeks spent in hiding, he suddenly reappeared, pallid and emaciated, in Shanghai on October 28. Immediately, he secretly moved to the Aili Garden, where he remained in comfortable exile until his death the following year.[34]

Over the following two decades, Hardoon consolidated and broadened his already close ties with the Shanghai gentry-merchant elite and with Chinese militarists. Of particular relevance is his involvement in the Chinese political arena between 1916 and 1928, an unstable period when political geography was characterized by chronic factionalism and volatile alliances. Remarkably, between 1917 and 1925 Hardoon established close ties with all the major conflicting factions and maintained contacts with the rival Beijing and Guangzhou governments. Perhaps the most appropriate remark that can be made is that Hardoon's foremost concern at the beginning of the 1920s seems to have been that of remaining at the center of political maneuvering in order to boost his own prestige and power among prominent Chinese political and military circles.

First, after a serious political crisis unfolded in Beijing in the late spring and summer of 1917, Hardoon provided Sun with a handsome donation to found a rival government in Guangzhou. Yet, at the same time Hardoon, whose pragmatism was always present in his political alliances, also curried friendly ties with the Anfu (Anhui-Fujian) clique. The Anfuites exerted a preponderant influence on Sun's major rival: the Northern regime based in Beijing and headed by Premier *Duan* Qirui. Most important for Hardoon, the Anfu clique held control over Chinese Shanghai and the nearby Zhejiang province. He further cemented his ties with this Northern group in the autumn of 1919, when he hosted *Wang* Yitang (1878–1946), a prominent member of the Anfu Club, the civil branch of the Anhui clique. Wang reached Shanghai on September 19 with the intention of reorganizing the peace talks between the Beijing and Guangzhou governments that had failed the previous May. However, Wang's attempt was from the beginning doomed to failure since the Guangzhou regime showed no intention of negotiating with him and his entourage. His mission came to an abrupt end on July 14, 1920, when a conflict between the two main Northern factions, the Anfu and Zhili cliques, broke out. The war was disastrous for the Anfu forces, which lost control over the Beijing government. Hardoon immediately switched his support to the Zhili clique, the winning side. It was not unusual for him to curry the favor of politicians and militarists who belonged to opposing groups.[35]

Hardoon's close involvement in factional politics and the vast network of exchange relationships he had set up with a number of militarists was a cause of concern among the British authorities in China. They closely watched his movements, as testified by the following report compiled in January 1920:

> Mrs. Hardoon, who is a Chinese by birth, recently went to Nanking with Joo Poo Ling (*Ji* Juemi), the Chinaman who lives with them, and had a long interview with the Military Governor. Mrs. Hardoon besides being a great intriguer is violently anti-British. Hardoon himself stated that all the Military and Civil Governors were his friends and adopted the views of his wife.[36]

A slightly different version was given in another report, saying "Hardoon himself is also stated to have been expressing very anti-British views."[37]

Hardoon's extraordinary connections with Chinese politicians and militarists also prompted widespread curiosity among Shanghainese and, to a lesser extent, among foreign residents of Shanghai. For example, in July 1923 the Chinese press reported the rumor that the disgraced president *Li* Yuanhong (1864–1928) would receive shelter in the Aili Garden after being forced out of office by *Cao* Kun (1862–1938), the nominal leader of the Zhili clique. Yet Hardoon firmly denied the allegation to a journalist of the *North China Daily News*.[38] Moreover, Hardoon and Cao's relations were confirmed during a visit of Hardoon to Beijing in the summer of 1924, when Cao appointed Hardoon to the position of high adviser to the Beijing government. In exchange Hardoon possibly offered Cao a loan of 2 million yuan, under the condition the latter would present Hardoon with valuable antiques from the Forbidden City.[39]

The aim was to use the antiques as prizes in charitable lotteries held during charity fairs, which aimed to raise money for Shanghai benevolent associations or for the Chinese population hit by natural disasters. Such events were regularly organized by Hardoon in collaboration with members of the Shanghai gentry-merchant elite and native-place organizations in the

Aili Garden after 1911. They represented a valid example of Shanghai hybrid treaty-port culture since they offered entertainments ranging from Chinese traditional opera to modern drama, from traditional colored lantern shows to foreign movies. What is of interest here is that Hardoon, who at time of the establishment of the republic had already acquired a profound understanding of the Chinese milieu, carried out benevolent activities according to local traditional practices. Significantly, his participation in relief activities with the Shanghai local elite represented one crucial aspect of his attempt to shape an image of himself as similar as possible to that of the traditional Chinese merchant-philanthropist. Hardoon's charitable activism also reveals that his interaction with the Chinese milieu was based on a complex and subtle balance between charitable endeavors, commercial interests, and political intrigues. In effect, through his involvement in Chinese charitable activities he promoted his *guanxi* with prominent individuals of the Shanghai gentry-merchant elite, Chinese militarists, and powerful native-place organizations.[40]

By the mid-1910s, and with the aim of building a new social identity in the host milieu, Hardoon also attempted to draw upon the Chinese elite's traditional repertoire of patronage of arts, scholars, and connoisseurship of antiques. Accordingly, he and his wife sponsored a number of conservative educational and cultural enterprises and "acquired a reputation of being fanatic admirers of traditional Chinese learning, customs, conventions, and moral values."[41] Between 1915 and 1925, the Hardoons, under the influence of Ji, attempted to transform the Aili Garden into a center of neotraditionalist studies opposed to the iconoclastic attitude toward China's past manifested by the New Culturalists, a pro-Western, anti-Confucian movement that flourished in China particularly after 1919. First, in February 1915 they set up the College to Propagate the Wisdom of the Sage *Cang Jie* (Cangsheng mingzhi daxue), with an attached higher primary and secondary school. A girls school was also established shortly afterward. The curriculum and organization of the schools were inspired by the 1913 "restore the ancient" (*fugu*) campaign, which fostered the worship of sages of antiquity and the return to Confucian teachings. The schools indeed cultivated the veneration of Cang, the mythical inventor of the Chinese script, and stressed the importance of Confucian studies. Within a more general discourse of neotraditionalist inclinations among Chinese conservative intellectuals, the schools might be seen as expressions of the national essence (*guocui*) school since they strongly advocated the national learning (*guoxue*). It is hence not surprising that the traditionalist scholar *Wang Guowei* (1877–1927), a staunch supporter of the national learning, taught in the schools of the Aili Garden. Between 1916 and 1923, under Hardoon's patronage, he also conducted considerable research on the Hardoons' collection of oracle bones and edited the *Xueshu congbian* (Journal of Scholarship). This journal, together with other works that fostered the maintenance of the national essence, was printed by a publishing house founded by Hardoon in his residence. Finally, the Society to Promote the Study of Language (Guang cangxue hui) together with its three attached organizations (founded by Hardoon in 1916) added another traditionalist and anachronistic touch to the Aili Garden. Many of its members were elderly Confucian literati still dressed in the traditional gown who congregated in the Aili Garden to escape from the increasingly westernized Shanghai.[42]

The above strongly suggests that, during his stay in Shanghai, Hardoon experienced a gradual process of cross-cultural adaptation in the Chinese host milieu, which can be seen from his increasing interaction with Chinese of all walks of life and his adoption of Chinese modes of thinking and behavior. However, it would be misleading to suggest that Hardoon relinquished ties with his coreligionists, since he maintained cordial relations with many individuals and families. Yet he never played a major role in the affairs of the Jewish community and his financial contributions to Jewish causes were meager, especially when compared to his handsome donations to Chinese philanthropy. The only remarkable project he financed was the building of the Beth Aharon synagogue in 1925, completed two years later. At times he also opened his residence to Jewish visitors such as the Zionist envoy Ariel Bension in 1925 and 1929. During Bension's first visit, Hardoon was among those who founded a committee of Jews and non-Jews to work for the promotion of Jewish culture in Palestine.[43]

Hardoon died on June 19, 1931, possibly of a heart attack, and two days afterward he was buried in his residence with a Jewish funeral. However, the presence of Buddhist monks, who might have performed some of their own rituals, prompted widespread criticism from the Jewish community. Even more shocking was the Chinese memorial service held at the end of July, which was a combination of a belated Chinese mourning service and a Chinese funeral. First, Hardoon's ancestral tablet was dotted by a Chinese scholar in front of his adopted male children on July 21. Immediately afterward the Hardoon children performed offerings to Hardoon's tablet to avoid the possibility of their father's becoming a malevolent and wandering ghost; undoubtedly a surprise for those who were supposed to educate them according to the Jewish faith. During the memorial service Buddhist monks and Daoist priests also performed esoteric rituals to facilitate the passage of Hardoon's soul through hell. According to Chinese custom, paper gifts were then also burned to purchase favors from the Chinese mandarins who inhabited hell.[44] The memorial service was organized by Hardoon's widow, yet there is no reason to believe that Hardoon would have opposed the dotting of his ancestral tablet and the performance of auspicious rituals by Chinese funeral specialists. In effect, it is arguable that the Jewish funeral and the Chinese memorial service reflected Hardoon's position in the last decades of his life, when as an old man he faced the challenging dilemma of attempting to reach some sort of balance between his deep involvement in the Chinese milieu and his attachment to his Jewish roots. As a whole, the relevance and peculiarity of Hardoon's stay in Shanghai lie in the fact that he underwent a remarkable process of cross-cultural adaptation in the Chinese host environment. In contrast, his Baghdadi coreligionists experienced a distinct process of Anglicization, but manifested an aloof attitude toward the Chinese milieu. In a few words, their choice was to adopt the mannerisms of the British gentlemen; Hardoon's was to imitate, as far as possible for a foreigner, the Chinese merchant-philanthropist.

Last but not least, the Aili Garden was almost completely destroyed by fire in 1943. Ten years later the local communist authorities ordered the removal of the Hardoons' mausoleum to the outskirts of Shanghai. Shortly afterward, on the former premises of the Aili Garden, the Sino-Soviet Friendship Building (nowadays the Shanghai Exhibition Center), was erected as a tribute to the fresh path followed by new (*xin*) socialist Shanghai in contrast with old (*jiu*) capitalist Shanghai. Despite the disappearance of Hardoon's most famous landmark, he and his wife are still widely remembered by Shanghainese. Elderly people still recollect salacious gossip and curious anecdotes on the Hardoons, and the youngest generation has often read fictional literature on the couple. On the whole, Hardoon remains a unique symbol of foreign presence in China since no other single foreigner has left such a lasting and distinctive mark on the collective memory of Shanghainese.

Notes

1. "Referring originally to Jews who came from the Tigris and Euphrates rivers, for centuries a center of Jewish learning and culture, the term *Baghdadi* or *Iraqi* soon came to include as well Jews from Syria and other parts of the Ottoman Empire, Aden and Yemen, all of whom were Arabic speaking, and even Jews from Persia and Afghanistan, who were not. In Bombay, the term *Baghdadi* was most common for all these groups." Joan G. Roland, *Jews in British India: Identity in a Colonial Era* (Hanover, NH: University Press of New England, 1989), p. 15.

2. On Hardoon see the recent Chiara Betta, "The Rise of Silas Aaron Hardoon (1851–1931) as Shanghai's Major Individual Landowner," *Sino-Judaica* 2 (1995), pp. 1–40; idem, "Silas Aaron Hardoon and Cross-Cultural Adaptation in Shanghai, 1874–1931" (paper presented at the symposium "Settlers and Sojourners: Foreign Communities on the China Coast," Nuffield College, Oxford, November 28, 1995); and idem,

"S.A. Hardoon (1851–1931): Marginality and Adaptation in Shanghai" (Ph.D. dissertation, University of London, School of Oriental and African Studies, 1997).

3. Carl Crow, *Foreign Devils in the Flowery Kingdom* (London: Hamish Hamilton, 1941), p. 62.

4. On Chinese literature on Hardoon, see Betta, "Hardoon: Marginality and Adaptation," chap. 7, *passim.*

5. See especially *Li* Changdao, *Da maoxianjia Hatong* (Hardoon the adventurer) (Beijing: Qunzhong chubanshe, 1979).

6. See, for example, Shen Ji, *Daban* (Taipan) (Shanghai: Shanghai wenyi chubanshe, 1993).

7. For the period considered in this chapter, Maisie Meyer's recent thesis has provided a first comprehensive presentation of the history of Baghdadi, Jews in Shanghai in the light of their Jewish, Baghdadi, and Sephardi identities. Maisie J. Meyer, "The Sephardi Jewish Community of Shanghai 1845–1939 and the Question of Identity" (Ph.D. dissertation, University of London, London School of Economics, 1994). The marginality of Baghdadi Jews within the Shanghai Western community has been discussed in Betta, "Hardoon: Marginality and Adaptation," chap. 1, *passim;* also presented as "Marginal Westerners in Shanghai: The Sephardi Jewish Community, 1845–1931," at the conference "Foreign Communities in East Asia (XIXth–XXth Century)," Institut D'Asie Orientale, Lyon, March 20–21, 1997.

8. Letter of Jakob b. Abraham d. Sudea reprinted in P.G. von Möllendorf, "Die Juden in China" (Jews in China), *Monatsschrift für Geschichte und Wissenschaft des Judenthums* 39 (1895), pp. 330–31. See also Stanley Jackson, *The Sassoons* (London: Heinemann, 1968), p. 23.

9. Shanghai shehui kexueyuan jingji yanjiusuo (Shanghai Academy of Social Sciences, Economic Research Institute), ed., *Shanghai dui wai maoyi, 1840–1949* (Shanghai foreign trade, 1840–1949) (Shanghai, 1989), vol. 1, p. 69; and *North China Herald,* August 3, 1850.

10. *The China Directory for 1874* (1874; repr. Taibei: Cheng Wen, 1971), 28J-29J. On the business of E.D. Sassoon and Company in Shanghai, see *Zhang* Zhongli and *Chen* Zengnian, *Shaxun jituan zai jiu Zhongguo* (The Sassoon group in old China) (Beijing: Renmin chubanshe, 1985). Zhang and Chen are the only scholars who have hitherto extensively used the archives of the Shanghai branch of E.D. Sassoon and Company.

11. British Jews were among the first to be buried in the Shanghai Jewish cemetery. Mendel Brown, "The Jews of Modern China," *Jewish Monthly* 3, no. 3 (June 1949), p. 161. Lewis Moore, the founder of the first auction house in Shanghai, came from Great Britain and was one of the most active members of the early Jewish community. See "An Enterprising Firm of Auctioneers," *Social Shanghai* 9 (January–June 1910), pp. 96–103.

12. Betta, "Hardoon: Marginality and Adaptation," pp. 26–29. Much of the early life of the community depended on the liberality of the Sassoon firms. David Sassoon sponsored the first Jewish cemetery in Shanghai in 1862. The Beth El Synagogue, established in 1887, was also funded by the Sassoon family. C.E. Darwent, *Shanghai: A Handbook for Travellers and Residents to the Chief Objects of Interests in and Around the Foreign Settlements and Native City* (Shanghai: Kelly and Walsh, 1920), p. 30; Meyer, "Sephardi Community," p. 99; Simon Adler Stern, *Jottings of Travel in China and Japan* (Philadelphia: Porter and Coates, 1888), p. 155 (courtesy of Michael Pollak).

13. London, Public Record Office (hereafter quoted as PRO), FO 369/2243, Abdullah Al Damluji (Minister of Foreign Affairs) to the Residency (Baghdad), 17/19 September 1931, enclosure, "Translation of Petition Dated 11th September, 1931, from Ezra Salih Hardun and Six Others of the Hardun family, to the Minister for Foreign Affairs";

Hanna Khayyat to the Legal Secretary (The Residency), 11 November 1931; and Shanghai, Shanghai House Property Administration Bureau Archives, Archives of the Hardoon Company hereafter quoted as HA), Yi 1986, "Power of Attorney. Rouben Shaul Abdoo Hardoon and Moshi Saleh Ishaq Hardoon in favor of Ezra Saleh Hardoon, known as Khan Bahadur (copy). Signed in front of Abdul Ghani, Notary Public, Baghdad North. Baghdad 15th day of Safar 1352 corresponding to the 8th of June 1933."

14. *Ji* Juemi, "Hatong xiansheng xingzhuang" (Life and deeds of Mr. Hardoon), in *Hatong rong'ailu* (S.A. Hardoon in commemoration) (Shanghai: Aili yuan, 1932), vol. 4. According to the Hardoons' marriage certificate, Hardoon's father was a merchant. H.A. Jia 271, SO105. Photographic copy of Hardoon's marriage certificate.

15. Ji, "Hatong," *Hatong rong'ailu,* vol. 4, and Jackson, *Sassoons,* p. 57. Jackson, however, wrongly affirms that the Hardoon family left Baghdad under the governorship of Daud Pasha.

16. Various samples of Hardoon's notes in Judeo–Arabic are held in the Hardoon archives. See especially HA, Yi 2123. See also Shanghai, Shanghai Municipal Archives, "Wu Kaisheng zhuanlue" (Profile of *Wu* Kaisheng), unpublished manuscript.

17. Betta, "Hardoon: Marginality and Adaptation," pp. 62–63, 100. The dismissal of Hardoon is reported in Maisie Meyer, "Three Prominent Sephardi Jews," *Sino-Judaica* 2 (1995), p. 98.

18. Jackson, *Sassoons,* pp. 65–66.

19. Betta, "Hardoon: Marginality and Adaptation," pp. 101–3.

20. *Shenbao* (Shanghai News), July 4, 1931.

21. *Yu* Bohai, "Hatong" (Hardoon), 1990, unpublished paper, p. 4.

22. Betta, "Hardoon: Marginality and Adaptation," pp. 107–16.

23. Jackson, *Sassoons,* p. 100.

24. Holmes Welch, *The Buddhist Revival in China* (Cambridge: Harvard University Press, 1968), p. 298–99 n 47.

25. H.A. Jia 271, SO105; and Robert Bickers, "Changing British Attitudes to China and the Chinese, 1928–1931" (Ph.D. dissertation, University of London, University of London, School of Oriental and African Studies, 1992), p. 117. On Baghdadi Jews and intermarriage, see Meyer, "Sephardi Community," pp. 78–81.

26. Betta, "Hardoon: Marginality and Adaptation," pp. 71–75, 84–90. Luo's adopted children were *Luo* Youliang, *Luo* Youlan, *Luo* Yousan, *Luo* Youqi, *Luo* Youren, *Luo* Youxiang, *Luo* Fuzhen, *Luo* Buqian, *Luo* Zhankun, *Luo* Xiumei, and *Luo* Huixiu. The Hardoons' adopted children were David George, Reuben Victor, Louis, Philip, Leo, Nora, Madeleine, Maple, Daphne, Emily, and Eva.

27. Ibid., pp. 76–69.

28. For a brief biographic sketch of *Huang* Zongyang, see *Li* Meishan, "Geming heshang: Huang Zongyang zhuanqi" (A Revolutionary Monk: The story of Huang Zongyang), *Zhongwai zazhi* (Kaleidoscope), no. 1 (January 1991), pp. 8, 72–75.

29. On the founding of the Chinese Educational Association, see Mary Backus Rankin, *Early Chinese Revolutionaries: Radical Intellectuals in Shanghai and Chekiang, 1902–1911* (Cambridge, MA: Harvard University Press, 1971), pp. 50–61. On the Hardoons and the Educational Association, see Betta, "Hardoon: Marginality and Adaptation," pp. 132–34, 174–75. The article published in *Nübao* was reprinted in *Xinmin congbao* in 1903. See "Luo Jialing nüshi zhuan," *Xinmin congbao* (The renovation of the people), no. 25, in *Xinmin congbao,* ed. Feng Zishan (Photolithograph, Taibei: Wenyi yinshuguan, 1966), vol. 5, pp. 165–67.

30. On the *Subao* case, see Rankin, *Early Chinese Revolutionaries,* chap. 4, *passim*; and Betta, "Hardoon: Marginality and Adaptation," p. 135.

31. See especially *Ruan* Renze and *Gao* Zhengnong, eds., *Shanghai zongjiaoshi* (A history of religions in Shanghai) (Shanghai: Renmin chubanshe, 1992), pp. 215, 276–77, 311.

32. Rankin, *Early Chinese Revolutionaries,* pp. 60, 209; *Gao* Wangzhi, "The Contributions of the Jewish Communities in Shanghai, Viewed in Their Sino-Judaic Prospective," *Points East* 2, no. 1 (February 1987), p. 7. See also Betta, "Hardoon: Marginality and Adaptation," pp. 138–42.

33. "Hardoon, Orient's Richest Individual Dies at Home Here," *China Press,* June 20, 1931, p. 1.

34. *Liao* Keyu with the collaboration of *Wang* Keng, "Hatong fufu yishi diandi" (A few anecdotes concerning the Hardoons), *Shehui kexue zhanxian* (Social Sciences' Front) 2, no. 3 (1979), pp. 161–62.

35. Betta, "Hardoon: Marginality and Adaptation," pp. 146–54.

36. PRO, FO 371/5350, "Appendix to Secret Abstract for January and February 1920. List of Suspected Persons. (Straits Settlements)," in Directory of Military Intelligence to Foreign Office, June 1, 1920.

37. PRO, FO 228/3214, "Summary of Intelligence of the Shanghai Intelligence Bureau for the week ending 8 January 1920."

38. Reprinted in "*Li* Yuan-Hung [Yuanhong] and Shanghai. Denial of Rumours That He Is on His Way Here: Political Camouflage," *North China Herald,* July 28, 1923, p. 243.

39. "Shanghai Jewish Money for Peking," *Celestial Empire,* August 2, 1924, p. 203; and "Shanghai Merchant Offer to Peking," *North China Herald,* August 2, 1924, p. 171.

40. On a charity fair organized in the Aili Garden, see "Hatong huayuan youlanhui zhi neimu" (Programme of the fete in the Hardoon Garden), *Shenbao,* August 13, 1914. On Hardoon's charitable activities in the Chinese milieu, see Betta, "Hardoon: Marginality and Adaptation," pp. 209–15.

41. Joey Bonner, *Wang Kuo-wei: An Intellectual Biography* (Cambridge, MA: Harvard University Press, 1986), p. 195.

42. Betta, "Hardoon: Marginality and Adaptation," pp. 181–99.

43. "Mr. and Mrs. Hardoon Tender Reception to Dr. Ariel Bension," *Israel's Messenger,* January 9, 1925, pp. 7–10; "Shanghai's New Synagogue," *Israel's Messenger,* December 4, 1925, p. 17; "Proposed Synagogue, Museum Road, Shanghai," *Israel's Messenger,* January 8, 1926, p. 10.

44. Rena Krasno, *Strangers Always: A Jewish Family in Wartime Shanghai* (Berkeley, CA: Pacific View Press, 1992), p. 161; "Buddhist Memorial Service," *Israel's Messenger,* August 31, 1931, p. 8; "Gejie gongji Hatong" (All circles pay their respects to Hardoon), *Shenbao,* July 31, 1931.

Chapter III.C.2

Jews and the Musical Life of Shanghai

Xu *Buzeng*

Many of the world-famous musicians who began to venture to China in the 1920s to share their music with the city of Shanghai were Jewish. Among the first to grace Shanghai was Leopold Godowsky, who toured the Far East at the end of 1922.[1] Godowsky dazzled audiences with two recitals: One consisted of works of Chopin only, while the other comprised works by Beethoven, Mendelssohn, Chopin, Liszt, and Debussy.[2] After Godowsky's arrival, other musicians soon began to flock to Shanghai. The list of musicians who performed includes such greats as the pianists Arthur Rubinstein, Ignaz Friedman, Benno Moiseiwitsch, and Lili Kraus; violinists Szymon Goldberg, Joseph Szigeti, Efrem Zimbalist, Jascha Heifetz, and Mischa Elman; and cellists Emanuel Feuerman and Gregor Piatigorsky. The presence of a galaxy of masters brightened Shanghai's musical scene and enlivened the cultural life of the music lovers of the city.[3]

Jewish musicians who had resided in Shanghai for ten, twenty, or thirty years had an even greater impact on the musical life of Shanghai. One such Jewish musician was Arrigo Foa (1900–1981). Born in Vercelli, a small town in Italy midway between Turin and Milan, Foa studied violin at the Milan Conservatory. At his graduation from the Conservatory in 1918, he was awarded the first prize. He was then invited to Shanghai in 1921 to become concertmaster and soloist for the Shanghai Municipal Symphony Orchestra. Founded in 1879, the orchestra was the oldest one of its kind in China and quickly established itself as one of the most renowned in the Far East. Foa gradually was promoted from concertmaster to assistant conductor and then to conductor.

Exemplifying many of the essentials required of a great conductor, Foa was blessed with a sense of perfect pitch, rhythm, and balance, which could be seen in his baton technique and allowed for his profound understanding of compositions. Thanks to his ceaseless efforts for more than thirty years, first as concertmaster and then as conductor, the orchestra experienced further growth and improvement. For more than a quarter of a century, the orchestra developed an extensive repertoire of symphonic music that was played at weekly concerts. The orchestra performed works by masters ranging from Bach and Handel to Stravinsky and Richard Strauss, and from Moussorgsky to de Falla. Many outstanding musicians from around the world performed with the Shanghai Municipal Symphony Orchestra, including Jacques Thibaud, Benno Moiseiwitsch, and Gregor Piatigorsky. Foa was also in charge of training and directing the Shanghai Songsters, a thirty-year-old institution with 120 singers.[4]

Besides gaining prestige for being a conductor, Foa was one of the first professors of the National Conservatory of Music in Shanghai. Founded in 1927, the Conservatory was the first of its kind in China. The prestigious *Cai* Yuanpei, the Chinese minister of education, served as president of the Conservatory, while *Xiao* Youmei, an accomplished Chinese composer and music educator with a doctorate in music from Leipzig University, acted as dean. The Conservatory was located in Shanghai with the idea of attracting the accomplished musicians of Shanghai's well-known and respected orchestra to teach at the Conservatory. Known for his exacting and conscientious teaching style, Foa was invited and soon became the head of the violin section. Many of the Chinese pupils that he trained over his twenty-year teaching career became quite prominent, such as *Dai* Cuilan, who later became director of the Conservatory. Foa left Shanghai for Hong Kong in 1952. His dream that the Orchestra would be composed entirely of Chinese musicians came true a few years after the establishment of the People's Republic.[5]

In Hong Kong, Foa served as permanent conductor of Hong Kong Philharmonic Orchestra until 1969. Foa was also head of the violin department at the Hong Kong Academy of Music from 1965. Foa was awarded the Star of Solidarity by the Italian government in 1952 in recognition of his work in the musical field in Shanghai and was honored as a "Cavalier Merito della Repubblica" by the Italian government in 1969.[6]

Of the numerous German and Austrian Jewish refugees who flooded into Shanghai, about ten professional musicians were lucky enough to find positions in the Shanghai Municipal Symphony Orchestra.[7] In turn, these new arrivals further enhanced the professional standard of the Orchestra. The most prominent figures in the orchestra were Otto and Walter Joachim and Wolfgang Fraenkel.

Otto Joachim, composer, teacher, and violinist, was born in 1910 in Duesseldorf, Germany, into the family of the Jewish opera singer Emil

Joachimsthal. He studied violin for eleven years at the Buths-Neitzel Conservatory and for four years at the Rheinische Musikschule in Cologne. In 1934, a year after Hitler's rise to power, Otto Joachim left Germany and traveled to East Asia, where he spent seven years in Singapore and then moved to Shanghai. Besides teaching, Joachim occasionally performed in the Shanghai Municipal Symphony Orchestra. He also organized a Jewish Orchestra composed of musicians dedicated to the performance of Jewish music, synagogue music, and secular pieces new to Shanghai.[8] In order to earn a living, Otto Joachim also opened a music store opposite the Lyceum Theater on Route Cardinal Mercier (now Maoming Nan Lu, where the Jinjiang Hotel is located). Since the Lyceum Theater was the site of the weekly symphony concerts of the Shanghai Municipal Orchestra, Otto Joachim's music store became a meeting place for musicians and music lovers alike. It was a place where music was discussed and instruments were carefully crafted and repaired. Musicians flocked to Joachim's store to acquire the instruments and musical scores they needed. If a specific score was not in stock, Otto Joachim would receive the customer's commission and somehow manage to get it from some fellow refugee musician who happened to have the music and was willing to spare it in order to meet his daily expenses. In the 1990s, a Chinese violinist, at more than eighty years old, recalled with gratitude that his collection of complete scores of Mozart, Schubert, and Brahms string quartets was made possible only with the help of Otto Joachim.[9]

In 1949, Otto Joachim emigrated to Canada, joined the Montreal Symphony Orchestra as principal violist, and began to teach at McGill University and at the provincial conservatory in Montreal, Quebec. In addition to these accomplishments, Otto Joachim made major contributions in the field of composition. His compositions generally fall into two categories: completely and conventionally notated twelve-note compositions, and works involving improvisation, new notations, synthesized sounds, mixed media, and theatrical elements. He is the only Shanghai Jewish musician listed in the authoritative *New Grove Dictionary of Music and Musicians*.[10]

Otto's brother Walter Joachim, born in 1912 in Duesseldorf, was a cellist and teacher who had studied music at the Stattliche Hochschule für Musik in Cologne. After graduation, Walter extensively toured Europe and Asia and finally traveled to Shanghai in 1940 from Kuala Lumpur, Malaya. Facing great privation upon his arrival, Walter worked during the day in a menial job while he played cello in a café and dancehall in the evening. Arrigo Foa, an avid dance fan, frequented the very dancehall where Walter was playing and was thoroughly impressed by his talent. At Foa's recommendation, Walter was invited to join the Shanghai Municipal Symphony

Orchestra and subsequently to teach in the Shanghai Conservatory of Music.

Walter worked conscientiously in both institutions for many years. It should be noted that among Walter Joachim's pupils was Miss *Situ* Zhiwen, who is now the chairwoman of the All-China Cellists' Association.[11] After leaving Shanghai for Canada in 1953, Walter joined the Montreal Symphony Orchestra, where he was first cellist until 1979. Continuing to share his musical expertise, Walter also taught for many years at McGill University and various other institutions throughout Canada. Walter Joachim proved as instrumental in producing talented, young cellists in Canada as he had been in Shanghai.[12] Among other honors, Walter Joachim in 1992 was named Knight of the Order of Quebec in appreciation of his extraordinary contribution to the cultural life of Canada.[13]

In 1987, Walter Joachim returned to Shanghai at the invitation of the Shanghai conservatory to attend its sixtieth anniversary celebration. After thirty-odd years, such a reunion with former colleagues and pupils from the Orchestra and the Conservatory brought all involved immense joy. In November 1991, he again visited China with his wife, Monique, this time giving lessons gratis to cello students in Shanghai, Jinan, and Beijing. Happy to be among the Chinese again, they gladly paid for their air tickets and sacrificed their salaries at home. Once back in Canada, they wrote to the Shanghai Conservatory and told of their plans to return to give further lectures.[14]

Another important Jewish musical figure to come to Shanghai from Germany was the composer Wolfgang Fraenkel (1897–1983). Born in Berlin, Fraenkel simultaneously studied violin, piano, and music theory at Klindworth-Scharwenka Conservatory in Berlin while he practiced law. Until his arrest and internment in a concentration camp, Fraenkel had served as a judge. After his release in 1939, he came to Shanghai, where he joined the Shanghai Municipal Symphony Orchestra and taught at the National Conservatory of Music. Blessed with a photographic memory, Fraenkel proved an extremely versatile musician in both composing and performing. Even though music had been just a hobby for him in Germany, he played both the piano and a variety of stringed instruments proficiently. In Shanghai, Fraenkel played in the string section of the orchestra and was able to switch with ease from violin to viola or vice versa whenever an additional player was needed.

Fraenkel's knowledge of musical repertoire was unsurpassable. A violinist once wanted to play Mozart's Violin Concerto No. 3 in G Major with the Municipal Symphony but had only the piano score and needed the full score to play the accompaniment. The distraught violinist turned to Fraenkel for help. Having neither the full nor the petite score, Fraenkel, depending solely on his memory and his profound knowledge of orchestration, wrote out the entire score for the orchestra by hand. Afterward Fraenkel's orchestration was checked against that of Mozart's original score, and there was remarkably little difference between the two.

At the Conservatory, Fraenkel taught composition as well as theory revolving around harmony and counterpoint. He was the first in China to introduce his pupils to the new composition systems and bold theories of the time, such as Arnold Schoenberg's Treatise on Harmony and Ernst Kurth's theory of linear counterpoint. Leading his pupils into new areas, hitherto unknown to them, Fraenkel expanded their minds. Fraenkel had a profound influence on *Ding* Shande, *Sang* Tong, and *Qu* Xixian, who later became foremost composers in China. Fraenkel himself did not write many compositions as he was busy with teaching at the Conservatory and playing in the Orchestra in order to make a living. The only compositions that he wrote in Shanghai consisted of three songs for mezzo-soprano and orchestra with Chinese poems as text. The treatise *Non-functional Music,* which had been written by Fraenkel in Germany during the 1930s but was barred from publication because of its Jewish authorship, was thoroughly revised and enlarged into a full exposition modeled after the New Viennese School.[15]

Fraenkel emigrated from Shanghai to the United States in 1947 and settled in Los Angeles. At the time of his departure and at the request of Conservatory authorities, he recommended the Jewish refugee composer Julius Schloss (1902–1973), a pupil of Alban Berg, to be his successor. In the United States, Fraenkel resumed his composition activities. Fraenkel successfully completed a great number of compositions in various forms, of which the *Symphonische Aphorismen (1965)* was awarded the first prize at the International Competition of the City of Milan.[16]

In 1990, an article entitled "Remembering My Teachers Wolfgang Fraenkel and Julius Schloss" was published in the Shanghai Conservatory of Music's journal, *The Art of Music.* The author, *Sang* Tong, a prominent Chinese composer and director of the Conservatory, described their teaching techniques and highly praised their contributions. Published in the same issue were three translated pieces about these two Jewish composers, the author of one of which was Carl Steiner, a fellow refugee pianist who is now living in Canada.

The most accomplished artist of the numerous German and Austrian refugee musicians was the violinist Alfred Wittenberg (1880–1952). Born in Breslau and educated in the Koeniglische Musikakademie of Berlin, Alfred Wittenberg was the first violinist of the Koenigsliches Operahaus from 1900 to 1903. He was one of the best pupils of the Hungarian violinist Joseph Joachim. In 1902, Wittenberg formed a trio (the first Schnabel Trio) with Dutch cellist Anton Hekking and Artur Schnabel, one of the most respected authorities and interpreters of Beethoven piano sonatas. Their concerts "gave masterly performances of virtually the entire trio literature" and "became an institution which lasted for years."[17]

Wittenberg arrived in Shanghai on February 25, 1939. A noted pianist as well as violinist, Wittenberg taught both violin and piano in the Conservatory and at a local university while he also gave private lessons. His virtuosity in performance, astonishingly accurate memory, and diligent and conscientious teaching technique won him the favor of the musical public and the general acclaim of his pupils. Wittenberg impressed faculty and pupil alike when he played from memory not only the violin solo, but also the piano accompaniment of the music he was to teach. Such erudite musicianship enabled Wittenberg to demonstrate the different interpretive techniques of such masters as Fritz Kreisler, Mischa Elman, Efrem Zimbalist, Joseph Szigeti, Jascha Heifetz, Nathan Milstein, and Bronislaw Huberman. At a time when Shanghai's music was still in a preliminary stage of development and gramophone records of Western classical music were scarce, such versatile demonstrations of musical technique played a tremendous role in expanding the musical perspective of his pupils.

At the same time, Wittenberg's relations with his pupils were so harmonious that some with spacious residences offered him a room gratis in exchange for his teaching other pupils. They also provided him regularly with meals after he gave lessons at their homes. Under such superb and caring instruction, pupils made notable progress and many became outstanding violinists. After World War II, Wittenberg's friends, Artur Schnabel and Efrem Zimbalist invited him to teach in the United States, but Wittenberg felt that he was too old to travel such a long distance. Preferring to remain in Shanghai with his beloved pupils, Wittenberg died and was buried in Shanghai in 1952.[18]

The reverence, warmth, and friendly affection Wittenberg enjoyed while teaching his Chinese pupils sharply contrasted with the fear and humiliation he experienced when asked to play a piano accompaniment for Ghoya (first name unknown), an amateur violinist and self-ordained "King of the Jews." Ghoya was the Japanese official in charge of Jewish affairs in the Shanghai ghetto from May 1943 to August 1945. The temperamental Ghoya proudly played his violin until his music began to clash with Wittenberg's piano accompaniment and then wildly shouted, "You play as I direct, or I kill you."[19]

Aaron Avshalomov (1894–1956) was born into a Russian Jewish family in the city of Nikolaievsk-na-Amure, not far from the Chinese–Russian border. Located north of Vladivostok, the region had been ceded by the

Chinese emperor to the tsar in the middle of the nineteenth century. During Avshalomov's childhood there was still a large Chinese population in Nikolaievsk (in Chinese, on a street called Miao Jie, meaning Temple Street) and the employees working in his father's fish market were mostly Chinese. Avshalomov was cared for by an elderly Chinese man who loved to sing Beijing Opera arias and Chinese folk songs and often brought the young Avshalomov to the theater to watch Beijing Opera performances. Avshalomov was fascinated by the way in which Beijing Opera ingeniously blended acting, posture, and facial expressions with singing, dancing, and orchestral accompaniment into an organic whole. Although he felt that the music of the opera was rich and colorful, he also believed that at times the music was a rough, tedious, and unceasing repetition of simple melodies. He thought that it was a pity that the vast musical treasury embedded in the Chinese folklore lay untouched. It was then that he resolved to devote his life to the advancement of Chinese national music and the Beijing Opera.

Focusing on music theory and composition, Avshalomov studied music at the Zurich Conservatory in Switzerland. He came to China in 1916, living and working successively in the northern cities of Beijing, Tianjin, and Qingdao, and collected folk songs and folk music that would be used in his future compositions. His first opera drawing from Chinese culture, *Guan Yin* (Avalokiteśvara), was produced in Beijing in 1925 and a year later in Portland, Oregon. In 1932 Avshalomov arrived in Shanghai, a metropolis still reeling from the full force and excitement of the New Culture movement. He quickly became acquainted with many outstanding Chinese musicians, such as *Nie* Er, the composer of *The March of the Volunteers*. Avshalomov produced the first orchestration of this song, which later became the national anthem of the People's Republic.

Drawing from authentic themes, Avshalomov went on to write a number of works in Shanghai based on Chinese culture. *The Soul of Qin*, a ballet, and *Incense Shadows*, a pantomime, were both composed in collaboration with the Chinese and Western music theory and composition technique. *Shen* Zhibai shared a common desire with Avshalomov to promote Chinese national music. The symphonic sketch *Peiping Hutungs* (*Beijing Alleys*), a tonal depiction of the carefree and leisurely life in the ancient city, was first performed in Shanghai in 1933 and again in 1935 in the United States by the Philadelphia Orchestra under the baton of Leopold Stokowski.

Avshalomov's masterpiece *The Great Wall* was a powerful music drama based on the tragic story of a woman named *Meng* Jiangnü, who lived during the ancient Qin dynasty (221–206 B.C.). Her husband was drafted by Qin Shi Huangdi (the first emperor of the Qin dynasty) to build the Great Wall in a remote mountain range and was never heard from again. *Meng*

Jiangnü slowly trekked to the Great Wall, only to discover that her husband had died from starvation and overwork. Her sorrow was so great that, when she wept, the Great Wall collapsed to symbolize the downfall of tyranny. Avshalomov elaborated on his aims in composing this outstanding work in his "'The Great Wall' and the Problem of Chinese Music Drama":

> The time has now come to search the ways for the Chinese classical drama to reflect the present civilization and to advance towards universal appreciation. *The Great Wall* is an experiment in this direction, conceived as a dramatic synthesis in which the elements of purely musical thought, poetic and vocal speech, pantomime and dancing are combined into a monolithic whole. The idiom of the music, acting, dancing and speech is basically that of the Chinese classical drama, and represents native spirit, while technique of composition and method of presentation are foreign.[20]

In November 1945, three months after the Japanese surrender and the end of World War II, *The Great Wall* made its world premiere in Shanghai and was hailed a great success. Many high-ranking American officials, such as General Albert C. Wedemeyer, the commander-in-chief of the U.S. Army stationed in China, attended the performance. Thoroughly impressed by the performance, they thought that this was an opera that they could understand and appreciate. Wedemeyer even encouraged Avshalomov to stage the opera in the United States. He later traveled there to plan and negotiate conditions for performing his work in the country. Unfortunately civil war (1946–49) broke out in China, and the situation in Shanghai was very grim. Unable to return to Shanghai, Avshalomov was stranded in the United States and later became a naturalized citizen. However, he continued to compose *The Twilight of Royal Lady Young,* another musical drama based on a Chinese subject. Avshalomov's works won the recognition of leading composers like Pierre Monteux and the above-mentioned Leopold Stokowski, both of whom had conducted his compositions. Serge Koussevitzky had even commissioned Avshalomov to write a symphony.[21]

Years later in 1985, Jacob Avshalomov, the Chinese-born son of Aaron Avshalomov and himself a composer and conductor of the Portland Junior Symphony Orchestra in Oregon, came to China to attend the belated commemoration of his father's ninetieth birthday in Beijing and Shanghai. Jacob delivered speeches and had the honor of conducting all his father's works in concert.[22] In the early 1990s Jacob Avshalomov discussed with Chinese authorities the possibility of touring China with the Portland Junior Symphony Orchestra.[23]

During one of the darkest chapters in world history, two separate worlds were drawn together for the sake of music. The bonds that were forged between the Jews and Shanghailanders under Axis pressure, Nazi persecution, and Japanese occupation were lasting bonds that continued to thrive and prosper.

Notes

1. *China Press* (Shanghai), January 3, 6, 1923.
2. *North China Daily News* (Shanghai), December 30, 1922.
3. *Xu* Buzeng, "Youtai yinyuejia zai Shanghai" (Jewish Musicians in Shanghai), Shanghai Conservatory of Music, *Yinyue yishu* (Art of Music), no. 3 (1991), pp. 36–38.
4. Ibid., pp. 38–40.
5. *Ding* Shande, ed., *Shanghai yinyeuxueyuan jianshi, 1927–1987* (An Outline History of the Shanghai Conservatory of Music, 1927–1987) (Shanghai: n.p., 1987), pp. 2–4. *Tan* Shuzhen, author interview, Shanghai, September 23, 1988; *Mao* Chuen, author interview, Shanghai, March 13, 1989.
6. "Arrigo Foa," *Hong Kong Who's Who—An Almanac of Personalities and Their History, 1958–1960* (Hong Kong: Rola Luzzato, 1960), p. 95. "Arrigo Foa," Hong Kong Who's Who—An Almanac of Personalities and Their History, 1970–1973 (Hong Kong: Rola Luzzato, 1973), p. 148.
7. David Kranzler, *Japanese, Nazis and Jews: The Refugee Community of Shanghai* (New York: Yeshiva University Press, 1976), p. 375.
8. *Shanghai Jewish Chronicle,* March 1, 1944.
9. *Chen* Zonghui, author interview, Shanghai, December 28, 1990.
10. Rick Macmillan, "Otto Joachim," in *Encyclopedia of Music in Canada* (Toronto: University of Toronto Press, 1981), pp. 479–80, and Udo Kasemets, "Otto Joachim," *The New Grove Dictionary of Music and Musicians* (London: Macmillan, 1980), vol. 9, p. 654.
11. Walter Joachim, author interview, Shanghai, October 23, 1991; *Tan* Shuzhen, interview.
12. Clair Repentigny, "Walter Joachim," in *Encyclopedia of Music in Canada* (Toronto: University of Toronto Press, 1981), p. 480.
13. Walter and Monique Joachim (Montreal), letter to *Xu* Buzeng, February 23, 1992.
14. Joachim, interview; Joachim, letter.
15. "Wolfgang Fraenkel," in *Baker's Biographical Dictionary of Musicians* (New York: Schirme Books, 1984), p. 754.
16. *Xu* Buzeng, "The Influence of Jewish Refugees on the Musical and Intellectual Life of Shanghai," *Points East* (August 1990), p. 10.
17. Cesar Saerchinger, *Artur Schnabel—A Biography* (London: Cassell, 1957), pp. 76–77.
18. *Tan* Shuzhen, interview; *Chen* Zonghui, interview.
19. Kranzler, *Japanese,* pp. 499–500.
20. Aaron Avshalomov, " 'The Great Wall' and the Problem of Chinese Music Drama," an article written in English for the synopsis to the première of the musical drama in Shanghai on November 24, 1945.
21. Jacob Avshalomov's speech at the commemoration, "Bring Back Aaron Avshalomov's Music to China" (May 13, 1985), *Guangming Daily* (Beijing), May 19, 1985.
22. Ibid.
23. Israel Epstein, author interview, Shanghai, December 5, 1991.

Chapter III.C.3

Jewish Musicians in Shanghai: Bridging Two Cultures

Harriet P. Rosenson

The arrival of Jewish musicians in China was a direct consequence of political upheavals erupting in their native lands. In the late nineteenth and early twentieth centuries, they fled anti-Semitic pogroms in Russia and Poland. The turmoil of the Russian Revolution also forced many Jewish musicians to leave Russia. When the rise of German and Italian fascism drove Jews to seek safety wherever it could be found, Shanghai became a refuge for Jews, musicians, and others alike. They were fortunate, able to escape annihilation.

Many of these Jewish musicians were graduates of great European musical institutions and had studied under illustrious music teachers.[1] Although penniless and deprived of their instruments, many still had the ability to teach, perform, and transmit their artistry to Chinese musicians. Some refugee musicians obtained teaching positions at Shanghai's Conservatory of Music; others had to give private lessons.[2] Some were engaged as regular members of the Shanghai Municipal Symphony Orchestra; others succeeded in getting jobs at night clubs and bars. Several became well-known soloists performing with the Shanghai Symphony Orchestra and with the resident opera company.[3]

Despite poor quality instruments, insufficient scores, improper heating conditions, and personal hardships that prevailed in their daily lives, they generated excitement in music. During the 1940s, they maintained regularly scheduled concerts at the Lyceum Theater (now called the Shanghai Arts Theater), with its seating capacity of nine hundred.[4] There was a summer outdoor series of concerts and opera performances held at Canindrome.[5] Operas were presented by Russian singers at what was called "the Jewish auditorium" of the Jewish Recreation Club. Many privately owned buildings, including the Jewish Recreation Club, were taken over and are now part of the Shanghai Conservatory of Music.[6] There were concerts given under the aegis of the Italian and French consulates and the Austrian Residents' Association.[7]

Initially, in the early 1920s, audiences consisted almost entirely of Westerners and some university students. By the 1930s, however, the number of Chinese in attendance had grown. During the 1940s, the audience included Chinese soldiers who overflowed the aisles, listening to the most avant-garde Western music.

When Jewish musicians arrived in China in the early 1920s, the technical level of playing Western music was, understandably, lower than in the West. In China, at the beginning of the twentieth century, there were only church schools where piano could be studied, which was not like studying at a conservatory.[8] In 1922, *Xiao* Youmei, just graduated from the University of Leipzig as doctor of philosophy, became the head of the newly created music department at Beijing University, under the presidency of *Cai* Yuanpei, one of China's most eminent educators and a strong proponent for the "Science and Democracy" movement. The Shanghai Conservatory of Music was founded by the government in 1927, with Cai serving briefly as director, then succeeded by Xiao.[9] Cai's tenure was brief since he was appointed president of the Central Research Institute in November 1927 precisely when the Shanghai Conservatory of Music opened.[10] Xiao was the guiding force behind the development of the conservatory. He induced prestigious artists like the Russian pianist Boris Zakharov, who had toured Asia, performing with his wife, the violinist, Cecilia Hanson, to remain in China: Zakharov as head of the conservatory's piano department. He similarly persuaded the highly acclaimed Russian bass singer Vladimir Shushlin to join the conservatory faculty. According to the Chinese musician *Ding* Shande, "both Zakharov and Shushlin were regarded as teachers of the 'first rank' at the conservatory."[11] They were instrumental in creating the tradition of excellence to which Dr. Xiao aspired. Except for the disastrous years of the Cultural Revolution (1966–76) when the conservatory's functions were severely disrupted, it has maintained the highest standards in music education.

The Shanghai Symphony orchestra had its embryonic beginnings as the Shanghai Municipal Band, founded in 1897. It developed into an orchestra of thirty-three musicians in 1907, under the direction of the German musician Rudolph Buck. In 1919, when Mario Paci took over as music director, he invited many well-trained musicians from Europe including the Italian Jew Arrigo Foa to join the orchestra. Originally, there were no Chinese members of the orchestra. Only in 1938 did several Chinese musicians join the orchestra as regular members.[12]

During the early twentieth century, many well-known foreign musicians occasionally performed in China as part of a larger tour of the Far East, for example, Mischa Elman, Jascha Heifetz, Benno Moiseiwitsch, and Arthur Rubinstein. They performed in Harbin, Shanghai, Beijing, Tianjin, and Guangzhou. In Shanghai, concerts were given in the International Settlement and provided additional excitement to the popular regular musical season. In all cities, however, performances, with few exceptions, were attended by foreigners living in China, much to the disappointment and perplexity of the visiting musicians, who wanted to meet with and play for Chinese audiences.

Touring in China was difficult, travel between cities was lengthy and possibly fraught with dangers. Those who traveled by boat were often caught in typhoons. The biography of Fritz Kreisler, a non-Jewish musician raised in the Catholic faith, provides a vivid description of his 1923 concert tour.[13] While en route from Korea to China, via Shenyang in Manchuria, General *Zhang* Zuolin commandeered for military purposes the train in which Kreisler and his wife were traveling. An impromptu concert was performed for the German residents at the Deutscher Klub in Shenyang before the Kreislers were put in a cattle car to continue their trip to Beijing and Shanghai. In Beijing, after Kreisler performed before entirely European audiences, he was asked to play for the Chinese exclusively in the Chinese quarter of the city. Kreisler was told that "the Chinese out of a feeling of national pride remained aloof from 'European concerts.' " He began his concert for the elegant Chinese audience with an unaccompanied Bach suite, which was so enthusiastically received that he had to repeat it before he continued with a Beethoven sonata and a traditional group of small pieces.[14]

Arthur Rubinstein's tour of China commenced in April 1935 with three highly successful concerts in Shanghai, then on to Beijing, Tianjin, and Guangzhou. In Beijing, the concert was scheduled to be performed in the "salle de fêtes" in the French-owned Hotel de Pekin. On the day of the performance before rehearsing, Rubinstein found, much to his "horror," that the piano was an old Schiedmeir and that there was no tuner to be found in Beijing. He announced that for the "first time in [his] life and [with] the best will in the world [he] could not give a concert on this instrument."[15] The prospect of canceling a concert for an audience that consisted of senior diplomats, some of them already en route from Nanjing, caused much agitation. An American, living in the hotel and hearing the ruckus, suggested that Mrs. Lyon, the wife of the American consul in Beijing and daughter of

Joseph Grew, the American ambassador in Tokyo, had a new Steinway grand, which she might be persuaded to lend for the performance. Mrs. Lyon's response was immediate; the piano would be sent right over. Rubinstein, deeply concerned about the care necessary to move a piano, waited apprehensively. Suddenly he heard what sounded like a chorus getting louder as it entered the hotel lobby. Twenty men singing rhythmically, "'cling, clang, tium, tium, clung, cling, clung, clung'" entered the room

> carrying, on ten huge bamboo poles, a Steinway grand with the legs and pedal well attached, using the singsong to keep their steps [so as] not to collide, as they could not see each other. The forty feet of the men moved rapidly toward the podium [slowing down] the singsong to walk up the steps. [After noiselessly placing the piano on the floor,] their heads and shoulders emerged from under the [poles].[16]

Rubinstein was filled with gratitude for Mrs. Lyon's generosity and for the great care with which the men had carried the piano. The concert was well received by the entirely European and American audience.

Caught in a typhoon, the Rubinsteins arrived in Hong Kong, after four frightening days at sea, to learn that a performance was scheduled for that very evening. Moreover, another concert had been scheduled for the next day in "nearby" Guangzhou. The concert in Guangzhou was to be held at the University of Guangzhou, for an entirely Chinese audience, predominantly students. Rubinstein, while chagrined at the unexpected scheduling of the performance, was enthusiastic about playing for a Chinese audience. He played Bach's Toccata in F major, which was new to them. The overwhelming response to this work, in contrast to the more subdued reaction to the more flamboyant compositions which followed it, astonished the pianist, prompting him to question the rector of the university about the difference. The rector's reply was,

> We Chinese are tremendously gifted with our hands, so great demonstrations of technical prowess or strength in the pieces you played do not impress them at all. But in your Bach, they felt the overwhelming greatness of the music. The ovation they gave you came from their appreciation of the nobility of a music they had never heard before.[17]

In 1923, when Kreisler played a heretofore unheard Bach Suite for Violin in Beijing, and, in 1935, twelve years later, when Rubinstein played Bach's Toccata in F for Piano in Guangzhou, both musicians evoked the same enthusiastic response from the Chinese audiences upon their first hearing this great Western composer's music.

Two of the Jewish musicians became committed to the study of music and musical instruments in ancient China as a consequence of their exposure to Chinese music and instruments during their sojourn in China.

Joseph Yasser was born in Lodz, Russian Poland, in 1893. He graduated with high honors from the Moscow Conservatory of Music in 1917. After the death of his teacher, Professor Sabanieeff, in 1918, Yasser succeeded him at the conservatory, becoming head of the organ department. He was also appointed organist at the Royal Opera House in Moscow, where he appeared as organ soloist under Koussevitsky.[18] In 1920, he toured Siberia with the State Quartet, giving concerts and lectures on chamber music, arriving finally in Shanghai. In 1897, in addition to the Shanghai Municipal Band, the Shanghai Songsters' Society was also founded. Dr. Yasser, newly arrived in Shanghai, was invited to become their conductor. He remained in China from 1921 to 1923. During this time, besides conducting the Shanghai Songsters' Society, he appeared as piano soloist in the municipal concerts and his Piano Quintet had its first public performance in Shanghai. He became interested in Chinese music, gathering a number of typical Chinese tunes, which he harmonized "according to Chinese principles." Simply stated, Chinese music is generally referred to melodically as pentatonic (music which uses a five-tone scale rather than the Western eight-tone scale or chromatic scale). Chinese music did not harmonize melodies or use counterpoint. The richness of coloring that comes from the addition of Western instruments and the accompanying instrumental techniques were still being developed in China in the first half of the twentieth century. It would seem that Yasser applied harmony and possibly instrumental coloring to Chinese pentatonic music. He also prepared material for a stage work. Because of his background as a professional organist he was drawn to investigating the origins and development of native Chinese organs. He came to the United States in 1923, where he became principally known as an organist and authority on Jewish music. He continued, however, to lecture and write about Chinese music.[19]

Fritz Kuttner (1903–91) arrived in China in May 1939, as a refugee from Nazi Germany. He, along with other German, Austrian, and Polish immigrants, arrived in his words "penniless and without any cultural preparation for a ten year [1939–49] stay in the country."[20] His earliest impression was that music was the most neglected of the arts in China. He maintained this view for several years, until he heard young Chinese students who were studying with Western teachers living in China. Initially, he felt insecure about teaching Chinese students. Gradually, however, he overcame his timidity and began giving lessons to Chinese pupils, concluding that his Chinese students were the equal of his Western students. In the spring of

1944, he was invited to join the faculty of St. John's University, in Shanghai, to teach Western music theory and history. Kuttner related his experience with the students at St. John's. The enrollment of his first semester classes

> amounted to over 200 students and had less to do with student interest than with [the rumor] circulating on campus [that music] is the easiest credit available.... You go and listen to some nice recorded music, or if you don't feel like hearing music, you [cut classes].... Over 75 percent of the students never did show up for classes, not even for midterm [or] final papers. And because I came from fussy Germany where an orderly presence list had to be maintained, I possessed at the end of the semester full proof of those who had taken the courses and those who had not.[21]

Faced with such evidence, all those students were failed. St. John's at that time had a "custom or near-requirement" that a failed course should be repeated to make up for the lost credit. The enrollment in the subsequent term went from 200 to 400, ultimately reaching over 1,100 students in his last teaching semester. Kuttner concludes, however, that the high enrollment was a positive development:

> For the first time in more than 100 years [or even longer, music courses] were being offered in an academic forum that were taken seriously by the teacher, and eventually by [the students]. And equally surprisingly, the subject offered was Western music rather than Chinese music.[22]

Kuttner became fascinated by Chinese instruments. The physical beauty of the instruments brought him to the conclusion that a "noble" music tradition must have existed during the late Tang and early Song dynasties. He was particularly taken by the exquisite beauty of a particular *pi-pa* (an instrument similar to a balloon shaped guitar or mandolin) he had seen at the home of a wealthy and highly respected scholar. His host dated the instrument back to the Northern Song dynasty, probably to the tenth or eleventh century A.D. "This insight pushed [his] search for the great music of China [back] by many centuries."[23] His book, *The Archaeology of Music in Ancient China,* published in the United States in 1990, is the culmination of his forty years of research into this topic. The purpose of his book is to determine acoustical experimentation in ancient China. Kuttner's esoteric and complex work is an investigation into the forms of experimentation used in ancient China in the development of ancient instruments such as bronze bells and bronze drums and instruments made of stones such as sandstone, limestone, marble, jade, jadeite, and nephrite.

During 1948 and 1949, Kuttner was music critic for Shanghai's *China Press.* His critiques of the performances defined the level of artistry of the many soloists, the conductor, and the orchestra. He castigated performers who had not performed so well as they should have and found fault with the musical selections chosen. He described the general conditions of the concert hall. The programs were varied in content, running from classical Western symphonies, chamber music, and vocal renditions to the most avant-garde music of the Western repertoire. There were also performances of a new Eurasian opera, "Love From the Sea," with music composed by a Mr. *Feng* and libretto by *Bi* Lihua and other Chinese musical selections composed by *Tan* Xiaolin, who had studied with Hindemith at Yale. His songs were performed by *Chao* Xiaoyan, a soprano, with *Chao* Janyan accompanying at the piano. Based upon Fritz Kuttner's reviews and copies of programs, as well as interviews with people who lived in China, it is possible to give a preliminary estimate of the number of Jewish musicians who appeared as soloists, or performed with chamber groups in Shanghai during this important period of time. That number would appear to be about fifty. There are still sources to be explored that will undoubtedly add to the number of Jewish musicians who lived and worked in China.

Kuttner wrote under the pseudonym "MARPURG," which he assumed from the name of Germany's first professional music critic and writer, Friedrich Wilhelm Marpurg.[24] In a farewell article mailed back to Shanghai Kuttner wrote that "we buried our occasional fits of homesickness behind the activities of Marpurg. Farewell to Shanghai! May the readers of our reviews keep the name of this 18th century musicologist in fond memory."[25]

Karl Steiner, a pianist, arrived penniless in Shanghai in 1939. He supported himself by playing in night clubs and giving piano lessons at the Jewish Refugee Club in Hongkew, not to be confused with the Shanghai Jewish Club located in the International Settlement of Shanghai. Young refugee composers and musicians who had been students of Arnold Schoenberg and Alben Berg survived the war years in Shanghai. Karl Steiner and Julius Schloss met, by chance, in the early morning hours (about 2:00 A.M.) after Steiner had finished playing at a night club. He told Schloss that he was resigning from his job at that club because he had obtained another position, which he hoped would be better. So desperate were they to work that Schloss quickly asked if he could apply for Steiner's old job. The unexpected encounter brought the composer, Schloss, and the pianist, Steiner, together.

There were, at this time, three well-known musicians from what is known as the "Second Viennese School" living in Shanghai.[26] They had all arrived in 1939. Wolfgang Fraenkel, a pupil of Arnold Schoenberg, became a member of the Shanghai Symphony Orchestra and also taught at the conservatory. Julius Schloss, who had been both pupil of and secretary to

Alben Berg, succeeded Fraenkel at the conservatory in 1947. In 1948, Schloss asked Karl Steiner, who was still struggling to gain some recognition in the musical world of Shanghai, to perform the work of one of his students, *Sang* Tong. Steiner had no piano on which to practice, but Schloss said he could provide him with a piano. The critics' response to Steiner's performance was very enthusiastic. After receiving this acclaim, Steiner continued to appear as a soloist in Shanghai until his departure from China in May 1949. *Sang* Tong, Schloss's Chinese protégé and composer, went on to become the highly esteemed director of the Shanghai Conservatory.[27]

In addition to the Shanghai Municipal Orchestra, other orchestras were formed. They were "pick up" orchestras. Since violinists predominated among the refugee musicians, the problem was finding brass and woodwind players. It was necessary to hire these scarce instrumentalists from the ranks of the Shanghai Municipal Orchestra. One of these orchestras was the Refugee Orchestra organized by Otto Joachim (1910–).[28] They performed at the Lyceum Theatre, giving no more than four or five performances. Joachim also organized a recording orchestra. The musicians were the same instrumentalists, drawn from the Refugee Orchestra and the Shanghai Municipal Orchestra. He also made the musical arrangements and conducted the orchestra. A song entitled "Roses, Roses Everywhere," composed by the Chinese musician, Svengali, made the list of "hit" songs. Svengali was the pseudonym of a Chinese composer who could scarcely read or write music. Otto Joachim arranged and recorded his music. Thirty sides of music were recorded at the Columbia Recording Studios in Shanghai.[29] An ensemble of musicians and a choir, composed of China's outstanding vocalists, recorded the Japanese *Anti-Opium March*. During the years of the Japanese occupation of Shanghai (1941–45) recordings had to be approved by the Japanese, who also took photographs of the musicians during recording sessions, much to the discomfort of the performers. The musicians lived as best they could, working at their chosen profession in night clubs and coffee houses playing dance music.[30]

Fraenkel, Schloss, and Steiner, members of the "Second Viennese School," students of Schoenberg, Berg, and Webern, were driven out of their homes by the Nazis, their promising careers disrupted. Chinese students received their initial exposure to advanced harmony, twelve-tone and atonal music from these important members of the new generation of Viennese musicians. It is reasonable to assume that contemporary Chinese music has been strongly influenced by these musicians. Conversely, the Western composers absorbed Chinese music and continued to incorporate Chinese melodies into their compositions after they had left China. Karl Steiner performed Julius Schloss's piano sonata as part of a concert sponsored by the United States Information Service. He also performed the world premiere of a work for piano by *Sang* Tong and was the piano accompanist for music written by *Can* Guolin. Conversely Julius Schloss, after many years of not composing, wrote two Chinese rhapsodies for violin and orchestra, based upon Chinese folk songs that *Sang* Tong had provided to him.[31]

When historical circumstance brought Jewish and Chinese musicians together in China, assimilation of each other's music began to take root. Evidence of this integration can be found in musical compositions written by Jewish composers who lived in Shanghai. Chinese melodies and tonal structures were utilized in many works, some composed after their departure from China. Several of the Western musicians devoted many years to the study of Chinese music. One of the most noteworthy of these musicians is Aaron Avshalomov.[32]

Jewish liturgical music was played and sung in Shanghai for the Jewish holidays. In the Orthodox synagogue, music was limited to music that is an integral part of the service and was sung by the cantor (*hazan*). Only in the privacy of their homes and at gatherings with close friends did Orthodox Jews sing Hebrew and Yiddish songs. Sitting around the table at the Passover seder they sang *Dayenu* and at Chanukah they sang *Rock of Ages*. At the services conducted by Reform Jews, men and women sat together and both participated in the musical portions of the service. They also had an organ to accompany the musical portions.[33] Jewish folk songs and Klezmer music was played at weddings, parties, and at Purim and Chanukah Balls held in Shanghai at the Jewish Refugee Club.

> A company performing Jewish folk music toured China. In 1918, a "Chamber Music Ensemble"—*Zimro* ("song") was organized in Petrograd by G. Mistechkin (first violin), G. Besrodney (second violin), K. Moldavan (viola), I. Cherniavski (cello), S. Bellison (clarinet) and L. Berdichevski (piano), trained at the conservatories of Petrograd and Leipzig.... Their objective was to ... propagate Jewish Folk Music "artistically cultivated" ... and to collect [the means to establish] ... a "Temple of Art in Palestine."[34]

To realize their goal, they went on a concert tour through Siberia, China, Japan, and via America to Palestine.

Conclusion

A.Z. Idelsohn, the noted Jewish musicologist, defines Jewish music as "the song of Judaism through the lips of the Jew. It is the tonal expression of Jewish life and development over a period of more than two thousand years. ... Its DISTINGUISHING CHARACTERISTICS are the result of the spiritual life and struggle of that people."[35]

The spiritual life of the refugee musicians in Shanghai played little, if any, role in their professional activities, They saw themselves as part of the modern, secular musical world and accordingly played music drawn from the repertoire of world-renowned compositions written by Jewish and non-Jewish composers. When the non-Jewish composer Max Bruch's[36] Salon Variations on the Kol Nidrei Theme was performed as part of the second International Cultural Committee concert, Fritz Kuttner (Marpurg) criticized it as "tasteless."[37] Kuttner's comment notwithstanding, Bruch's work illustrates that religious affiliation is not a constraint in musical creativity.

Since the beginning of the nineteenth century when Jews in Europe were admitted into the social and cultural life of Europe, the Jewish composer has written not as a Jew but as a contributor to the cultures that accepted his presence in their midst. The unique situation for Jewish musicians, dispersed in different parts of the world, resulted in the creation and performance in the style of their adopted homes. The components of foreign music often were integrated and synthesized with the elements and characteristics of Jewish music.

While living in China, a dilemma for Jewish musicians was how to bridge the differences between the two musical heritages. Stylistically and instrumentally, Chinese native music and traditional Chinese opera differ markedly from the Western musical forms. It was particularly difficult to present a performance of a Western opera before a Chinese audience that would not appear to them to be a caricature. Nevertheless, performances were presented in China with the hope that the Chinese members of the audience would not find the music too exotic. In traditional Chinese opera the singing is highly stylized, with vocal usage that sounds harsh and artificial to Westerners. Music and dialogue are separate entities. When the singing commences, the action is interrupted. In Western opera the music and the story flow together uninterrupted. For the Chinese it was funny because they were singing while they were talking. Furthermore, the audience was newly exposed to recitative, when a singer delivers a narrative text in a declamatory or rhetorical manner. The music was sung from deep in the chest. They heard Bel Canto singing, quartets, sextets, and octets singing in harmony. It was perplexing and amusing, and, for some Chinese, it was attractive.

Jewish musicians who arrived in China as late as 1939 considered it a stop along their journey to another country. They did not anticipate a stay that would last ten years for some of them. The influence of these musicians, however, in relation to the number of years they spent in China, is significant. *Xiao* Youmei had realized that for Chinese students to become professional musicians, on a par with others in the mainstream of the musical world, they would require a Western musical education. The influx, especially of Jewish musicians in 1939, gave Chinese musicians easy access to many highly trained and respected professionals. Chinese performers could learn in a short span of time what had taken Western musicians centuries to evolve. The musical repertoire was enlarged, exposing both musicians and audiences to works that had not been heard in China before this time.

Jewish musicians were impressed by their students' enthusiasm and eagerness to learn. Set adrift in Shanghai, their careers disrupted, these Westerners welcomed the opportunity to impart scholarship and musical inventiveness. Their knowledge and creativity now resides in their Chinese pupils. These former students are the teachers of today's young Chinese artists, some of whom are among the most promising musicians in the world. Prominent among the musicians who studied with Fraenkel and Schloss was *Sang* Tong, who was until recently director of the Shanghai Conservatory of Music. After 1978, when the conservatories began to function again, young musicians began reexploring the use of twelve-tone and atonal music. They found it difficult to understand and hard to play. Among the new generation of musicians, *Ge* Ganru, *Tan* Dun, Bright Sheng, and *Zhou* Long are receiving worldwide recognition for their work. The current musical scene provides ample testimony to the willingness of peoples of diverse cultures to share and enrich each other's musical lives.

Notes

1. Arrigo Foa (1900–1983) studied at Milan Conservatory; Otto Joachim (1910–) at Buths-Neitzel Conservatory and the Rheinische Musikschule at Cologne; Walter Joachim (1912–) at Cologne's Stattliche Hochscule für Musik; Wolfgang Fraenkel (1897–1983) at Berlin's Klindworth-Scharwenka Conservatory; Alfred Wittenberg (1880–1952) at Berlin's Koeniglische Musikakademie; Aaron Avshalomov (1894–1965) at the Zurich Conservatory; Joseph Yasser (1894–1981) at Moscow Conservatory.
2. Foa, Walter Joachim, Wittenberg, and Fraenkel all taught at the conservatory.
3. Otto and Walter Joachim.
4. Author interview with *Ding* Shande, March 30, 1987, Shanghai.
5. Twelfth Open-Air Concert Program, August 10, 1946, *Gao* Zhilan Collection, Shanghai.
6. Author interview with *Gao* Zhilan, April 7, 1987, Shanghai.
7. Music Reviews, 1948–1949, Fritz Kuttner Collection.
8. *Ding,* author interview, March 30, 1987.
9. Shanghai Conservatory of Music Catalogue (Shanghai Conservatory of Music Publication, undated), Harriet P. Rosenson Collection.
10. Colin McKerras, *Modern China: A Chronology from 1812 to the Present* (San Francisco: W.H. Freeman, 1982), pp. 313, 317.
11. *Ding,* interview, March 30, 1987.
12. Program of the Shanghai Symphony Orchestra (Shanghai Symphony Orchestra publication, 1987), unpaginated, Harriet P. Rosenson Collection.

13. Louis P. Lochner, *Fritz Kreisler* (New York: Macmillan, 1950), pp. 34, 36. Kreisler is included to illustrate hazardous situations musicians encountered.

14. Ibid., pp. 217–19.

15. Arthur Rubinstein, *My Many Years* (New York: Alfred A. Knopf, 1980), p. 373.

16. Ibid., p. 374.

17. Ibid., p. 390.

18. J.A.H. (author's full name is not given), "Russian Musician Finds Queer Organs in Chinese and Philippine Monasteries," *Musical America* 39, nos. 7–8 (December 1923), p. 4.

19. Ibid.

20. Fritz Kuttner, *The Archaeology of Music in Ancient China* (New York: Paragon House, 1987). Reprinted with permission of the author's estate.

21. Ibid., p, 230.

22. Ibid., p. 230.

23. Ibid., p. 231.

24. In 1750, Marpurg published a little volume entitled *The Critical Musicus on the Spree River,* that is, the river on which the German capital Berlin is situated. Quoted from a letter in Fritz Kuttner's scrapbook. Fritz Kuttner Collection now held by Robert Mok, Larchmont, New York.

25. Ibid.

26. The "Second Viennese School" refers to Schoenberg, Berg, and Webern. The "First Viennese School" refers to Haydn, Mozart, and Beethoven.

27. The current director, as of April 1992, is *Jiang* Mingdun. Telephone interview with U.S.–China Arts Exchange, New York, June 26, 1997.

28. See chapter III.C.2. by *Xu* Buzeng in this volume for further background on Otto Joachim.

29. Telephone interview with Otto Joachim, December 7, 1994, Montreal, Canada.

30. Ibid., May 18, 1993, Montreal, Canada.

31. Telephone interview with Karl Steiner, December 14, 1994, Montreal, Canada.

32. See chapter III.C.2 in this volume for further background on Aaron Avshalomov.

33. Author interview with Esther Ashkenazi Funk, daughter of Rabbi Meir Ashkenazi, chief rabbi of Shanghai, November 28, 1994, New York, and telephone interview with Rose Tanner, December 7, 1994, East Williston, New York.

34. A.Z. Idelsohn, *Jewish Music in Its Historical Development* (New York: Tudor, 1944), p. 464.

35. Ibid., p. 24.

36. Ibid., pp. 276, 465, 513 n 22.

37. Marpurg, "Music Review," *China Press* (Shanghai), February 8, 1949, unpaginated.

D. Zionism, the Holocaust, and the Sino–Judaic Exodus

Chapter III.D.1

The Shanghai Zionist Association and the International Politics of East Asia Until 1936

Maruyama Naoki

With several notable examples, most literature on the history of Zionism makes scant mention of its presence in East Asia. The Jewish communities there were small and isolated in contrast to those of Europe.[1] Yet on close examination, it can be seen that the Jews of East Asia also made valuable contributions to Zionism. This chapter concerns those Zionists who lived in East Asia until 1936. Some of these ardent Zionists lived to see their national homeland, but others died before Israel was created.

The Origins of Zionism in China

In 1897, the first World Zionist Congress in Basel, Switzerland, established the World Zionist Organization. The event immediately exerted an influence on the Jews of Shanghai. At that time, the Jewish community in Shanghai had only several hundred souls. Most were of Baghdadi origin, had come to China via India, and held British citizenship. Many were wealthy merchants. Because of the miserable experiences of their forefathers in the Diaspora as well as their possibly exaggerated perception of British sympathy toward Zionism, they generally supported the Zionist movement. Some, such as Elly S. Kadoorie, who had accumulated a fortune, generously endowed the movement. However, it was not Kadoorie who set up the first Zionist organization in Shanghai. Nissim E. Benjamin Ezra, who had come to China from India, launched the Shanghai Zionist

Association (SZA) in 1903 and was its chief leader for many years. The association was one of the three earliest Zionist organizations in Asia, the other two being in Iraq and Turkey.[2]

In April 1903, Shanghai Jews first met and discussed establishing a branch of the Zionist movement. According to a letter addressed to Moses Gaster, Haham of British Jewry and one of the founders of the English Zionist Federation, the Shanghai delegates unanimously approved this idea.[3] On April 22, 1904, the SZA and the Jewish National Fund Commission for China began publishing their biweekly official organ *Israel's Messenger*, with N.E.B. Ezra as editor-in-chief. Although publication of *Israel's Messenger*, which was later issued monthly, was interrupted from February 1910 to September 1918 because of financial hardships, it survived difficult periods and lasted until October 17, 1941.

Shanghai Zionists numbered around one hundred in March 1905. Although few in number, they extended their full support to the worldwide Zionist movement, raised their voices from their corner of East Asia in sympathy with their brethren being persecuted in Europe, entered into negotiations for the aims of Zionism with local governments, and thus contributed to the creation of the Jewish state.

When Shanghai Jews held their first meeting and agreed to create a Shanghai branch of the Zionist movement in 1903, they also passed a resolution to send their delegation to the Sixth Zionist Congress, which was to be held in Basel that summer. Considering the geographic distance, they asked Moses Gaster to officially represent the SZA at the coming congress.[4] The Sixth Zionist Congress, at which Shanghai was represented for the first time, was a turning point for Zionism. Controversy over a British proposal for Jewish settlement in Uganda split the Zionist "rank and file" in Basel. The British who would then become settlers in Uganda suspected they could tap into a reservoir of persecuted Eastern European Jews. The English Zionist Federation supported their government's proposal. What was the stance of the SZA? The Uganda proposal was reported upon in detail. An editorial appearing in *Israel's Messenger* of June 17, 1904, supported the Uganda proposal. It was hardly surprising that Shanghai Zionists concurred with British Zionists, arguing that "we see no reason why a colony of Jews should not exist in Africa as well as in Palestine. We do not see why there should be any hitch in the Palestinian scheme if Uganda become [sic] a Jewish settlement." A May 5, 1905, editorial urgently advocated the East African scheme on the grounds that "the position of the Jews in Eastern Europe calls for immediate and drastic measures for improvement." On May 7, 1905, the SZA met at the Shanghai Jewish School to discuss the

British offer concerning Uganda. According to a report in *Israel's Messenger*, "prior to the opening of the meeting the Zionist National anthem, the *Hatikvah*, was sung, which was very much appreciated by the audience and tended greatly to enliven the meeting. This is the first occasion in Shanghai on which this Zionist song was recited."[5] In his address Jacques Blumenfeld, the Ashkenazi president of the then-overwhelmingly Baghdadi SZA, emphasized humanitarian principles and asked the audience "to approve the acceptance of the magnanimous offer made to the Zionists by the British Government of forming a Jewish autonomous colony in East Africa, provided that the Commissioners' report is favorable for the purposes of Jewish Colonization."[6] Subsequently that resolution won unanimous support.

However, when the East African Commissioners' survey was eventually issued, it was totally pessimistic, pointing to the inadequacy of the area for Jewish settlement. Finally the British offer was dismissed at the Seventh Zionist Congress in 1905. Since the destiny of the Uganda scheme had been made clear, Shanghai's response to it was quick. A June 16, 1905, *Israel's Messenger* editorial changed the SZA position, adopted just a month earlier, arguing that "East Africa is not to displace Palestine."[7]

The SZA, the Balfour Declaration, and Siam

From 1903 to 1917 the Shanghai Zionist movement did not achieve much. It could only maintain its daily activities, and *Israel's Messenger* ceased publication in 1910. This was in part because the Zionist movement as a whole was in a dilemma over the Uganda scheme. In addition, after Germany declared war on Great Britain in 1914, the World Zionist Organization split into pro-British and pro-German factions, leaving many members in a quandary. However, since the SZA was under the control of Jews with British citizenship, the city's Zionists inclined toward Britain and the other Entente countries. In 1915, E.S. Kadoorie was elected chairman of the SZA. He, together with N.E.B. Ezra, strongly argued that the Zionist movement could progress only by cooperating with Britain.[8]

The SZA's tilt toward Britain became irrevocable once Turkey, the colonial occupier of Palestine, entered World War I. In a dramatic effort to bolster Jewish and especially Zionist support for their war effort, on November 2, 1917, the British government issued its Balfour Declaration, favoring "the establishment in Palestine of a Jewish national home." Since this declaration was an expression of political commitment only of the British government to the Zionist leaders, Zionists worldwide felt obligated to obtain similar commitments from other powers. They started their diplomatic efforts with other Western nations. France, Italy, and the United States ultimately supported the Zionist cause. It was on this occasion that the Shanghai Zionists approached the Asian nations.

Immediately after the Balfour Declaration was issued, the SZA sent a telegram of thanks to British prime minister David Lloyd-George and accelerated publicity by distributing pamphlets and organizing lectures.[9] At that time, exclusive of Russia, there were three independent nations in East Asia: Siam (Thailand), China, and Japan. The SZA immediately took steps to obtain support for the declaration from these three nations.

First, it asked Captain David I. Sandelson of the British Army, Charles S. Lobingier, judge of the U.S. Court for China, and John B. Powell, editor of *Millard's Review* (later *China Weekly Review*) to act as intermediaries between the SZA and the Royal Siamese government.[10] As a result of their intermediary efforts, in July 1918, Elly S. Kadoorie, president of the SZA, wrote a letter to Devawongse, foreign minister of Siam, requesting support of the Siamese government for the establishment of a Jewish national home in Palestine.[11] The same letter was sent to Elden R. James, American legal adviser to the Royal Siamese government. In August James met with the French chargé d'affaires to Siam to ask about the French position on Zionism. During the meeting James disclosed that the Siamese government was being solicited to declare its sympathy toward the movement, which was aiming at the creation of a Jewish state in Palestine.[12] The French chargé d'affaires, who was surprised to hear the phrase *Etat juif,* or "Jewish state," indicated to James that as far as he knew, the Zionists' desire was for no more than a national home for the Jews as also specified in the Balfour Declaration. Immediately he cabled this information to French foreign minister Stephen Pichon.

On August 22, 1918, ten days after the French chargé d'affaires dispatched the cable to Paris and apparently before any clarification was received, the Siamese foreign minister sent a letter of support for Zionism to Kadoorie.[13] *The Bangkok Times* of September 27, 1918, reported that Elden R. James, Judge Lobingier, and John B. Powell had made "a great contribution." In other words, these official and unofficial channels succeeded in gaining the support of the Siamese government for the Zionist movement. At the request of Nahum Sokolow of the World Zionist Organization, Foreign Minister Devawongse said in his letter to Kadoorie that he had instructed the Siamese ambassador to Great Britain to inform the English Zionist Federation of Siam's support for Jewish aspirations.[14] The Zionist Organization, London Bureau, expressed its gratitude to the Siamese minister in its letter of November 29. The Zionist Organization of America also thanked Shanghai Zionists for their efforts vis-à-vis Siam in Jacob de Haas's letter dated December 26.[15] Siam was the first Asian and the first non-Christian nation to issue a pro-Zionist declaration.

The SZA, the Balfour Declaration, and China

Chinese recognition of Zionism was delayed mainly for technical reasons. The American ambassador to China, Paul S. Reinsch, who was to play the role of intermediary between the Zionists and the Chinese government, together with Judge Lobingier and George E. Morrison, an Australian who occasionally advised the Chinese government, suddenly took leave in early July 1918. United States chargé d'affaires John V.A. MacMurray succeeded to Reinsch's post in his absence but was less enthusiastic about intermediation between the SZA and the Chinese government.[16] In June, Lobingier had talked to Reinsch about obtaining Chinese support for the Balfour Declaration. Reinsch had promised to bring the matter to the attention of the Chinese government.[17] However, Lobingier was astonished to receive a letter from MacMurray dated July 5 containing the letter from the SZA to the Chinese foreign minister. MacMurray told Lobingier that he could not transmit the letters to the Chinese foreign minister because of "standing instructions," and instead suggested that Lobingier approach the U.S. Department of State through American Zionist organizations.[18] Lobingier returned the SZA letter to MacMurray, calling his attention to the fact that Reinsch had promised to transmit it and asked him to hold it pending Reinsch's return.[19] Consequently, the SZA's negotiations with the Chinese government were suspended until Reinsch's return.

Meanwhile, there were communication difficulties between London and Shanghai Zionists concerning the negotiations with China and Japan for declarations of support for the Balfour statement. In August 1918, Shanghai Zionists were annoyed to learn that Zionist leaders in London had already contacted the Japanese and Chinese embassies there.[20] Yet in his letter to N.E.B. Ezra on November 29, 1918, Samuel Landman of the Zionist Organization's London Bureau, said that he thought that local Zionists should procure declarations of support from the Chinese and Japanese governments.[21] On September 15, G.E. Morrison, who thought that everything had been arranged during Lobingier's recent visit to Beijing, wrote a letter to Ezra, expressing his surprise that Ezra had not yet obtained from the Chinese government the communication that Ezra was expecting. Then he asked Ezra to privately send the wording of the letter that the latter required.[22] Immediately Ezra sent a draft of the declaration to Morrison.[23]

On November 1, 1918, Lobingier wrote to Reinsch, who had just returned to Beijing, that "the local Zionists are earnestly hoping that you may be able to obtain in [sic] behalf of their cause a favorable expression by the Chinese Government."[24] Reinsch replied that he had taken the necessary steps to bring the matter to the notice of *Chen* Lu, China's deputy minister of foreign affairs. Chen promised an answer to the communication and expressed personal sympathy with the aspirations of the Jewish people for a national home.[25] On December 14, 1918, Chen sent an official letter to E.S. Kadoorie that "I have the honor to inform you that the Chinese Government had adopted the same attitude toward the Zionist aspirations as the British Government."[26] On April 24, 1920, Dr. *Sun* Yat-sen, founder of the Republic of China, also expressed his sympathy for the Zionist movement. In reply to a letter from the editor of *Israel's Messenger,* Sun wrote:

> Dear Mr. Ezra:
> I have read your letter and the copy of *Israel's Messenger* with much interest, and wish to assure you of my sympathy for this movement, which is one of the greatest movements of the present time. All lovers of Democracy cannot help but support ... the movement to restore your wonderful and historic nation, which has contributed so much to the civilization of the world and which rightfully deserve [sic] an honourable place in the family of nations.
> I am,
> Yours very truly,
> Sun Yat-sen[27]

To further advance the cause of Zionism within Shanghai, the SZA organized lectures and gatherings when famous Jewish personalities and Zionist activists visited Shanghai. In 1920, Shanghai Zionists warmly greeted Israel Cohen, representative of the World Zionist Organization. (For more information on the Cohen mission to both China and Japan, see below.) In 1923, Albert Einstein visited Shanghai and addressed a pro-Zionist meeting. In 1925, Uriel Bension, a representative of the Palestine Foundation Fund (Keren Hayesod), visited Shanghai.[28]

Most significantly, between 1917 and 1927, the Shanghai Zionist movement broadened its base beyond its Baghdadi roots. After the Russian Revolution of 1917, many Russian Jews with Zionist sympathies arrived in Shanghai via Harbin and Tianjin. This led to a swift expansion of the Ashkenazi membership in the Shanghai Zionist Association and a change in the earlier situation, when Baghdadi Jews generally led the movement. By August 1920, the Russian Zionist weekly *Siber Palestina* appeared in Shanghai.[29] The Shanghai Zionist movement added a purely Ashkenazi organization called Kadimah and a Baghdadi group named Ezra, derived from the Hebrew word for "help" but unrelated to N.E.B.'s name. In 1925,

Dr. Bension helped establish a pro-Zionist support organization with non-Jewish members, including Chinese, Japanese, Parsees, Hindus, and Muslims. This was seldom seen elsewhere in the world.[30]

In the period 1900 to 1929, Shanghai Zionists increased their support of Jewish emigration to Palestine and attempts to rebuild the national homeland there. In 1900, Zionists set up the Shanghai Branch of the Palestine Foundation Fund with E.S. Kadoorie as chairman. One project of the foundation was to collect funds to finance a "Hebrew University" in Jerusalem, a project that came to fruition in the early 1920s. The Foundation also funded the Beth Sepher Kadoorie agricultural school in Palestine.[31] In 1920, Shanghai Zionists established a colony of immigrants in Palestine fittingly called the China Jewish Colony. In 1921, Shanghai Zionists set up a second settlement named for Laura Kadoorie, the late wife of E.S. Kadoorie. The two "China" settlements later merged into one, with funding mostly from E.S. Kadoorie. During World War I the Jews of Shanghai raised more than 10,000 yuan for Jewish settlements in Palestine.[32] During the clashes between Arabs and Jews that erupted in Palestine in 1929, Shanghai Zionists appealed widely for support for Palestine's Zionist movement. In October 1929, Ezra wrote an open letter to Mohandas K. Gandhi. Ezra protested a statement purportedly made by Gandhi to the viceroy of India in which Gandhi offered to send twenty thousand Hindus to Palestine to protect the Muslim holy places against supposed Jewish aggression. In reply, Gandhi sent a denial, which was published in *Israel's Messenger*.[33]

In 1928, Mrs. Raymond Elias Toeg, from another notable Baghdadi family, took the place of E.S. Kadoorie as chairman of the Shanghai Zionist Association. The following year, at the official invitation of the Chinese government, Toeg and Ezra attended the ceremonies when Dr. *Sun* Yat-sen's remains were reentombed in the memorial built for him in Nanjing. These and other prominent Shanghai Zionists were well received and recognized by China's government.[34]

The SZA, the Balfour Declaration, and Japan

Japan also responded sympathetically responses to the Balfour Declaration at the request of the SZA. Since E.S. Kadoorie spent his summer vacations in Japan, most of the SZA's summer correspondence with China and Japan were handled by Ezra, who remained in Shanghai. As with China, the response of the Japanese government was delayed because of unexpected problems, causing Kadoorie to extend his stay in Japan to resolve matters.

There are several reasons why Japan's statement vis-à-vis Zionist aspirations was late.[35] First, as mentioned earlier, in the middle of August 1918, the SZA secretary Ezra learned that Zionists in London had started contacting the embassies of Japan and China. Shanghai Zionists thought that they should withhold their approaches to these governments at least temporarily. Second, the French ambassador to Japan, whom Kadoorie had contacted as an intermediary between the Japanese government and the SZA, suddenly left for home in October. This reduced the capability of the French embassy in a manner similar to the American situation in China. Third, Japan's domestic politics were in turmoil at that time. Rice riots followed Japan's dispatch of an expeditionary force to Siberia in August 1918. The Terauchi cabinet resigned on September 21. On September 29 the Hara cabinet was installed. Viscount *Uchida* Yasuya took office as foreign minister. Kadoorie, who waited out this development, asked French ambassador Marcel François Delanney to transmit the letter of the SZA to the Japanese government on September 24.[36] Kadoorie considered support from this growing Asian power vital for the Zionist movement and therefore extended his stay in Japan.

In October 1918, French ambassador Delanney informed the SZA that he had given Foreign Minister Uchida his government's letter asking for Japan's support of British policy on Palestine.[37] There is no record in the government archives in Japan of an immediate Japanese government response to Delanney. However, when the San Remo Conference was held in April 1920, Japanese ambassador to France *Matsui* Keishiro said: "The Imperial Government replied to the SZA that it was not opposed to the aspirations of establishing the Jewish 'National Home' after inquiring about the opinions of the British Government."[38]

In November 1918, in the absence of a concrete reply from Japan, Ezra wrote to the French embassy in Tokyo, requesting that the French government approach Viscount Uchida and obtain Japan's recognition of the British declaration on Palestine.[39] In his December 27, 1918, letter to Kadoorie, the French chargé d'affaires in Japan, Roger Maugras, stated that the Japanese government "informs me, and I have the honor to advise you, that it is pleased to learn of the ardent desire of the Zionists to establish in Palestine a National Jewish Homeland, and that it will accord its sympathy to the realization of your aspirations."[40] The SZA cabled the news to Zionist organizations in London and New York.

On January 3, 1919, Chaim Weizmann, president of the English Zionist organization, asked the Japanese ambassador to Great Britain for an official letter to the Zionist organization. *Chinda* Sutemi, the Japanese ambassador, issued the official letter of the Japanese government on January 6. It says: "The Japanese Government gladly take [*sic*] note of the Zionist aspirations to establish in Palestine a national home for the Jewish people and they look forward with a sympathetic interest to the realization of such desire upon the basis proposed."[41]

Aside from the activities mentioned above, Zionists in Shanghai and London were in a special hurry to obtain official declarations from Siam, China, and Japan. Why? The Paris Peace Conference was to begin on January 18, 1919. Zionists wanted to get Japan's official statement before the conference's opening. On January 10, after receiving the letter from the Japanese ambassador, London-based Zionists informed Ezra that "this brings all the important allied powers into unanimity on this subject."[42] In their January 16, 1919, letter to Nahum Sokolow, Kadoorie and Ezra came to the same conclusion, saying, "now that the Peace Conference has commenced to deliberate on the problem of all Nations, we hope that you shall have no difficulty in securing the unanimity of all the Powers for a Jewish Palestine."[43] Obtaining unanimity of all the powers on the Jewish National Home in Palestine was the main goal for the Zionist movement after the British Declaration in November 1917.

On January 15, 1919, the SZA thanked Viscount Uchida: "We venture to give expression to our firm conviction that your great country will rise to still further greatness in the near future, and we feel confident that Japan is destined to occupy a loftier place in the very forefront of the Great Powers of the world."[44]

In April 1920, when the allied powers, including Japan, met in San Remo and discussed mandates over Palestine and other former Turkish territories, Shanghai Zionists appealed again to Japan. In his letter of April 27, Ezra requested Japan's foreign minister Uchida to "direct a few lines to be cabled to us for publication in our Organ on the eve of the realization of our two-thousand-year-old dreams."[45] Uchida replied on May 12, 1920: "Accept my hearty congratulations on the achievement of your two thousand year old aspirations. Have followed with keen interest the progress of your movement for which you now enjoy the well-earned reward."[46]

The Council of the League of Nations confirmed the mandate agreement for Palestine on July 24, 1922. In advance of this, Ezra dispatched two letters to Foreign Minister Uchida. The letter of May 9, 1922, reads:

> The delay in the ratification of the Palestine Mandate by the League of Nations has, unfortunately, greatly impeded the reconstruction work in Palestine and gave an opportunity to the agitators to advocate for the abrogation of the Balfour Declaration which had been supported and endorsed by all the Allied Powers, including Japan. At the present moment when the Conference at Genoa is expected to ratify the Palestine Mandate it would be a graceful act on the part of your Excellency to give further public expression of your sympathy with and interest in the cause of the Jewish people and your ap-

proval of the terms of the Palestine Mandate insofar as they relate to the establishment of the Jewish National Home.[47]

And in Ezra's second letter of May 19, 1922, Viscount Uchida was urged again to "give further public expression of your sympathy with and interest in the cause of the Jewish People."[48] Faced with these requests, Uchida instructed Japan's consul general in Shanghai, *Funatsu* Tatsuichiro, to inform Ezra that Japan would consider the matter favorably when it was placed before the meeting of the Council of the League of Nations.[49] On June 8, 1922, Funatsu gave his foreign minster's reply to Ezra.[50]

At the height of its enthusiasm, the SZA decided to inscribe the name of Foreign Minster Uchida in the Golden Book of the Jewish charitable organization Keren Kayemet, in commemoration of Japan's and especially Uchida's contribution to Zionism.[51] Foreign Minister Uchida was the first Japanese whose name was inscribed in the Jewish Golden Book in acknowledgment of his contribution to Zionism. The SZA's organ also praised Uchida in a two-page special account in its July 7, 1922, issue. On March 4, 1923, a presentation ceremony of the "Diploma of the Golden Book" in which the name of Uchida was inscribed was held in the Seymour Road synagogue. Japanese consul general Funatsu and his wife attended on behalf of Foreign Minster Uchida.[52]

Israel Cohen's Mission to China and Japan in 1920

With growing concern about Japan's elevated position in international politics after World War I, the Central Executive of the World Zionist Organization in London fully realized the need to strengthen ties with the Jewish communities in East Asia and decided to send its first mission there. After the San Remo conference, Zionist leaders asked Israel Cohen, the WZO's director of publicity and propaganda, to visit East Asia.[53] In his autobiography, Cohen recalls, "The Executive lost no time in deciding that among the urgent measures to be taken was the despatch of emissaries to North and South America and other parts of the world to expound the implications of the Balfour Declaration and to raise the funds that were necessary. They invited me to undertake a mission for this purpose to Australia and East Asia."[54]

Israel Cohen left London on May 15, 1920, and returned there on May 8, 1921. What did the Zionist leaders expect from his mission to Asia? He carried with him testimonials on behalf of his mission from significant Zionist and pro-Zionist personalities: Chaim Weizmann, Nahum Sokolow, Lord Lionel Walter Rothschild (the recipient of the Balfour Declaration), Max Nordau, Lord Robert Cecil, and Sir Herbert Samuel. Cohen gave lectures and raised funds at each place he visited. The Asian Jewish communities enthusiastically welcomed their first Zionist emissary. In Shanghai, where he gave several speeches, *Israel's Messenger* devoted seven pages of its December 17 issue to Cohen's visit.[55] In Japan, where Cohen stayed from December 8 to 18, he held two meetings at Yokohama and Kobe. His visit was covered by several local papers, which expressed fascination with Jews and their struggling national movement.[56]

The SZA, Ezra, Manchuria, and Jewish Refugees

International tensions in East Asia intensified in the 1920s with unanticipated consequences for the SZA. After the Bolshevik Revolution in Russia in 1917, Japan had intervened and dispatched forces to Siberia. There, some Japanese army and navy officers contacted anti-Semitic White Russians and learned of Europe's traditional "Jewish question": "What can we *do* about the *problem* of the Jews?" Several "Jewish experts" appeared from among these officers, most notably *Yasue* Norihiro. In October 1927, the War Ministry dispatched Yasue to Palestine and Europe on a fact-finding mission about the "Jewish problem." After returning to Japan in May 1928, he published several books on his travels. In these books he admired the rapid development of the Jewish communities in Palestine and related his strong impression of the elated nationalist consciousness of the Jewish people.[57] In the late 1930s, when the Jewish refugees came to East Asia looking for a haven, Yasue came to the fore as an expert on Jewish affairs. He was one of the organizers of the Far Eastern Jewish National Conferences held in Harbin in 1937, 1938, and 1939.

In Manchuria, the economic situation deteriorated after the New York stock market crash of 1929, with a consequent upsurge in anti-Semitic violence. Japan's occupation of Manchuria began on September 18, 1931, and soon spread into large-scale Sino–Japanese conflict. Japan's international isolation led the country to withdraw from the League of Nations on March 27, 1933. The SZA maintained its neutral position during this sensitive period, stating on October 1, 1931, that "we take no sides in the conflict between China and Japan, since *Israel's Messenger* has made it a rule to shun politics and rely upon the spirit of fairness and impartiality which should animate all impartial observers. We cling to the hope that the two great Asiatic nations will not plunge into armed conflicts but settle their differences amicably."[58] Despite their hope, the situation continued to deteriorate. In August 1933, Simeon Kaspe, son of Joseph Kaspe, owner of the Hotel Moderne in Harbin, was kidnaped and murdered by White Russians. This cold-blooded incident shocked all the Jewish communities in East

Asia. Although most anti-Semitic acts were carried out by White Russian Fascists, Japanese gendarmes were deeply connected with many of these crimes.[59] Ezra, as editor of *Israel's Messenger,* asked the Japanese Foreign Ministry to suppress anti-Semitism in Manchuria. In early 1934, he asked his Japanese friend *Oyabe* Zenichiro, a Christian priest who believed that the Japanese were the descendants of the Ten Lost Tribes of Israel, to appeal to the Foreign Ministry.[60] Ezra requested at a minimum that Deputy Minister *Shigemitsu* Mamoru suppress the White Russian Fascists' violently racist propaganda.[61] Because Shigemitsu's response was very slow in coming, Ezra decided to go to Japan and appeal to him personally. This was his first and last trip to Japan. On August 18, 1934, he sailed for Japan, arriving in Tokyo on August 24. On the same day, he was received by Shigemitsu at the Foreign Ministry. According to his account, which appeared in *Israel's Messenger,* his impression of Shigemitsu was favorable.[62] The atmosphere of the meeting was friendly.

Ezra reminded Shigemitsu of his recent pleas regarding anti-Semitism in Harbin. In response, Shigemitsu said that the government was not unmindful of the state of affairs. The deputy minister assured Ezra that steps would be taken to suppress lawless agitation and remove disruptive elements.[63]

Even before Ezra's mission to Japan, the Japanese had already begun to investigate. On May 7, 1934, the Harbin chief of police sent a report to the director of police of the civil administration in Manchukuo. It emphasized that "the essential matter was that the White Russians, who were the underdogs for a long time, were encouraged by the outbreak of the Manchurian Incident and the establishment of Manchukuo, and started their retaliations against Jews and communists. However the Jews exploited these persecutions for their counter propaganda against the White Russians."[64] The anti-Semitic campaign in Harbin did not stop. On December 8, 1934, the Shanghai Ashkenazi Jewish Communal Association, set up in December 1932, passed a resolution stating that "this meeting views with regret the persistent anti-Semitic campaign and the ill-treatment of the Jews in Harbin at the hands of the Japanese judicial officials employed by the Manchukuo Government, who encourage the anti-Semitism of a part of the White Russians."[65] Anti-Semitism in Harbin further provoked criticism of Japan in foreign countries. Japan's chargé d'affaires in Britain queried Tokyo and Harbin concerning the matter. Faced with such scrutiny from abroad, the Manchukuo authorities considered easing the tensions generated by White Russian Fascist bodies in Harbin. But these authorities do not appear to have taken any further steps to intervene in this matter.[66]

Meanwhile, with the rise of nazism in Germany in the early 1930s, the European Jews faced a critical period unparalleled since the days of the

Spanish Inquisition. One possible haven was Shanghai, where Russian Jewish refugees from the Bolshevik Revolution and from instability in Manchuria had already begun to settle. The Central and East European exodus to Shanghai, beginning in the 1920s, transformed the demographics and politics of a traditional Baghdadi Jewish community. The European Jews established their own community structures and synagogues. Before long, a branch of the heavily Russian Jewish Zionist Revisionist movement appeared. (For more information on the Revisionist movement, see chapter III.D.2 by *Pan* Guang in this volume.)

Faced with the crises of his brethren in Europe, on September 15, 1933, Ezra wrote Shigemitsu suggesting Manchukuo as a refuge for fifty thousand Jewish refugees from Germany.[67] Two days later, Ezra wrote Israel Cohen of the World Zionist Organization that "as it is impossible to take away all the Jews from Germany to our homeland [i.e., Palestine —*Ed.*], I thought Manchukuo would be a nice country where the future centre of Judaism may well take rest. In the hands of Asiatic powers we Jews have not been persecuted."[68] In a reply to Ezra dated October 17, Cohen objected to the proposal as follows:

> The Jewish exiles from Germany are naturally anxious to settle in a land where they can be assured perfect peace, liberty and protection. They are hardly likely to find such conditions in a land that has been wrested by Japan from China.... The whole problem of the settlement of the German refugees is to be taken in hand by a special High Commissioner of the League of Nations, acting in conjunction with a Governing Body appointed by the Council. It is hardly likely that this Governing Body would favor a settlement of refugees in a country that has been conquered by Japan in direct defiance of the wishes and decisions of the League.[69]

Japan's response to Ezra's proposal was also negative. In August 1934, when Ezra met Shigemitsu at the Foreign Ministry, the deputy minister told him that "it is not possible to say anything definite just yet. The country has many problems to adjust, it is just in its embryo, and, to my mind, such a movement is too big for the present."[70]

N.E.B. Ezra died of a heart attack on December 3, 1936, while working indefatigably to aid his embattled European brethren. It might have been small gratification to him had he lived a little longer to see the Japanese side briefly reconsider his Manchukuo scheme. From their point of view, the scheme was considered a way to attract American–Jewish financial investment and thereby salvage deteriorating Japanese–American relations.[71] Nor did Ezra live to fulfill another aspiration about which he had written Nahum Sokolow in 1918: to serve in a future Jewish government in Palestine.[72]

What he and his SZA colleagues had achieved was to demonstrate repeatedly their concern about their European brethren. The fullest expression of the efforts of N.E.B. Ezra, E.S. Kadoorie, Mrs. R.E. Toeg, and other early Shanghai Zionists would be the reborn State of Israel. Their few successes before 1936 are all the more impressive when one considers the formidable obstacles they confronted and the turbulent state of China's international relations in the first four decades of the twentieth century.

Notes

    1. The notable exceptions that mention Shanghai Zionism are Herman Dicker, *Wanderers and Settlers in the Far East: A Century of Jewish Life in China and Japan* (New York: Twayne, 1962); Hyman Kublin, ed., *Studies of the Chinese Jews: Some Western Views* (New York: Paragon, 1971); David Kranzler, *Japanese, Nazis and Jews: The Refugee Community of Shanghai 1938–1945* (New York: Yeshiva University Press, 1976); and Michael Pollak, *Mandarins, Jews, and Missionaries: The Jewish Experience in the Chinese Empire* (Philadelphia: Jewish Publication Society, 1980).

    2. *Encyclopedia Judaica* (hereafter, cited as *EJ*) (Jerusalem: Keter, 1978), vol. 16, p. 1127; Pan Guang, "Zionism in Shanghai, 1903–1949," *Studies in Zionism* 14, no. 2 (Autumn 1993), p. 170.

    3. N.E.B. Ezra, Shanghai, to Moses Gaster, April 30, 1903, Moses Gaster Papers, Mocatta Library, University College, London.

    4. Ibid. At the congress, however, instead of Gaster, Joseph Cowen of the English Zionist Federation represented Shanghai.

    5. *Israel's Messenger* (hereafter, cited as *I.M.*), May 19, 1905.

    6. Ibid.

    7. *I.M.*, June 16, 1905.

    8. Pan, "Zionism," *passim*.

    9. This was mentioned in Ezra's letter addressed to Nahum Sokolow dated August 20, 1918. N.E.B. Ezra, Shanghai, September 11, 1918, Record group Z_4/176, Central Zionist Archives (hereafter, cited as C.Z.A. with appropriate record group indicated), Jerusalem. See also *I.M.*, October 27, 1918.

    10. Lobingier to Ezra, Shanghai, September 11, 1918, Z_4/176, C.Z.A., Jerusalem. See also *I.M.*, October 27, 1918.

    11. *I.M.*, November 4, 1927.

    12. Chargé d'affaires de France to Monsieur Stephen Pichon, Bangkok, August 13, 1918, no. 42, Ministère des affaires étrangères, Direction des affaires politiques et commerciales, série E 312/4. The author is grateful to Professor David Vital of Tel Aviv University for providing a copy of the letter.

    13. Chargé d'affaires to Pichon, Bangkok, September 28, 1918, no. 63. Courtesy David Vital.

    14. Devawongse to E.S. Kadoorie, Bangkok, November 2, 1918, C.Z.A. Z_4/176.

    15. *I.M.*, November 4, 1927.

    16. MacMurray to Lobingier (copy), Peking, July 5, 1918, C.Z.A. Z_4/176.

    17. Lobingier to Reinsch, Shanghai, November 1, 1918. The copy of this letter was enclosed in the former's letter to Ezra, November 5, 1918, C.Z.A. Z_4/176.

    18. MacMurray to Lobingier.

    19. This was mentioned in Lobingier's letter to Ezra, Shanghai, September 11, 1918, C.Z.A. Z_4/176.

    20. Ezra to Sokolow, Shanghai, August 20, 1918, C.Z.A. Z_4/176.

21. Landman to Ezra, London, November 29, 1918, C.Z.A. Z₄/176.
22. Morrison to Ezra, Peking, September 15, 1918, C.Z.A. Z₄/176.
23. Ezra to Morrison, Shanghai, September 20, 1918, C.Z.A. Z₄/176.
24. Lobingier to Reinsch.
25. *I.M.,* November 4, 1927.
26. Tcheng Log [sic] to Kadoorie (copy), Peking, December 14, 1918, C.Z.A. Z₄/2039.
27. *Sun* Yat-sen to Ezra, April 24, 1920, in *The Complete Works of Dr. Sun Yat-sen* (Taibei: Committee of Party History, Central Committee of the Guomindang, 1973), vol. 5, pp. 426–27; *I.M.,* November 4, 1927.
28. *Xu* Buzeng, "Einstein's Two Visits to Shanghai" (in Chinese), *Shanghai Archival Journal,* no. 5 (1991), pp. 49–50, cited in *Pan,* "Zionism," p. 171.
29. Rudolf Loewenthal, "The Religious Periodical Press in China," *Sinological Series,* no. 57 (1940), p. 263, cited in *Pan,* "Zionism," p. 171.
30. Raphael Patai, ed., *Encyclopedia of Israel and Zionism* (New York: Herzl Press, 1971), vol. 1, pp. 184–85, cited in *Pan,* "Zionism," p. 171.
31. *EJ,* vol. 10, p. 667; J. Zeitlin, "The Shanghai Jewish Community," *Jewish Life,* 41 (October 1973), pp. 56–57, cited in *Pan,* "Zionism," p. 171.
32. Patai, *Encyclopedia,* vol. 1, p. 184, cited in *Pan,* "Zionism," p. 171.
33. Ibid.
34. Ibid.
35. See *Maruyama* Naoki, *Barufoa sengen to Nihon* (The Balfour Declaration and Japan), *Hitotsubashi Review* 90 (July 1983).
36. *The North-China Herald,* January 25, 1919.
37. It was referred to in Ezra's letter to Sokolow dated October 10, 1918, C.Z.A. Z₄/176.
38. *Matsui* Keishiro to foreign minister (in Japanese), telegram, San Remo, April 26, 1920, no. 14, foreign ministry Archives (hereafter, cited as F.M.A.), Tokyo.
39. This was described in Ezra's letter to Sokolow dated November 14, 1918, C.Z.A. Z₄/176.
40. The original letter was in French. Roger Maugras to Kadoorie, Tokyo, December 27, 1918, F.M.A. See also the English translation in *Three Asiatic Powers Complete World Endorsement of the Jewish National Movement* (Shanghai: Shanghai Zionist Association, 1919), and *I.M.,* November 4, 1927.
41. *Chinda* Sutemi to Chaim Weizmann (copy), London, January 6, 1919, Weizmann Archives, Rehovot, and also C.Z.A. Z₄/2039.
42. Zionist Organization, London Bureau to N.E.B. Ezra (copy), London, January 10, 1919, C.Z.A. Z₄/176.
43. Kadoorie and Ezra to Sokolow, Shanghai, January 16, 1919, C.Z.A. Z₄/176.
44. Kadoorie and Ezra to Viscount Uchida, Shanghai, January 15, 1919. This letter appeared in *I.M.,* November 4, 1927.
45. Ezra to Uchida, Shanghai, April 27, 1920, F.M.A.
46. Viscount Uchida to Ezra, Tokyo, May 12, 1920, F.M.A.
47. Ezra to Uchida, Shanghai, May 9, 1922, F.M.A.
48. Ezra to Uchida, Shanghai, May 19, 1922, F.M.A.
49. Uchida to Funatsu (in Japanese), Tokyo, no. 82, May 27, 1922, F.M.A.
50. Funatsu to Ezra, Shanghai, June 8, 1922, F.M.A.
51. D.E.J. Abraham (vice-president of the SZA) and Ezra to Uchida, Shanghai, June 12, 1922, F.M.A. At the same time, the SZA decided to take steps to inscribe the names of E. James, Lobingier, and Reinsch in the Golden Book in memory of their contributions to Zionism.

52. Funatsu to Foreign Minister Uchida (in Japanese), telegram, Shanghai, no. 32, February 6, 1923; Uchida to Funatsu (in Japanese), telegram, Tokyo, no. 22, February 7, 1923; Funatsu to Uchida (in Japanese), Shanghai, no. 169, February 20, 1923; Funatsu to Uchida (in Japanese), Shanghai, no. 232, March 7, 1923, F.M.A.

53. See *Maruyama* Naoki, "Japan's Response to the Zionist Movement in the 1920s," *Bulletin of the Graduate School of International Relations, International University of Japan* 2 (December 1984).

54. Israel Cohen, *A Jewish Pilgrimage: An Autobiography of Israel Cohen* (London: Vallentine, Mitchell, 1956), p. 173.

55. Ibid., p. 154.

56. For example, *Kokumin Shimbun* carried the following headline: "The judgement for the reconstruction of the lost nation at the meeting; Mr. Cohen, Jewish royal family, weeping for the Holy Mission" (December 13, 1920).

57. Yasue's account of his tour to Palestine is contained in his book, *Kakumei undo wo abaku* (Inside the Revolutionary Movement) (Tokyo: Shoka sha, 1931).

58. *I.M.,* October 1, 1931.

59. See Amleto Vespa, *Secret Agent of Japan: A Handbook to Japanese Imperialism* (London: Victor Gollancz, 1941).

60. Oyabe to Shigemitsu (in Japanese), Tokyo, January 22, 1934, F.M.A.

61. Ezra to Shigemitsu, Shanghai, April 24, 1934; June 15, 1934; June 29, 1934; November 5, 1934; December 7, 1934; and December 14, 1934, F.M.A.

62. *I.M.,* September 7, 1934.

63. Ibid.

64. The chief of the Harbin police office to the director of the police department of the civil administration (in Japanese), confidential, no. 283, May 7, 1934, F.M.A.

65. The Resolution of the Shanghai Ashkenazi Jewish Communal Association (copy), F.M.A.

66. Chargé d'affaires to Great Britain Fujii to consul general to Harbin Sato, no. 25, November 7, 1935, F.M.A.; *I.M.,* March 6, 1935.

67. Ezra to Shigemitsu, Shanghai, September 15, 1933, C.Z.A. Z₄/3225 II. A copy of this letter was enclosed in Ezra's letter to Cohen, September 17, 1933.

68. Ezra to Cohen, Shanghai, September 17, 1933, C.Z.A. Z₄/3225 II.

69. Cohen to Ezra, London, October 17, 1933, C.Z.A. Z₄/3225 II.

70. *I.M.,* September 17, 1934.

71. For example, *Yudayajin taisaku yoko* (Outline of Policy Toward Jews), December 6, 1938, F.M.A. This was decided at the Five Ministers' (prime minister, foreign minister, army, navy, and finance) Conference.

72. Ezra to Sokolow, Shanghai, October 10, 1918; Secretary to the Zionist Organization to Ezra, London, November 29, 1918, Z₄/176, C.Z.A.

Chapter III.D.2

Zionism and Zionist-Revisionism in Shanghai, 1937–1949

Pan *Guang*

To understand Zionism in Shanghai after 1937 it is essential to discuss the origins and activities of an array of Zionist groups that emerged alongside the mainstream Shanghai Zionist Association (SZA) beginning in 1929. The most prominent of these dissident groups was the Zionist-Revisionist group. (For a discussion of the SZA up to 1936, see chapter III.D.1 by *Maruyama* Naoki in this volume.)

Discord and Unity, 1929–1937

From 1929 to 1937, the Shanghai Zionist movement underwent a process of internal reorganization because of discord within the world Zionist movement. The Shanghai Zionist Association could no longer exclusively represent Shanghai Zionists.

In the early 1920s there were different viewpoints in the world Zionist movement on Britain's policies toward Palestine. In 1925, as noted in Israel Epstein's paper in volume 2 of this publication, Vladimir (Zev) Jabotinsky set up his own organization, the World Union of Zionists-Revisionists. Jabotinsky insisted on statehood in all of Palestine and toward that end pledged more militant tactics than either the mainstream World Zionist Organization (WZO) or its Shanghai affiliate, the SZA. In 1930, Lord Passfield (Sidney Walsh), the British colonial minister, issued a "White Paper" stressing that Palestine's "economic absorptive capability" should be a factor in receiving Jewish immigrants.[1] Many Jews interpreted this verbiage as a rationalization for Britain to cut off Jewish immigration to Palestine. The 1930 White Paper was opposed by many Jews, but especially by the Revisionists. In 1935, the Revisionist group withdrew from the World Zionist Organization altogether and reorganized itself as the New Zionist Organization.

In Shanghai, Russian Zionists inclined toward the Revisionists because of their familiarity with Jabotinsky and experience with virulent anti-Semitism in their homeland. In the late 1920s many Russian Zionists in Shanghai joined Jabotinsky's ranks. According to *Wang* Qingyu, Shanghai had a group called the "China Union of Zionist-Revisionists" in 1929, which had separated from the SZA.[2] In 1931, when Betar, the Revisionist Zionist youth organization, set up its branch in Shanghai, the city's Revisionist presence significantly expanded. Shanghai Betar was established through the efforts of young Revisionists from Harbin and Tianjin, led by Lela Kotovitch from Tianjin.[3] The group at first had only nine members. After one year, according to leader Leo Hanin, the number jumped to seventy. A "Friends of Betar" organization composed of middle-aged and elderly people also was set up.[4] Thanks in part to the efforts of Shanghai Betar in 1931, a mainly Jewish company was set up within the ranks of Shanghai Volunteer Corps. In 1932, this company, with 101 soldiers and four officers, was the world's sole legal Jewish army at the time.[5]

Shanghai Betar sent young Revisionist members with military training to Palestine. Lela Kotovitch left Shanghai for Palestine in 1934.[6] By 1936, Shanghai Betar had more than four hundred members, while sympathizers toward the organization, according to Leo Hanin, far surpassed that number.[7] In 1933, Shanghai Revisionists established an English monthly, *The Jewish Call,* to publicize their viewpoint.[8] In 1935, a branch of the New Zionist Organization (NZO) was also set up in Shanghai. *The Jewish Call* had originally been issued by the "Shanghai Zionist Revisionists and Berith Trumpeldor," but after the middle of 1939 it had become the "Organ of the New Zionist Organization of China." Shanghai Betar, the NZO, and the above-mentioned "China Union of Zionist-Revisionists" might have been organized by the same group of Revisionist activists.

Just as the Zionist Revisionists developed step by step in Shanghai, branches of other Zionist organizations appeared, including Mizrachi, Poalei Zion, and the left-wing Poalei Zion. Shanghai Poalei Zion began publishing its short-lived magazine *The Jewish Voice* in English and Russian in 1935.[9]

Between 1929 and 1939, despite dissension within the Shanghai Zionist movement, increased European anti-Semitism exerted a countervailing unifying influence on Shanghai Jews. This unity was reflected in vigorous, broad-based Zionist activity. One example of this was the Shanghai Jewish Club (Shanghai Jewish Communal Association), set up in 1932. As an activity center for Jews of all persuasions, the club was originally non-Zionist.[10] But by the late 1930s it was actively publicizing Zionist views in its wall newspapers.[11]

The Challenge of War, 1937–1945

Between 1937 and 1945 China waged a full-scale war against Japanese aggression. Simultaneously Shanghai experienced an increase in Zionist ranks due to the arrival of thousands of German and Central European Jewish refugees from Hitler.

As noted in *Maruyama* Naoki's and Marcia Ristaino's articles in volumes one and two of this publication, this movement to Shanghai originated from both the Nazi Holocaust of European Jews and simultaneous restrictions imposed by many countries on Jewish immigration (see chapter III.D.1 in this volume). Unlike the restrictive countries, Shanghai from 1937 to 1939 was the world's only place that demanded no entry visas or financial guarantees.

Among the Jewish refugees who came to Shanghai, some were already members of Betar or held Revisionist leanings. Others who originally had not favored Zionism became receptive to it after undergoing Nazi persecution. Therefore many of the Jewish refugees, upon arrival in Shanghai, joined Zionist organizations or took part in Zionist activities. Shanghai's Kadimah organization had originally conducted activities mainly in Russian with English as subsidiary language. After 1937, the organization set up a German branch for newly arrived Jewish refugees led by Bernard Rosenberg and Ossie Lewin.[12] At the same time, Betar established a branch for more than three hundred German-speaking young people in Hongkew's Ward Road Synagogue. On September 9, 1939, German-speaking Jewish refugees set up their own independent mainstream Zionist organization, the Theodor Herzl Allgemeine Zionist Organization (THAZO), under Jacob Wachtel and Otto Kortischoner. In a year, it took in more than two thousand members, far surpassing in number the Baghdadi or Russian Zionist groups.[13]

More than a thousand Jewish refugees came to Shanghai from Poland between 1940 and 1941. Many were highly cultured, Orthodox, and Yiddish-speaking. This group included rabbis, religious scholars, writers, and artists. All the teachers and students of the yeshiva (Jewish theological seminary) of the Polish city of Mir, some four hundred in number, came to Shanghai and accounted for nearly half the city's Polish Jewish population.[14] There were dozens of Zionist leaders among the Polish refugees, who represented many of the political tendencies within the worldwide

Zionist movement. They included Zorach Warhaftig, Israel's future minister of religion, and Leon Ilutovich, future executive director of the Zionist Organization of America.

But World War II was intensifying long-existing differences within the Zionist movement in Shanghai. Should Zionists support Britain in the struggle against European fascism and Japanese militarism? How should Zionism push forward during the war? What attitude should Shanghai Zionists take toward the Japanese occupation authorities? How should Zionist activities be conducted in the special environs of Shanghai? The differences resulted in a split within THAZO and appearance of another two organizations: Zion Zioni and the Zionist Association. After December 1941, Japanese troops occupied the international part of Shanghai and viewed British and American citizens as enemy aliens. This was a heavy blow to the Shanghai Zionist Association, which was made up mainly of Jews of British nationality. As a result, the association came to a standstill, finding it difficult to continue its activities. In February 1943, the Japanese authorities established a special settlement in Hongkew for "stateless refugees," ordering most refugees who had arrived in Shanghai from Europe since 1937 to move into the settlement within three months. This placed the Zionists from Central Europe in difficult straits, but also offered them a chance to unite. After they entered the so-called Hongkew Ghetto, the tiny Zionist groups THAZO and Zion Zioni merged with the Zionist Association to form one organization called the "Zionist Organization Shanghai," with Paul Parnes as chairman.[15] Because of the nonaggression pact between Japan and the Soviet Union, Russian Zionist organizations and all USSR passport holders could still freely conduct their activities in Shanghai.

In eight years of warfare from 1937 to 1945, Shanghai Zionist activity can be summarized as follows:

First, because all the Zionist groups were well-organized with a fixed membership and strong leadership core, they played an important organizational and coordinative role in assisting Jewish refugees. As soon as Jewish refugees arrived in Shanghai, Baghdadi Zionists called on members of the Jewish community to help their suffering compatriots. Members of all walks of Jewish life in Shanghai participated in the first meeting in October 1938, sponsored by Horace Kadoorie, son of Elly S. Kadoorie, to discuss the issue of aiding the Jewish refugees. The Kadoories also financed a Hongkew school for the free education of refugee children.[16] Russian Zionist groups, though not so rich as the Baghdadis, contributed significantly by virtue of their numbers and strong organizational abilities. In 1941, they set up a Committee for Assistance to Jewish Refugees from Eastern Europe.[17] Significantly, after the establishment of the special settlement for "stateless refugees," Russian Zionists utilized their neutral status and Soviet passports to play a role impossible for non-Soviet passport holders.

Second, Zionists ran a number of newspapers and magazines to publicize their cause, especially among refugees. After 1941, *Our Life* [Nasha zhizn'], a weekly sponsored and edited by David Rabinovich, came out in Russian, English, and Yiddish and actively publicized Zionism. The German and English-language *Shanghai Jewish Chronicle,* with Ossie Lewin as editor-in-chief, also popularized Zionism. Other newspapers with a Zionist bent included the *Gelbe Post,* The *Shanghai Woche* (later renamed *8 Uhr Abendblatt*), *The Shanghai Post, Das Wort, Unser Welt,* and *Davar* (mimeographed).[18]

Third, Shanghai Zionists took part in political activities in coordination with the international Zionist movement when they sent representatives to attend the Conference of Far Eastern Jewish Communities in Harbin. In 1940, when Jabotinsky died, all the Zionist Revisionist organizations in Shanghai held memorial meetings publicizing his principles and platform. After Japanese troops occupied the international part of Shanghai, relations between the Shanghai Zionist organizations and outside Zionist organizations were terminated by the Japanese.

Fourth, Zionists organized recreational and sports activities among the Jewish young people to reinforce the unity of the Jewish community. Shanghai Betar organized physical and military training for Jewish youth. After large number of refugees reached Shanghai, participation in Betar activities increased. After February 1943, Betar, with Russian Zionists among its main activists, persisted in its activities. But, to avoid any possible suspicion and interference from the Japanese authorities, military training had to be abandoned. They continued to hold football, basketball, boxing, tennis and swimming matches, dances, chamber music concerts, and Yiddish dramas.[19] These activities helped sustain Jewish morale in hard times.

During this period Shanghai Zionists also struggled against nazism. After 1937, Shanghai Zionist groups demonstrated against the German slaughter of Jews and gained sympathy from Jews and non-Jews alike. Jewish refugees also protested Nazi "victory" celebrations in Shanghai.[20] Early in 1943, when Japanese authorities established a "designated area for stateless refugees," Zionist groups organized Jewish refugees, especially Poles, to resist the practice.[21] According to David Kranzler, one prominent Zionist was allegedly arrested and tortured for helping to secure the escape of downed American pilots.[22] Although there existed some differences among the Zionists as to whether to fight for Britain, some Betar members who had received military training joined the British army and navy and lost their lives on the battlefields of Southeast Asia.[23]

Fruition and Dissolution, 1945–1949

From 1945 to 1949, because of rapid changes in Palestine and the steady exodus of most Shanghai Jews, the Shanghai Zionist movement gradually ceased activity.

When the war ended in 1945, Zionism was a major trend in the Shanghai Jewish community.[24] Shanghai's Zionist organizations consisted mainly of General Zionists and Zionist-Revisionists. General Zionists belonged to the Kadimah organization, the Shanghai Zionist Association (the Ezra organization), and the newly established Shanghai branch of the Women's International Zionist Organization (WIZO). The Shanghai Zionist Association, though it had not officially disbanded, had existed in name only after the eruption of the Pacific War. Zionist-Revisionists had become the strongest postwar force in the Shanghai Zionist movement. As soon as the war ended, Betar and the NZO immediately reactivated. That the Revisionists exerted much influence over the Shanghai Zionist movement can be seen in elections for representatives to the twenty-second World Zionist Congress. Of three representatives elected (two from Shanghai, one from Tianjin), two were Revisionists, including Judith Hasser, a leader of the Shanghai Revisionists.[25] Shanghai Revisionists published their *Hadegel* [The Flag] weekly in Russian and *Tagar* [Challenge] biweekly in English and Russian. Apart from the two major groups of Zionists, postwar Shanghai also had smaller branches of other Zionist parties.

In less than three years after the end of World War II, events in Palestine stimulated the Shanghai Jewish community to further action. Judith Hasser made several addresses after she returned from the 1946 22nd World Zionist Congress. By early 1947 she was vigorously explaining the situation the Zionist movement was facing.[26] In March, when conflict in Palestine intensified, Gedalio Zulhovitsky, a representative of the Zionist umbrella fundraising group Palestine Foundation Fund (Keren Hayesod), visited Shanghai. At a meeting in the Shanghai Jewish Communal Association, he explained the latest developments in Palestine and appealed for support.[27] On April 22, more than eight thousand Jews gathered in Huishan Park (now the Worker's Club in Yangpu district) to protest the hanging in Palestine of the Revisionist activist Dov Gruner by the British on April 16. Speakers at the meeting condemned Britain for "following Hitler's policy against Jews." The meeting approved a resolution to call on all Jews to unite in a struggle against Britain and to reestablish a Jewish state.[28] This mass meeting, attended by so many Jews, was the largest political act in the century-long history of the Shanghai Jewish community. In November, Shanghai Betar activated a Shanghai branch of the National Defense Organization (*Irgun*

Zva Leumi), also called the "China" or "Far East" Branch, with more than two hundred members and more than three hundred "Friends of Irgun."[29] The group had a secret armory and a military training base in Betar headquarters at 20 Rue Pichon (now Fenyang Road).[30]

As conflict intensified in Palestine between Englishman and Jew and Arab and Jew, Shanghai Zionist groups, especially the Revisionists, vigorously sought support from Chinese officials and noted personalities. The united Zionist-Revisionists wrote Chinese government officials, explaining their views on the Palestine conflict. On July 4, 1947, *Sun* Fo, president of the Legislative Council of the Chinese government in Nanjing, wrote Judith Hasser, leader of the Shanghai Revisionists, that he fully agreed with the support for Zionism expressed by his father, Dr. *Sun* Yat-sen.[31] At the same time, Shanghai Betar and the Irgun made every effort to obtain weapons and ammunition from the Chinese. They tried to ship munitions and young Jewish trainees to Palestine. Although the plan may have been given tacit consent by Chinese officials, it was cancelled at the last minute because of the destruction of the Irgun arms ship *Altalena* on orders of David Ben-Gurion, who feared an independent army outside the command of his Jewish National Council.[32] His Vaad Leumi became the government of the State of Israel on May 14, 1948, a moment that all Shanghai Zionist organizations celebrated.

With the near-simultaneous eruption of full-scale war between Jews and Arabs, Irgun headquarters urgently demanded that the Shanghai branch dispatch men as soon as possible. Shanghai Betar and the Irgun sent two groups of young volunteers. The first was led by Samuel Muller and the second by Arye Marinsky. They arrived in Palestine in the fall of 1948 and were immediately sent into action. Several of the China volunteers later rose to prominence in the Israeli army.[33]

After 1945, Jews rapidly left Shanghai for the United States, Canada, Australia, South Africa, and Europe. In December 1948, Moshe Yuval, Israel's consul general in New York, arrived in Shanghai as a special diplomatic representative to distribute seven thousand visas for Israel.[34] From the fall of 1948 to the spring of 1949, about four thousand to five thousand Jews from Shanghai, including many leaders of the Shanghai Zionist movement, arrived in Israel.[35] Zionist organizations and the State of Israel had actively encouraged the emigration of these Shanghai Jews. Among the many ex-Shanghai leaders who rose to prominence in Israel are the aforementioned Zorach Warhaftig; Yosef Tekoah, Israel's ambassador to the United Nations and president of the Ben-Gurion University of the Negev; Brigadier General Yehuda Halevy, since his retirement, active as a fund raiser for Ben-Gurion University of the Negev; industrialist Shaul Eisenberg, founder of Israel Corporation; and Hebrew University professor

Ellis Joffe, arguably the world's leading academic authority on the Chinese military. After their departure from Shanghai, the activities of the Zionist organizations ceased, although individual Zionists lingered on through the mid-1950s.[36]

Conclusion

The Shanghai Zionist movement was a part of world Zionism but also had distinctive characteristics due to its Chinese context.

1. Reflecting similar developments elsewhere in the Diaspora, Shanghai Zionism was pluralistic: all the major movements, from Socialist to Revisionist, were represented in the city.[37]

2. The environment, which was not anti-Semitic, enabled Shanghai Zionists to take legal, nonviolent forms of action. In the 1930s and 1940s, Shanghai witnessed few anti-Semitic articles, and almost all of those derived from ethnic Germans, White Russians, and Japanese rather than from Chinese. Apart from the fact that Zionists were interned along with other enemy aliens during World War II, Shanghai Zionists were never persecuted for their specific political beliefs—unlike Zionists in Europe, Palestine, the Soviet Union, and its Eastern bloc allies. Shanghai Zionists freely published newspapers and magazines and held public meetings.

3. Shanghai Zionists maintained good relations with many of China's outstanding democratic and patriotic personalities (see chapter III.D.1 in this volume).

4. Shanghai Zionists enjoyed significant economic backing. In the early twentieth century, when Zionist organizations emerged in Shanghai, sympathetic Baghdadi Jews enjoyed world-class prosperity. Among them were eminent families like the Sassoons, Hardoons, Kadoories, Ezras, Abrahams, Arnholds, and Toegs. Although they held differing attitudes toward Zionism, they were basically supportive. At critical points in the development of the Shanghai Zionist movement, especially when European Jewish refugees swarmed into Shanghai, financial support from Baghdadi business circles was critical. The need to meet common threats caused the branches of Shanghai Zionism to cooperate and, on occasion, even unite. What distinguished the community was that Israel's birth combined with the draw of the West resulted in the peaceful and gradual emigration of almost the entire Jewish population.[38]

Shanghai Zionists and Zionist-Revisionists ultimately made small contribution to the establishment of the State of Israel. In so doing, their experience constitutes a unique chapter in the history of Western activity on the China coast.

Notes

An earlier version of portions of this paper appeared in English as *Pan* Guang, "Zionism in Shanghai, 1903–1949," *Studies in Zionism* 14, no. 2 (autumn 1993), pp. 169–81.

1. Haim Ben-Sasoon, ed., *A History of the Jewish People* (London: Weidenfeld and Nicholson, 1976), p. 1008.
2. *Wang* Qingyu, "Jiu Shanghai de youtairen" (The Jews in Old Shanghai) *Shanghai shehui kexueyuan xueshu jikan* (Quarterly Journal of the Shanghai Academy of Social Sciences), no. 2 (1987), p. 172.
3. *Betar in China 1929–1949: Commemorative anthology for the fiftieth anniversary of Betar, 1923–1973* (Israel, n.d., ca. 1971), p. 86.
4. Author interview with Leo Hanin, Los Angeles, June 9, 1992.
5. Shanghai Municipal Council, Annual Report, 1933, p. 68.
6. *Betar in China,* p. 87.
7. Hanin interview.
8. Rudolf Loewenthal, "The Religious Periodical Press in China," *Sinological Series* (Beijing), no. 57 (1940), pp. 258–59; Avraham Kaufman, "The Zionist Press in the Far East" (in Hebrew), n.d., n.p.
9. Loewenthal, "Religious," p. 259. See also Kaufman, "Zionist Press," *passim.*
10. Shanghai Municipal Police Dossier (SMPD) 4749, United States National Archives, Washington, DC.
11. Wang, "Jews in Old Shanghai," p. 170.
12. Alphons Kraemer, "Der Zionismus in der Immigration," [Zionism and Immigration] *Shanghai Herald,* German Language Supplement (SE), April 1946, p. 5.
13. Author interview with William Schurtman, New York, January 17, 1989.
14. See Elchonon Y. Hertzman, *Escape to Shanghai,* trans. Chaim U. Lipschitz (New York: Maznaim, 1984).
15. Ossie Lewin, ed., *Shanghai Jewish Almanac* (Shanghai, 1947); *Shanghai Echo,* p. 59. See also Kraemer, "Zionismus," *passim.*
16. Lord Lawrence Kadoorie, *"The Kadoorie Memoir"* Memorial (Hong Kong: Jewish Historical Society of Hong Kong, 1985), p. 82.
17. Herman Dicker, *Wanderers and Settlers in the Far East: A Century of Jewish Life in China and Japan* (New York: Twayne, 1962), p. 102. See also the name list of the leading board of the Committee for Assistance to Jewish Refugees from Eastern Europe.
18. YIVO Institute (New York) Shanghai File (YF) No. 52. See also Rena Krasno, "Jewish Publications in Shanghai During the First Half of the twentieth Century," *Points East* 6, no. 1 (March 1991), p. 7.
19. David Kranzler, *Japanese, Nazis and Jews: The Jewish Refugee Community of Shanghai 1938–1945* (New York: Yeshiva University Press, 1976), chap. 13. See also Lewin, *Shanghai,* p. 59; and "*Betar* Corner," in *Nasha Zhizn'* (Our Life) (in Russian), published every Friday from 1941 to 1949.
20. Gerd Kaminski and Else Unterrieder, *Von Osterreichern und Chinesen* [Regarding Austrians and Chinese]. (Vienna: Europaverlar, 1980), p. 791.
21. Author interview with Leon Ilutovich, New York, October 15, 1992.
22. Kranzler, *Japanese,* p. 534.
23. *Betar,* p. 88.
24. "Jews in Shanghai," one of an "Information Series" of pamphlets issued by the Institute of Jewish Affairs of World Jewish Congress, New York, February 1949, p. 5.
25. *Betar,* p. 90.
26. Ze'ev Kronish, "Impressions of Shanghai Jewry," *The Reconstructionist,* April 2, 1948, p. 15.

27. Author interview with Yechiel Dobekirer, New York, October 13, 1992.
28. *China Press,* April 23, 1947. See also *Tagar* (Struggle), May 1, 1947, pp. 3 and 15.
29. Wang, "Jews in Old Shanghai," p. 172.
30. *Betar,* p. 90.
31. Ibid., p. 109.
32. Ibid., pp. 90, 110.
33. Author interview with Ellis Joffe, Jerusalem, October 25, 1991.
34. Dalie Ofer, "The Israeli Government and Jewish Organizations: The Case of the Immigration of Jews from Shanghai," *Studies in Zionism* (Tel Aviv), 2, no. 1 (spring 1990), p. 79.
35. Joffe interview. See also Ofer, "Israeli," p. 67.
36. *Pan* Guang, "Zionism in Shanghai, 1903–1949," *Studies in Zionism* 14, no. 2 (autumn 1993), p. 181.
37. Ibid.
38. Ibid.

Chapter III.D.3

Who Can See a Miracle? The Language of Jewish Memory in Shanghai

Vera Schwarcz

Attachment to historical memory is a cornerstone of Jewish identity. It has ensured cultural continuity over scattered geographies. Those who survived the Diaspora as Jews were unwilling to silence the echo of remembering that bound them to Torah, to Jerusalem, to other Jews. It is not only the psalmist who warns, "If I forget you, oh Jerusalem, let my tongue cleave to my mouth." Every Jew who has been forced to leave home, to build a community in a strange land, has come to know the value of memorial roots. These roots are often slender, textually transmitted, and vulnerable to assimilation. And yet, as Abraham Heschel put it aptly: "We are a people in whom memory endures, in whom the present is inconceivable without moments gone by."[1]

The enduring impact of memory may be glimpsed in the experience of Jewish refugees in twentieth-century Shanghai. Here, in a far-flung corner of the Asian world, in the midst of a devastating war, Jews found refuge and cultural renewal. Their survival is not a historical accident. It is intentional in ways that mirror cultural continuity in Chinese tradition as well. Although Chinese culture has been more geographically anchored than the Jewish one, it too has endured over time as a result of conscious attachment to historical memory. In China, faithfulness to the ways of the ancients has been nurtured by Confucian sages rather than biblical prophets. And yet prophets and sages alike required their communities to value the legacy of the past as a source of individual solace and communal compassion.

These two disparate champions of historical memory were brought together on the cover of a 1991 booklet commemorating the wartime rescue of the Mirrer Yeshiva. On the winding path of an inkbrushed mountain stand two figures. Although their faces are indistinct, their garb embodies their worlds. The Asian scholar wears long robes and a straw hat. The student of the Talmud is clad in dark pants and a dark hat. The two men stand close together on the lonely mountain capped by one ragged pine—symbol of moral rectitude in Chinese art. Above them shines the moon and two messages in finely crafted calligraphy. The Chinese brush expresses a core belief of Confucian historiography: "Jianshan tianxia" (Seek to unify and benefit all under Heaven). In Hebrew script we read Rabbi Hillel's famous dictum: *Ukhshe'ani le'atzmi ma 'ani?* (If I am for myself alone, what good am I?)[2] Each man appears comforted by these few words from his own tradition—as if tradition allowed him to become more fully human, to understand others while remaining true to himself.

It is no accident that the Mirrer Yeshiva chose to recall its wartime experience through this distinctive symbolism. As the only institution of Jewish learning to be fully salvaged from the Holocaust, it bears witness to a distinctive history. Its institutional memory is significant beyond the circle of its own students and teachers, many of whom recall with vividness their years in Japan and China. The Mirrer Yeshiva's commitment to commemoration bespeaks a deeper Jewish commitment to recalling the past in order to guide and to inspire the present. In the words of Rabbi Yecheskel Leitner, who was himself a Mirrer student in China: "The miraculous rescue of the Mirrer Yeshiva, together with the remnants of other yeshivas, proved to be a Divine vehicle for translating the eternal Torah to a new continent, to open up the new era of post-Holocaust rebirth."[3]

To secular ears, Rabbi Leitner's words run counter to the belief that meaning is what we create rather than discover in history.[4] Nonetheless, for the religiously observant Jews who escaped from the Nazi persecution to Japan and then China, meaning is found in the memory of their refuge. Their lives—individually and collectively—were transformed, not just saved, by this forced migration out of Europe. In this way, they share Heschel's belief that to be a Jew is to be born through, not just into, history. Wrestling with historical events has enabled these Jews to deepen their identity. They looked out upon a world at war through Torah-informed eyes and found increasing meaning in Rabbi Hillel's question: "If I am for myself alone, what good am I?" A particular appreciation of Jewish tradition was their pathway to more universal understanding.

The Chinese thinker Mencius followed a similar road in developing his understanding of moral and historical responsibility. Rooted in the Confucian tradition that valorized the ancients, he searched historical precedent for moral guidelines in the present. Trying to make sense of the upheavals in the Warring States period (403–221 B.C.), not unlike the Jews who sought refuge in Shanghai and solace in Rabbi Hillel's teachings, Mencius wrote: "When the ancients found opportunity, they used their power to enhance the world. Deprived, they focused on self-cultivation. In obscurity a man makes perfect his own person, but in prominence he seeks to perfect the whole world (*jianshan tianxia*)."[5]

This determination to ground universal moral concerns in the fabric of a particular attachment to the "ancients" is captured on the cover of the Mirrer commemoration booklet. It also emerged strongly in the four interviews I conducted with survivors of the Shanghai experience. Rabbi Anshel Wainhaus (b. 1911), a former student of the Mirrer Yeshiva; Rabbi Solomon Schwartzman (b. 1917), a former student of the Mesivta Yeshiva; Rabbi Shimon Goldman (b. 1925), former student of the Lubavitch Yeshiva; and Dr. Robert Sokal (b. 1927), a graduate of Shanghai's St. John's University; all spoke about the enduring impact of the Shanghai years upon their identity as Jews. I also had an opportunity to view the videotaped testimony of Kathe K. (b. 1915), former coeditor of a German–Jewish newspaper in Shanghai.[6] Starting with this tapestry of voices, I have tried to surmise what was distinctively Jewish about the way in which survivors recall their years in Shanghai.

My goal in this project has not been to capture a representative sample of Jewish voices. Rather, as a China historian, I sought out a few individuals who would enable me to hear the inner meaning of the Shanghai experience. After a decade of oral history projects focused upon Chinese intellectuals traumatized by war and revolution,[7] I wanted to hear more from the Jewish side—from a cultural world that is intimate to me through my own family's experiences in Romania, yet a world that I never explored beyond my parents' fractured recollections. Hearing Jewish refugees talk about communal life in Shanghai, I was reminded of Chinese immigrants' deep feeling for their native place. Shanghai, the city that enabled Jews to survive the war, was also, in the language of a local gazetteer, "a hybrid place that mixes up people from all over China. The number of outsiders outnumbered natives. Accordingly, the people from each locality establish an association of fellow provincials to maintain their connections with each other . . . each established *huiguan* [native place associations]. From this it is possible to know that Chinese people have the moral excellence of loving the group."[8]

The "moral excellence of loving the group" is also the main thread in Jewish recollections of the war years in Shanghai. Russian, German, and Central European refugees carried native worlds with them to China. They, too, created trade, cultural, and religious associations in wartorn Shanghai. It is conscious attachment to the group and to Jewish tradition that sustained them. And this attachment is vividly embroidered in the process of remembrance. Consequently, I chose to dwell on the language in which the Jewish "excellence of loving the group" is expressed, rather than the details of escape from Europe.[9] What I tried to listen for is how Jews were affected by their experience and how they give meaning to their history in the process of testimony itself.

The voices of religiously observant Jews are especially valuable for understanding the ways in which Jewish tradition helps shape historical memory. These refugees were the ones who took to heart the biblical injunction to *zachor*—to remember. For Torah-literate Jews, memory is a God-given responsibility.[10] Although they comprised a small fraction of the Shanghai refugees, religious Jews from Poland and Russia brought with them a world of learning that affected many more—including the more assimilated, more numerous German refugees. They looked back to the Torah and out onto the Nazis and the Japanese with a double vision that enriches the memorial process even today. Pieces of the Shanghai episode continue to be assembled on the prophetic model of recollection that glorifies God by recounting His goodness in the details of personally experienced salvation. Faith and knowledge of biblical and rabbinic literature, in this sense, is the golden thread weaving the refugees' memories into a coherent and morally compelling narrative. This thread also runs through David Kranzler's scrupulously documented history of the Jewish experience in Shanghai. Kranzler concludes his introduction to *Japanese, Nazis, and Jews* with the often-used passage from Genesis in which Joseph tells his brothers: "Although you intended me harm, God intended it for the good, so as to bring about the present result—the survival of many people."[11] Unlike Kranzler, however, I am not a scholar of Jewish history. As a woman trained in Chinese history, I have less familiarity with the Torah-learning world that informs the memories of the rabbis I was privileged to interview. I began this journey into the language of Jewish memory armed only with a familiarity with the Chinese landscape and the details of Chinese history.

It is this China-centered perspective that allows me to look at the Jewish experience in Shanghai in terms of cultural interaction and resistance. Chinese and Jewish culture met and rubbed up against each other in rather harsh ways during the war years. Some of the Jewish refugees were more aware, more open to the Chinese culture around them, than others. Among religious Jews, ritual observance and dietary laws forbade deeper exploration of the Asian world in which they found themselves. On the Chinese side, war, poverty, and imperialist occupation did not allow Chinese culture to show its best face to European refugees. Nonetheless, rickshaw drivers, petty merchants, unemployed Confucian scholars, Polish yeshiva students, and German doctors were forced to live alongside one another in the alleys of Shanghai.

It is this cacophony of interactions and its enduring legacy that concerns me here. In the spirit of two sages beneath the scruffy pine, I also took the winding path of cultural memory to discover how Jews lived and thought in Shanghai. And I discovered that, as on the cover of the Mirrer commemorative booklet, Jews stood apart from the Asian landscape in which they found themselves thrust by war and persecution. Yet they became more deeply Jewish in Shanghai. Their memories bear out the truth of the other half of Rabbi Hillel's dictum: "If I am not for myself, who will be for me? If I am for myself alone, what am I?"

Oral History of Shanghai: A Journey Through Jewish Memory

I first heard the story of Rabbi Anshel Wainhaus's years in Shanghai through the ears of Dr. Dori Laub—the psychoanalyst who conducts interviews for Yale University's Fortunoff Video Archive for Holocaust Testimonies. In an essay on "Bearing Witness" Laub writes that Holocaust testimonies often begin when the victim "testifies to an absence, to an event that has not yet come into existence in spite of the overwhelming and compelling reality of its occurrence.... The listener, therefore is party to the creation of knowledge *de nuovo*.[12] Rabbi Wainhaus was not a victim of the Holocaust in the same sense as were Auschwitz inmates. He was a relatively privileged survivor who took part in the Mirrer Yeshiva's collective escape from Poland to Shanghai. And yet when he gave testimony for the Yale archives, Rabbi Wainhaus spoke with the same intensity as other Jews who have come forth to make sense of their war years in public. One sign of that determination not just to speak but to bear witness was apparent in the first moments of the interview. Dr. Laub invited the conservatively dressed rabbi to speak in Yiddish, the language of his youth and most Jewish learning in the Mirrer Yeshiva. Rabbi Wainhaus chose instead to speak in English—a clear sign that he intended to speak to subsequent generations that know little about the Yiddish-speaking world of his Polish childhood and even less about the rigors of Torah learning embodied by the Mirrer Yeshiva.

In English then—on camera as in his own home in Borough Park, where I met with him on July 24, 1991—Rabbi Wainhaus retells the "miracle" of the rescue of his school from the hamlet of Mir to the International Settlement in Shanghai. But this is not an institutional history. Rather, it is the memory of an individual who lived through extraordinary events and now pieces them together in front of a sympathetic listener. And so, along with the details of the "miracle" comes the *de nuovo* knowledge of Rabbi

Wainhaus's own distinctive journey from his parents' home in Poland to the Beth Aharon Synagogue on Museum Road in Shanghai.

The public history of the Mirrer Yeshiva begins in 1815 with the impact of enlightenment ideas upon Jewish institutions of higher learning. The highly intellectual current of the *haskala,* in turn, evoked a vigorous, rationalistic response within the observant community. The Mirrer Yeshiva represented this approach and became one of the most prestigious institutions of Talmudic scholarship in prewar Poland.[13] Rabbi Wainhaus's personal story, however, does not begin with the *haskala* but, rather, with 1939. In the safety of his home in Brooklyn, the eighty-year-old survivor dwells on the vulnerability of Polish Jews caught between the Soviet and German struggles for power. In the same way the Rabbis Schwartzman and Goldman also emphasized in their recollections, Anshel Wainhaus as a young man is drawn to Vilna [also known as Wilno and Vilnius —*Ed.*], the capital of a briefly independent Lithuania. It is in Vilna that the long journey to China begins. It begins with the good fortune of obtaining transit visas to Japan from *Sugihara* Chiune, the Japanese consul in Kovno [Kaunas] and ends with different strategies used to outwit the NKVD, the dreaded secret police of the Soviet Union.

Each man left behind a whole world. Each man lost parents and siblings, and that loss is the animating force for bearing witness today. Immaculately dressed and strong voiced when talking about world events or Talmud scholarship, Rabbi Wainhaus now speaks briefly, softly about a younger brother: "I had already obtained the life saving visa for him. . . . Then I tried to meet him at a train station. . . . No luck. This brother, with my mother and three other children left behind in Poland, was betrayed by a shepherd. They were all taken to the gas chambers."[14]

Rabbi Schwartzman also recalls the turning point in 1939, when he returned home as a recently demobilized soldier. We are sitting in the conference room of a New Haven synagogue when this energetic, clear-voiced seventy-four-year-old starts to recall the skinny young man who came home in 1939. Later, Rabbi Schwartzman shows me a photograph of himself as a young yeshiva student in Warsaw: The young boy's face is still beardless, his head covered by the square hat worn by Gerrer Hasidim. This young man, too, had awakened to the dangers of Jewish life in German-occupied Poland. He, too, decided to leave and seek safety through Lithuania. Like Rabbi Wainhaus, Rabbi Schwartzman did not find out about the fate of his family until after the war, when he stopped in Chicago on his way from Shanghai to New York: "My older brother Chaim, two sisters, and their spouses and children had been taken to the gas chambers, . . . all except a younger brother who was killed jumping off the transport train."[15]

Rabbi Shimon Goldman comes from the same Polish town of Shedlitz as Rabbi Schwartzman. In the comfort of his Crown Heights dining room, this soft-spoken survivor drifts into Yiddish often as he recalls the color of the wallpaper at the Schwartzman home after a Sabbath kiddush. The youngest of the three men (born in 1925), Rabbi Goldman was only fourteen when he fled from home out of his own initiative. Without the army experience of Rabbi Schwartzman and unsupported by the communal contacts of the Mirrer Yeshiva that organized Rabbi Wainhaus's escape, Shimon Goldman left stealthily one day, with just one extra layer of clothing on his back. Having witnessed the bombing of his hometown and the local rabbi's begging permission to bury the Jews killed in 1939, this precocious young man understood that Jewish life in German-occupied Poland had reached a dead end. How deadly that end would be, he found out only after the war, "when I learned that my parents died in the gas chambers."[16]

These three young men who were to come together in Shanghai seemed to share little with the German and Austrian refugees, who far outnumbered the Polish group in wartime China. Yet beyond the vast differences in religious observance lies a shared tale of fear and loss. The year 1939, the same year that witnessed the escape of the three young men from Poland, also saw the end of the known world for Robert Sokal in Vienna and for Kathe K., in Breslau, Germany (Wroclau, Poland in 1998). For the Polish Jews, the German bombing of Warsaw on the eve of Sukkot 1939 spelled the beginning of the end. For Dr. Sokal's father, the German occupation of the capital of Austria had brought disaster earlier. In the safety of his daughter's home in New Haven, the eminent biologist who relies on scientific reason for research as well as for recollection now speaks of unreasonable events: "My father was taken to Dachau and Buchenwald from July 1938 to February 1939 . . . so we knew we had to get out. We left for Shanghai two months after my father was released from the labor camp, in April 1939. In China, we moved in with an aunt and uncle who had preceded us to Shanghai."[17]

Kathe K. also arrived in Shanghai in 1939, but she was alone and disabled. Having suffered from cerebral palsy since childhood, this remarkably modern woman is nonetheless a kindred spirit of the young men who also left family and the known world to seek refuge in the alien alleys of Shanghai. Krystallnacht in 1938 had already demolished much of Kathe K.'s world in Breslau. By 1939 her younger brother had left on a children's transport to England, and three sisters had also found refuge abroad: "Finally my parents started to look around for a way to leave. But it was too late. . . . We were too late. . . . We were too late for everything, so my father tried to get us to Shanghai. That was the only way out."[18] When family funds proved too scanty for collective salvation, the young woman left for Shanghai alone.

Forty-five years later this vigorous sixty-nine-year-old survivor faces the videocamera with lively eyes behind dark glasses. Her cropped gray hair dances along with the animated tale while the disabled body remains rigid in its metal brace. Good humor and articulate precision mark Kathe K.'s recollection: "On the day I left, France was invaded; the war spread.... When I arrived in Shanghai, I had no one, I stood alone on the pier, not knowing what to do until a member of the greeting committee brought me to a 'Home,' a *heime* as we called them, a terrible place. I shared a room with six others, five of them deaf mutes. I decided I would not stay there. Not for me! I did not know where I would sleep but I would not go back there."[19]

Sheer willpower is the hallmark of survivors. As a disabled woman, Kathe K. had plenty of it. But willpower is not all. Mindfulness of the collective fate of the Jewish people adds an edge of passion—and significance—to the years in wartime China. Each survivor brought his or her separate pain along with the few belongings that accompanied them on this journey to a strange, often unheard-of country. For the religious young men leaving Poland, God showed the way through a series of miraculous "coincidences." For most German-speaking refugees, China was a place of adventure, dimly glimpsed—from German camp songs, as in the case of Robert Sokal. But, whether they were observant or not, Shanghai transformed the Jewishness of their lives greatly.

Dr. Sokal, for example, came from a highly assimilated family. His parents did not keep kosher, went to synagogue only on holidays, and sought to educate their son as an Austrian citizen. In China, his father's only contact with religious Jews occurred when yeshiva boys came to have their *tefillin* straps refurbished in the little shop below the family's apartments. Wrapping those leather straps, or phylacteries, around one's arm and forehead is a morning prayer ritual for Orthodox Jewish men. And yet Dr. Sokal interrupts our conversation just as I am about to pop the question of what difference China made to his family's Jewishness.

"You did not ask about *me*," the soft-spoken scientist interjects, "how *I* became more Jewish in Shanghai.... Until China, I had only the minimal Jewish education required by Austrian state law. We thought of ourselves as Austrians. Then we became stateless. In China I realized that Jewish identity transcends national boundaries. In China, being Jewish acquired a positive connotation.

"In Shanghai I became friends with an Orthodox boy from Germany. With him, I went to the Beth Aharon synagogue on Museum Road. In China, I joined a Zionist youth organization and planned to go to Israel.... In Shanghai I met all different kinds of Jews including a 'poor millionaire' from Iraq. My roommate at St. John's University was Polish. I learned how to read Yiddish from him. . . . Yes, in China, I became more Jewish than if we had stayed in Vienna before the war."[20]

Forging, maintaining, and transmitting a Jewish identity is a communal experience. It echoes what the Chinese gazetteer called the "moral excellence of loving the group." For Dr. Sokal this "moral excellence" included an exploration of religious ritual, Hebrew and Yiddish language, and Zionism in a way that went far beyond his parents' secularism. For the young men who came with the Mirrer Yeshiva to Shanghai, the forging of a Jewish commitment was an easier undertaking. They already knew how to speak Yiddish and how to pray in Hebrew. And yet for them, as for Dr. Sokal, Shanghai remains the high point of a strengthened sense of Jewish identity. Rabbi Anshel Wainhaus still prays every day with a group of men who shared the Mirrer experience in Shanghai. In Borough Park, Brooklyn, more than four decades after their communal refuge in China, aged Yeshiva graduates gather to share intense Talmudic discussions. "We studied with more intense concentration in China, published more in Shanghai than we ever thought possible," Rabbi Wainhaus insists, "and we could not have done that alone. We had a mission. Nothing happened which was an accident. We were taken to China for a reason: to get ready for Jewish life, Jewish learning after the Holocaust."[21]

Rabbi Wainhaus did not remain a Torah teacher after the war. Rather, he became a businessman with strong connections to the Talmud-studies world and to the men who shared his formative years in China. Dr. Robert Sokal did not end up going to Israel as he had planned while in China. He married the Chinese woman who was his schoolmate at St. John's University and raised their children to be Jewish in New York. Yet, Dr. Sokal, too, maintains close friendships with comrades from the China years. Because memory matters, it takes on density in proportion to conscious reflection upon the significance of the Shanghai interlude. In the words of Kathe K., who was made to stop for six weeks in San Francisco after the war: "They wanted us to stay so that we [could] forget the years we suffered. You *cannot* forget in six weeks. I did not forget! . . . Now I could write not only one book but three books about that time!"[22]

And what about us, those who never went through the war in China? What do we hear through the voices bearing testimony to the refuge in Shanghai? Minimally, that history makes a difference to the evolving meanings of Jewish identity. And those meanings are more complex than we might have imagined. The spiritual barriers between religiously observant and non-religious Jews, for example, become more permeable through the perspective of memory. Dr. Sokal and Rabbi Wainhaus probably never spoke to each other in the alleys of the Hongkew ghetto. The young man riding his bike to St. John's University each day might have had little to say to the bearded young Torah students who came into the shop where tefillin were repaired. But Rabbi Wainhaus was not one of those bearded Jews. In one of the photographs he shared with me during our interview, I glimpsed—with surprise—a clean-shaven, hatless young man astride a marble turtle in a park in Shanghai.

Was this a Mirrer Yeshiva student in China? Then Rabbi Wainhaus's Russian wife, Bella, brings out more photographs. One striking one shows four Mirrer comrades in Poland: They are still clean shaven, still hatless, still with a fiercely intellectual look in their eyes. Their glance across the decades demands that we, the hearers of their tale, do not dismiss their insistence upon meaning in Jewish history as the delusion of old world fundamentalists. These are distinctly modern men, who, like Dr. Sokal, are intensely alert to the enduring significance of their years in China.

With Shanghai in Mind

Wartime Shanghai was not an optimal vantage point from which to understand and appreciate Chinese culture. Not surprisingly, the Jewish refugees had little opportunity and not much incentive to stray beyond the boundaries of the foreign concessions or beyond the parameters of the ghetto set up in 1943. From their forcibly limited perspective, European Jews might readily understand Barbara Tuchman's apology in her introduction to the book on General Stilwell's career in China (which overlaps in time with that of the refugees):

> I am aware that this book by the nature of its subject does not do justice to China and the Chinese people. Because it concentrates, especially in the second half, on low points in China's history and on the military function which has never been of high repute in China, the negative aspects predominate. The likeableness, the artistic vision, the philosophic mind, the strength of character, intelligence, humor and capacity for work which have put the Chinese in the forefront of the world's civilized people, have not come through in proper proportion.[23]

Most Jews in China did not have General Stilwell's familiarity with the Chinese language. They did not count Chinese intellectuals among their friends. They were largely unaware that the same city in which they endured great economic hardships was also a "lonely island" for Chinese laborers who dared to strike against the Japanese, for Nationalist politicians who plotted military resistance, and for writers like *Zhen* Zhenduo, who mourned the spiritual depredation of his countrymen under the Japanese occupation.[24] Few of the Jewish refugees knew about the loneliness and misery of patriotic Chinese. Instead, they crowded into small alleys surrounded by fellow Jews and impoverished, uneducated natives who lived day to day through bitter strength—*ku li*. It was these "coolies," starving children, and dead bodies left out to rot in the night that dominate the Shanghai of the refugee's mind.

One Jewish artist captured a corner of this utterly unglamorous world in a drawing entitled "Life in the Lanes of Hongkew." Reproduced in David Kranzler's book, this image centers on a little boy with split pants relieving himself in the open street. An angry Chinese mother drags her daughter away from this all-too-familiar scene while a German Jewish family in the background rushes out to receive an envelope from the alley's postman. The European refugees grasp that piece of paper as if it were a life line to a world of cleanliness and material well-being left behind. Above the anticipation-filled Jews hang tattered Chinese robes—a concrete reminder of the new and strange world in which these Europeans now found themselves.[25]

The stench-filled alleys that Jews were forced to inhabit during the days of the Hongkew ghetto led Polish refugees to look back with nostalgia to their brief stay in Japan. Rabbi Shimon Goldman, for example, recalls fondly the civility of Japanese women who started bowing to the yeshiva students, assuming that their praying gestures were a form of greeting commonly used among polite Japanese. "Also I recall the shock of stores: wide open, no owner nearby. No one dared to take anything, such was the fear and respect for the law."[26] Rabbi Wainhaus also emphasized the cleanliness and politeness that the Mirrer Yeshiva encountered in Japan as well as the welcomed supply of food after the long suffering endured on the train through Siberia. "I recall how impressed we were to be met by a Japanese professor, Kahzuka [Professor Setzuso (Abraham) *Kotsuji*] I think was his name, who spoke Hebrew and was a member of the royal family. He pressed our case with the Japanese officials and eventually converted to Judaism. He took on the name Abraham and asked to be buried in Israel."[27]

No such Jewishly literate Chinese greeted the refugees in Shanghai. They were not greeted by blue and white flags as they had been in Kobe, or by plentiful food. Certainly they were not given spacious houses with stone tiles like the one that housed the Mirrer Yeshiva in Japan. Instead, German refugees like Kathe K. were taken to crowded, unsanitary group "homes" by harried American aid officials. After the clean streets of Kobe, the littered alleys of wartime Shanghai provoked a rude awakening that grew more acute each day: "I will never forget the first morning I went out and saw the bodies of dead children left out because they had died of starvation or had frozen overnight," whispers Rabbi Wainhaus after he finishes talking about the exuberance of emigration out of Soviet Russia. "Then we had to get used to riding rickshaws. Imagine, using a human being as an animal. We were not trained for that, it is not the Torah way.... But you get used to it after a while. You realize that it helps a poor man make a living."[28] Dr. Sokal also recalls the human debris encountered on his way to the British "public school" that prepared young men for Oxford and Cambridge: "Each day one would pass three, four bodies on the way."[29]

Rabbi Solomon Schwartzman dwells more on how one survived life in Shanghai and less on the death so prevalent in the streets. He describes with excitement one of his own survival tactics: selling a certain kind of bowler hat, unsuited for religious Jews, to the rickshaw drivers in his corner of Hongkew: "For days after this business venture, I took delight in seeing our hats grow more and more popular among rickshaw pullers in other parts of Shanghai."[30] Being curious about other corners of life in China, Rabbi Schwartzman also ventured to look at an opium den and saw for himself the wasted lives of those who tried to forget the war by responding to hawkers peddling the pleasures of oblivion. He ventured one day to the outskirts of the city, far beyond the foreign settlements: "There I saw Chinese huts—no windows, just newspapers on the wall. So utterly poor, so utterly primitive."[31]

In contrast to the Chinese poverty glimpsed through a hut window or inscribed on the stiff body of the abandoned dead, Jewish refugees lived relatively cultured lives. The Mirrer Yeshiva was most fortunate in this respect. Its students arrived in Shanghai from Japan before the High Holidays in 1941 to find an empty synagogue with exactly the right number of seats to accommodate them. Both Rabbi Wainhaus in his conversation and Yecheskel Leitner in his written memoir emphasize this extraordinary "coincidence": that the great Beth Aharon synagogue—built by the highly assimilated Kadoorie family—turned out to meet the precise needs of the Polish yeshiva. It had two kosher kitchens, and 250 seats for students to study and was in a convenient location on Museum Road. Thus the Mirrer group was able to go on immediately with its prewar Jewish purpose. The large, imposing, mostly unused *beth keneset* (hall of worship) was now turned into a spacious *beth midrash* (study hall).

Unlike German refugees such as Kathe K., who came alone and was destitute, Mirrer students did not have to suffer the humiliations of a group home. They were also able to resume a rigorous Talmudic curriculum more rapidly than the two smaller Hasidic yeshivas, the Lubliner and the Lubavitch (numbering thirty or so persons each), which had to find accommodations in the already crowded working class district of Hongkew and had to hire special trained cooks for the kosher requirements of their students. The Mirrer Yeshiva was also more vigorously supplied by funds from abroad than the other smaller institutions of Jewish learning. In New York, Rabbi Abraham Kalmanowitz of the Vaad Hatzalah rescue organization was tireless in fundraising for the Mirrer students in China, going so far as to break the Sabbath prohibition against riding in a car in order to go from synagogue to synagogue asking for funds. All this because he believed that the predicament of the Mirrer Yeshiva in Shanghai was a case of *pekuach nefesh* (the salvation of a life in danger).[32] As a result of Rabbi Kalmanowitz's energetic efforts, the Mirrer students were able to find individual accommodations with respectable Jewish families, they were able to have a proper Sabbath meal most of the time—all privileges that were unavailable for other yeshiva students, who were not entitled to funds from the Vaad Hatzalah.

Money, however, was not the only prerequisite for spiritual life among the Jews of Shanghai. Certainly it helped provide a minimum stipend needed for ongoing study and ritual observance. But, through the eye of memory, the presence of two great religious leaders also accounts for the vitality of Jewish life in wartime China. Rabbi Meir Ashkenazi, the leader of the Russian Jewish community in Shanghai from 1927 to 1947, certainly imprinted himself deeply upon the life and imagination of refugees in Shanghai. Although he himself was a Lubavitch Hasid, Rabbi Ashkenazi was scrupulously fair to all the various communities that congregated in Shanghai during the war. His white-bearded face was familiar to Anshel Wainhaus and Solomon Schwartzman as well as to the young Lubavitch follower Shimon Goldman. Each had occasion to be invited for a Sabbath meal at the home of this distinguished leader; each had occasion to hear him share his Torah learning.

An equally powerful reminder of the resilience of the Jewish spirit in times of adversity was the presence among the refugees from Poland of Rabbi Shimon Kalish, known as the Amshenover Rebbe. Not so publicly visible as Rabbi Ashkenazi, the Amshenover Rebbe was a different kind of "pillar of light."[33] He shared the hardships of the yeshiva students in their escape from Poland and the Soviet Union. He blessed their prayers and study sessions with fervent affirmation of life, even in the midst of fear, bombings, and material deprivations. Rabbi Goldman recalls one morning when the physically small but spiritually towering rabbi stamped his foot on the ground and corrected a student's prayer, "God who causes one to *live* . . . is not just the King who causes one to die."[34]

In May 1942, when the first volume of the Talmudic tractate *Gittin* appeared as an offprint in Shanghai, a public celebration was organized at the Russian Jewish club. Although bombs had already fallen on Pearl Harbor and although Shanghai itself had already been damaged by bombs from

Japanese planes, the Jewish community celebrated the continuation of Torah study with fervor. Rabbi Kalish was at the heart of the celebration and bore witness to the joy of spiritual life in spite of—and especially in the midst of—a world gone mad. In the words of a 1942 observer: "Those who did not witness the Amshenover Rabbi and Yeshiva students dance at receiving this marvelous gift had never seen true Jewish joy and felt the secret of the Jew's eternity."[35]

Retrospectively, this briefly glimpsed "secret" of Jewish endurance grows more compelling. Rabbi Wainhaus, like Rabbi Goldman and Rabbi Schwartzman, emphasized the extraordinary determination it took to maintain an unchanging study schedule in spite of all the dislocation. It was as if the war, with its fearful news, with the dead bodies on the streets of Shanghai, with the material deprivations of the German refugees, paled before the urgency of Torah study. Isolation from news about the war in Europe certainly helped this feat of religious commitment. But the "secret" of Jewish endurance is not found in Japanese-imposed isolation from world events. Rather it lies in willful concentration upon the ultimate sources of Jewish life. Rabbi Wainhaus talked at length about his impression of how the Allies' war with Japan spread to China and how, even after the bombing of Pearl Harbor, he heard bombing over Shanghai and could even remember an Italian boat overturned in the river. Every day on his way to the study hall at the Beth Aharon Synagogue, Anschel Wainhaus had seen the overturned boat, yet what mattered was not the battered present but the eternally compelling Talmud. The present, though manifestly there in the reminder of the scuttled ship, did not ignite the same passionate curiosity as the texts to be studied, to be freshly appropriated in Shanghai.

Dr. Robert Sokal also recalled the upturned boat. He even recalled its name—*Conte Verde*—and the explosion of shrapnel that had accompanied the Japanese bombings of Allied ships in Shanghai harbor. But for him, too, what mattered was something else—a life of study, though in mostly secular subjects. An interest in biology, in Zionism, and in learning more about other Jews in Shanghai consumed Dr. Sokal as much as Talmud study riveted the Mirrer Yeshiva students. A capacity to turn inward—to books, to Jewish community, to newspaper publishing, and to Yiddish musicals and theater productions—all this is part of the "secret" of Jewish endurance.

In Abraham's Footsteps: Jewish Historical Consciousness

Jewish refugees in Shanghai are living proof of the will to survive as a distinctive community. Whereas Jews in India, or Chinese Jews in Kaifeng, had centuries to negotiate strategies of acculturation, those who escaped to Shanghai had been cast upon China's shores in one dark wave occasioned by European anti-Semitism. The historical pressures that drove Jews out of Germany, the Soviet Union, and Central Europe, however, do not explain the vitality of Jewish life in China. The forcible ghettoization of different Jews in the summer of 1943 does not account for the rich texture of communal solidarity or the vivid density of refugee recollections. Rather, the ability—indeed, determination—to anchor the novel, and at times humiliating, Shanghai experience in the language of tradition accounts for a vigorously *Jewish* survival.

In Shanghai, unlike in the European death camps, many aspects of life went on relatively unassaulted by war. Whereas all efforts at sense-making were, in the words of Jean Amery "emptied by Auschwitz,"[36] in China new meaning could be found in old models of cultural survival. In the wake of the European nightmare, it is difficult to find inspirational messages in the testimony of survivors. Lawrence Langer, who has researched hundreds of hours of such oral testimonies, has made a very powerful argument against those who would heroicize the experience of Jews who survived the death camps in Europe. Instead, he suggests, we need new narrative and conceptual tools to grasp the utter "ruin of memory."[37]

Testimonies by Jews who found refuge in Japan and China, by contrast, do not convey this sense of inner devastation. Instead, there is a sense of pride, of exhilaration at having snatched spiritual victory from the jaws of a life-denying juggernaut. Rabbi Schwartzman, for example, used *lech lecha* as the historical precedent that inspired his escape out of the European nightmare. *Lech lecha* are the first words that God speaks to Abraham in Genesis II.1: "Get thee out of thy country and from thy kindred and from thy father's house into a land that I will show you." Recalling this passage, the soft-spoken, elderly gentleman moves back to the time before he left Poland: "I had pleaded with my family," he mourns in retrospect, "I argued with my uncle about the need to leave the old country. But my uncle was well established, he had a shop. He was making a good living. He would not leave."[38] Although a whole community had studied the sacred texts, only a few of its youth was actually willing to follow in Abraham's footsteps—to actually forsake the familiar world of the Jewish shtetl for unknown Asian lands.

Rabbi Wainhaus, recalling a talk by Professor Kotsuji Setzuso to the Mirrer students in Kobe, also dwells on *lech lecha*. The marvel of this "descendant of the Mikado royal family" who addressed yeshiva students in Hebrew increased their sense of purpose: to bear witness to God's will in an unfamiliar land.[39] The Japanese linguist who later chose to name himself

Abraham understood enough already by 1942 to welcome the Mirrer Yeshiva with this particular passage from Genesis that demands displacement of the first Jew.

Shimon Goldman, the fourteen-year-old boy who left the town of Shedlitz in Poland, was also following in Abraham's footsteps. He, too, picked up and left the familiar world of his parents and ended up in the strange-smelling, crowded streets of Shanghai. This willingness to go—and, more significantly, to look back decades later and reconnect one's own scattered actions to a tradition of Jewish self-becoming—is the essence of a distinctive historical consciousness. Among Lubavitcher Hasidim, this sense of mission finds expression in the *Ha yom yom*—a collection of daily teachings that insists "wherever our feet tread, it is all in order to cleanse and purify the world with words of Torah and *tefilah* (prayer). We, all of Israel, each of us as Divine Providence has decreed for us. None is free from this sacred task placed on our shoulders."[40]

Emphasis on this "sacred task" sets Jews apart. It also links them, indirectly to be sure, to the Confucian tradition with its emphasis upon the sacred burden of recollection. Both the Chinese and Jewish traditions carry a wealth of memory metaphor that cements the individual's connection to communal continuity. In Hebrew, for example the word *zachor* connotes simultaneously "memory" and "permanent engraving." In Chinese the character *ming* means to "engrave" and is also the root of *minggan*—"to remember with gratitude." Both traditional Judaism and Confucianism assume that individual life gains meaning through *zachor* and *minggan*—through sacred connectedness to the communal past.[41]

Few Jewish refugees in Shanghai had time or interest to tease out these cultural and linguistic echoes. Yet they had taken refuge in a culture with a fierce attachment to the ways of the ancients. Without reference to divine providence, Confucius had emphasized the need to "love the ancients," to bear witness to the wisdom of the past in new and changing circumstances.[42] The heirs of Confucius became China's greatest historians, antiquarians, poets, and essayists. Their passionate connection to the Chinese past endured even in wartorn Shanghai. The writer *Zheng* Zhenduo, for example, devoted his time to finding and buying old books. At the very hour when Japanese aggression threatened to destroy his country, Zheng used whatever little money he had to buy and preserve old books—his people's "national treasures."[43]

The obsession with preserving books, preserving one's cultural identity *through books* was thus not limited to Jews alone. Zheng Zhenduo might have used money spent on buying ancient Chinese texts to feed a few of the thousands of beggar children in Shanghai. Yet he sought to preserve something else. He was not immune to the physical deprivations of his countrymen; rather, he knew that, dispossessed of their tradition, they would be even more crushed by the Japanese. Without *minggan,* without *zachor,* without textually anchored memory, survival becomes more difficult, maybe less meaningful.[44]

War-ravaged Shanghai was a world in which Jewish as well as Chinese refugees tried to preserve themselves and their cultural identity. For the Chinese, the predicament of having become refugees in their own country was particularly painful. This world of physical and spiritual deprivation surfaces briefly in Dr. Sokal's recollection when he speaks about a Chinese language teacher at his British preparatory school. "He was a highly educated old gentleman, who had been an official of the Qing dynasty consulate in New York. Now he had to make a living by teaching language to largely uninterested foreign boys in Shanghai. I remember the day he was forced to substitute for an English class. And he surprised us all by his perfect recitation of passages from Shakespeare's *Tempest.*"[45]

The pathos of Chinese dislocation, however, touched the lives of Jewish refugees only lightly, like the brushing of sleeves in a crowded street. Chinese intellectuals like Zheng Zhenduo and Dr. Sokal's language teacher lived on their lonely island while Jews remained enclosed in their cacophonous world. One sign of the relative insularity of Jewish culture in Shanghai turned out to be food. Recalling his meals in the kosher restaurants in Hongkew, Rabbi Schwartzman goes on to say: "The only time I had Chinese food was at a friend's wedding, where the Russian-trained cook made kosher chop suey."[46] Dr. Sokal, who did not observe the laws of kashruth, also recalls that he did not eat native food "until much later, at the house of my Chinese in-laws."[47]

As if the boundaries of *kashrut* (observance of dietary laws) were not solid enough, the geography of Shanghai also kept Jewish refugees far from Chinese life. Dr. Sokal, whose wife was a Shanghai native, tells me that he never ventured to the Chinese part of the city during the war. The foreign settlements, and later the Hongkew ghetto, were worlds onto themselves. Culturally curious refugees such as Kathe K. did glimpse bits of China before 1943: "Such wonderful buildings! Such wonderful paintings! Such beautiful gardens!" Forty years after the war, she still takes great pleasure in retelling her China "adventures" for posterity. In her video testimony for the Yale archives, she speaks with pride about the adversities she overcame as a disabled refugee in Shanghai. In China, Kathe K. became truly self-sufficient. In China, she met her husband and became coeditor of a German Jewish newspaper. In China, she learned what it means to be part of an endangered community of stateless Jews. In China, as she phrased it: "I became a survivor."[48]

To survive *as a Jew* required the ability to live in different geographies and disparate temporalities both at once. Religiously observant Jews had to negotiate these complexities with extra care. They continued to mark time in China according to the Jewish calendar. Holidays like Rosh Hashanah, Yom Kippur, and the weekly Sabbath figure prominently in the recollections of those who used Jewish temporality to strengthen cultural identity in a foreign land. On the boat from Russia to Japan, for example, Rabbi Wainhaus and the other Mirrer students celebrated Purim with extra zest, using it as an occasion to mark not only victory over Haman long ago but also triumph over the Soviet secret police. In Kobe, yeshiva students became engaged in debates about when exactly to celebrate the Sabbath because of the change of time occasioned by crossing the international date line. Such disputes underscore the refugees' determination to transcend local time and local conditions in order to forge links with the world of Jewish tradition.

This ability to live in more than one world and to draw from each what was needed to strengthen identity is evoked vividly on the cover of Yecheskel Leitner's book on the Mirrer escape to China. In the far backdrop burn two candle sticks. The brass candle holders are clearly Chinese, but the flames are an unmistakable reminder of the Jewish Sabbath. In front of the candle sticks are laid out three thoroughly Chinese objects: a piece of embroidered silk, a fan, and a celadon spice jar. The candle light of Jewish observance casts a warm glow in each. The foreground is reserved for a worn copy of the open Talmud. The binding of the large text is frayed, but the book holds. Literally and figuratively, the text with its layer upon layer of commentary embodies the attachment of Jews to their tradition.[49]

It is textually anchored memory that gives increased coherence to the survival experience in China. Without the connecting fabric of Jewish history, without conscious reference to its sense-making potential, the Shanghai years might have been just another interlude in the long record of Jewish persecution. Instead, however, they take on a new light in the conclusion of Rabbi Wainhaus's testimony for the Yale Video Archives:

> They ask, why is. In old times happened miracles. We don't see miracles now. People ask. I tell you: Old times also did not see it. For instance, the story of Haman and Ahashverosh, it happened in twenty years. One year a fraction. Five years a fraction. Here Vashti killed. Here Esther taken away. Ten years later Mordechai nominated. It is only a fraction. But when you are back of it already, look with an eye on all twenty years, you see a miracle. The same thing with us. When we went through it, who can see a miracle?[50]

These words capture the power of precedent. Who can see a miracle indeed? Rabbi Wainhaus suggests that "miracles" happen to those prepared to see them. This same conviction comes through in Rabbi Schwartzman's insistence that the concluding passage from Psalm 27 gave him the inner strength to live through his years of refuge in Asia: *Kave el Hashem, chazak veyaametz libecha, vekave el Hashem* (Hope in God, strengthen yourself and he will give you courage, hope in God).[51] Why the repeated injunction to hope? Is it not enough that God gave the Jews strength to survive? No. It is clear from the recollections of these Shanghai refugees that courage had to be rooted in a double-layered hope: hope that they would escape the ravage that fell upon their kin in Europe and hope that their survival would augment the possibilities for Jewish life after the war. Having come face to face with anti-Semitism, the Jews who congregated in Shanghai did more than survive. They forged a way of living out of adverse circumstances that was, in the words of Rabbi Wainhaus, nothing short of a "miracle."

For those of us who were born after those terrible years, the "miracle" takes on yet another meaning. We, who are heirs to Jewish assimilation in the West, must find a way to return to the sources that animate the refugees' ability to make sense of senseless deprivations. When we manage to grasp fully Rabbi Hillel's question—*Ukhshe'ani le'atzmi ma 'ani?* (If I am for myself alone, what good am I?)—we will have understood something important about the distinctive nature of Jewish humanism. A concrete appreciation of this particularistic concern will enable us to understand Chinese humanism better in turn. *Jianshan tianxia*—(seek to unify all under Heaven) becomes practicable only in a world in which Chinese history and Jewish memory each have their due.

Notes

1. Abraham Joshua Heschel, *Israel: An Echo of Eternity* (New York: Knopf, 1969) p. 128.

2. *Pirkei-avot* (Ethics of the Fathers), chapter I, verse 14. My translation follows the Art Scroll Version (New York: Mesorah, 1984), p. 13.

3. Yecheskel Leitner, *Operation: Torah Rescue* (Jerusalem: Feldheim, 1987), p. 11.

4. The belief that providence triumphed in the twentieth century also runs against post-Holocaust Jewish theologians who assert that divine guardianship of history was terminally questioned in Auschwitz. The foremost representative of this latter view is Emil L. Fackenheim, whose book, *God's Presence in History* (New York: Harper, 1970), discusses traditional Jewish views about providential history as well as the doubts ignited by the Holocaust.

5. Mencius, "Xinzheng" (rectifying the heart)—which is also the name of Book VII of the Chinese classic *Mengzi*. My translation differs slightly from the one found in *Mencius,* trans. D.C. Lau (New York: Penguin Books, 1970), p. 183.

6. The Fortunoff Video Archive for Holocaust Testimonies at the Yale University Library has a policy of preserving the anonymity of interviewees by releasing *first*

names and last initials only. I am especially indebted to Joanne Rudof, archivist of the Fortunoff Video Archive, for bringing the China interviews to my attention.

7. The most comprehensive presentation of these oral history projects is found in Vera Schwarcz, *Time for Telling Truth Is Running Out: Conversations with Zhang Shenfu* (New Haven: Yale University Press, 1992).

8. *Li* Weiqing, *Shanghai xiangtuzhi* (Shanghai Local Gazetteer), item 153 (Shanghai, 1907), quoted and discussed in Bryna Goodman, "The Moral Excellence of Loving the Group" (unpublished manuscript), n.d.

9. Other historical studies, notably David Kranzler, *Japanese, Nazis and Jews: The Jewish Refugee Community of Shanghai, 1938–1945* (New York: Yeshiva University Press, 1976), and Marvin Tokayer and Mary Swarz, *The Fugu Plan: The Untold Story of the Japanese and the Jews During World War II* (New York: Paddington Press, 1979), explore the details of the flight from Europe and of the Hongkew ghetto with much insight.

10. For a fuller discussion of the role of memory in Jewish religious consciousness, see Bernard Childs, *Memory and Tradition in Israel* (London: Allenson, 1962), and Yosef Yerushalmi, *Zachor* (Seattle: University of Washington Press, 1982).

11. Kranzler, *Japanese, Nazis and Jews*, p. 17.

12. Shoshana Feldman and Dori Laub, *Testimony: Crises of Witnessing in Literature, Psychoanalysis and History* (New York: Routledge, 1992), p. 57.

13. For a fuller history of the Mirrer Yeshiva in Poland, see Yosef D. Epshtayn, "Yeshivot Mir" (the Mirrer Yeshiva), in *Institutions of Higher Learning in Europe: Their Development and Destruction,* ed. Samuel K. Mirsky (New York: Ogen, 1965), pp. 87–132. I am especially indebted to Professor Jonathan Goldstein, who made a copy of this essay available to me.

14. Author interview with Rabbi Anshel Wainhaus, July 24, 1991. This particularly painful moment does not come up in the video testimony for the Yale archives. I was able to touch upon it briefly, only because Rabbi Wainhaus's son, Rabbi Alvin Wainhaus, was kind enough to speak with me before the interview in Borough Park. It was the son who first broke the silence surrounding the loss of his father's brother.

15. Author interview with Rabbi Solomon Schwartzman, January 29, 1992. The return home from the army is also vividly recalled in Rabbi Solomon Schwartzman's video testimony for the New York Holocaust Museum, recorded on November 27, 1990.

16. Author interview with Rabbi Shimon Goldman, February 23, 1992. I am indebted to Rabbi Solomon Schwartzman and to Dr. Lawrence Harris for helping me locate Rabbi Goldman in Crown Heights and thus open up for me the distinctive voice of a Hasidic student who journeyed to China with the remnants of the Lubavitch Yeshiva.

17. Author interview with Dr. Robert Sokal, February 28, 1992. I am indebted to Hannah Sokal Holmes, Dr. Sokal's daughter, and to her husband, Dr. Oliver Holmes, for arranging this interview in their own home.

18. "Kathe K.," T-292 (10:32), Fortunoff Video Archive for Holocaust Testimonies, Yale University Library. This interview was taped on June 25, 1984.

19. Ibid. (20:50).

20. Sokal interview.

21. Wainhaus interview.

22. "Kathe K." T-292 (1:10:00–1:20:26).

23. Barbara Tuchman, *Stilwell and the American Experience in China* (New York: Norton, 1980), p. xiii.

24. For a fuller discussion of the Chinese experience in wartime Shanghai, see *Tao Juyin, Gudao jianwen* (Life on lonely island) (Shanghai: Renmin chubanshe, 1979).

"Lonely Island" is the name used by patriotic Chinese intellectuals to describe their life in Japanese-occupied Shanghai.

25. Kranzler, *Japanese, Nazis and Jews,* p. 614.

26. Goldman interview; see also Abraham *Kotsuji, From Tokyo to Jerusalem* (New York: Bernard Geis Associates, 1964).

27. Wainhaus interview.

28. Ibid.

29. Sokal interview.

30. Schwartzman interview.

31. Ibid.

32. Rabbi Abraham Kalmanowitz, *Letters and Documents* (New York: Mirrer Yeshiva, 1962).

33. Rabbi Shimon Goldman has recorded his recollections of the Amshenover Rebbe years in China in "Amod Ohr" ("A Pillar of Light"), *Kfar Chabad* (November 13, 1991), pp. 22–24.

34. Ibid. p. 23.

35. A Polish journalist quoted in Kranzler, *Japanese, Nazis and Jews,* p. 434. Tractate Gittin opens with a lengthy discussion of the laws of divorce in foreign lands and concludes with God's grief over the dissolution of first marriages. It was of particular significance to Jewish refugees who could readily identify with earlier periods of exile and the need to preserve Jewish law in inhospitable lands.

36. Jean Amery was Primo Levi's bunkmate in Auschwitz. He is the author of *At the Mind's Limits* (New York: Simon & Schuster, 1986), which gives a devastating account of the intellectual's spiritual defeat in the face of the illogic of the death camps.

37. Lawrence Langer, *Holocaust Testimonies* (New Haven: Yale University Press, 1991), pp. 162–206.

38. Schwartzman interview.

39. Wainhaus interview.

40. *Ha Yom Yom: 5 Adar 1* (Daily teachings: 5th day of Adar 1) (New York: Kehot, 1980), p. 117.

41. For a preliminary comparison of Chinese and Jewish memory metaphors, see Vera Schwarcz, "Mnemosyne Abroad: Reflections on the Chinese and Jewish Commitment to Remembrance," *Points East* 6, no. 3 (October 1991), pp. 1–16.

42. The sacred meanings of memory in Chinese tradition are discussed by Stephen Owen in *Remembrances: The Experience of the Past in Classical Chinese Literature* (Cambridge: Harvard University Press, 1986), pp. 13–15.

43. *Zheng* Shenduo, *Zhiju sanji* (Random reminisces of life in hibernation) (Shanghai: Renmin chubanshe, 1951).

44. This concern with meaningful survival led observant Jews in Shanghai to seek out offset publishers such as *Chow* Si-tsing of 220 Szechuan Road, who reproduced for them much-needed prayerbooks and of the Talmud. One of the books from the Shanghai years that Rabbi Schwartzman showed me with care and pride is a Torah commentary by Alexander Zisha Friedman, who died in the Warsaw Ghetto uprising. Friedman's work *Torah Kval* (The Torah Source) lived on among the Shanghai Jews as part of a collection entitled "Migulei Poland" (Refugees from Poland).

45. Sokal interview.

46. Schwartzman interview.

47. Sokal interview.

48. "Kathe K.," T-292 (54:52).

49. This richly textured evocation stands in marked contrast to the cover of Rabbi

Elochon Y. Hertzman's recollection of the Mirrer Yeshiva's years in Shanghai. Published in 1981, only six years before the Leitner work, the book shows on its jacket a fear-ridden Jew, who is hugging and running with a Torah scroll on the outer edges of a walled Chinese city. The Jew, like the Chinese coolie in vague lines behind him, seems to rise out of a nightmare—a time of rushed flight.

50. "Anshel W.," T-612 (22:13), Fortunoff Video Archive for Holocaust Testimonies, Yale University Library. This interview was conducted by Dr. Dori Laub on August 11, 1985.

51. Telephone conversation with Rabbi Solomon Schwartzman, August 16, 1992.

Concluding Essay
Jews and China: Past and Present Encounters

Benjamin I. Schwartz

Stories of encounters between disparate human groups separated from one another by geography as well as by enormously diverse cultures and histories will always retain their fascination. They not only provide rich material for comparative reflections in every area of human experience but also force us to think hard about the very vexing problem of the "otherness" of other cultures. Such encounters may also lead to totally unanticipated consequences in the home territories of those who are the direct participants in the encounter. In the case of the Jews in China, it is thus intriguing to note that the Hebrew biblical manuscripts found by the Jesuit missionaries in Kaifeng during the seventeenth century differed in no significant respect from the versions of the Hebrew Bible available to Christian theologians in Europe. This discovery was to have an enormously dampening effect on a belief long prevalent in Christian circles that the post-Talmudic Western versions of the Hebrew Bible had been tampered with by rabbinical scholars bent on suppressing all references to the coming of Christ. Since the Jesuits were fairly convinced on the basis of the evidence available to them that the biblical manuscripts that the Chinese Jews possessed represented a much earlier, more authentic version of the Bible, they were most disappointed with their findings.

Yet the stubborn fact remains that not all encounters are equally significant. The objective circumstances surrounding such encounters set formidable limits to their effects on both sides of the encounter. While we have references to the presence of Jews in China from post-Han times on and while there is reason to think that these Jews came by land and by sea, most of our more solid evidence about Jews in China is based on the history of the Jewish community in the Northern Song capital of Kaifeng. These Jews had most likely found their way to China across the central Asian trade routes and were also most likely itinerant merchants whose Judaism seemed to reflect the Jewish culture of the medieval Persian cultural sphere. From the beginning to what might be called the end or fading away of the community in the nineteenth and twentieth centuries, the disparity in numbers between the Jews and their Chinese hosts remained overwhelming. There were probably few, if any, highly trained "religious specialists" among them, and their contacts with the centers of the Jewish Diaspora elsewhere remained minimal or nonexistent.

To the extent that one can speak of a meaningful encounter, it largely affected the Jewish side. On the Chinese side, the existence of this tiny group hardly entered the consciousness of the vast bulk of the population apart from those few Chinese in and out of government who were in direct contact with them. The fact that they could survive only by intermarriage and by "acculturation" to the Chinese family system may not have been the decisive factor in their weakness. The Chinese Muslims among whom they lived had undergone a similar "biological" acculturation. Yet here the difference in numbers as well as the kind of social power conferred by numbers, by the presence of aggressive spiritual leaders, and by the ongoing ability to communicate with the spiritual homelands of Islam in Central Asia and the Middle East made all the difference. The Chinese were highly conscious of their presence, and the state regarded them as a potential and later an actual threat to its interests and even to the official state Confucian creed. When we turn to the Catholic missionary enterprise of the seventeenth century, we find that while the missionaries were small in numbers, both the Jesuits and their ecclesiastic opponents were exceptionally highly trained "religious specialists" very much in touch with the "worldly" secular culture of Western Europe, in constant touch with their home bases, and above all, highly conscious of their missionary goals and strategies. They thus came to be recognized by their elite hosts as both an intellectual challenge and a potential menace.

To the extent that the Chinese establishment was conscious of the separate existence of the Jews, in the words of Michael Pollak, it probably regarded them as "an insignificant sect attached to the nation's Islamic population."[1] Yet it may have been precisely because of this insignificance that it represented neither a cultural nor a political threat and was thus accorded both permission to practice its religion and opportunities to participate in the cultural, economic, and political life of the larger society.

For their part, the Jews, like those in various Diaspora lands of the medieval and modern worlds, had little illusion of their power to resist the overwhelming hegemony of the ruling establishments of the countries in which they lived. As Jews, they were basically bent on preserving their own separate identities based mostly on interpretation of their cherished religious tradition. To the extent that they were allowed to participate in the cultural, economic, and political life of other societies, such as Hellenistic Alexandria, Moorish Spain, or Ming China, the majority of them tended to respond with enormous gratitude and, often, highly positive responses to many of the universalistic claims of the host culture as well as an eagerness to find compatibilities between the Jewish tradition and the host cultures.

When we examine the stone stele inscriptions found at the Jewish synagogue site at Kaifeng (which cover the years from 1489 to 1679) that provide us with our main source (thus far) of knowledge concerning the attitude of some of the more articulate members of the community on the question of the relationship of their Judaism to their Chineseness, we are not surprised to find that the emphasis is wholly on compatibility and complementarity between the teachings of the Jewish tradition and generally accepted Confucian views. On the one hand, one need not doubt that the Jewish literati who composed these inscriptions fully and sincerely believed in the compatibility. On the other hand, we are aware that these are official documents and that compatibility does not necessarily imply identity. One continues to wonder whether documents such as the two lost essays on Judaism by the most famous Jewish literati of seventeenth-century China, *Zhao* Yingchen and his brother *Zhao* Yingdou, would throw more light on what their Jewishness added to their Chineseness.

Yet, in the end, for all the reasons mentioned above, we remain unsurprised by the slow erosion of the numbers of those who maintained a sense of separate identity. The question is not one of why the community faded away and why the content of the identity became more and more attenuated, but why we still find in the accounts of foreign visitors from Matteo Ricci to the late nineteenth century a certain remarkable tenacity with which some in the community clung to their identity no matter how attenuated. Whether it took the form of ritual practices, of modes of resistance to aspects of Chinese popular religion, of specific ways of dealing with ancestor worship, of a fervently expressed desire to be in touch with the world Jewish community, or finally of a stubborn resistance to the claims of Christian missionaries that they were the true interpreters of the "Old Testament" tradition, one remains struck by this residual tenacity. Professor Irene Eber has, to be sure, suggested that the tenacity itself may owe more to the Chinese tradition of lineage loyalty than to the hold of the Jewish heritage per se (see chapter I.A.2). It may reflect the fact that the familial piety of the Chinese often involved loyalty to particular intellectual and religious commitments passed down through the family line. Whatever may be the case, it is possible that sustained contacts with the world Jewish Diaspora might have made an enormous difference.

When we turn to the second encounter between Jews and China in the nineteenth and early twentieth centuries, we are again struck by the limits of the encounter. We now find ourselves in a radically transformed world on both sides. The Jews from the West, the Middle East, and Russia who find their way to China have all been exposed, to a greater or lesser degree, to the post-Enlightenment national cultures in which they live. In the Jewish world, it is a period of deep religious crisis. The Middle Eastern mercantile Jewish families such as the Hardoons and Sassoons, which were to play such an important role in China's international commerce, were born in a world still dominated by Islamic tradition and Middle Eastern Jewish orthodoxy. Yet they were to become caught up in the world of the British-sponsored "treaty port" system. The Russians Jews of the late nineteenth and early twentieth century who settled in the Manchurian city of Harbin were able to maintain an integrated community that reflected all the diversity and tensions to be found in the world of East European Jewry. They were able to maintain this autonomy largely because they were walled off from the surrounding society by the same system of "foreign concessions" that prevailed in Shanghai. One might say that the main encounter of these nineteenth- and twentieth-century Jews from abroad was with the treaty port culture of China. One assumes that most of them shared the negative attitude toward what they perceived to be the backward impoverished, superstitious, and corrupt Chinese society, which had become the dominant image of China in the nineteenth-century West. There were no doubt many anonymous individuals who did interest themselves in various aspects of Chinese culture and even exotic figures such as Silas Hardoon, who become involved both in Chinese culture and contemporary political life. On the whole, however, we are light years away from the Kaifeng Jews of late imperial China, whose perceptions were so deeply affected by the universalistic claims of Chinese culture.

Nevertheless, there is one Jewish impulse that can often be found even among fairly indifferent Jews that can also be found among some members of the Jewish community in Shanghai: the impulse to seek out traces of the presence of Jews in the countries in which they find themselves. Thus in 1900 a small group of committed Shanghai Jews organized the Society for the Rescue of Chinese Jews, which engaged in strenuous efforts both to create a link with and to revitalize the remnants of the Kaifeng Jewish community and to encourage worldwide Jewish support abroad.[2] This effort was to prove largely abortive.

In the mid-twentieth century, there was what might be called a second wave of the modern Jewish encounter with China. The catastrophes of the rise of Nazism and World War II were to bring to the treaty ports of China a new and a much more variegated assortment of Jews desperately engaged in seeking a haven for survival. Here we find Orthodox yeshiva students, German professionals, East European Jews of all types and persuasions as well as the old Sephardic stratum of treaty port Jews herded together in a time of great desperation. While again there were individuals who interested themselves in Chinese matters both modern and ancient, it is difficult to speak of a meaningful encounter with China.

At the Harvard Conference Jews in China, we were privileged to have the presence of many Jews who had lived through this entire "Chinese experience." We were thus able to re-experience an important page in the living history of twentieth-century Jews. The particular environment within which these Jews found themselves highlighted the power of their will to survive and to maintain their ways of life as well as some negative accounts of inner Jewish conflicts and intercommunal strife. On the whole, however, it was not basically an account of a meaningful cultural encounter with Chinese society.

On the Chinese side, the multiple turmoils and crises of the nineteenth and twentieth centuries did not lead to any greater concern with the role of the Jews either in China or in the larger framework of Western culture. There has been, to be sure, no systematic study of this subject. It was thus a revelation to learn from Chinese colleagues at the conference that German Jewish musicians in Shanghai had greatly stimulated the appreciation of Western classical music in China. Occasionally leading intellectuals of twentieth century China such as *Yan* Fu (Yen Fu) and *Liang* Qichao (Liang Ch'i-ch'ao) would wonder about the status of modern Jews in the West as a nation without a territory. Yet, more often than not, stereotypes about the nature of Judaism as a religion would be derived from Christian missionary sources even by Chinese who were decidedly not Christian.

Indeed, one is tempted to say that some of the most meaningful encounters between the Jews and China have occurred only in the past few years. For various reasons, the number of scholars of Jewish origin who have become interested in both "traditional" and modern China has grown significantly in recent years, both in the West and in Israel. In the case of Israel, the recent improvement in state-to-state relations with mainland China may be based mainly on considerations of Realpolitik on both sides. It has, however, greatly encouraged an already existing scholarly interest not only in modern Chinese studies but in the study of literature, religion, and philosophy of the past as well. We thus now have a considerable corpus of Hebrew translations of Chinese texts as well as independent scholarly works. While most of the Jewish scholars in America and elsewhere who deal with China are not inclined to find "Jewish" dimensions in their work, some Chinese intellectuals have become interested, rightly or wrongly, in how the Jewishness of these scholars may have affected their approach to China. This in itself suggests some growing interest in the phenomenon of Jews and Judaism within the Chinese academic world. We now have Chinese writings both on the history of Jews in China and on Jews and Judaism in general. Whether this will spur the efforts to revive the prospects of a Jewish community in China of which some dream or lead more Jews to seek wisdom in China, this new encounter cannot but enrich and complicate our comparative global discourse.

Notes

1. Michael Pollak, *Mandarins, Jews and Missionaries: The Jewish Experience in the Chinese Empire* (Philadelphia: Jewish Publication Society, 1980), p. 12.
2. For a short account of this effort to link the two encounters, see ibid.

Contributors

Wendy R. Abraham, a director of the Sino–Judaic Institute in Menlo Park, California, wrote her Columbia University Teachers College doctoral dissertation on Kaifeng Jews. She has also written about them in the "Afterword" to a 1990 edition of Pearl Buck's novel *Peony* and in an article "A Chinese Jewish Identity," *Hadassah Magazine* 69, no. 1 (August/September 1987), pp. 20–25.

Chiara Betta is writing her doctoral dissertation on Silas Aaron Hardoon for the University of London's School of Oriental and African Studies.

Boris Bresler is Professor Emeritus of Engineering at the University of California at Berkeley and archivist of Tel Aviv's Igud Yotzei Sin, an association of Jewish former residents of China. He resided in Harbin, Tianjin, and Dalian before emigrating to the United States in 1937. He wrote "The Excellence of Harbin's Public Commercial School—Fact or Nostalgia?" (in Russian), Igud Yotzei Sin *Bulletin* (July–August 1996).

Lane Earns teaches East Asian history at the University of Wisconsin-Oshkosh. He is the author of "Life at the Bottom of the Hill: A Jewish-Japanese Family in the Nagasaki Foreign Settlement," *Crossroads: A Journal of Nagasaki History and Culture* (Nagasaki), no. 2 (summer 1994), pp. 79–90, and "The Foreign Settlement in Nagasaki, 1859–1869," *The Historian* 56, no. 1 (spring 1994), pp. 483–500.

Irene Eber, the Leo Friedberg Professor of East Asian Studies at the Truman Research Institute of the Hebrew University of Jerusalem, is the author of *Voices From Afar: Modern Chinese Writers on Oppressed Peoples and Their Literature* (1980). She has written introductions for the catalogs of Sino–Judaic exhibitions at Tel Aviv's Museum of the Diaspora (Beit Hatefutsot) (1984) and at Harvard University (1992).

Jonathan Goldstein is professor of history (East Asia) at the State University of West Georgia and research associate at Harvard University's John K. Fairbank Center for East Asian Research. He is author of the award-winning *Philadelphia and the China Trade, 1682–1846* (1978) and editor of *America Views China* (1991) and *China and Israel, 1948–98: A Fifty Year Retrospective* (forthcoming 1998).

Shirley Isenberg, an anthropologist, is author of *India's Bene Israel: A Comprehensive Inquiry and Sourcebook* (1988) and of an introduction to the catalog of the Jews of India exhibit at Jerusalem's Israel Museum (1995).

Barbara C. Johnson, an Ithaca College anthropologist, wrote her 1985 University of Massachusetts doctoral dissertation on India's Cochin Jews. It is entitled " 'Our Community' in Two Worlds: The Cochin Paradesi Jews in India and Israel." She is the author, with Ruby Daniel, of *Ruby of Cochin: An Indian Jewish Woman Remembers* (1995).

Nathan Katz, chairman of Florida International University's Department of Religious Studies, is author of *An Annotated Bibliography About Indian Jewry* (1991) and, with Ellen S. Goldberg, *The Last Jews of Cochin: Jewish Identity in Hindu India* (1993). He edited *Studies of Indian Jewish Identity* (1995).

Dennis A. Leventhal studied Chinese history at the University of Pennsylvania under Derk Bodde and Schuyler Cammann. An American Jew, he has resided in Hong Kong for more than twenty years. He is chairman of the Jewish Historical Society of Hong Kong and published *The Jewish Community of Hong Kong: An Introduction* (1985) and, with Mary Leventhal, *Faces of the Jewish Experience in China* (1990).

***Maruyama* Naoki** teaches international relations at Japan's Meiji Gakuin University. His publications in Japanese, Chinese, and English include "Barufoa Sengen to Nihon" (The Balfour Declaration and Japan), *Hitosubashi Review* 90 (July 1983); "1920 Shionisuto Tokushi no Nihon houmon" (A Zionist Mission to Japan in 1920), *Meiji Gakuin Ronso* 589 (March 1997); and "Nagasaki no yudayajin shakai" (The Jewish Community of Nagasaki), *Meiji Gakuin University Annual Law Review* 8 (August 1992).

Pan **Guang,** dean of the Center for Israel and Judaic Studies at the Shanghai Academy of Social Sciences' Institute of World History, is the author of "The Holocaust Survivors in Shanghai" (1990), *The Development of Jewish and Israel Studies in China* (1992), and "Zionism in Shanghai, 1903–1949" (1993).

Andrew H. Plaks is a director of the Sino–Judaic Institute and a professor of East Asian Languages and Civilization at Princeton University. He has published a translation into Hebrew of the 1489 stele of the Kaifeng Jews entitled *Remembrances in Stone: A Five Hundred Year Old Testimony Regarding Jewish Life in China* (Jerusalem: Israel Museum, 1989).

Michael Pollak, second vice president of the Sino–Judaic Institute, is the author of *The Torah Scrolls of the Chinese Jews* (1975), *Mandarins, Jews, and Missionaries* (1980), and *The Jews of Dynastic China: A Critical Bibliography* (1993).

Joan G. Roland, a professor of history at Pace University, is the author of *The Jews in British India* (1989), "Indian-Jewish Identity of the Bene Israel During the British Raj" (1995), and "Baghdadi Jews in India" (1995).

Harriet P. Rosenson, a musicologist and a director of the Sino–Judaic Institute, has interviewed Chinese and Jewish musicians from Shanghai. She is former director and moderator of World Affairs Seminars in Great Neck, New York.

Vera Schwarcz holds the Mansfield Freeman Chair of East Asian Studies at Wesleyan University. She is the author of *The Chinese Enlightenment: Intellectuals and the Legacy of the May Fourth Movement of 1919* (1988), "Mnemosyne Abroad: Reflections on the Chinese and Jewish Commitment to Remembrance" (1991), "Chinese History/Jewish Memory" (1994), and "The Burden of Memory: The Cultural Revolution and the Holocaust" (1996).

Benjamin I. Schwartz is Leroy B. Williams Professor of History and Political Science Emeritus at Harvard University. His books include *The World of Thought in Ancient China* (1985) and *In Search of Wealth and Power: Yen Fu and the West* (1964). A graduate of Boston's Hebrew Teachers College, he has lectured on "Chinese Inscriptions: Speculations on Judaism in China" and "A Layman's View of Judaism" (both 1988).

Zvia Shickman-Bowman was born in Beijing of Russian Jewish and Chinese parentage. In 1968 she and her family emigrated to Israel. She received her Ph.D. in Chinese literature from the University of Toronto. She is the author of "The Harbin Jewish Community," *China Review* (autumn–winter 1996), pp. 18–21.

Nancy Shatzman Steinhardt, associate professor of East Asian art at the University of Pennsylvania, is the author of *Chinese Traditional Architecture* (1984), *Chinese Imperial City Planning* (1990), and *Liao Architecture* (1997).

Xu **Buzeng,** a member of the Shanghai Academy of Social Sciences, has extensively researched and published about the cultural experiences of Shanghai Jews.